EDUCATION IN A COMPETITIVE AND GLOBALIZING WORLD

HANDBOOK OF ACADEMIC PERFORMANCE

PREDICTORS, LEARNING STRATEGIES AND INFLUENCES OF GENDER

EDUCATION IN A COMPETITIVE AND GLOBALIZING WORLD

Additional books in this series can be found on Nova's website
under the Series tab.

Additional e-books in this series can be found on Nova's website
under the e-book tab.

EDUCATION IN A COMPETITIVE AND GLOBALIZING WORLD

HANDBOOK OF ACADEMIC PERFORMANCE

PREDICTORS, LEARNING STRATEGIES AND INFLUENCES OF GENDER

ROLF HAUMANN
AND
GEORGE ZIMMER
EDITORS

nova
publishers
New York

NOTICE TO THE READER

The Publisher has taken reasonable care in the preparation of this book, but makes no expressed or implied warranty of any kind and assumes no responsibility for any errors or omissions. No liability is assumed for incidental or consequential damages in connection with or arising out of information contained in this book. The Publisher shall not be liable for any special, consequential, or exemplary damages resulting, in whole or in part, from the readers' use of, or reliance upon, this material. Any parts of this book based on government reports are so indicated and copyright is claimed for those parts to the extent applicable to compilations of such works.

Independent verification should be sought for any data, advice or recommendations contained in this book. In addition, no responsibility is assumed by the publisher for any injury and/or damage to persons or property arising from any methods, products, instructions, ideas or otherwise contained in this publication.

This publication is designed to provide accurate and authoritative information with regard to the subject matter covered herein. It is sold with the clear understanding that the Publisher is not engaged in rendering legal or any other professional services. If legal or any other expert assistance is required, the services of a competent person should be sought. FROM A DECLARATION OF PARTICIPANTS JOINTLY ADOPTED BY A COMMITTEE OF THE AMERICAN BAR ASSOCIATION AND A COMMITTEE OF PUBLISHERS.

Additional color graphics may be available in the e-book version of this book.

Library of Congress Cataloging-in-Publication Data

Handbook of academic performance : predictors, learning strategies and influences of gender / editors, Rolf Haumann and George Zimmer.
     pages cm
 Includes bibliographical references and index.
  ISBN 978-1-62417-888-7 (hardcover)
 1. Academic achievement. 2. College students--Psychology. 3. Women college students. I. Haumann, Rolf, editor of compilation. II. Zimmer, George, 1968-, editor of compilation.
  LB1062.6.H357 2013
  378.1'6082--dc23
                        2012051474

Published by Nova Science Publishers, Inc. † New York

CONTENTS

PREFACE

In this book, the authors gather and present current research in the study of the predictors, learning strategies and influences of gender on academic performance. Topics discussed include the gender effect on academic results and whether personality is a factor; the consequences of evening preference of adolescents on school achievement; performance standards in higher education; developments in the measure of intelligence; disciplinary consequence effects on the achievement of students with disabilities; teacher and student ethnicity in Texas elementary schools; and a study of gender and ethnic differences and success in the enrollment of advanced placement courses.

Chapter 1 - The purpose of this study is to disentangle the complex relationship between gender, personality and academic performance. Previous work has shown higher levels of performance for female students. Further, a bulk of studies stressed the role of personality, conceptualized within the Big Five framework, with respect to academic achievement. The literature, however, is unclear with respect to personality as an underlying factor in the relationship between gender and academic outcomes. In this chapter, the authors investigate whether the gender effect on academic results can partly be explained by differences between men and women in personality and whether academic motivation could be the missing link to fully understand the gender effect on academic performance. The authors make a distinction between three different approaches towards academic motivation: motivation as a trait, motivation regulation and academic effort. They theoretically and empirically focus on the possible role of Self-Determination Theory and Regulatory Focus Theory in explaining gender differences in academic effort and performance. The sample consisted of 233 college freshmen in a Business Administration program at a University college in Belgium. The data for this study were collected in a survey and completed with the end-of-semester exam results. Models with academic effort and performance as dependent variables were tested. The results reveal that gender differences in academic effort and performance can be explained, both as a whole and in the particular parts, by differences in personality, especially conscientiousness as the trait component of study motivation. In explaining academic performance, effort (the state component of study motivation) as well as the dimension of intrinsic versus extrinsic motivation (motivation regulation) seem to be the essential elements.

Chapter 2 – The authors live in a changed and changing world where knowledge is being generated at unprecedented rates. In this chapter, the authors discuss how institutions of higher education can incorporate appropriate and valid new knowledge into their curricula through a process that examines the strengths, weaknesses, opportunities and threats associated with doing so. The authors also discuss the timely and responsive development of learner performance standards and their inclusion into a strategic plan that provides timely feedback on whether these standards are having the anticipated results. They discuss how these activities create a four way dilemma: 1) Students who resist the effort to meet the performance standards, but still want a degree; 2) Institutions of higher education who must maintain or grow budgets and hence must attract and retain students; 3) Faculty members who wish to become tenured and/or promoted and require favorable student opinion of instruction; and, 4) Employers who expect that a university degree certifies that the student possesses certain levels of knowledge.

Chapter 3 - This study compared the academic performance, perceived competence, attitudes, and perceived level of momentary skill of 244 (n =129 male, n = 115 female) high school students in science. While males and females did not differ from one another in their science grades, there were significant gender differences in factors that promote motivation and persistence in science. Female students reported lower perceived competence in science and more negative general science attitudes than male students. Males and females also differed systematically from one another in their perceived level of momentary skill while in science as measured by the Experience Sampling Method. The authors sought to understand more about the role that teachers' beliefs and practices may play in fostering these experiential and motivational differences. Students' high school science teachers (n=13) were interviewed about their beliefs pertaining to gender and science. Observational data from their classrooms also were coded and examined to describe teachers' interactions with male and female students. In general, teachers spent an average of 39% more time addressing male than female students, which was not explained by student initiation. In particular, teachers addressed males more often than females about content knowledge, elaboration of course content, and classroom management. Most teachers explicitly denied that there were gender differences in science performance, but their talk about males and females in their classrooms revealed implicit beliefs that suggested gender bias. Some consistency was found between the science teachers' implicit beliefs, teachers' practices, and the gendered motivational patterns of their students.

Chapter 4 - Unsatisfactory academic performance is a recurring theme to many education and related studies. Numerous methods and techniques have been suggested on improving academic performance. However there seem to be limited data on the opinions of the students with regard to academic performance and improvement strategies. There is also limited data on the influence of these opinions on the lecturer's (facilitator's) practices. The current study is aimed at eliciting students' opinions on academic performance as well as the influence of these on the lecturer's (facilitator's) developmental process.

Method: A qualitative study using the phenomenological and the autoethnographic approaches was employed. The phenomenological section of the study was conducted using a questionnaire with open ended question items as a data collection tool in order to acquire rich qualitative data from a cohort of 35 final year diagnostic radiography students. The autoethnographic approach was utilised to demonstrate the developmental process through a transformative reflective report from the educator (facilitator).

Results: Five themes emerged from the qualitative data that could possible shed light into possible causes of students' unsatisfactory academic performance. These were (i) the application of poor or non existent assessment preparation strategies, (ii) the absence of independent study time, (iii) lack of understanding, (iv) the utilisation of inadequate studying techniques as well as (v) strategies to improve academic performance. The autoethnographic approach demonstrated a developmental transformative reflection (reflective practice) of a junior lecturer (facilitator) in acquiring the necessary skills to act and respond to students educational and psychosocial needs.

Conclusion: The impact of the students' input within the education environment cannot be underestimated. Furthermore reflective practice should be utilised by both educators and students to allow for maximum developmental transformation within the educational.

Chapter 5 - Using data from 30 different countries, this investigation is among the first to analyze the impact the education level of the person who one chooses to marry or cohabit with has on personal earnings and if a certain combination in levels of education (qualifications) between the couple leads to higher total family remuneration when compared to other combinations. The results describe something quite new in the area: the education level of the person who one chooses to live or cohabit influences the total remuneration of the other member of the couple; the impact of the husband's education level on the wife's total remuneration is higher than when the inverse is compared; and when it is the man who has the higher educational level, on average, total family earnings are higher than when it is the woman. Finally the total earnings of the other member of the couple and a person's own remuneration are influencing factors which drive male or female to spend more time on housework. The findings of this paper are very important, essentially to executive compensation area, because until the moment literature only focuses on the impact of executive personal characteristics in terms of total executive compensation, but the education level of the person who married or cohabites with this executive seems to have also a positive effect in his personal compensation.

Chapter 6 - Variables that predict work performance are often the same variables that predict academic performance. For example, both job performance and class performance are affected by achievement motivation, cognitive ability, personal characteristics, and self-efficacy, just to name a few commonly investigated factors. Research in organizational psychology and education seems to converge on a common model that applies to both academic and work performance.

The purpose of this chapter is to report on a test of a predictive model of academic performance based largely on findings from organizational psychology and education. The model was tested using a path model framework. The critical components of the model were (a) motivation, (b) ability, (c) personal attributers (e.g., locus of control, self-esteem, self-efficacy), (d) class performance, (e) satisfaction, and (f) outcome. The results showed that the model was a plausible representation of the relationship among these different components.

The findings revealed that motivation and ability predicted student expectations, expectations predicted exam performance, exam performance predicted grade satisfaction, and grade satisfaction predicted the final course grade and estimated college grade point average. Limitations, implications, applications, and future research directions are noted. In general, this chapter shows how research in organizational psychology and education can be integrated into a common predictive model.

Chapter 7 - This chapter shows the different conceptions of intelligence and the procedures that have been developed to measure it. First, the authors are going to explain the main models that have been used to define the concept of intelligence. Subsequently, are going to be developed the first techniques to quantify the intelligence and how they have evolved into the theories that today allow the development of intelligence tests.

Chapter 8 - In this investigation, the authors analyzed the effect of disciplinary action (i.e., in-school suspension, out-of-school suspension, and disciplinary alternative education program placement) on the academic achievement (i.e., reading and math) of Texas Grade 9 students (n = 33,389) with disabilities (i.e., Learning Disability, Emotional Disturbance, and Other Health Impairment) for the 2008-2009 school year. Students with a disability who received a disciplinary consequence had statistically significantly lower scores in reading and in math on the Texas state-mandated assessments than did students with a disability who did not receive a disciplinary consequence. Effect sizes were small. Implications of our findings are discussed.

Chapter 9 - In this study, the authors examined 5 most recent years of data (2003-2004 through 2007-2008) from the Academic Excellence Indicator System of the State of Texas regarding new teachers on high school campuses (n of schools > 1000). In particular, the authors focused on the accountability rating of each high school as it was related with new teachers, new teacher salaries, and minority students. Across all 5 years, statistically significant differences were present, primarily between the Exemplary and Academically Unacceptable high school campuses, in the percent of minority students and in teacher salaries. In 3 of the 5 years, Academically Unacceptable schools had higher percentages of new teachers than did Exemplary high schools. Results were quite consistent across the 5 years of data analyzed. Implications of these findings and suggestions for further research are discussed.

Chapter 10 - Education has been of concern to different groups from time immemorial; there have been many efforts of professionals, politicians, families, etc., so that children have a quality education. And yet, the problem of low performance is unresolved. Although there are many resources for education, changes of models and laws, the school failure is still a pending issue for many countries. Researchers from different disciplines have tried to find the cause of poor academic performance and what variables are associated with good performance in order to intervene and achieve more successes in education.

Chapter 11 - In this study, relationships between teacher ethnicity and student ethnicity in Texas public elementary schools were investigated. Data from all public elementary schools in the state of Texas were gathered for the school years 1999-2000 through 2009-2010 using the Academic Excellence Indicator System. Data on both student enrollment by ethnic membership and teacher employment by ethnic membership at the elementary school level were downloaded. Statistically significant, positive relationships, with large effect sizes, were yielded between teacher ethnic diversity (i.e., Black, Hispanic, and White) and student ethnic diversity (i.e., Black, Hispanic, and White) respectively in Texas elementary schools. As more Hispanic students were enrolled in an elementary school, the tendency was present for more Hispanic teachers to be employed at that school. The same result was yielded for Black and for White teachers and students. Implications of these findings are provided.

Chapter 12 - *Introduction. Coping Strategies* and *Resilience* have emerged as two variables that determine behavior when facing stress in academic situations. Current research examines their role among other motivational-affective variables of a cognitive type. The objective of this study was to establish how the gender of university students relates to strategies for coping with stress and to resilience. An interdependence relationship was hypothesized between students' gender and the type of coping strategies used, and between gender and resilience behavior.

Method. The participants were 243 students from the Psychology degree program at the University of Almería (Spain). An ex post-facto design was used. The assessment instruments were: (1) for *Coping Strategies,* the *Escalas de Estrategias de Coping,* a Spanish version of the Coping with Stress Questionnaire by Lazarus and Folman, assessing coping strategies that either focus on the problem or focus on emotion, when managing academic stress; (2) for *Resilience,* the CD-RISC inventory, Spanish version. The latter is a likert-type scale made up of 25 items and five factors: (1) personal competence, high standards and tenacity, (2) tolerance of negative affect and strengthening effects of stress, (3) positive acceptance of change, and secure relationships, (4) control and (5) spiritual influences. Cluster analyses, correlation and ANOVAs were performed.

Results. Significant differences appeared in the variables assessed as a function of gender. Female university students scored higher on total coping strategies, and on coping strategies focused on emotion and on the problem. As for resilience, male students had higher scores in withstanding stress, while female students scored higher on the spirituality factor.

Discussion. The results provide evidence of the importance of coping strategies and resilience in the life of the university student, according to students' gender. Furthermore, they concur with other prior evidence. An important line of research is thus marked out for the study of motivational and affective variables involved in how university students learn.

Chapter 13 - Enrollment in Advanced Placement courses in one Texas school district was examined for two years to determine the extent to which student diversity was present. A higher percentage of girls were enrolled in Advanced Placement courses for both years than was boys. In this urban school district, Whites comprised the largest ethnic group of students enrolled in Advanced Placement courses and Black students had the lowest percentage of students for both years. Language Arts, Social Studies, and Math were the three areas with the largest percentage of student enrollment for both years, with Foreign Language having the lowest percentage of student enrollment (4.4%) for the most recent year. Boys had higher percentages than girls in Computer Science and Math Advanced Placement courses for both years. Statistically significant differences were present in Advanced Placement subject area enrollment as a function of gender and ethnicity for both years. Regarding student success, White students had the highest percentage of students with exam scores of at least 3, with Black students having the lowest percentage of exam scores of at least 3. Implications of these findings are discussed.

Chapter 14 - In this study, the researchers examined the science achievement of Hispanic students and of White students on the Texas state-mandated assessment for students in Grades 5, 8, and 11 for 3 years (i.e., 2005-2006, 2006-2007, and 2007-2008) for all schools in Texas (*n of schools* > 1,000). Statistically significant differences were present for all comparisons, within each grade level and within each year of data analyzed. All effect sizes were very large, with White students having statistically significantly higher science pass rates than Hispanic students. With the accountability mandates of the No Child Left Behind Act focused in reading and math, the achievement gap in science remains wide.

Chapter 15 – The authors examined the extent to which boys and girls differed in their performance on the Texas state-mandated science assessment in grades 5, 8, and 11 for three consecutive school years (i.e., 2005-2006, 2006-2007, and 2007-2008) for all public schools in Texas (*ns* > 7,000 schools). For all three grade levels and for all three years, boys demonstrated higher passing rates in science than girls. Given the need for qualified people working in science, the lack of accountability for science proficiency in the No Child Left

Behind Act, and the consistent achievement gaps in science documented in this study, the authors believe that this presence of a gender gap is cause for concern.

In: Handbook of Academic Performance
Editors: Rolf Haumann and George Zimmer

ISBN: 978-1-62417-888-7
© 2013 Nova Science Publishers, Inc.

Chapter 1

GENDER, PERSONALITY AND ACADEMIC PERFORMANCE: SELF-DETERMINATION THEORY AND REGULATORY FOCUS THEORY AS LEVERS TO OPEN THE BLACK BOX BETWEEN GENDER, PERSONALITY, ACADEMIC EFFORT AND PERFORMANCE

Dries Berings, Tim De Feyter*, Lieven Brebels,
Anja Van den Broeck and Karin Proost
Human Relations Research Group, Hogeschool-Universiteit Brussel,
K.U.Leuven Association, Belgium

ABSTRACT

The purpose of this study is to disentangle the complex relationship between gender, personality and academic performance. Previous work has shown higher levels of performance for female students. Further, a bulk of studies stressed the role of personality, conceptualized within the Big Five framework, with respect to academic achievement. The literature, however, is unclear with respect to personality as an underlying factor in the relationship between gender and academic outcomes. In this chapter, we investigate whether the gender effect on academic results can partly be explained by differences between men and women in personality and whether academic motivation could be the missing link to fully understand the gender effect on academic performance. We make a distinction between three different approaches towards academic motivation: motivation as a trait, motivation regulation and academic effort. We theoretically and empirically focus on the possible role of Self-Determination Theory and Regulatory Focus Theory in explaining gender differences in academic effort and performance. The sample consisted of 233 college freshmen in a Business Administration program at a University college in Belgium. The data for this study were collected in a

---
* Corresponding author. Tim De Feyter, Hogeschool-Universiteit Brussel, Warmoesberg 26, B-1000 Brussels, Belgium. Tel: +32 2 609 8274. Email: tim.defeyter@hubrussel.be.

survey and completed with the end-of-semester exam results. Models with academic effort and performance as dependent variables were tested. The results reveal that gender differences in academic effort and performance can be explained, both as a whole and in the particular parts, by differences in personality, especially conscientiousness as the trait component of study motivation. In explaining academic performance, effort (the state component of study motivation) as well as the dimension of intrinsic versus extrinsic motivation (motivation regulation) seem to be the essential elements.

1. INTRODUCTION

Within the debate concerning gender and academic performance (AP), attention has recently shifted from the subordination of women in higher education to the underachievement of male students (Severiens & ten Dam, 2012). A lot of studies published in recent decades, show that women often outperform men in higher education (Betts & Morell, 1999; Bridgemen & Wendler, 1991; Evers & Mancuso, 2006; Hyde & Kling, 2001; Kim, Rhoades & Woodard, 2003; Leonard & Jiang, 1999; Wainer & Steinberg, 1992) even in situations where the under-representation of female first year students is still a fact (Dayioglu & Serap Türüt-Asik, 2004).

Post hoc explanations for this gender effect in higher as well as in secondary education are related to differences in several predictors of AP. Although general cognitive ability is widely recognized as explaining individual differences in academic achievement (Chamorro-Premuzic & Furnham 2008), the gender effect on academic performance is attributed to nonintellectual rather than to general cognitive ability differences (Feingold, 1988). Wilberg and Lynn (1999), for example, argue that females work more conscientiously combined with a higher level of work ethics. Female students also surpass male students in language abilities like writing skills, vocabulary and verbal fluency. Other possible explanations for gender-related scholastic performance lie in differences in course taking and classroom behavior (Byrnes, Hong & Xing, 1997; Young & Fisler, 2000), study skills (Leonard & Jiang, 1999), learning attitudes and strategies like time management skills (Trueman & Hartley, 1996), levels of discipline and regard for authority, and differences in goals and aspirations (Grebennikov & Skaines, 2009; Severiens & ten Dam, 2012; Younger, Warrington, & Williams, 1999). After reviewing the literature, Woodfield, Jessop and McMillan (2006) summarized it as 'women work harder and more consistently'.

Thus, in order to understand better why female students outperform their male colleagues in higher education, it is useful to focus on gender differences in nonintellectual predictors of AP. Such general characteristic differences are possibly embedded in personality, which can be defined as (relatively) stable behavior patterns that distinguish individuals from each other. By the end of the past century, psychologists reached a consensus on the dimensions underlying individual differences (Costa & McCrae, 1992a; Goldberg, 1993). Five factors emerged as fundamental dimensions of personality, usually labelled as conscientiousness, neuroticism, openness, extraversion and agreeableness. The Big Five model or the so-called Five-Factor model serves as a framework to conduct systematic research and is broadly recognised as an integration of the diversity of individual differences measures.

De Feyter, Caers, Vigna, and Berings (2012) found in their study that the gender effect on academic results can partly be explained by personality differences between men and women.

Several studies indeed report gender differences concerning the Big Five personality traits (Budaev, 1999; Costa, Terracciano, & McCrae 2001; Lippa, 2010). Generally the results reveal higher scores for females on agreeableness and neuroticism. Moreover, these differences have been found among adults and older people as well as in student populations (Chapman, Duberstein, Sörensen, & Lyness, 2007; Woodfield, Jessop, & Mc Millan, 2006). Finegold (1994) reported gender differences for facets of neuroticism and agreeableness, i.e. anxiety and tender-mindedness respectively, but also for orderliness as a facet of conscientiousness. Concerning conscientiousness De Fruyt, Van Leeuwen, De Bolle and De Clercq (2008) obtained higher scores for female students on concentration, perseverance and orderliness.

Another bulk of literature shows that personality can explain a certain amount of variance in AP (e.g., Bickle, 1996; Chomorro-Premuzic & Furnham, 2003a; De Raad & Schouwenburg, 1996; Farsides & Woodfield, 2003; Komarraju & Karau, 2005; Poropat, 2009; Rindermann & Neubauer, 2001; Wolfe & Johnson, 1995). In the following paragraphs, we give a short overview of those studies in which personality is conceptualized within the Big Five framework.

Conscientiousness. A positive relationship between conscientiousness and academic outcomes is well documented (Busato, Prins, Elshout, & Hamakers, 1999; Chamorro-Premuzic & Furnham, 2003a; De Feyter et al., 2012; De Fruyt & Mervielde, 1996; Furnham & Monson, 2009; Komarraju, Karau, & Schmeck, 2009; Noftle & Robins, 2007) and interpreted in terms of a parallelism between facets of conscientiousness like working hard, self-discipline, persistence and order and requirements and expectations in higher education (MacCann, Duckworth, & Roberts, 2009; Paunonen & Ashton, 2001).

Neuroticism. In contrast to conscientiousness, the majority of studies reveal a negative correlation between neuroticism and AP (Furnham & Monson, 2009; Lounsbury, Sundstrom, Loveland, & Gibson, 2003; Sanchez-Marin, Rejano-Infante & Rodriguez-Troyano, 2001) which is attributed to the anxiety component of neuroticism. At first glance it seems logical that neurotic individuals could be hindered in their performance because of their high levels of anxiety and restlessness, especially in the context of exams. But anxiety to fail can also induce a higher level of effort during preparation for the exams. With this argument in mind it is not surprising that some studies find a positive instead of negative impact of neuroticism on academic performance (De Feyter et al., 2012; Komarraju et al., 2009; Nguyen, Allen, & Fraccastoro, 2005; Rosander, Bäckström, & Stenberg, 2011). The lack of inconsistent results concerning neuroticism and academic performance may be explained by the role of motivational aspects as partial mediator in the relation between neuroticism and academic achievement. De Feyter et al. (2012) argue that neuroticism can have a direct negative effect on AP, especially in stressful situations like exams, but this adverse influence may be neutralized or even reversed by a supplementary positive indirect effect through motivation.

Extraversion. De Raad and Schouwenburg (1996) suggest two distinctive processes leading to opposing effects of extraversion on AP. First, because they are very sociable and seek excitement, extrovert students may prefer a variety of social activities to hard study efforts (Chamorro-Premuzic & Furnham, 2003b; Furnham & Monsen, 2009). Second, as enthusiasm, a high energy level and desire to learn are positively related to extraversion, this personality trait may be associated with a motivational surplus (Poropat, 2009), especially in educational settings where students learn by social interaction during lectures (Chamorro-Premuzic & Furnham, 2003a).

Agreeableness. In general, it is accepted that there is no impact of this personality trait on academic motivation and performance (Chomorro-Premuzic & Furnham, 2003a). However, some studies did find a positive relationship between agreeableness and a student's achievement, which can be explained by the fit between this personality characteristic and the learning environment (Farsides & Woodfield, 2003; Poropat, 2009). Cooperative and trusting students, for example, are more likely to learn in an educational setting where team work and group projects are important.

Openness. Because intellectual curiosity is one of the facets of openness as defined by Costa and McCrae (1992b), a positive correlation with academic achievement could be expected. Indeed, Blickle (1996) found a positive relation between openness and academic performance. Such a positive correlation seems obvious knowing that the drive to learn and explore things, the tendency to be creative, the hunger for knowledge and insight and open-mindedness are all elements of openness and may be part of the requirements and expectations formulated towards students in higher education. Another argument is that there exists evidence that openness is correlated with intelligence (Holland, Dollinger, Holland, & MacDonald, 1995) and general knowledge (Ashton et al., 2000; Goff & Ackerman, 1992) and that creativity, a concept strongly related to openness, is also positive correlated with academic performance (Sen & Hagtvet, 1993).

Knowing this, it is surprising that in several studies no correlation or only a weak correlation has been found between openness and AP (Chamorro-Premuzic & Furnham, 2003a; De Feyter et al., 2012). One possible explanation could be that nowadays rule compliance is more reinforced in higher education than creativity and open-mindedness. The clear positive correlation between rule compliance and conscientiousness, the fact that anxiety as a component of neuroticism seems to have a positive impact on academic performance especially in situation where rule compliance is important (De Feyter et al., 2012) and the fact that some studies find that introverted and agreeable students on average perform better than extraverted students (Chamorro-Premuzic & Furnham, 2003a) give some support to such a proposition.

As the gender effect on academic performance might be explained by personality differences between men and women, the purpose of this chapter is to contribute to the disentanglement of the complex relationship between personality and gender on the one hand and academic performance on the other hand. In the discussion above, several motivational aspects are part of the theoretical explanation for the impact of the Big Five traits on AP. Therefore, in order to explore the black box between gender, personality and academic achievement, we introduce some supplementary components into the research model. More specifically, in line with the research of Komarraju et al. (2009) and De Feyter et al. (2012) we focus on academic motivation (AM) as mediator in the personality-performance relationship.

However, inspection of the literature concerning motivation in education teaches that 'motivation' is a too large a concept to be conceptualized and assessed by one simple measure (Shah & Gardner, 2008). First, some authors approached *motivation as a trait* that comes near to personality characteristics (Rindermann & Neubauer, 2001). Second, other measures come near to the *behavioral component of motivation*. Elements like intentions, effort and real study behaviors are facets of such measures. For example, Lockwood, Jordan and Kunda (2002) developed a questionnaire measuring 'academic motivation'. Inspection of the items teaches that respondents are asked to evaluate their own intention to expend effort in the near future. Further, motivation is also one of the subscales of the Learning and Study Strategies Inventory (LASSI; Cano, 2006). This scale contains items referring to behavioural expectations and duties as formulated in higher educational contexts. Such behavioural approaches to academic motivation are largely embedded in 'common sense' beliefs concerning desirable student behaviours rather than in well-established motivation theories. Third, some motivation measures are related to specific theories like the Self-Determination Theory (SDT; Deci & Ryan, 1985, 2012) or the Regulatory Focus Theory (RFT; Lockwood et al, 2002). These measures approach *motivation as an internal regulation process* that can make the bridge between motivation as a trait and the behavioral component of motivation.

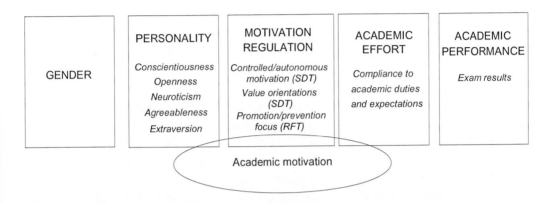

Figure 1. Conceptual model of the relation between gender, personality, academic motivation and performance.

We present all three motivation approaches (motivation as a trait, behavioral component of motivation, motivation as internal regulation) in one conceptual model (see Figure 1) that we will use in this chapter to explore theoretically and empirically the different possible links between gender, personality and academic performance. Two paradigms concerning motivation regulation are explored theoretically as well as empirically. The first paradigm is the Self-Determination Theory (Deci & Ryan, 1985, 2012; Kasser & Ryan; 1993; Komarraju et al., 2009; Vansteenkiste, Lens & Deci, 2006; Vallerand, Pelletier, Blais, Brière, Senécal, & Vallières, 1992; Vallerand, Pelletier, & Koestner, 2008; Vansteenkiste, Simons, Lens, Soenens, Matos & Lacante, 2004), the second is the Regulatory Focus Theory (Higgins, Friedman, Harlow, Idson, Ayduk, & Taylor, 2001; Lockwood, Jordan, & Kunda, 2002; Molden, Lee, & Higgins, 2007; Vaughn, Baumann, & Klemann, 2008). Individual differences measured in line with the concepts used in those paradigms probably could result in a better understanding of the relationship between gender, personality and performance. In particular the distinction between promotion focus and prevention focus (Lockwood et al., 2002; Molden et al., 2007) and the different levels of motivation regulation from controlled to autonomous motivation, as conceptualized by the SDT framework (Deci & Ryan, 2002; Vallerand et al., 1992), could throw some light on the black box between gender and personality differences on the one hand and academic effort and performance on the other hand. First, in Section 2 and 3, we will explain the basic concepts and central propositions of respectively SDT and RFT. We pay special attention to the relationship with academic performance, and in so far these relationships have already been the subject of study, we report the main results from the scientific literature. In other words, we will give an overview of research findings that throw light on the predictive validity of the concepts used in the two motivation regulation paradigms for Academic Performance. Next, we look for empirical indications that these motivation regulation parameters are embedded in personality traits as conceptualised within the Big Five tradition. Therefore, we empirically explore the proposed relations in data from a sample of first year students enrolled in a Business Administration program at a University college in Belgium. In Section 4, the methodology of this study is discussed. The results are presented in Section 5. Finally, in Section 6, the results are discussed and we provide some directions for further research.

2. SELF-DETERMINATION THEORY AND ACADEMIC PERFORMANCE

2.1. Autonomous and Controlled Motivation

Over the past 40 years, Self-Determination Theory has developed into a grand theory of human motivation and optimal functioning (Deci, 1975; Deci & Ryan, 2000, 2012). Initially, Deci and colleagues studied intrinsic motivation, which can be defined as the enactment of a form of behavior for its own sake, that is, for the pleasure experienced during the course of the activity. Extrinsic motivation, in contrast, relates to the engagement in a particular behavior to obtain an outcome that is separable from the activity itself. For example, students studying because they are genuinely interested in the course material are intrinsically motivated. Extrinsically motivated students in contrast study to obtain high grades or the rewards they would get from their parents upon their achievement. Several older motivation theories (e.g., Vroom, 1964) assume that intrinsic and extrinsic motivation are additive components of one's total motivation.

Studies within SDT however challenge this interpretation (see Deci, Ryan, & Koestner, 1999 for a meta-analysis). These studies indicated that paying individuals for conducting an intrinsically challenging task, subsequently leads to a decrease in intrinsic motivation. Rather than adding to one's total motivation, the provision of extrinsic rewards diminished one's total motivation. Various studies replicated this finding showing that monetary rewards, deadlines and close supervision may have a detrimental effect on intrinsic motivation. Not all types of extrinsic motivation, however, seemed to evoke such negative effects. This finding has led to the differentiation of four types of extrinsic motivation within SDT. These types differ in the degree to which the reason for the behavior is external to the individual or has been adopted as part of one's self, i.e. has been internalized (Ryan & Connell, 1989).

First, external regulation refers to engagement in an activity to obtain rewards or avoid punishments given by others. These rewards can be material or social in nature, and include for example prizes, financial rewards or positive feedback or recognition from teachers or parents. Extrinsically oriented students may, for example, put effort into their studies just because they want to obtain their diploma or desire to please their parents. Second, introjected regulation is defined as being motivated by internally pressuring reasons such as the wish to avoid guilt and shame or feel proud of one's behavior. Studying late because one's self-worth is dependent upon good grades is an example of introjected regulation. In the case of external regulation the ratification of the behavior stems from the social environment. No complete internalization has taken place. In case of introjection the individuals are granting themselves rewards and punishments. However, they haven't accepted the reasons for their behavior, so their behavior is accompanied by inner feelings of conflict and compulsion (Vansteenkiste, Sierens, Soenens, Luyckx, & Lens, 2009) Hence, the behavior has only partially been internalized. Both in the case of external regulation and that of introjection, the locus of causality is external. Therefore these types of extrinsic motivation are labeled controlled motivation.

Not all types of extrinsic motivation are characterized by an external locus of causality. According to SDT, the third type of extrinsic motivation, identification, is typified by an internal locus of control. Identification refers to carrying out an activity because its goal is considered important and has been personally endorsed. Business students, for example, identify with mathematics study because they feel this course will help them in becoming trustful and decent accountants. The reason for conducting the behavior has been accepted and the internalization process has been completed. In the case of identification, the reason to conduct the behavior thus lies within the individual. Notably, this is also the case with intrinsic motivation, when students are spontaneously and freely following their interests. Vallerand and colleagues (1992) further differentiate between three types of intrinsic motivation. Intrinsic motivation to know refers to students inherent interest in learning. Intrinsic motivation towards accomplishments details students' enjoyment of an activity because they create or accomplish something. Finally, intrinsic motivation to experience stimulation relates to students' search for novelty and stimulating sensations such as excitement about the learning material. Identification and intrinsic motivation are both indicated as autonomous types of motivation. Throughout the development of SDT, the conceptual distinction between intrinsic and extrinsic motivation thus became replaced by the distinction between autonomous and controlled motivation.

Within SDT, it is argued that adopting an autonomous regulation style yields a host of positive effects, while controlled motivation leads to less optimal results. Empirical evidence supports this assumption. Holding higher autonomous and lower controlled motivation relates to higher well-being, for example, in terms of more vitality, satisfaction and lower levels of depression (Niemiec, Lynch, Vansteenkiste, Bernstein, Deci, & Ryan, 2006). It is also associated with higher levels of engagement, and particularly more dedication and absorption and with lower levels of burnout (Stoeber, Childs, Hayward, & Feast, 2011). Being autonomously rather than controlled motivated for studying also relates to better cognitive processing such as organizing learning material and critical thinking, as well as to more adaptive meta-cognitive strategies, including better time management and goal setting (Vansteenkiste et al., 2010). Autonomously motivated students furthermore persist longer and tend to drop out less (Vallerand, Fortier, & Guay, 1997). They seem to refrain from cheating behavior (Vansteenkiste et al., 2010). Although controlled motivation might enhance students' performance in terms of rote learning, conceptual learning seems to be conditional upon autonomous motivation (Vansteenkiste et al., 2010; see also Jang, 2008). Autonomous motivation has therefore repeatedly been related to better performance, including higher GPA and exam scores (e.g., Phillips, Abraham & Bond, 2003; Soenens & Vansteenkiste, 2005; Vansteenkiste et al., 2010). Such results have been found cross culturally, including European (Stoeber, et al., 2011; Vansteenkiste et al., 2010) and American students, but also students from China (e.g., Pan & Gauvain, 2012), Japan (Nishimura, Kawamura, & Sakurai, 2011), and the Middle-East (Katz, Kaplan, & Buzukashvily, 2011).

As autonomous as opposed to controlled motivation relates to several desirable outcomes, scholars have examined potential antecedents of these types of motivation. At the institutional level, it has been shown that autonomous motivation is fostered when the learning institution supports the connections between freshmen and higher level students as well as between students and teachers (Pan & Gauvain, 2012). Autonomy support of parents (e.g., Niemiec et al., 2006), teachers (Katz et al., 2011; Soenens, Sierens, Vansteenkiste, Dochy & Goossens, 2012) and peers (Pan & Gauvain, 2012) seems equally important. Autonomous motivation is most likely to develop when students perceive that others provide them with choices, grant them freedom to work in their own way, provide meaningful rationales for the requested behaviour and empathically try to understand their point of view. When others try to evoke particular behaviour by using intrusive behaviour such as directives, threats or love withdrawal, controlled motivation is likely to emerge.

Apart from stressing the importance of the social environment, the personal antecedents of autonomous and controlled motivation have also been examined. Most importantly, it has been found that students' autonomy orientation is a strong predictor of autonomous motivation to study (Williams & Deci, 1996).

Unlike autonomous motivation, which is context specific, a general autonomous orientation is one's general tendency to be oriented to and enact upon contextual autonomy support. Other personal aspects increasing autonomous motivation include a strong future time perspective (De Bilde, Vansteenkiste, & Lens, 2011) and holding high personal standards, one of the aspects of perfectionism (Gaundreau & Antl, 2008). Holding high standards in combination with being concerned about mistakes, in contrast, relates to controlled motivation. As regards personality traits, some studies have explored the associations of autonomous and controlled motivation with the personality aspects as defined in the Big Five. First, Ingledew, Markland, and Sheppard (2004) found in a sample of adults that neuroticism associated positively with introjection and negatively with intrinsic motivation to engage in excercising, after controlling for the other aspects of the Big Five. Extraversion yielded positive relations with introjection, identification and intrinsic motivation. Second, initial research with respect to behavioural regulations for studying indicated that conscientious students are more likely to display intrinsic motivation and identification. They are less likely to act out of introjection. Neurotic and extraverted students, in contrast, are more likely to experience introjection (Phillips, Abraham & Bond, 2003). Related to this issue, Olesen, Thomsen, Schnieber, and Tonnesvang (2010) found that extraverted, conscientious, open and agreeable students were also characterised by an autonomous orientation, while a controlled orientation was negatively related to agreeableness and showed a slight positive relationship with extraversion.

As regards demographic differences, it might be expected that autonomous motivation increases with age, because of the advancing internalisation process. De Bilde and colleagues (2011), for example, provided evidence for this assumption among a sample of college and university students.

These authors also indicated that female students displayed higher levels of identification and intrinsic motivation compared to their male counterparts, but other studies failed to determine significant gender differences in terms of autonomous and controlled motivation (e.g., Hui, Sun, Chow, & Chu, 2011; Stoeber et al., 2011). The current study aims to further explore this issue.

2.2. Values Orientations

Apart from examining the regulations underlying behaviour, or 'why' of motivation, SDT also taps into the goals or values individuals might aspire to, or the 'what' of behaviour. The pursuit of values is a critical aspect for individuals' motivation (Latham & Pinder, 2005). Values are considered to function as general standards and criteria that determine individuals' attitudes, preferences and behaviour (Berings, De Fruyt, & Bouwen, 2004; Feather, 1992). SDT differentiates intrinsic values from extrinsic values. Students valuing an intrinsic values aim to develop themselves, build meaningful relations with others and contribute to the society as a whole (Kasser & Ryan, 1996). In contrast, students holding extrinsic values attach importance, for example, to financial success, status and power.

The pursuit of intrinsic values is considered to be inherently rewarding, as they allow for the satisfaction of the basic human psychological needs for autonomy (i.e., the inherent desire for volitional functioning), competence (i.e., the inclination to be efficacious) and relatedness (i.e., the propensity to care and to be cared for). Within SDT, the satisfaction of these needs is said to be as essential for optimal psychological functioning as the satisfaction of physical needs such as thirst and hunger is essential in order to feel physically well. Rather than allowing for the satisfaction of the basic psychological needs, extrinsic values concern external manifestations of worth and may therefore even frustrate the basic human psychological needs. Therefore, they will likely run against students well-being and performance.

Research supports this assumption. Students valuing intrinsic values experienced higher levels of well-being as indexed by life satisfaction, positive affect and vitality and were less likely to experience somatic or psychological distress, negative affect, smoke or do drugs (Sheldon & Krieger, 2004; Vansteenkiste, Duriez, Simons, & Soenens, 2006). Extrinsic value pursuit relates to various aspects of anti-social behaviour, including feeling threatened by others (Duriez, Meeus, & Vansteenkiste, 2012), feeling superior to others and prejudice (Duriez, Vansteenkiste, Soenens, & De Witte, 2007). Value pursuit also predicts academic-related outcomes. Intrinsic values are positively related to persistence in a learning activity (Vansteenkiste, Timmermans, Lens, Soenens, & Van den Broeck, 2008).

These results have been found in terms of the importance students attach to these values, as well as considering the degree to which these values were attained (Niemiec, Ryan, & Deci, 2009). Interestingly, similar results have been established among educational sciences and economics, although it might be believed that their learning environments are relatively diverse (Vansteenkiste et al., 2006). Notably, the values that are stressed within the learning context seem to impact students' functioning as predicted by SDT. For example, students learning about recycling in a manner based on intrinsic (i.e., for saving the environment) rather than extrinsic values (i.e., saving money) engaged less in superficial learning and more in deep level processing and, hence, also performed better (Vansteenkiste et al., 2004).

To date, research has focused upon the consequences of intrinsic and extrinsic value pursuit. Few studies tapped into their antecedents (Kasser, Ryan, Zax, & Samerhoff, 1995; Kasser, 2002). One study also examined the associations between personality and the pursuit of intrinsic and extrinsic values (Romera, Gomez-Fraguela, & Villar, 2012). Among a sample of adults, the pursuit of extrinsic life values correlated positively with neuroticism, extraversion and conscientiousness, but negatively with openness and agreeableness. Extraversion, openness agreeableness and conscientiousness related positively to the pursuit of intrinsic values in one's life. The current study aims to further disentangle these relationships with respect to the values students pursue in their academic life. As respects gender, some studies suggest that males give higher priority to extrinsic goals compared to females, who scored higher on intrinsic values (e.g., Kasser & Ryan, 1996; Romero et al., 2012; Williams, Cox, Hedberg, & Deci, 2000). Other studies, however, failed to establish such gender differences (Schmuck, Kasser & Ryan, 2000). Interestingly, in the study of Ryan and colleagues (1999) American females considered intrinsic values as more important than men did, Russian females attached less importance to such values as compared to Russian men. These findings suggest that potential gender differences might be culture specific. The current study aims to explore potential gender differences in intrinsic and extrinsic values among Belgian students and wants to explore the mediating role of work values between gender and academic achievement.

3. REGULATORY FOCUS THEORY AND ACADEMIC PERFORMANCE

3.1. Central Concepts and Propositions

Regulatory Focus Theory (Higgins, 1997; 2000) provides another relevant paradigm for examining student academic motivation and performance. Although RFT builds on the classic psychological distinction between advancement and maintenance-related goals (e.g., Maslow, 1955), it also extends this distinction by proposing that each goal-type not only originates from different needs, but also fosters different modes of *goal-pursuit* (Higgins, 1997). That is, RFT argues that people experience and represent advancement-related goals in an entirely different manner than maintenance-related goals (Molden, Lee, & Higgins, 2007). We will elaborate on these distinct modes of goal-pursuit below.

Advancement-related goals activate and are best met through a *promotion focus* that is oriented toward gains or positive end-states. In a promotion focus, people view themselves as striving toward the presence of positive outcomes (i.e., gains) and toward avoiding the absence of positive outcomes (i.e., non-gains). Put differently, self-regulation with a promotion focus is characterized as the motivation to attain growth by bringing one's actual self into alignment with one's ideal self (i.e., one's perceived hopes, aspirations, and accomplishments). For instance, students with a strong promotion focus toward improving their exam grades may represent this goal as actively picking up on any opportunity to increase their insights into the course material and avoiding any missed opportunity for doing so. As a consequence, a promotion focus typically involves goal-pursuit in a willful and eager manner.

By way of contrast, maintenance-related goals activate and are best met through a *prevention focus* that is oriented toward losses and negative end-states. In a prevention focus, people view themselves as striving toward the absence of negative outcomes (i.e., non-losses) and toward avoiding the presence of negative outcomes (i.e., losses). Put differently, self-regulation with a prevention focus is characterized as the motivation to attain security by bringing one's actual self into alignment with one's ought self (i.e., one's perceived duties, obligations, and responsibilities). For instance, students with a strong prevention focus toward avoiding failure in an exam may represent this goal as actively eliminating any possible threat to their concentration while studying and avoiding social events that would keep them from studying. As a consequence, a prevention focus typically involves goal-pursuit in a vigilant or avoidance-oriented manner.

Central to RFT is the proposition that the effects of regulatory focus occur both as a function of state differences and as a function of trait differences (Higgins, 1997). That is, although contextual cues may influence the extent to which people temporarily rely more or less on their promotion or prevention focus strategies for goal-pursuit (i.e., state regulatory focus), relatively stable differences also exist between individuals (i.e., trait or dispositional regulatory focus). Besides the effects of trait and state differences in regulatory focus, a well-documented part of the literature emphasizes the particularly strong influence of the interaction between both. This concerns the compatibility between trait and state regulatory focus in the process of goal-pursuit. More specifically, as expressed by Shah and colleagues 'Motivation and performance are greater when the dispositions, task incentives, and means of goal attainment all share the same regulatory focus than when they do not.' (Shah, Higgins, & Friedman, 1998; p. 291).

In the current contribution, we started off by measuring trait regulatory focus differences between students in order to examine whether these differences contribute to a better understanding of the relations between personality, gender, and academic outcomes.

3.2. Predictive Validity towards Academic Performance

Over the past fifteen years, a variety of disciplines and applied domains have incorporated the role of regulatory focus into their research. These include, among others, decision-making (e.g., Crowe & Higgins, 1997), perception and social cognition (e.g., Friedman & Förster, 2005), social psychology and organizational behavior (e.g., Brebels, De Cremer, & Sedikides, 2008), leadership and management (e.g., Brebels, De Cremer, van Dijke, & Van Hiel, 2011; Kark & Van Dijk, 2007), marketing and consumer behavior (e.g., Adams, Faseur, & Geuens, 2011; Pham & Avnet, 2004). Although some prior research examined the influence of a regulatory focus upon academic or other indications of cognitive task effort and performance, not much clarity exists on how exactly regulatory focus applies to the domain of academic effort and performance. Next, we will highlight some relevant findings to this end.

In general, promotion and prevention focus are considered to reveal equal performance levels on cognitive tasks. Yet relevant distinctions have been observed between both regulatory foci when looking at more specific performance differences. For example, a promotion (relative to prevention) focus has been associated with faster, but less accurate problem-solving and decision-making (Crowe & Higgins, 1997; Foerster, Higgins, & Bianco, 2003). Other research has revealed that prevention-focused individuals prefer to initiate goal pursuit on academic tasks sooner and ultimately also outperform promotion-focused individuals under conditions of distraction, but not under non-distracting conditions (Freitas, Liberman, Salovey, & Higgins, 2002). With respect to task characteristics, research demonstrated that promotion-focused individuals outperform prevention-focused individuals on creative tasks, but the reverse is true on analytical tasks (Friedman & Foerster, 2005; Seibt & Foerster, 2004). Finally, promotion-focused individuals are more likely than prevention-focused individuals to develop illusions of control over the extent to which their actions positively influence intended outcomes (Langens, 2007). This should make them more susceptible to over-confidence and underestimation of the actions needed to pass the exams or get high grades in terms of studying.

In sum, the available evidence, albeit in short supply, clearly suggests that the prevention focus mode of goal-pursuit should be more effective at regulating students' academic effort and performance than the promotion focus mode of goal-pursuit. As mentioned above, however, a significant body of evidence demonstrates that the effects of trait regulatory focus are often qualified by the interaction of the regulatory focus with the task itself or the environment in which the task is performed (i.e., regulatory fit); a phenomenon that likely also holds in the domain of academic effort and performance (Shah et al., 1998; Keller & Bless, 2006). We will return to this point in the discussion.

3.3. Relatedness to Personality and Gender

How do both regulatory foci map onto Big Five personality traits? Although promotion and prevention focus are conceptually related primarily and respectively to Extraversion and Neuroticism (Higgins, 1997), recent empirical contributions (i.e., mainly in the field of organizational psychology) have suggested the existence of additional relations between regulatory foci and personality dimensions of the five factor model (Gorman et al., 2011; Vaughn, Baumann, & Klemann, 2008). For instance, besides a positive relation with Extraversion and a negative relation with Neuroticism, promotion focus also related positively to Conscientiousness. Likewise, besides a negative relation with Extraversion, prevention focus was also positively related to Conscientiousness (Gorman et al., 2011). Other research also revealed that people higher (as compared to lower) in Openness to experience are more motivated by promotion-related and gain-framed goals and they were less motivated by prevention-related and loss-framed goals (Vaughn et al., 2008), as such suggesting additional relationships with Openness to experience.

Despite the fact that personality traits share variance with both regulatory foci, recent contributions reveal that regulatory focus can influence performance-related outcomes beyond the effects of Big Five personality traits (Lanaj, Chang, & Johnson, 2012). In the current contribution, we test this in the realm of academic effort and performance.

Unlike the above-mentioned relatedness with personality traits, no significant differences are observed when gender is used to predict regulatory focus differences. Males are often found to be slightly more promotion-focused and females slightly more prevention-focused, but these patterns remain largely non-significant. Apart from the absence of a relation between gender and regulatory focus, interesting research on stereotype threat has thrown a somewhat different perspective on the combined effects of gender and regulatory focus (Brazy & Shah, 2005). In this research, participants were asked to complete a mathematical task. Before completion, however, half of the participants were made to believe that males usually outperform females on this task, whereas the other half did not receive this information. Results revealed that prevention-focused female participants felt more threatened while completing the task and also performed worse relative to their promotion-focused counterparts and females who did not believe the task was gender-biased. These findings suggest that the influence of gender on academic effort and performance on exams for which there is a strong belief in gender bias, depends upon students' trait regulatory focus, such that particularly prevention-focused students' effort and performance is affected by these beliefs.

4. METHOD

4.1. Data

For the purpose of this study, we collected data from 233 college freshmen (64% men and 36% women) enrolled in the first year of a Business Administration program at a University college in Belgium. To measure personality, motivation regulation and academic effort, the participants completed an online questionnaire during a mandatory class 10 weeks before the end-of-semester exams. Afterwards, those data were merged with the exam results, based on the student registration numbers. The age of the participants ranged between 18 and 24 years (63% aged 18 years; 19% aged 19 years; 18% aged 20-24 years).

4.2. Measures

Personality. Mowen's Personality Scale (2000) was used to measure the Big Five personality factors. This compact inventory consists of only 15 items and is derived from Saucier's (1994) version of the much longer Five-Factor Personality Scale of Goldberg (1992). Mowen's instrument has already been used in several studies (Emmerik et al. 2004; Mowen and Sujan 2003) in which the convergent as well as the predictive validity of the measures has been demonstrated. In line with these results we found good to acceptable internal consistency with the Dutch version of this instrument (Cronbach's Alpha between .61 and .87; Berings & Adriaenssens, 2012). Each item consist of a short formulated characteristic (e.g., 'imaginative' or 'orderly') that is evaluated on a seven point scale (1: *does not correspond at all*; …; 7: *corresponds exactly*).

Amotivation, Intrinsic and Extrinsic motivation. To measure amotivation, intrinsic motivation (IM) and extrinsic motivation (EM), we used the Academic Motivation Scale of Vallerand et al. (1992). The questionnaire is based on the basic concepts of Self-Determination Theory (Deci & Ryan, 1985). The original distinction between IM and EM (Deci, 1975) is incorporated in the inventory, as well as the third motivational construct introduced by Deci and Ryan (1985), termed Amotivation. Along with the idea of the self-determination continuum (Deci & Ryan, 1985) distinct stages in EM are measured: External regulation (ER), Introjected regulation (IR) and identification (ID). The fourth stage formulated by Deci & Ryan termed 'integrated regulation' has not been included in the Academic Motivation by Vallerand et al. (1989; 1992) because it was difficult to make the empirical distinction from 'identified regulation'. Furthermore the instrument incorporates a differentiation within IM. Inspired by the original work of Deci (1975), Vallerand et al. (1989) developed a tripartite taxonomy of intrinsic motivation. The three correspondent scales in the inventory are: IM to Know (IK), IM to accomplish (IA) en IM to experience stimulation (IE). The Academic Motivation Scale consists of 28 items divided into seven subscales: three for EM, three for IM en one for AM. A sample item is "Why do you go to college?", followed by a statement that can be confirmed or not by the respondents on a seven point Likert scale going from 1 (= *does not correspond at all*) to 7 (= *corresponds exactly*). For each of these subscales satisfactory internal consistency values are found with values between .62 and .91. The reported Test-retest correlations are all above .70. The assumed underlying factor structure of the instrument has been confirmed fairly well by confirmatory Factor Analyses (LISREL) (Vallerand et al., 1992).

Work Value Orientations. In order to measure work value orientations, we used the Aspiration Index developed by Kasser and Ryan (1996) and adopted by Timmermans, Vansteenkiste and Lens (2004). Specifically, students are confronted with a set of extrinsic goal contents (EWV, e.g., wealth, fame, and image) and a set of intrinsic goal contents (IWV, e.g., affiliation, growth, and community) and are asked to estimate the importance of each goal to them on a seven point scale from 1 (= *not important*) to 7 (= *very important*).

Regulatory Focus. In order to measure the regulatory focus we used the Promotion/Prevention Scale (Lockwood et al., 2002) (PPS), which is one of the two distinct measures of regulatory focus that have been used in research. The alternative scale of Higgins et al. (2001), the Regulatory Focus Questionnaire (RFQ), reflects the conceptualization of regulatory focus in term of 'self-guide', while the Promotion/Prevention Scale reflects more the 'reference point' definition (Summerville & Roese, 2008). The 'self-guide'-approach focuses on the standards students use in their motivational self-regulation, respectively internal versus socially based standards for promotion versus prevention focus. The 'reference point' definition rather refers to the end state that students have in mind, respectively an end state formulated as a 'gain' versus a 'non-loss'. Other differences between the two scales are that RFQ induce a 'past'-orientation while the PPS is priming the respondents toward the future. Further, PPS contains emotional elements like 'hope' and 'anxiety', while RFQ does not focus on the affective component (Haws, Dholakia, & Bearden, 2010). Examples of items for each of the two focuses in the PPS are: "I typically focus on success I hope to achieve in the future" (Promotion) and "I frequently think about how I can prevent failures in my life" (Prevention). Each item is evaluated on a scale going from 1 (does not correspond at all) to 7 (corresponds exactly). In the original article of Lockwood et al. (2002) a Cronbach's alpha's of .81 and .75 is reported for promotion goal strength and prevention goal strength respectively. Also other studies report comparable levels of internal consistency and results of confirmatory factor analyses reveal acceptable goodness-of-fit measures (Haws et al., 2010). The assumption that promotion and prevention focus are independent dimensions is only partially confirmed. Correlations are found of .17·(Lockwood et al., 2002) and .27 and .12 (Haws et al., 2010).

Academic effort. Effort, as the behavioral component of Academic Motivation, has been measured by the motivation scale of the Learning and Study Strategies Inventory (LASSI; Cano, 2006; Olaussen & Braten, 1998; Olejnik & Nist, 1992; Weinstein et al., 1987). The items in this scale reflect what is expected of students or what their duties are (e.g., "I read textbook assigned for my classes") as well as forms of persistence (e.g., "I work hard to get a good grade, even when I don't like the course").

The scale consists of 8 items and all items are answered on a seven point Likert-type scale (1: *not at all like me*; …; 5: *very much like me*). De Feyter et al. (2012) reported, based on a comparable sample, a Cronbach's alpha of .83.

Academic performance. In this University college the study programs are composed of a number of courses that in total represent 60 European credits per year. The courses differ in the number of assigned credits. For each course included in the program the student is evaluated during the end-of-semester exams and given maximum of 20 marks. For each student in our sample we computed four indicators of academic performance.

- The first indicator (APa) is the number of obtained marks divided by the theoretical maximum number of marks based on his/her study program (in %).
- In the second indicator (APb) the nominator is the same as in the first indicator, but the denominator here is the total number of obtained marks only for the exams the student has participated in (in %).
- The third indicator (APc) is the ratio of the total number of obtained credits divided by the total number of credits in the study program (in %).
- The fourth indicator (APd) is a dummy variable (successful or not successful) which is derived directly from the third indicator. A student is called 'successful' if he/she has obtained as least 75% of the credits in the study program.

5. RESULTS

Table 1. Descriptive statistics and Cronbach's alpha's for the variables in this study.

	Mean	SD	α
Neuroticism	3.19	1.15	.783
Extraversion	4.48	1.27	.873
Openness	4.42	0.88	.759
Agreeableness	5.54	0.70	.731
Conscientiousness	4.60	1.21	.833
Amotivation	1.95	0.92	.828
Extrinsic motivation	5.57	0.67	.823
EM external regulation	5.96	0.73	.675
EM introjected regulation	4.98	1.12	.827
EM identification	5.76	0.73	.729
Intrinsic motivation	4.31	0.84	.896
IM to know	4.90	0.96	.832
IM to accomplish	4.45	1.05	.823
IM to experience stimulation	3.59	0.93	.770
Extrinsic work values	5.10	0.97	.827
EWV financial	5.64	0.95	.830
EWV social recognition	4.94	1.09	.819
EWV power	4.74	1.20	.871
Intrinsic work values	5.58	0.60	.754
IWV personal growth	5.95	0.63	.696
IWV community	4.92	0.91	.538
IWV affiliation	5.88	0.76	.687
Prevention focus	4.20	0.85	.790
Promotion focus	5.08	0.75	.823
Academic effort	4.72	0.80	.823

Table 1 shows the descriptive statistics as well as the Cronbach's alpha for all the variables in this study. For most scales, acceptable levels of internal consistency were obtained. The scale measuring extrinsic work values - community, however, only had a

Cronbach's alpha of .54. The results with this scale, therefore, need to be interpreted with caution.

5.1. Antecedents of Academic Effort

In this first part of the result section, we explore several antecedents of the effort students invest in their studies. We first consider gender as an antecedent of academic effort. Next, we look at personality and motivation regulation as possible antecedents of effort. Effort, in turn, is an important antecedent of academic performance, at which we take a closer look in the second part of the results section (see paragraph 5.2). Table 2 shows the bivariate correlations of the five personality traits and the different aspects of motivation regulation with academic effort and performance.

Table 2. Correlations of personality and motivation regulation with academic effort and performance.

	Academic effort	APa	APb	APc
Neuroticism	-.180**	-.061	-.049	-.031
Extraversion	.067	.071	.093	.040
Openness	.089	.105	.067	.066
Agreeableness	.253***	-.057	-.052	-.047
Conscientiousness	.493***	.189**	.208**	.185**
Amotivation	-.358***	-.158*	-.198**	-.130‡
Extrinsic motivation	.252***	.056	-.028	-.003
EM external regulation	.154*	.053	-.017	-.013
EM introjected regulation	.158*	.001	-.081	-.042
EM identification	.302***	.101	.067	.070
Intrinsic motivation	.299***	.103	.048	.065
IM to know	.278***	.068	.029	.049
IM to accomplish	.264***	.158*	.086	.119‡
IM to experience stimulation	.227**	.027	.000	-.011
Extrinsic work values	.103	-.042	-.059	-.057
EWV financial	.098	-.006	.008	-.028
EWV social recognition	.084	-.062	-.085	-.069
EWV power	.084	-.040	-.072	-.052
Intrinsic work values	.284***	.117	.057	.087
IWV personal growth	.306***	.164*	.101	.105
IWV community	.149*	-.023	-.042	-.030
IWV affiliation	.227**	.162*	.096	.150*
Prevention focus	.105	-.021	-.074	-.024
Promotion focus	.227**	.011	-.001	-.003

Note. ‡ p<.10 * p<.05; ** p<.01; *** p<.001.

5.1.1. Gender and Personality as Antecedents of Effort

A gender effect on academic effort was found. Women and men differed in the effort invested in their studies, $t(217) = -2.91$, $p < .01$. Women invested more effort in their studies than men ($M = 4.92$, $SD = .83$ and $M = 4.28$, $SD = 1.14$, respectively).

With respect to personality (see Table 2), neuroticism was negatively related to effort, $r = -.18$, $p < .01$, whereas conscientiousness and agreeableness were positively related to effort, $r = .49$, $p < .001$, and $r = .25$, $p < .001$, respectively. Students who scored low on neuroticism and high on conscientiousness and agreeableness invested more effort in their studies.

5.1.2. Motivation Regulation As Antecedent of Effort

In this section, we take a closer look at the relationship between the concepts of motivation regulation and work values as proposed by SDT and RFT, on the one hand and invested effort on the other hand.

The results showed that several aspects of motivation regulation were positively related to the effort invested by students (see Table 2). A significant positive relationship was found with both intrinsic and extrinsic motivation. More specifically, for extrinsic motivation, the subscales external regulation, introjected regulation as well as identification were all positively related to effort. For intrinsic motivation, the three subscales of intrinsic motivation to know, to accomplish and to experience stimulation, were all significantly positively related to effort.

The results were less supportive for the regulatory focus paradigm. A significant positive relationship was found for promotion focus but no relationship was found between prevention focus and effort.

With respect to work value orientation, the results showed no significant relationships for the extrinsic work values. The intrinsic work values, on the contrary, were all significantly positively related to effort. Specifically, students who scored higher on the intrinsic values of personal growth, contributing to society and affiliation, also scored higher on the effort invested in their studies.

5.2. Antecedents of Academic Performance

In this second part of the results, we look at several antecedents of the academic performance of students. First, we look at the correlation between academic effort and performance. A significant positive relationship of effort with APa ($r = .31$, $p < .001$), APb ($r = .27$, $p < .001$) and APc ($r = .26$, $p < .001$) was found. Students who invested more effort in their studies, also performed better. Next, parallel to the previous section, we look at more trait like concepts (i.e., gender and personality) as well as motivation regulation (i.e., SDT, regulatory focus and work value orientation).

5.2.1. Gender and Personality as Antecedents of Academic Performance

Besides the bivariate correlations of the personality traits with academic effort (see Section 5.1) Table 2 also shows the correlations with three measures of academic performance. Only conscientiousness was significantly positively related to academic performance. For all the other personality traits, the relationship with academic performance did not reach significance.

Table 3. Gender and academic performance.

		Male			Female		
Population (N=277)	%	Mean	SD	%	Mean	SD	T-test
% obtained marks (APa)		37.9	18.6		44.3	16.2	-2.91**
% obtained marks participated exams (APb)		43.7	13.7		47.7	12.5	-2.28*
% obtained credits (APc)		41.3	30.0		49.3	28.3	-2.14*
Successful students (dummy) (APd)	17.7			23.1			
Sample (N=233)	%	Mean	SD	%	Mean	SD	T-test
% obtained marks (APa)		39.3	17.7		46.1	16.5	-2.63**
% obtained marks participated exams (APb)		44.9	13.2		49.9	12.2	-2.81**
% obtained credits (APc)		44.4	29.8		52.3	28.1	-2.01*
Successful students (dummy) (APd)	19.6			27.1			

Note. ‡ p<.10 * p<.05; ** p<.01; *** p<.001.

Further, we conducted some t-tests in order to investigate gender differences in academic performance (see Table 3). We did these analyses for the sample (students who participated in this study) as well as the whole population (all the students enrolled in this educational program, including those who were absent during the lecture in which the survey was taken). For all our measures of AP, the results of the t-tests showed that women outperform men. Remark that the gender differences are similar for the sample and the population. The results of the whole population are slightly lower than those for the sample, reflecting the lower results of students that not attend classes.

5.2.2. Motivation Regulation as Antecedent of Academic Performance

As can be seen in Table 2, amotivation was significantly related to academic performance. Students who were amotivated performed less well. Both extrinsic and intrinsic motivation were unrelated to academic performance. Also for prevention and promotion focus, no significant relationships were found with academic performance. And finally, also for work values, no significant relationships were found with academic performance.

5.3. Interrelationships between the Antecedents of Effort and Academic Performance

In this section, we investigated how the different antecedents of effort and academic performance, that were studied in Section 5.1 and 5.2, were related to each other. We first investigated the relationship between gender on the one hand and personality and motivation regulation on the other hand. Second, we looked at the relations between personality and motivation regulation.

5.3.1. Gender Differences in Personality and Motivation Regulation

We looked at gender differences with respect to motivation regulation, both in terms of SDT and in terms of regulatory focus, as well as in respect to work value orientations (see Table 4).

For motivation regulation, no gender differences were observed. Women and men did not differ in intrinsic, extrinsic or amotivation, or in any of the subscales. However, there was a marginally significant difference in amotivation, in the sense that men scored slightly higher than women. Also, no differences between women and men were found with respect to promotion and prevention focus.

With respect to work value orientation, several significant gender differences were observed, especially with respect to extrinsic work value orientations, for which men obtained higher scores than women. Specifically, men were found to attach more importance to financial aspects of the job and power. The difference with respect to social recognition was only marginally significant. Women, on the other hand, attached more importance to affiliation than men.

Table 4. Gender differences in personality and motivation regulation.

	Male		Female		
	Mean	SD	Mean	SD	T-test
Neuroticism	3.19	1.18	3.17	1.09	0.09
Extraversion	4.49	1.23	4.47	1.35	0.11
Openness	4.54	0.78	4.22	1.01	2.49*
Agreeableness	5.45	0.66	5.72	0.75	-2.77**
Conscientiousness	4.28	1.14	5.16	1.12	-5.53***
Amotivation	2.03	0.92	1.79	0.89	1.89‡
Extrinsic motivation	5.56	0.65	5.58	0.72	-0.12
EM external regulation	6.00	0.71	5.88	0.75	1.18
EM introjected regulation	4.95	1.17	5.03	1.08	-0.52
EM identification	5.73	0.73	5.82	0.73	-0.82
Intrinsic motivation	4.27	0.79	4.39	1.09	0.09
IM to know	4.87	0.89	1.94	1.09	0.11
IM to accomplish	4.37	1.03	4.60	1.08	-1.55
IM to experience stimulation	3.57	0.87	3.62	1.04	-0.39
Extrinsic work values	5.23	0.94	4.85	0.98	2.85**
EWV financial	5.77	0.91	5.40	0.97	2.75**
EWV social recognition	5.03	1.08	4.75	1.09	1.80‡
EWV power	4.93	1.15	4.39	1.20	3.27**
Intrinsic work values	5.53	0.62	5.66	0.55	-1.57
IWV personal growth	5.93	0.64	5.98	1.61	-0.57
IWV community	4.89	0.91	4.97	0.92	-0.68
IWV affiliation	5.79	0.77	6.03	0.71	2.32*
Prevention focus	4.14	0.82	4.31	0.90	-1.42
Promotion focus	5.11	0.75	5.03	0.75	0.71

Note. ‡ p<.10 * p<.05; ** p<.01; *** p<.001.

5.3.2. Relationships between Personality and Motivation Regulation

Table 5 shows the bivariate correlations between the five personality traits on the one hand and the different aspects of motivation regulation on the other hand.

Neuroticism was significantly positively related to amotivation while extraversion, agreeableness and conscientiousness were significantly negatively related to amotivation. Neuroticism was negatively related to the extrinsic motivation subscale of identification. Extraversion, openness and agreeableness on the other hand, were significantly positively related to identification.

With respect to intrinsic motivation, significant relationships were observed with openness and conscientiousness. Especially the intrinsic motivation to know and to accomplish were significantly positively related to both personality traits. The intrinsic motivation to experience stimulation was only significantly related to openness while the intrinsic motivation to know was also positively related to agreeableness.

Students who scored higher on prevention focus scored higher on the personality traits of neuroticism and conscientiousness but lower on extraversion and openness. Students who scored higher on promotion focus, on the contrary, scored higher on extraversion, openness, agreeableness and conscientiousness.

With respect to the extrinsic work values, students higher on extraversion attach more importance to extrinsic work values, especially financial values and power. Also students higher on openness, attach more importance to power. For the intrinsic work values, personal growth was positively related to extraversion, openness and agreeableness. The latter was also related to the intrinsic value of community and affiliation.

Table 5. Correlations of personality and motivation regulation with academic effort and performance

	Neuroticism	Extraversion	Openness	Agreeableness	Conscientiousness
Amotivation	.150*	-.215**	.036	-.091*	-.215**
Extrinsic motivation	-.077	.113‡	.100	.144*	.180**
EM external regulation	-.131‡	.138*	.005	.106	.125‡
EM introjected regulation	.052	.008	.109	.048	.185**
EM identification	-.159*	.162*	.104*	.221***	.091
Intrinsic motivation	.052	.075	.297***	.079	.208**
IM to know	.044	.117‡	.315***	.125*	.143*
IM to accomplish	.042	.070	.174*	.079	.271***
IM to experience stimulation	.048	.005	.285***	-.003	.109
Extrinsic work values	.044	.179**	.173**	-.003	-.004
EWV financial	-.400	.201**	.089	.034	-.005
EWV social recognition	.093‡	.070	.131	.042	.013
EWV power	.072	.199**	.240***	-.080	-.011
Intrinsic work values	-.086*	.141*	.039*	.305***	.138*
IWV personal growth	-.103	.220**	.247***	.200**	.084
IWV community	-.025	.056‡	.056‡	.209**	.077
IWV affiliation	-.059	.067	-.169*	.290***	.178**
Prevention focus	.136*	.200**	-.159*	.075	.163*
Promotion focus	.067	.124*	.241***	.230***	.209**

Note. ‡ p<.10 * p<.05; ** p<.01; *** p<.001.

5.4. Relative Weight of the Antecedents of Effort and Academic Performance

Two stepwise multiple hierarchical regression analyses were used to investigate the relative unique predictive validity of each of the antecedents discussed in the previous section for effort and academic performance. At each step of the process the criteria for inclusion and exclusion in the model are respectively $p < .10$ and $p > .15$. In the first step, gender was added as a predictor. In the second step, the five personality traits of the Big Five were added to the regression equation, followed by the motivation regulation variables in the third step. In the fourth step, the different work value orientations were added. The regression analyses with respect to academic performance also contained a fifth step in which effort was added as a final predictor.

Table 6. Results of the hierarchical regression analysis of academic effort.

	Academic effort			
	Step 1	Step 2	Step 3	Step 4
Step 1: Gender	-.194**	-.030	-.010	-.007
Step 2: Big Five personality traits				
Conscientiousness		.464***	.383***	.383***
Neuroticism		-.175**	-.156**	-.147**
Openness		.128**	.113‡	.078
Agreeableness		.122*	.114*	.086
Step 3: Motivation regulation				
Amotivation			-.263***	-.233***
IM to experience stimulation			.119*	.100‡
Prevention focus			.113‡	.119*
Step 4: Work value orientation				
IWV personal growth				.155**
ΔR^2	.038**	.271***	.083***	.020**
Total adjusted R^2	.033**	.292****	.368***	.385***

Note. ‡ p<.10 * p<.05; ** p<.01; *** p<.001. The standardized regression coefficients are presented.

The results of the regression analysis on academic effort are reported in Table 6. The results showed significant gender differences in effort in step one. This effect, however, became insignificant when controlling for conscientiousness, neuroticism, openness and agreeableness in step 2. Whereas the relationship between neuroticism and effort was significantly negative, students who scored higher on conscientiousness, openness and agreeableness were found to invest more effort in their studies. With respect to motivation regulation (step 3), amotivation was significantly negatively related to effort while the intrinsic motivation subscale of stimulation was related positively to effort. The relationship to prevention focus was only marginally significant in this step but became significantly positive only after controlling for work values. Of the latter, the work value of growth was related significantly positively to effort invested. The proposed model explained 39% of the variance in effort.

Table 7 shows the results of the regression analysis with respect to AP. For this multivariate analysis, we have chosen to use indicator APb (i.e., the number of obtained marks divided by the total number of obtained marks, but only for the exams the student has participated in) as measure for academic performance. This indicator meets best the assumption of normality (Kolmogorrov-Smirnov-statistic=.036; v=228; p=.200) while the other indicators deviate significantly from the normal distribution. Similar to the results of the regression analysis on academic effort, a negative relationship was found between gender and academic performance in the first step of the regression equation. This means that female students outperformed their male colleagues. This relationship, however, became smaller after entering the personality traits in the second step. Specifically, conscientiousness was related positively to academic performance whereas agreeableness was related negatively to academic performance. Conscientiousness seemed to be the most important personality trait with respect to both effort and academic performance. In the third step of the regression analysis, motivation regulation was added. Amotivation and introjected regulation were related significantly negatively to academic performance and IM to accomplish was related positively to it. There was no significant relationship with prevention and promotion focus. In Step 4 of the stepwise regression procedure, we entered work value orientation into the regression equation. However, work values did not significantly explained the variance in APb, above gender, personality and motivation regulation. In the last step, academic effort was added to the model, which was related significantly positively to academic performance. Remark that the effect of conscientiousness and amotivation was no longer significant after including academic effort in the model. The regression coefficient of introjected regulation however did not change after adding effort to the model. This suggests that academic effort mediates the relation of conscientiousness and amotivation to academic performance, but does not mediate the relation between introjected regulation and AP. Gender, personality, motivation regulation and academic effort explained a significant amount of variance in academic performance, namely 12%.

Table 7. Results of the hierarchical regression analysis of academic performance

	APb				
	Step 1	Step 2	Step 3	Step 4	Step 5
Step 1: Gender	-.184**	-.141‡	-.123‡	-.123‡	-.125‡
Step 2: Big Five personality traits					
Conscientiousness		.187*	.156*	.156*	.078
Agreeableness		-.121‡	-.127‡	-.127‡	-.156*
Step 3: Motivation regulation					
Amotivation			-.143*	-.143*	-.091
EM introjected regulation			-.240**	-.240**	-.238**
IM to accomplish			.191*	.191*	.163‡
Step 4: Work value orientation					
Step 5: Academic effort					.208*
Δ Adjusted R²	.034**	.037*	.055**	0	.029*
Total adjusted R²	.029**	.057**	.099***	.099***	.124***

Note. ‡ p<.10 * p<.05; ** p<.01; *** p<.001. The standardized regression coefficients are presented.

CONCLUSION

In this chapter, we explored the black box between gender and academic performance. We explored our theoretical expectations using a sample of 233 college freshmen in a Business Administration program. Also in this sample, we found gender differences in academic performance. Female students outperformed their male colleagues. We expected that academic motivation could be the missing link to fully understand this gender effect on AP. Exploration of the literature however reveals that we can distinguish different ways to approach academic motivation. On the one hand, we can recognize a trait component in motivation that possibly could be captured in personality traits like conscientiousness and openness. On the other hand, there exists a behavioral component in academic motivation that reflects the way students perceive and evaluate their own study effort. In this study, we explored whether motivation regulation processes could mediate the relation between personality (motivation as trait) and academic effort (behavioral component of motivation). We focused on two paradigms concerning motivation regulation that can bring more clarity in the chain between traits and study outcomes, namely SDT and RFT.

Our results confirm the positive effect of academic effort on performance. Although female students clearly showed higher levels of study effort than male students, our findings suggest that this can only partly explain the gender difference in AP. Therefore, it was even more interesting to explore the effects of personality and motivation regulation, because they might have a direct effect and/or an indirect effect on academic performance through study effort. This exploration could further reveal the underlying mechanisms explaining the gender difference in AP.

Our findings suggest that personality was related to AP, and certainly to effort. We found support for the well documented and substantial positive correlation between the personality trait conscientiousness on the one hand and academic effort and performance on the other hand. Moreover, the relation between conscientiousness and academic achievement was fully mediated by effort. This sheds some light on the black box between gender and AP, because, as already reported in previous studies, female students scored higher on conscientiousness than male students.

Although we also found gender differences in openness and agreeableness, these personality traits did not contribute to the explanation of the gender difference in AP. While openness (and neuroticism) had a unique predictive validity for academic effort, these effects eventually had no significant influence on academic performance. Thus the theoretically expected, but empirically not confirmed relationship between openness and academic performance is also not found in our dataset. Further, agreeableness was positively related to effort. But it had a unique negative effect on academic achievement. Because we also found a positive correlation of agreeableness with the IM dimension 'identification' and the 'promotion focus', these findings raise the question of whether high scores on certain aspects of motivation might not be contaminated by social desirability. The results show no relation of extraversion with academic effort, nor to performance, which could be explained by two opposite and neutralizing effects of this personality trait on academic effort and performance.

In conclusion, while conscientiousness and agreeableness fully explained the difference between male and female students in academic effort, conscientiousness is the only Big Five personality trait for which our results indicate a partial explanation for the gender effect on AP.

Concerning motivation regulation, the results show that the concepts borrowed from SDT and RFT only had a small unique predictive validity for academic effort and performance. From SDT we theoretically expected that intrinsic motivation and the nearest forms of extrinsic motivation would predict study effort and academic performance. Our findings show that the dimensions of extrinsic and intrinsic motivation were positively correlated with academic effort. Nevertheless, the intrinsic motivation to accomplish was the only dimension of extrinsic and intrinsic motivation for which a positive correlation with AP was found. Moreover, it had a unique effect beyond personality and academic effort. Amotivation had a significant negative effect on academic effort and performance. As with the conscientiousness effect, the relation between amotivation and AP was fully mediated by study effort.

The concepts of motivation regulation were clearly related to some personality traits. Our findings suggest that, except for the intrinsic motivation to experience stimulation, the impact of extrinsic and intrinsic motivation on study effort seemed already to be included in personality, especially in conscientiousness. The intrinsic motivation to experience stimulation was the only dimension of extrinsic and intrinsic motivation that had a unique significant impact on academic effort and that was not related to the strongest predictor of academic effort, i.e. conscientiousness. This personality trait was also negatively related to amotivation. However, both conscientiousness and amotivation had unique predictive validity for academic effort. Study effort seems to be composed of three elements: sense of duty, interest and pleasure in learning.

Although the results on extrinsic and intrinsic motivation are valuable to understand the relation between personality, academic effort and performance, they do not contribute to the explanation of gender differences in study effort and AP. The reported gender differences in the dimensions of extrinsic and intrinsic motivation are in line with expectations, but they are statistically not significant. However, we did find a significant gender difference in amotivation. Male students showed higher levels of amotivation than female students and thus, besides conscientiousness, partially explained the gender effect on AP through study efforts.

From RFT, we expected that promotion and prevention focus both contribute to study effort and academic performance, because higher educational approaches evoke and support both orientations. We expected the highest predictive power from prevention focus because we observed that the educational approach evolved in the direction of more formalized educational learning outcomes and paths whereby academic motivation could be more regulated by external established objectives and criteria rather than by personal goals and aspirations. The results show that promotion focus was positively correlated with academic effort, but this effect was fully captured by the personality traits conscientiousness, openness and agreeableness. Prevention focus on the other hand had no a significant correlation with study effort nor with AP. Only after controlling for other significant predictors of effort, prevention focus had a modest unique positive relation to effort. As no significant gender differences in promotion and prevention focus were found, RFT did not contribute to the explanation of the gender effect on study effort or on AP.

Besides current motivational regulation, the literature suggests that distant work goals or aspiration could also possibly influence study effort and academic performance. Our empirical exploration of the valence of distant work goals, conceptualized within the SDT framework, reveals that male students attached more value to extrinsic work goals than female students. This could have contributed to the explanation of the effect of gender on AP, because the literature suggests that extrinsic value pursuit is likely to harm performance. However, extrinsic work goals were not significantly related to study effort, nor to academic performance. Intrinsic work goals, on the other hand, were clearly correlated with study effort, especially personal growth. However, the results did not show gender differences in intrinsic work goals.

Explaining the variance in academic performance was shown to be a tricky endeavor. All our possible predictors together explained only a modest fraction of academic performance. Maybe other factors, above all talent and competence, could explain academic performance.

The results suggest that we must not overestimate the role of motivation regulation. The reason for this may be twofold. One the one hand, the theoretical concepts supplied by the two paradigms under consideration might have limited predictive power. On the other hand, it is possible that the measures used are not optimal. One possible critique is that the measures used for the motivation regulations are too much trait based. A suggestion for future research on this topic is to complement the measures used in this study, especially the measures for prevention and promotion focus, with more situation specific measures that assess the regulation focus in a specific educational situation like lectures, assignments and exams.

To study gender differences in academic performance, it seems worthwhile to explore the expectations induced by the educational approach on the one hand and the personality and motivation regulations of the students on the other hand, and how the fit or misfit between both can have an impact on academic performance. However, in the present study, we restricted ourselves to the individual level because only one educational context is taken into account. In future research we want to broaden the research design by including educational programs taken from different fields of study (economy, health care, social work, education, linguistics, …) and belonging to different higher educational institutions. Such a design will allow us to explore the effect of individual difference as well as domain and institution related characteristics on academic effort and performance. It also opens perspectives to explore further the concept of 'student-approach'-fit by measuring both sides of the fit in a commensurate way using concepts of SDT or RFT discussed and explored in this chapter at the individual level.

REFERENCES

Adams, L., Faseur, T., & Geuens, M.(2011). The Influence of the Self-Regulatory Focus on the Effectiveness of Stop-Smoking Campaigns for Young Smokers. *Journal of Consumer Affairs,* 45, 275-305.

Ashton, M., Lee, K., Vernon, P., & Jang, K. (2000). Fluid intelligence, crystallized intelligence, and the openness/intellect factor. *Journal of Research in Personality,* 34, 198-207.

Berings, D., & Adriaenssens, S. (2012). The role of business ethics, personality, work values and gender in vocational interests from adolescents. *Journal of Business Ethics,* 106, 325-335.

Berings, D., De Fruyt, F., Bouwen, R. (2004). Work values and personality traits as predictors of enterprising and social vocational interests. *Personality and Individual Differences,* 36, 349-364.

Betts, J. R., & Morell, D. (1999) The Determinants of Undergraduate Grade Point Average: The Relative Importance of Family Background, High School Resources, and Peer Group Effects, *The Journal of Human Resources,* 34, 268-293.

Blickle, G. (1996). Personality traits, learning strategies, and performance. *European Journal of Personality,* 10, 337-352.

Brazy, C. P., & Shah, J. Y. (2005). Regulatory focus as a moderator of stereotypethreat. *Unpublished manuscript.*

Brebels, L., De Cremer, D., & Sedikides, C. (2008). Retaliation as a response to procedural unfairness: A self-regulatory approach. *Journal of Personality and Social Psychology, 95,* 1511-1526.

Brebels, L., De Cremer, D., van Dijke, M., & Van Hiel, A. (2011). Fairness as social responsibility: A moral self-regulation account of procedural fairness enactment. *British Journal of Management, 22,* 47-58.

Bridgeman, B., & Wendler, C. (1991) Gender Differences in Predictors of College Mathematics Performance and in College Mathematics Course Grades, *Journal of Educational Psychology, 83,* 275-284.

Busato, V.V., Prins, F.J., Elshout, J.J., & Hamaker, C. (1999). The relation between learning styles, the Big Five personality traits and achievement motivation in higher education. *Personality and Individual Differences, 26,* 129-140.

Byrnes, J.P., Hong, L., & Xing, S. (1997). Gender differences on the Math Subtest of the Scholastic Aptitude Test may be culture-specific, *Educational Studies in Mathematics, 34,* 49-66.

Cano, F. (2006). An in-depth analysis of the Learning and Study Strategies Inventory (LASSI). *Educational and Psychological Measurement, 66,* 1023-1038.

Chamorro-Premuzic, T., & Furnham, A. (2003a). Personality predicts academic performance: evidence from two longitudinal university samples. *Journal of Research in Personality, 17,* 319-338.

Chamorro-Premuzic, T., & Furnham, A. (2003b). Personality traits and academic examination performance. *European Journal of Personality, 17,* 237-250.

Chamorro-Premuzic, T., & Furnham, A. (2008). Personality, intelligence and approaches to learning as predictors of academic performance. *Personality and Individual Differences, 44,* 1596-1603.

Chapman, P.B., Duberstein, P.R., Sörensen, S., & Lyness, J.M. (2007). Gender differences in Five Factor Model personality traits in an elderly cohort: Extension of robust and surprising findings to an older generation. *Personality and Individual Differences, 43,* 1594-1603.

Costa, P. T., & McCrae, R. R. (1992a). *NEO-PI-R. Professional manual.* Odessa, FL: Psychological Assessment Resources.

Costa, P. T., & McCrae, R. R. (1992b). *Revised NEO personality inventory and five-factor inventory professional manual.* Odessa, FL: Psychological Assessment Resources.

Costa, P. T., Terracciano, A., & McCrae, R. R. (2001). Gender differences in personality traits across cultures: Robust and surprising findings. *Journal of Personality and Social Psychology, 81,* 322-331.

Crowe, E., & Higgins, E. T. (1997). Regulatory Focus and Strategic Inclinations: Promotion and Prevention in Decision-Making. *Organizational Behavior and Human Decision Processes, 69,* 117-132.

Dayioglu, M., & Türüt-Asik, S. (2004). *Gender differences in academic performance in a large public university in Turkey. ERC Working Papers in Economics* (17). Ankara: Economic Research Center, Middle East Technical University.

De Bilde, J., Vansteenkiste, M. & Lens, W. (2011). Understanding the association between future time perspective and self-regulated learning through the lens of self-determination theory. *Learning and Instruction, 21, 332-344.*

Deci, E.L. (1975). *Intrinsic motivation.* New York: Plenum Press.

Deci, E. L., Koestner, R., & Ryan, R. M., (1999). A meta-analytic review of experiments examining the effects of extrinsic rewards on intrinsic motivation. *Psychological Bulletin,* 125, 627-668.

Deci, E. L., & Ryan, R. M. (1985). *Intrinsic Motivation and Self-determination in Human Behavior.* New York: Plenum Press.

Deci, E. L., & Ryan, R. M. (2000). The 'what' and 'why' of goal pursuits: Human needs and the self-determination of behavior. *Psychological Inquiry,* 11, 227-268.

Deci, E.L.,& Ryan, R.M. (2002). *Handbook of self-determination research.* Rochester:The University of Rochester Press.

Deci, E. L., & Ryan, R. M. (2012). Self-determination theory. In P. A. M. Van Lange, A. W. Kruglanski, & E. T. Higgins (Eds.), *Handbook of theories of social psychology: Vol. 1 .* (pp. 416-437). Thousand Oaks, CA: Sage.

De Feyter, T., Caers, R., Vigna, C., & Berings, D. (2012). Unraveling the impact of the Big Five personality traits on academic performance : The moderating and mediating effects of self-efficacy and academic motivation. *Learning and Individual Differences,* 22, 439-448.

De Fruyt, F., & Mervielde, I. (1996). Personality and interests as predictors of educational streaming and achievement. *European Journal of Personality,* 10, 405-425.

De Fruyt, F., Van Leeuwen, K., De Bolle, M., & De Clercq, B. (2008). Sex differences in school performance as a function of conscientiousness, imagination and the mediating role of problem behaviour. *European Journal of Personality,* 22, 167-184.

De Raad, B., & Schouwenburg, H.C. (1996). Personality in learning and education: A review. *European Journal of Personality,* 10, 303-336.

Duriez, B., Meeuws, J., & Vansteenkiste, M. (2012). Why are some people more susceptible to ingroup threat than others? The importance of a relative extrinsic to intrinsic value orientation. *Journal of Research in Personality,* 146, 164-172.

Duriez, B., Vansteenkiste, M., Soenens, B., & De Witte, H. (2007). The social costs of extrinsic relative to intrinsic goal pursuits: Their relation with social dominance and racial and ethnic prejudice. *Journal of Personality,* 75, 757-782.

Evers, F., & Mancuso, M. (2006). Where are the boys? Gender imbalance in higher education. *Higher Education Management and Policy,* 18, 1-13.

Farsides, T. L., & Woodfield, R. (2003). Individual differences and undergraduate academic success: The roles of personality, intelligence and application. *Personality and Individual Differences,* 34, 1225-1243.

Feather, N. (1992). Values, valences, expectations, and actions. *Journal of Social Issues,* 48, 109-124.

Feingold, A. (1998). Cognitive gender differences are disappearing. *American Psychologist,* 43, 95-103.

Förster, J., Higgins, E. T., & Taylor Bianco, A. (2003). Speed/accuracy in performance: Trade-off in decision making or separate strategic concerns? *Organizational Behavior and Human Decision Processes,* 90, 148-164.

Freitas, A. L., Liberman, N., Salovey, P., & Higgins, E. T. (2002). When to begin? Regulatory focus and initiating goal-pursuit. *Personality and Social Psychology Bulletin,* 28, 121-130.

Friedman, R. S., & Förster, J. (2001). The effects of promotion and prevention cues on creativity. *Journal of Personality and Social Psychology,* 81, 1001-1013.

Furnham, A., & Monson, J. (2009). Personality traits and intelligence predict academic school grades. *Learning and Individual Differences, 18*, 28-33.

Gaudreau, P., & Antl, S. (2008). Athletes' broad dimensions of dispositional perfectionism: Examining changes in life satisfaction and the mediating role of sport-related motivation and coping. *Journal of Sport & Exercise Psychology, 30*, 356-382.

Goff, M., & Ackerman, P. (1992). Personality-intelligence relations: Assessment of typical intellectual engagement. *Journal of Educational Psychology, 84*, 537-552.

Goldberg, L. R. (1992). The development of markers of the Big-Five structure. *Psychological Assessment: A Journal of Consulting and Clinical Psychology, 4*, 26-42.

Gorman, C. A., Meriac, J. P., Overstreet, B. L., Apodaca, S., McIntyre, A. L., Park, P., & Godbey, J. N. (2012). A meta-analysis of the regulatory focus nomothetical network: Work-related antecedents and consequences. *Journal of Vocational Behavior, 80*, 160-172.

Grebennikov, L., & Skaines, I. (2009). Gender and higher education experience: A case study. *Higher Education Research & Development, 28*, 71-84.

Haws, K. L., Dholakia, U. M., & Bearden, W.O. (2010). An assessment of chronic regulatory focus measures. *Journal of Marketing Research, 47*, 967-982.

Higgins, E. T. (1997). Beyond pleasure and pain. *American Psychologist, 52*, 1280-1300.

Higgins, E. T., Friedman, R. S., Harlow, R. E., Idson, L. C., Ayduk, O. N., & Taylor, A. (2001). Achievement orientations from subjective histories of success: Promotion pride versus prevention pride. *European Journal of Social Psychology, 31*, 3-23.

Hui, E. P., Sun, R. F., Chow, S., & Chu, M. (2011). Explaining Chinese students' academic motivation: filial piety and self-determination. *Educational Psychology, 31*, 377-392.

Holland, D., Dollinger, S., Holland, C., & MacDonald, D. (1995). The relationship between psychometric intelligence and the five-factor model of personality in a rehabilitation sample. *Journal of Clinical Psychology, 51*, 79-88.

Hyde, J. S., & Kling, K. C. (2001). Women, Motivation and Achievement, *Psychology of Women Quarterly*, 25, 364-378.

Ingledew, D. K., Markland, D., & Sheppard, K. E. (2004). Personality and self-determination of exercise behaviour. *Personality and Individual Differences, 36*, 1921-1932.

Jang, H. (2008). Supporting Students' Motivation, Engagement, and Learning During an Uninteresting Activity. *Journal of Educational Psychology, 100*, 798-811.

Kark, R., & Van Dijk, D. (2007). Motivation to lead, motivation to follow: The role of the self-regulatory focus in leadership processes. *Academy of Management Review, 32*, 500-528.

Kasser, T. (2002). *The high price of materialism.* Cambridge Mass./London, England: The MIT Press.

Kasser, T., & Ryan, R. M. (1993). A dark side of the American dream: Correlates of financial success as a central life aspiration. *Journal of Personality and Social Psychology, 65*, 410-422.

Kasser, T., & Ryan, R. (1996). Further examining the American dream: Differential correlates of intrinsic and extrinsic goals. *Personality and Social Psychology Bulletin, 22*, 280-287.

Kasser, T., Ryan, R. M., Zax, M., & Sameroff, A. J. (1995). The relations of maternal and social environments to late adolescents' materialistic and prosocial values. *Developmental Psychology*, 31, 907-914.

Katz, I., Kaplan, A., & Buzukashvily, T. (2011). The role of parents' motivation in students' autonomous motivation for doing homework. *Learning and Individual Differences,* 21, 376-386.

Keller, J., & Bless, H. (2006). Regulatory fit and cognitive performance: The interactive effect of chronic and situational self-regulatory mechanism on cognitive test performance. *European Journal of Social Psychology,* 36, 393-405.

Kim, M. M., Rhoades, G., & Woodard, D. B. (2003). Sponsored Research versus Graduating Students? Intervening Variables and Unanticipated Findings in Public Research Universities. *Research in Higher Education,* 44, 51-81.

Komarraju, M., Karau, S. J., & Schmeck, R.R. (2009). Role of the Big Five personality traits in predicting college students' academic motivation and achievement. *Learning and Individual Differences* 19, 47–52.

Komarraju, M., & Karau, S. J. (2005). The relationship between the Big Five personality traits and academic motivation. *Personality and Individual Differences,* 39, 557-567.

Latham, G., & Pinder, C. (2005). Work motivation theory and research at the dawn of the twenty-first century. *Annual Review of Psychology,* 56, 485-516.

Lanaj, K., Chang, C-H., & Johnson, R. E. (2012). Regulatory focus and work-related outcomes: A review and meta-analysis. *Psychological Bulletin,* 138, 998-1034.

Langens, T. A. (2007). Regulatory focus and illusion of control. *Personality and Social Psychology Bulletin,* 33, 226-237.

Leonard, D. K., & Jiang, J. (1999) Gender Bias and the College Predictors of the SATs: A Cry of Despair. *Research in Higher Education,* 40, 375-407.

Lockwood, P., Jordan, C. H., & Kunda, Z. (2002). Motivation by positive and negative role models: Regulatory focus determines who will best inspire us. *Journal of Personality and Social Psychology,* 83, 854-864.

Lounsbury, J. W., Sundstrom, E. J., Loveland, J. M., & Gibson, L. W. (2003). Intelligence, 'Big Five' personality traits, and work drive as predictors of course grade. *Personality and Individual Differences,* 35, 1231-1239.

MacCann, C., Duckworth, A. L., & Roberts, R. D. (2009). Empirical identification of the major facets of conscientiousness. *Learning and Individual Differences,* 19, 451-458.

Maslow, A. (1955). Deficiency motivation and growth motivation. In M.R. Jones (Ed.), Nebraska symposium on motivation (Vol. 3, pp. 1–30). Lincoln: University of Nebraska Press.

Molden, D. C., Lee, A. Y., & Higgins, E. T. (2007). Motivations for Promotion and Prevention. In J. Y Shah and W.L. Gardner (Eds.) *Handbook of motivation science.* New York: Guilford Press.

Mowen, J. C. (2000). *The 3M Model of motivation and personality: Theory and empirical applications to consumer behavior.* Boston: Kluwer Academic.

Nguyen, N. T., Allen, L. C., & Fraccastoro, K. (2005). Personality predicts academic performance: exploring the moderating role of gender. *Journal of higher education policy and management,* 27, 105-116.

Niemiec, C. P., Lynch, M. F., Vansteenkiste, M., Bernstein, J., Deci, E. L., & Ryan, R. M. (2006). The antecedents and consequences of autonomous self-regulation for college: A self-determination theory perspective on socialization. *Journal of Adolescence,* 29, 761-775.

Niemiec, C. P., Ryan, R. M., & Deci, E. L. (2009). The path taken: Consequences of attaining intrinsic and extrinsic aspirations in post-college life. *Journal of Research in Personality*, 43, 291-306.

Nishimura, T., Kawamura, S., & Sakurai, S. (2011). Autonomous Motivation and Meta-Cognitive Strategies as Predictors of Academic Performance: Does Intrinsic Motivation Predict Academic Performance ? *Japanese Journal of Educational Psychology*, 59, 77-87.

Noftle, E. E., & Robins, R. W. (2007). Personality predictors of academic outcomes: big five correlates of GPA and SAT scores. *Journal of Personality and Social Psychology*, 93, 116-130.

Olaussen, B. S., & Braten, I. (1998). Identifying latent variables measured by the Learning and Study Strategies Inventory (LASSI) in Norwegian college students. *The Journal of Experimental Education*, 67, 82-96.

Olejnik, S., & Nist, S. L. (1992). Identifying latent variables measured by the Learning and Study Strategies Inventory (LASSI). *The Journal of Experimental Education*, 60, 151-159.

Olesen, M. H., Thomsen, D. K., Schnieber, A., & Tonnesvang, J. (2010). Distinguishing general causality orientations from personality traits. *Personality and Individual Differences*, 48, 538-543.

Pan, Y., & Gauvain, M. (2012). The continuity of college students' autonomous learning motivation and its predictors: A three-year longitudinal study. *Learning and Individual Differences*, 22, 92-99.

Paunonen, S. V., & Ashton, M. C. (2001). Big five factors and facets and the prediction of behavior. *Journal of Personality and Social Psychology*, 81, 524-539.

Pham, M. T., & Avnet, T. (2004). Ideals and oughts and reliance on affect versus substance in persuasion. *Journal of Consumer Research*, 30, 503-518.

Phillips, P., Abraham, C., & Bond, R. (2003). Personality, cognition, and university students' examination performance. *European Journal of Personality*, 17, 435-448.

Poropat, A. E. (2009). A meta-analysis of the five factor model of personality and academic performance. *Psychological Bulletin*, 135, 322-338.

Rindermann, H., & Neubauer, A. (2001). The influence of personality on three aspects of cognitive performance.: Processing speed, intelligence and school performance. *Personality and Individual Differences*, 30, 829-842.

Romero, E., Gómez-Fraguela, J. A., & Villar, P. (2012). Life aspirations, personality traits and subjective well-being in a Spanish sample. *European Journal of Personality*, 26, 45-55.

Rosander, P., Bäckström, M., & Stenberg, G. (2011). Personality traits and general intelligence as predictors of academic performance: A structural equation modelling approach. *Learning and Individual Differences*, 21, 590-596.

Rothstein, M., Paunonen, S., Rush, J., & King, G. (1994). Personality and cognitive ability predictors of performance in graduate business school. *Journal of Educational Psychology*, 86, 516-530.

Ryan, R. M., & Connell, J. P. (1989). Perceived locus of causality and internalization: Examining reasons for acting in two domain. *Journal of Personality and Social Psychology*, 57, 749-761.

Ryan, R. M., Chirkov, V. I., Little, T. D., Sheldon, K. M., Timoshina, E. & Deci, E. L. (1999). The American dream in Russia: Extrinsic aspirations and well-being in two cultures. *Personality and Social Psychology Bulletin*, 25, 1509-1524.

Sanchez-Marin, M., Rejano-Infante, E., & Rodriguez-Troyano, Y. (2001). Personality and academic productivity in the university student. *Social Behavior and Personality, 29,* 299-305.

Saucier, G. (1994). Mini-markers: A brief version of Goldberg's unipolar big-five markers. *Journal of Personality Assessment, 63,* 506-516.

Schmuck, P., Kasser, T., & Ryan, R. M. (2000). The relationship of well-being to intrinsic and extrinsic goals in Germany and the U.S. *Social Indicators Research, 50,* 225-241.

Seibt, B., & Förster, J. (2004). Stereotype Threat and Performance: How Self-Stereotypes Influence Processing by Inducing Regulatory Foci. *Journal of Personality and Social Psychology, 87,* 38-56.

Sen, A., & Hagtvet, K. (1993). Correlations among creativity, intelligence, personality, and academic achievement. *Perceptual and Motor Skills, 77,* 497-498.

Severiens, S., & ten Dam, G. (2012). Leaving College: A gender comparison in male and female-dominated programs. *Research in Higher Education, 53,* 453-470.

Shah, J., &, Gardner, W.L. (Eds.) (2008). *Handbook of motivation science.* New York: Guilford Press.

Shah, J., Higgins, E. T., & Friedman, R. S. (1998). Performance incentives and means: How regulatory focus influences goal attainment. *Journal of Personality and Social Psychology, 74,* 285–29.

Sheldon, K. M., & Krieger, L. (2004). Does law school undermine law students? Examining changes in goals, values, and well-being. *Behavioral Sciences and the Law, 22,* 261-286.

Soenens, B., & Vansteenkiste, M. (2005). Antecedents and outcomes of self-determination in three life domains: The role of parents' and teachers' autonomy support. *Journal of Youth and Adolescence, 34,* 589-604.

Soenens, B., Sierens, E.,Vansteenkiste, M., Dochy, F., & Goossens, L. (2012). Psychologically controlling teaching: Examining outcomes, antecedents, and mediators. *Journal of Educational Psychology, 104,* 108-120.

Stoeber, J., Childs, J. H., Hayward, J. A. & Feast, H.R. (2011). Passion and motivation for studying: predicting academic engagement and burnout in university students. *Educational Psychology, 31(4),* 513-528.

Summerville, A., & Roese, N. J. (2008). Self-Report Measures of Individual Differences in Regulatory Focus: A Cautionary Note. *Journal of Research in Personality, 42,* 247-254.

Timmermans, T., Vansteenkiste, M., & Lens, W. (2004). *Does an extrinsic values induction result in higher performance and persistence among extrinsically oriented individuals? A test of the self-determination theory versus the match hypothesis.* Internal research report, University of Leuven.

Trueman, M., & Hartley, J. (1996). A comparison between the time-management skills and academic performance of mature and traditional-entry students. *Higher Education, 32,* 199-215.

Vallerand, R.J., Blais, M.R., Brière, N.M., & Pelletier, L.G. (1989). Construction et validation de l'Echelle de Motivation en Education (EME). *Revue Canadienne des Science du Comportement, 21,* 323-349.

Vallerand, R. J., Fortier, M. S., & Guay, F. (1997). Self-determination and persistence in a real-life setting: Toward a motivational model of high school dropout. *Journal of Personality and Social Psychology, 75,* 1161-1176.

Vallerand, R.J., Pelletier, L.G., Blais, M.R., Brière, M.R., Senécal, C., & Vallières, E.F. (1992). The Academic Motivation Scale: A Measure of Intrinsic, Extrinsic, and Amotivation in Education. *Educational and Psychological Measurement, 52,* 1003-1017.

Vallerand, R. J., Pelletier, L. G., & Koestner, R. (2008). Reflections on self-determination theory. *Canadian Psychology, 49,* 257-262.

Vansteenkiste, M., Duriez, B., Simons, J., & Soenens, B. (2006). Materialistic values and well-being among business students: Further evidence for their detrimental effect. *Journal of Applied Social Psychology, 36,* 2892-2908.

Vansteenkiste, M., Lens, W., & Deci, E.L. (2006). Intrinsic Versus Extrinsic Goal Contents in Self-Determination Theory: Another Look at the quality of Academic Motivation. *Educational Psychologist, 41,* 19-31.

Vansteenkiste, M., Niemiec, C. P., & Soenens, B. (2010). The development of the five mini-theories of self-determination theory: An historical overview, emerging trends, and future directionsIn T. C. Urdan & S. A. Karabenick (Eds.), *Advances in motivation and achievement, v. 16A—The decade ahead: Theoretical perspectives on motivation and achievement* . (pp. 105-165). London: Emerald Group Publishing Limited.

Vansteenkiste, M., Sierens, E., Soenens, B., Luyckx, K., & Lens, W. (2009). Motivational profiles from a self-determination theory perspective: The quality of motivation matters. *Journal of Educational Psychology,* 101*(3),* 671-688.

Vansteenkiste, M., Simons, J., Lens, W., Sheldon, K. M., & Deci, E. L. (2004). Motivating learning, performance, and persistence: The synergistic role of intrinsic goals and autonomy-support. *Journal of Personality and Social Psychology, 87,* 246-260.

Vansteenkiste, M., Simons, J., Lens, W., Soenens, B., Matos, L. & Lacante, M. (2004). Less is sometimes more: Goal content matters. *Journal of Educational Psychology, 4,* 755-764.

Vansteenkiste, M., Timmermans, T., Lens, W., Soenens, B., & Van den Broeck, A. (2008). Does extrinsic goal framing enhance extrinsic goal oriented individuals' learning and performance? An experimental test of the match-perspective vs. self-determination theory. *Journal of Educational Psychology, 100,* 387-397.

Vaughn, L.A., Baumann, J., & Klemann, C.(2008). Openness to Experience and regulatory focus: Evidence of motivation from fit. *Journal of Research in Personality, 42,* 886-894.

Vroom, V. (1964). *Work and motivation.* New York: Wiley.

Wainer, H., & Steinberg, L. S. (1992) Sex Differences in Performance on the Mathematics Section of the Scholastic Aptitude Test: A Bidirectional Validity Study, *Harvard Educational Review, 62,* 323-336.

Weinstein, C. E., Schulte, A., & Palmer, D. R. (1987). *The Learning and Study Strategies Inventory.* Clearwater, FL: H & H Publishing.

Wilberg, S., & Lynn, R. (1999). Sex differences in historical knowledge and school grades: A 26 nation study. *Personality and Individual Differences, 27,* 1221-1229.

Williams, G. C., Cox, E. M., Hedberg, V., & Deci, E. L. (2000). Extrinsic life goals and health risk behaviors in adolescents. *Journal of Applied Social Psychology, 30,* 1756-1771.

Williams, G. C., & Deci, E. L. (1996). Internalization of biopsychosocial values by medical students: A test of self-determination theory. *Journal of Personality and Social Psychology, 70,* 767-779.

Wolfe, R., & Johnson, S. (1995). Personality as a predictor of college performance. *Educational and Psychological Measurement, 55,* 177-185.

Woodfield, R., Jessop, D., & McMillan, L. (2006). Gender and higher education experience: A case study. *Studies in Higher Education, 31,* 1-22.

Young, J.W., & Fisler, J.L. (2000). Sex differences on the SAT: An analysis of demographic and educational variables. *Research in Higher Education, 41,* 401-416.

Younger, M., Warrington, M., & Williams, J. (1999). The gender gap and classroom interactions: Reality and rhetoric? *British Journal of Sociology of Education, 20,* 325-341.

Reviewed by Prof. Dr. Willy Lens and Prof. Dr. Marlies Lacante, K.U. Leuven.

In: Handbook of Academic Performance
Editors: Rolf Haumann and George Zimmer

ISBN: 978-1-62417-888-7
© 2013 Nova Science Publishers, Inc.

Chapter 2

PERFORMANCE STANDARDS IN HIGHER EDUCATION: TRUTH AND CONSEQUENCES

William Swart[*], *Steve Duncan and Cathy Hall*

East Carolina University
Greenville, NC, US

ABSTRACT

We live in a changed and changing world where knowledge is being generated at unprecedented rates. In this chapter, we discuss how institutions of higher education can incorporate appropriate and valid new knowledge into their curricula through a process that examines the strengths, weaknesses, opportunities and threats associated with doing so. We also discuss the timely and responsive development of learner performance standards and their inclusion into a strategic plan that provides timely feedback on whether these standards are having the anticipated results. We then discuss how these activities create a four way dilemma: 1) Students who resist the effort to meet the performance standards, but still want a degree; 2) Institutions of higher education who must maintain or grow budgets and hence must attract and retain students; 3) Faculty members who wish to become tenured and/or promoted and require favorable student opinion of instruction; and, 4) Employers who expect that a university degree certifies that the student possesses certain levels of knowledge.

INTRODUCTION

Performance standards should guide an institution of higher learning to do the right things well. Few would argue that an institution of higher learning should prepare students to lead full and productive lives in the future. Yet, we know of few institutions that have taken an ongoing look at what the future holds and how to adapt *what* it does and *how* it does it, including being able to adapt its performance standards, to that future. We subscribe to Yogi Berra's (Berra, 1998) saying that "the future ain't what it used to be" – in other words,

---

[*] Email: swartw@ecu.edu

tomorrow the future will not look like it does today. Nevertheless, without adopting a view of the future, we will surely find ourselves subject to another Yogi Berra saying: "You got to be careful if you don't know where you are going because you might not get there."

One way to conjure up a vision of the future is to examine current trends. Karl Fisch (2012) presents a series of facts about Globalization, demographics, and the information age that will continue to have a significant impact on industry, academia and society in general. These are:

- China will soon become the number one English speaking country in the world.
- The 25% of India's population with the highest IQ is greater than the entire population of the United States. This means that India has more honor kids than America has kids.
- The top 10 in-demand jobs in 2010 did not exist in 2004.
- We are currently preparing students for jobs that do not exist yet, using technologies that haven't been invented in order to solve problems we don't even know are problems yet.
- The U.S. Department of Labor estimates that today's learner will have 10-14 jobs by the age of 38.
- 1 in 4 workers has been with their current employer for less than a year. 1 in 2 has been there for less than 5 years.
- 1 out of 8 couples married in the U.S. last year met online.
- There are 845 million monthly active users of Facebook. Facebook is now available in more than 70 languages. If Facebook were a country, it would be the third largest (behind China and India).
- Twitter is currently seeing about 50 million tweets per day. That breaks down to about 600 Tweets per second.
- There are 31 Billion searches on Google every month. In 2006, this number was 2.7 Billion.
- The first commercial text message was sent in December of 1992. Today, the number of text messages sent and received everyday exceeds the total population of the planet.
- Years it took to reach a market audience of 50 million:
  o Radio 38 years
  o TV 13 years
  o Internet 4 years
  o iPod 3 years
  o Facebook 2 years
- The number of internet devices in 1984 was 1,000. In 1992 it was 1,000,000 and in 2008 it was 1,000,000,000.
- There are 540,000 words in the English Language, about 5 times as many as during Shakespeare's time.
- It is estimated that a week's worth of New York Times contains more information than a person was likely to come across in a lifetime in the 18th century.

- It is estimated that 4 exabytes (4.0 x 10^19) of unique new information will be generated worldwide this year. That's estimated to be more than in the previous 5,000 years.
- The amount of new technical information is doubling every 2 years.
- For students starting a four year technical or college degree, half of what they learn in their first year of study will be outdated by their third year of study.
- TT Japan has successfully tested a fiber optic cable that pushes 14 trillion bits per second down a single strand of fiber.
- Digital music sales in 2011 outstripped physical sales for the first time ever.
- Revenue from the iPhone and iPad now account for 72 percent of Apple's revenue. Neither could be bought 5 years ago.
- Prediction: by 2013 a supercomputer will be built that exceeds the computation capability of the human brain.
- Predictions are that by 2049 a $1,000 computer will exceed the computational capabilities of the entire human species.
- In the time it would take to watch the "Did you know" video (approximately 5 minutes):
  - 67 babies were born in the U.S.
  - 274 babies were born in China.
  - 395 babies were born in India.
  - And, 694,000 songs were downloaded illegally.

This chapter examines some of the approaches that are being developed by individuals, business and academia in response to this changed and changing future. Particular emphasis will be given to institutions of higher learning since they are already in the midst of a dilemma that seeks to find an appropriate balance between meeting the needs of: 1) Students who are more interested in obtaining a degree than acquiring the knowledge that it implies; 2) Employers that are finding that new graduates do not possess expected skills; 3) Academic institutions who must attract and retain students to meet their budgetary requirements; and, 4) Faculty that face pressure to relax academic performance standards in order to receive good student evaluations, a necessary requirement for them to achieve promotion and tenure (Hall et al., 2012).

DIRECTIONS OF CHANGE

The global, demographic, and technology facts listed above indicate that we are living in "Exponential Times" and that, in Karl Fisch's words, "Shift Happens." This has a direct impact on everything that we do — everywhere. It requires significant adaptation by individuals, business/industry and academia. How they respond will dictate their future. Not surprisingly, pundits in all three areas have given their view on how the information presented has created trends of change in their areas.

Trends for Individuals

These facts indicate that we are currently experiencing "Exponential Times" and how entities, including individuals, respond will dictate their future. Michelle Trip (2009) points out that in the past, the Renaissance Man was revered but that in the Exponential Age, it will be the Exponential Man (or Woman) that will be revered. She characterizes such an individual as someone that can create value individually with broad impact. In other words, an Exponential Person is someone taking small actions with big results such as an independent iPhone developer. Because of technology, it no longer requires a corporation to launch great ideas or inventions that yield exponential value. She then states that a life of value in the future will require the following set of new skills:

Skill # 1: Rule-Breaking – Be ready to consider possibilities that others are told "don't make sense."

Skill # 2: Entrepreneurial – The ability to carve out personal opportunities and being able to find them.

Skill # 3: Self-Educating – Don't sit back and wait to be taught.

Skill # 4: Bonding – The ability to add value to people's lives much beyond just adding Facebook friends and having numerous twitter followers.

Skill # 5: Revolutionary – Understand that small ideas can create big revolutions.

Skill # 6: Visionary – Be able to imagine what is possible, imagine what is next, and predict the needs and values of tomorrow.

These skills, if successfully acquired, can profoundly affect the way we learn and work during Exponential Times.

Trends for Business/Industry

Haydn Shaughnessy (2011) writes the trends that are shaping business in response to their view of the future and lists them as:

- *New business platforms*: The new platforms should consist of highly scaled interactions in order to decrease the amount of time they take and increase their volume overall. Previously, platforms worked to lock users in, but we should work to create a set of simple, defined rules under which deals are carried out.
- *New business ecosystems*: The development and management of a new type of business ecosystem to gain and maintain a larger partner base than would be available under a direct contract basis.
- *'Universal connectors'*: These are devices through which business can be conducted anonymously and at a large scale, and examples of this are RSS and APIs. RSS and APIs are a set of standardized codes and standards that allow businesses to collaborate, often without even meeting. Through automated relationships, information is transferred more efficiently.

- *Cloud infrastructure*: Although a recent technology, cloud infrastructure allows for IT support and immediate access to data, files, and skills at a low cost. Additionally, it allows information to be stored remotely by a third party so that information is not harmed or destroyed if a disaster should occur.
- *Sapient Leaders*: These new leaders should be sapient, possessing a "sense of worldliness and wisdom beyond the reach of normal command and control management."
- **Radical Adjacency**: This concept refers to "an acquisition or market move that takes the buyer or executing company into markets where management has no current experience."
- **New ways to scale businesses**: Typically, we think of scaling businesses in terms of profitability or number of employees; however, we should consider new methods for which we scale ourselves and competition.
- **The rise of the global middle class**: There will be 1.15 billion people in the global middle class by 2030, up from 400 million in 2000.
- **The new global division of labor:** As China attempts to move up the value chain, its leaders will seek new sources of cheap labor elsewhere. Similarly, the demand for outsourcing skilled and unkilled labor in India will most likely increase dramatically. As a result of these changes, cheap labor will most likely shift to Africa and the middle class in the United States and Europe will crumble even further.
- **The externalizing of talent, and particularly the rise of the bottom of the pyramid as a source of information**: Modern technologies that are seen as high cost are also in demand in Western civilizations; however, these regions often cannot afford the high-cost of advances available in the United States.

The above trends that are italicized are considered to be the most important and are referred to the five pillars to success. The term pillar is used to denote an area of strong and solid competency (Vitalari and Shaugnessy, 2012).

Trends for Education

The New Media Consortium (DeSantis, 2012) through their Horizon's project identified 28 "metatrends that will influence education in the future. The top 10 of these are:

- The world of work is increasingly global and increasingly collaborative. As more companies move to the global marketplace, it is common for work teams to span continents and time zones. Not only are teams geographically diverse, they are also culturally diverse.
- People expect to work, learn, socialize, and play whenever and wherever they want to. Increasingly, people own more than one device, using a computer, smartphone, tablet and e-reader. People now expect a seamless experience across all their devices.
- The internet is becoming a global mobile network – and already is at its edges. Mobithinking reports there are now more than 6 billion active cell phone accounts.

1.2 billion have mobile broadband as well, and 85% of new devices can access the mobile web.

- The technologies we are using are increasingly cloud based and delivered over utility networks, facilitating the rapid growth of on-line videos and rich media. Our current expectation is that the network has almost infinite capacity and is nearly free of cost. One hour of video footage is uploaded every second to YouTube; over 250 million photos are sent to Facebook every day.

- Openness – concepts like open content, open data, and open resources, along with notions of transparency and easy access to data and information – is moving from a trend to a value for much of the world. As authoritative sources lose their importance, there is a need for more curation and other forms of validation to generate meaning in information and media.

- Legal notions of ownership and privacy lag behind the practices common in society. In an age when so much of our information, records, and digital content are in the cloud, and often clouds in other legal jurisdictions, the very concept of ownership is blurry.

- Real challenges of access, efficiency, and scale are redefining what we mean by quality and success. Access to learning in any form is a challenge in too many parts of the world, and efficiency in learning systems and institutions is increasing an expectation of governments – but the need for solutions that scale often trumps them both. Innovations in those areas are increasingly coming from unexpected parts of the world, including India, China, and central Africa.

- The Internet is constantly challenging us to rethink learning and education, while refining our notion of literacy. Institutions must consider the unique value that each adds to the world in which information is everywhere. In such a world, sense making and ability to assess the credibility of information and media are paramount.

- There is a rise in informal learning as individual needs are redefining schools, universities, and training. Traditional authority is increasingly being challenged, not only politically and socially, but also in academia – and worldwide. As a result, credibility, validity and control are all notions that are not givens when so much learning takes place outside school systems.

- Business models across the education ecosystem are changing. Libraries are deeply reimagining their missions; colleges and universities are struggling to reduce costs across the board. The educational ecosystem is shifting, and nowhere more so than in the world of publishing, where efforts to reimagine the book are having profound success, with implications that will touch every aspect of the learning enterprise.

Institutions of higher learning are expected to prepare individuals for success in life and work. Thus, they play a most critical role in making their two most important customers: new graduates and businesses, match each other's current and future needs while simultaneously preparing to contribute to creating a better world. Thus, the remainder of this chapter will focus on the issues facing institutions of higher learning in accomplishing this task.

SETTING PERFORMANCE STANDARDS FOR INSTITUTIONS OF HIGHER LEARNING IN A CHANGED AND CHANGING WORLD

It is interesting that all the trends for education defined earlier in this chapter focused exclusively on *how* to deliver credible learning and not on *what* to deliver (e.g. the content of that learning should be in the first place). In Exponential Times, the content of appropriate and relevant knowledge is also changing at exponential rates, and it is critical to determine which of this new knowledge should become part of the curricula.

Determining What New Knowledge to Introduce in the Curricula

In Exponential Times, the relevance and validity of information, technical in particular, is changing VERY rapidly (recall that for students starting a four year technical or college degree, what they learn in their first year of study will be outdated by their third year of study). This creates a major onus on institutions of higher learning because the faculty is typically resistive to curricular change and the time that is required by most university curriculum approval processes is usually measured in years. In order to maintain their relevance in Exponential Times, institutions of higher learning must become agile, flexible, and relevant. In other words, they must be able to incorporate new relevant and appropriate knowledge into their curricula (and take obsolete knowledge out), identify the risk and returns of doing so, and select that knowledge which will attract and retain the best students and make them valuable entrepreneurs and associates to the most rewarding companies.

New knowledge is generated through research and development and often involves university faculty members. It reaches the classroom only after (and if) it is presented at conferences and published in journals and, eventually, textbooks. This process can take years. Instead, institutions of higher learning must short circuit this process and identify early, through their research faculty, what knowledge is a candidate to be introduced into their curriculum now. One proven method to determine this is through a systematic process of identifying and analyzing the strengths, weaknesses, opportunities and threats (SWOT analysis) that are associated with the introduction of this new knowledge into the curriculum and whether it is consistent with the strategic plan of the institution (Swart, 2010).

Once the determination is made to include certain new knowledge into the curriculum, then the SWOT analysis has created expectations of how this new knowledge, appropriately packaged into new courses or made part of existing courses, will impact student enrollment, student recruitment by employers, and research productivity. However, for these expectations to become reality, appropriate and valid performance standards for the courses have to be developed.

Setting Performance Standards

Performance standards in institutions of higher learning exist at every level of the institution. In the classroom, they are typically specified in course syllabi. They specify the student performance required on a number of criteria (exams, term papers, homework assignments, etc.) to merit a specific grade. It is the instructor's responsibility to assess how well a student met the course standards and assign a corresponding grade. For instructors, performance standards are typically set and assessed by the department chair based on criteria agreed to via joint governance processes (faculty committees, faculty senates, etc.). These criteria are usually related to teaching effectiveness, research productivity, and service to the institution, profession and community. At the academic department and college levels, the performance standards are usually set by the academic deans and the vice chancellor for academic affairs respectively and usually include student enrollment as well as aggregate measures for research productivity, service to the university, profession and community, and teaching effectiveness. At the institution level, the performance standards for public institutions are set by legislative bodies through a board of governors and/or boards of trustees. These standards generally involve criteria that include benefits delivered to the region, state and society in general. The performance standards at one level of the institution must be *aligned* with the performance standards of the next higher and lower levels of the organization and this can be achieved via an appropriate strategic plan.

Performance standards are specifications of what outcomes are desired and can be thought of as constituting a roadmap for an automobile journey or a flight plan for a pilot. However, by themselves, they serve little purpose unless it can be assessed how actual performance compares to the standard, *and* corrective action is specified to close the gap between actual and standard. A system that achieves this purpose is referred to as a feedback control system. A strategic plan constitutes a feedback control system if it includes the following eight activities (Swart, 2010):

1) The development of an **ideal vision** that specifies survival, self-sufficiency, and positive quality of life for all stakeholders. Such an ideal vision is about societal value added, and recognizes that a university is a vehicle for achieving such an outcome (Bernardez et al., 2005; Kaufman, 2000, 2006). The institutional strategic plan and the college and department tactical plans, if there are any, can serve, for example, as the flight plan as long as they focus on *results* (where we are going and how will we know when we get there safely), in addition to (we are going to fly you in comfort, show you great movies, and serve you with a smile).

2) Develop a **mission** that specifies in measurable terms what results the academic system aspires to produce over a period of time in pursuit of the ideal vision. Note that statements such as "We will excel in research…" do not specify a destination in that there is no yardstick provided to indicate when you have arrived. They focus on means, rather than ends. One measurable result might be that the unit wishes to generate an average of $x per faculty member per year in externally supported research and/or that it wishes to generate an average of y refereed publications per faculty member per year.

3) Break down the mission into a *tactical plan* that specifies the sequence of yearly measurable **results** that, if accomplished, will result in the fulfillment of the mission. A key requirement of such a tactical plan is to forecast the "causes and effects" between the results and the operations, processes, and educational products.

4) Develop a timeline for each activity of the integrated set of operations and processes so that each of the yearly measurable results can be achieved.

5) Measure **performance** by collecting data on the results that have actually been achieved (actual average $/faculty member per year in externally supported research, number of graduates, number of graduates that are self-sufficient and self-reliant, etc.).

6) Compare actual yearly performance results to desired yearly results.

7) After comparing yearly performance to desired results, assess the *lessons learned*. One way to accomplish that is to perform the following exercise:

    a) Review each operation and process that has been undertaken and each product that has been produced over the past year.

    b) Compare the forecasted impact of each operation, process, and product to the actual results achieved.

    c) Conduct a **variance analysis** on those operations and processes whose result was different than forecasted. For each, search for an *assignable cause* for the variance. An assignable cause consists of a specific explainable reason for the discrepancy. If that cause or reason is likely to persist into the future, add the operation or process to a discussion list.

8) Update the strategic plan to reflect the lessons learned. This includes: 1) Updating old information and readjusting the plan accordingly; 2) Considering the inclusion of promising new operations and processes; 3) Considering the elimination of some of the underperforming operations and processes; and, 4) Revising the tactical plan, including the measurable results to be expected as a results of the updates.

In such a plan developed for a large southeastern university, the performance standards are for research expenditures, enrollment, and teaching evaluations because these are the criteria that influenced the allocation of budget by the state to the university, the university to the colleges and the college to the departments (Swart, 2010). Each department developed their own strategic plan. The departments are the deliverers of the academic products, principally courses, of the university. How well these courses, or the results of those courses – namely knowledge, are delivered by the faculty and received by the various customers of the university (students as well as employers) is the driver of the higher level performance standards (research expenditures, enrollment, and teaching evaluations) that are used in the college and university strategic plans. Thus, the performance standards for individual courses, which are spelled out in the course syllabi, indicate how students must perform in each in order to earn a particular grade and, presumably, utilize the knowledge gained to help them to lead full and productive lives. Instructors for each course assess how well each student meets the performance standards specified in the course's syllabus and assign a corresponding grade.

In Exponential Times, institutions of higher learning must change their educational products frequently in order to keep up with the rapid global changes in demographics and technology. To assess whether these new educational products are effectively meeting the needs of its customers, institutions of higher education must have an effective strategic plan that will assess whether these new products are meeting the performance standards set for them and, if not, to take rapid corrective action. Thus, in Exponential Times, strategic plans must be able to be updated in Logarithmic Times. In other words, even though change is Exponential, the impact of educational products designed to incorporate that change will continue to be periodic. Traditionally, the term 5-year plan and strategic plan are often used synonymously. This is no longer acceptable due to the amount of change that is occurring every five years. At the most, strategic plans must be updated every year *and* they must provide reliable feedback on the effectiveness of new academic products. This feedback must lead to the rapid reconfiguration of academic programs that discard ineffective academic products and adopt promising new ones.

Change is ubiquitous. Employers demand that new products be developed faster and processes be done better, faster, or cheaper or they will not be able to compete and hence become history quicker than ever before. With industry demanding new products and better processes, institutions of higher learning are challenged to adjust curricula and to develop learning approaches that complement what is needed by those that employ their graduates. For institutions of higher learning, this has created a four way dilemma: 1) Students do not necessarily want to exert the effort to learn more quicker as required by course standards, but yet do want to earn a good grade and receive a degree; 2) Institutions of higher learning need to maintain and/or increase their enrollments in order to be allocated a desirable budget; 3) Instructors, particularly new instructors, want to earn promotion and tenure which requires good student evaluations of instruction; and, 4) Employers want to hire students who can perform according to academic standards.

BALANCING STUDENT GOALS, EMPLOYER EXPECTATION, AND HIGHER EDUCATION PERFORMANCE STANDARDS

At the 2012 Society for College & University Planning national conference, one of the presenters expressed the belief that a number of colleges and universities could be out of business in the coming years. If that opinion is only partly true, it still serves as a preview of a paramount issue plaguing institutions of higher learning. Bluntly put, institutions that rely primarily on student tuition to pay their bills will be forced to address business strategies that balance student recruitment, retention, and graduation rates with the quality concerns of the students who are recruited. Some of the institutions of higher learning may have to come to grips with the fact that not all students are legitimate college material, and high dropout rates coupled with high college debt is a disaster currently in the making.

Secondarily, as revealed by the trends presented earlier in this chapter, higher education will increasingly find itself attempting to define and serve a changing customer market. While colleges and universities may have not considered the point of view that suggests the student is actually the consumer of their commodity (knowledge), business and industry is starting to let some of those institutions know that certain graduates may not be hired due to the performance gaps between what the students are bringing to the job and what the employer requires of its new hires.

In a September 2008 issue of the Chronicle of Higher Education (Basken, 2008), a Boeing Corporation representative reported that Boeing would no longer seek to recruit graduates from certain engineering programs because those graduates did not bring the expected skill sets to the company. In this example, one would have to question who the customer is and who is the consumer of the graduates of our universities? If the customer is the business community, then Boeing, in this example, said the provider failed to achieve the required product quality (the educated student). If the customer is the student and success was measured by the fact that the student graduated, then by that definition the educational institution achieved success. In the Chronicle article, Boeing is seen as "raising the possibility that employers could become a major force for college accountability."

Student Perspectives

Universities historically have been seen as places where students went to seek knowledge. This could occur by reading, research, lectures, and even ad-hoc discussion sessions. Students were expected to be in class and often attendance was taken. Today, with the technology that brings knowledge to us in a variety of methods, the need to seek the traditional educational experience is greatly impacted. Instead of sitting in standard classrooms and listening to knowledgeable people "push" knowledge out in lecture formats, the ubiquitous nature of information is such that most people today "pull" the knowledge they need in a "just in time", "just enough" format. While the traditional college classroom experience still exists, it has given way somewhat to distance education. The thought that a student can graduate without ever having attended a traditional classroom experience still bothers some educators and creates all kinds of new questions about amounts of classroom and study time a student invests, as well as whether the student actually did his or her own work. The literature is rich with studies where technology has improved on the quality, timeliness, and quantity of work that can be accomplished. Students attend business classes where professors are intent on convincing them that the company that does not change and adapt will not survive when compared with its competitors.

Against this backdrop of efficiency and economy discussions, the traditional university class experience remains much as it has for years. Students may well ask why they must sit through finite periods of classroom exposure when they feel competent and capable of accessing the knowledge in far less time.

In a recent focus group conducted at a large university in the southeast (Duncan et al., 2008), students expressed a surprising lack of disinterest in the content that was in the syllabi of business, psychology, and communications curricula. Almost to the student they were willing to do the minimum amount of work that led to a letter grade of "A" or at a minimum "B". These students indicated that they were very busy with their daily routines which included a heavy social life and often working a job. For these students, college was a requirement "to get the paper" that signified graduation. They then felt that they would learn what to do on the job once they had been selected by an employer.

The student behavior discussed above is not restricted to U.S. students alone. In another study (Swart, et al., 2009), the study behaviors of Asian and American students were compared. The results indicated that students from both the U.S. and Asia exhibited limited self-regulation in the pursuit of behaviors leading to academic success in comparison to what they reported they should be doing. There was not a significant difference between U.S. and Asian students in self-reported actual engagement in pro-academic behaviors. However, Asian students presented less of a discrepancy between actual and intended engagement in pro-academic behaviors in comparison to their U.S. counterparts. A notable difference was also found in that the Asian students self-regulated better than their U.S. counterparts in terms of pro-academic behaviors that were not directly observable. For Asian students, there was not a discrepancy in self-reported engagement of observable vs. non-observable behaviors

The U.S. students, however, appeared to be more amenable to external motivation (e.g. having the instructor be able to observe their behavior) and less likely to engage in non-observable behaviors leading to academic success.

While it cannot be said that these attitudes are prevalent at all universities in all countries, there are indications that universities in the U.S. seem to be catering more to students and seeing them as the customer of the academic experience, and the ones to be satisfied. In one southern state legislature a movement is underway to tie university funding to a series of academic markers such as retention rates, graduation rates, and how long it takes a student to graduate (Ferreri, 2010). This can be justified in the sense that the business of education is to provide the opportunity for knowledge with a certain probability that those that start the venture will complete the journey and receive a degree. If a legislature simply funds new enrollment growth and does not monitor for graduation rates, what becomes their indicator of a successful investment of funds? Universities have been forced to review their educational processes and are busy working to set retention and related goals that can ensure the continuation of funding.

This "retention attention" has led to some creative answers. Tutoring centers are starting up on campuses. Tutoring has long been an element of sports programs on campus with the expressed intent of keeping those students eligible for participation. We now find a new incentive to keeping the other college students academically qualified to continue in school, namely the funding models of certain state legislative assemblies. To continue the flow of dollars students need to be retained in school and successfully graduated. During the previously mentioned focus groups, students frequently expressed that they need high grades (A or B) in order to retain financial aid, scholarships or grants. However those same students when asked whether they were willing to invest their time in the study behaviors necessary to make the grades they required, relayed that they knew what it entailed, but were not totally willing to do the work. So, a fundamental question needs to be addressed in regard to whether learning is a student responsibility, assisted by faculty, or is it the university's responsibility to ensure that students learn. The current emphasis seems to be on the latter, and consequently a lot of money, personnel, and time are being invested to ensure the college student of today has every opportunity to get the diploma. With employers demanding more highly qualified graduates across a broad spectrum of employment opportunities, we must challenge ourselves to determine if the approach to keeping schools funded is consistent with producing the highest quality of graduates to meet employer requirements.

There have been numerous studies done on grade inflation and the relationship to student evaluations of faculty. Almost without exception, grades in higher education have crept upwards. If this inflation is positively correlated with more knowledgeable students, that is a good thing. But if the higher grades are more of an indication of faculty adjusting standards to allow students to make a "grade of choice", that could be at least partly explanatory of the hiring approach Boeing started using relative to certain schools and programs of study.

Student/Faculty Interactions

A recent study of American college and university grading practices from 1940-2009 found that on average across a wide range of schools, the letter grade of "A" represented 43% of all grades, an increase of 28 percentage points since 1960, and 12 percentage points since

1988. The authors conclude that GPA's are so saturated with high end grades that they have little use as a motivator for students and as an evaluation tool for graduate and professional schools and employers. They go on to suggest that with instructors gradually lowering their performance standards, the most common grade on college campuses is now an "A", but that the grade of "A" will likely continue to have less and less meaning (Rojstaczer and Healy, 2012).

In a study on important and vital student study behaviors (Duncan et al., 2008), business students stated they complied with the necessary study behaviors 71.4% of the time, psychology students 71.2% of the time, and communication students 81% of the time. When one considers these numbers and realizes that colleges and universities are being "pressured" to show higher retention and graduation rates, the institutions may be faced with "watering down" the instructional experience or accept a fate of higher attrition and the associated issue of lower state funding.

While students may not be that interested in performing the study behaviors associated with earning good grades, they do remain interested in receiving good grades. As mentioned earlier, student grades are often associated with financial aid packages, grants, scholarships, or even athletic eligibility. Students who are not achieving the grades they need or desire characteristically seek to negotiate the course standards that are generally specified in the course syllabus (Hall et al., 2012). All too frequently we read of cheating scandals. If students are seriously intent on learning material, cheating should be minimal. But even at our military academies where students take an oath to never "lie, cheat or steal or tolerate those who do", cheating scandals are not unheard of (Novotney, 2011). Professors have been asked to drop the lowest grade, allow re-takes on exams, or grant requests for extra credit activities. The sole intent of these three examples, and there are others, is to achieve a grade that is pre-determined to be enough to protect the interests of the student. Couple the student's need for success with the recent pressure on schools to retain and graduate students and a nexus of cooperation may now be formed based on an approach that says "if A or B is the answer, what is the question?" The caution is that the grade received may not have any correlation to the knowledge required and expected of someone with such a course in the business world.

Faculty Perspectives

The ultimate goal of any faculty member entering academia is to obtain tenure and achieve what in essence is life-long job security. However, they no longer are free to independently set performance standards in their courses without some fear of repercussions. Students today exercise some power in the instructional picture. In many universities, the process of reviewing the progress of faculty members toward achieving promotion and tenure includes the student opinion of the course as an important factor in the decision. Students who specify that a particular teacher is "too hard", or "unfair", can at a minimum create some issues for professors looking to advance. Thus, there is a subtle pressure on the new professors to help students out or be subjected to condemning evaluations.

For example, a personal acquaintance teaching online at a mid-western university had received exceptional teaching evaluations since she was hired three years ago. However, because one student felt she was treated unfairly, the professor was subjected to a formal inquiry. It mattered not that no other student in the class had any issues or difficulties with the professor, and that the student in question had not done her work satisfactorily, the full blown inquiry was still initiated. The ability to extract some form of retribution in the faculty input process does not go unnoticed by students. Many use online professor rating systems that give professors value ratings based on difficulty of the content and the flexibility of the professor in ensuring the student passes. Systems such as "Rate my Professor.com", "My Edu.com", and many other similar sites are focused on condemning some professors and lauding others. Comments often refer to the academic rigor of a particular class. While some professor profiles in these on line systems can be flattering, it generally seems that the professors who require more rigorous adherence to performance standards set for their courses and may also check roll and deduct for absences are frequently singled out for negative comments.

These issues simply point to the fact that the student perceives him or herself as the customer of the educational experience. A few students in the aforementioned focus group stated that they pay a lot of money for the college experience, and it should be their decision to attend class or not and that they should not be penalized for missing. Some also stated they felt it was the professor's responsibility to provide a way for the student to make an acceptable grade, regardless of whether that involved extra credit or re-taking a failed exam (because they are paying to take the course).

Professors who are not "meeting the needs" of the student, as defined by the students, often get denigrated in evaluations. Thus, the pressure on professors, in particular those that have not yet earned tenure or aspire for a promotion, to try and find a way for students to get good grades, even if it means "stretching" the course performance standards as published in the course syllabi, can be intense.

Employer Perspectives

If we re-structure the paradigm that shows the student as the consumer of the educational experience and look at business as the ultimate customer it puts the nature of a college degree into a different perspective, especially in light of the Exponential Times and the demands this has placed on employers. We have to ask ourselves whether it is the ultimate goal of the college experience for every student to graduate. If not, then what is an acceptable graduation rate, especially in light of funding models that are now being appended to retention and graduation rates? Today approximately 25% of the population of this country has received a bachelor's degree. That suggests that 75% do not have the college degree. We might need to question if a college degree has become a goal in and of itself. If so, we could end up with a nation of college degreed people who may or may not have the skill sets to go into industry and perform. As a nation, we must consider if a college degree has become a status symbol, much like high end clothes or cars. Employers must also be honest in their assessment of the college degree. Does the degree signify skills and knowledge attained, or might it simply signify maturity achieved through at least four years of post -secondary study, and as an employer are they seeking to hire skills and knowledge or maturity?

If you take the students in the aforementioned focus groups as indicative of the college students in general, as customers you must ask if they are suggesting that the four years in an academic setting is doing little more than proving they can endure the academic experience and "get the paper." Whether they can manage projects, communicate effectively, manage their time and get work completed seems immaterial to many students who were in the focus group sessions. So, maybe the ultimate goal of American education might be to see that every student has the opportunity to attend college? If this became the view of higher education, then we would have to face the fact that colleges might be serving as a part of the "great sifting process" whereby the best and brightest graduate and those who do not achieve standards do not? If higher education is allowed to be a piece of the sifting experience, this would allow some latitude to put academic rigor front and center of the student experience without fear of attrition rates, student criticism, or reduced state funding.

In 2006, the Society for Human Resource Management published the results of interviews with various human resource personnel and senior executives and reported astounding results (Cassner – Lotto, 2006). The primary finding showed that the United States is not doing enough, fast enough to prepare for the economic future. Students entering the workforce were described as woefully ill-prepared. In discussing what steps were necessary to continue to remain competitive in the global economy, the need was noted for a strong link between academia and industry (Morton, 2007). Things do not seem to have gotten any better. The December 2011 issue in the Chronicle of Higher Education contains an article that states that "many employers believe colleges aren't adequately preparing students for jobs" (Johnson, 2011). This statement is based on analysis of a study by the Accrediting Council for Independent Colleges and Schools where 1,000 employers were surveyed from a variety of industries. More than half of the employers said finding qualified applicants is difficult, and fewer than half thought students should receive workplace training rather than a broad based education. Less than 10 percent of employers thought colleges did an excellent job of preparing students for work. This last report prompted Representative Virginia Foxx of North Carolina who chairs the House Sub-committee on higher education to state that "colleges and universities are pandering to the students and giving them what they want, instead of what the employers want (Johnson, 2011)."

Some would argue that the changing nature of the college student, along with the impact of social media should force the universities to change the way they disseminate learning. Some argue that learning should not be defined by how much one can hold inside the head, but rather the speed and accuracy by which one can find answers. In this regard, you must now begin to question the accreditation processes which define courses by hours of class time and hours of study and preparation. For sure, the student of today is certainly unlike the student of only 20 years ago. It is safe to say that every student graduating from high school today is computer capable, if not totally literate. Students do research and compose their college papers on line. Students who feel they are more comfortable with technology than their professors may well question why traditional instructional processes are still used.

The Dilemma

There is obviously a dilemma developing in the world of higher education. Schools who count on tuition monies to pay their bills need to make sure their consumer is pleased with the educational experience. Pleasure can be defined by the student as achieving good grades without exerting too much intellectual capital. When students are viewed as the consumers and funding models are built around keeping a healthy flow of students enrolled, retained and graduated, the educational experience may become one of adjusting the curriculum and teaching methods to accommodate the funding models. This can obviously create situations where the graduates of certain programs are not deemed employee ready to enter the workforce, and can consequently cause employers to take on the added cost and time of producing the needed skills for the new employee.

Students in the focus group cited earlier were consistent in the thought that the business world would teach/train them to do their jobs, which relegated the collegiate experience to a lesser level of importance. If this happened to be the prevailing student opinion, the most recent college graduates are not benefitting from the on-the-job exposure. In a May 2011 Worktrends survey released by the John J. Heldrich Center for Workforce Development, data on recent college graduates who are working revealed that only about a quarter of graduates felt their first job was the beginning of a career. Still 46% did feel the first job was a step toward a career. Many graduates expressed the thought that they took a job in an area that was not their first choice because they needed to work just to get by. Three in ten who responded felt they were working below what they felt was their skill level. The odd part of this statement is that it conflicts with the belief coming out of the focus group that higher education did not teach enough "real life" job skills, and those would be learned in the workplace. Now, we read that the workplace of on the job training and on the job experience is less challenging than the curriculum of the collegiate classroom (Godofsky et al., 2011).

We may have to ask ourselves how we got to this place. Are we guilty of recruiting students who may not be collegiate material? Are we guilty of giving passing grades for work that is not up to industry standards? Are we graduating students who are poor writers, or poor communicators, especially in light of the fact that social media does not emphasize these practices? Are our schools de-emphasizing a strong work ethic through our assignments, the amount of work required and the rigor of our assessments, and are we failing to give our students a realistic view of the demands of the corporate work environment?

Has college become a place for people to "be" while they are waiting for something to break for them in the business world? Student loans are at an all- time high and constitute an amount in excess of one trillion dollars. Based solely on student loan data a lot of people are in college. Couple that with military downsizing which periodically puts several hundred thousand former service members on the streets and you have another market of people who are either looking for work, or will choose to attend college.

If our colleges become a form of a job for unemployed or underemployed people, can we expect those students to be college material? Some may well be but others may be doing just enough to get by so they can continue to borrow funds, or use the GI bill. Colleges who cater to the less than serious student may not be concerned with graduation rates but eventually these students will either finish or leave school with the likelihood of some serious debt.

Institutions of higher learning that are being scrutinized for retention and graduation rates may have their numbers impacted by the behaviors of the less than serious student. Should colleges then invest whatever it takes to tutor and mentor these students to graduation? Will professors feel pressure to adjust the evaluation procedures in order to reduce the number of failures? If graduation rates increase but the graduates fail to measure up to what business needs, have the universities been successful or not?

Can America stay competitive in a global economy if it re-defines the collegiate experience so that the goal of everyone graduating may mean some of the traditional academic rigor must be toned down?

Does this country risk the competitive edge going to foreign governments in areas such as aerospace, energy, automotive, medicine, farming, and information technology, just to name a few of the areas that have drawn intense international competition?

Will American business rely on higher education to train its workforce, or will they choose to do it themselves? Do we see a future where students go to college to learn specific jobs that are directly employable into industry or medicine? Has the broad based general studies value of college waned, especially in light of the immediacy of knowledge via the internet?

CONCLUSION

In this chapter, it has been shown that our world is going to become more global, technology is going to increase and those who do not prepare for the future will indirectly become shaped by it. Employment opportunities will become increasingly open to the educated, trained, and skilled. This means that institutions of higher learning must become able to rapidly incorporate new knowledge into innovative educational products for their curricula. They must be able to develop appropriate and relevant performance standards and have a strategic plan in place that allows for timely assessment and, if necessary, corrective action when performance does not meet standards.

If, in their attempts to accomplish the above, institutions of higher learning focus on satisfying students as their primary customers, they may negatively affect another customer group—employers— because the two customer groups have significantly different ways of defining and measuring expectations. There are no easy solutions to addressing the negotiation of standards that undermine quality human performance. All customers of higher education deserve the best we can offer, as higher education, business/industry, and the economic success of the United States are intricately connected and are dependent upon one another. As noted in the Delta Project (Wellman, 2009), the United States is quickly losing ground in the global race for talent. Institutions of higher education, faculty, students, and businesses can serve as contributing architects in ensuring education establishes quality standards. They are all consumers, and they all have a vested interest in maintaining standards in order for graduates to be fully prepared for the Exponential Times ahead.

REFERENCES

Basken, P., "Boeing to Rank Colleges by Measuring Graduates' Job Success," *The Chronicle of Higher Education,* Sept. 19, 2008, pp. A1, A14-16.

Bera, Y., *The Yogi Book,* Workman Publishing, 1998.

Casner-Lotto, J. and Brenner, M.W, *Are They Really Ready to Work? Employers' Perspectives on the Basic Knowledge and Applied Skills of New Entrants to the 21st Century U. S. Workforce,* The Conference Board, Inc., the Partnership for 21st Century Skills, Corporate Voices for Working Families, and the Society for Human Resources Management, 2006.

DeSantis, N., "New Media Consortium Names Top 10 "Metatrend" Shaping Educational Technology", http://chronicle.com/blogs/wiredcampus/new-media-consortium-names-10-top-metatrends-shaping-educational-technology/35234, February 1, 2012.

Duncan, S., Swart W., Hall C., and Eribo, F., "A Quantitative Analysis of the Quality of Human Performance Among University Students," *American Journal of Educational Studies,* No. 1, November, 2008, pp. 5-14.

Ferreri, E, "UNC system rethinks the way to fund its campuses," http://www.newsobserver.com/2010/11/06/784463/colleges-push-funding-changes.html, Nov. 6, 2010.

Fisch, K., Did you know 3.0 (Officially updated for 2012) HD, http://www.youtube.com/watch?v=YmwwrGV_aiE

Godofsky, J., Zukin, C., and Van Horn, K. (May, 2011)."Unfulfilled Expectations: Recent Graduates Struggle in a Troubled Economy." www.heldrich.rutgers.edu/sites/.../Work_Trends_May_2011.pdf

Hall, C., Swart, W. and Duncan, S. (2012), "Balancing Customer Needs and Standards in Higher Education," *Quality Approaches in Higher Education*, Vol. 3, No. 1.

Johnson, L., "Employers Say College Graduates Lack Job Skills," Chronicle of Higher Education. http://chronicle.com/article/Employers-Say-College/130013/, December 5, 2011.

Morton, J. (2007, April), *Engineering Skills: The Threat from China and India?* Paper presented at the meeting of European Engineers Forum, Hanover, England.

Novotney, A. (June, 2011), "Beat the Cheat," *Monitor on Psychology*, Vol. 42, N0. 6.

Rojstaczer, S. and Healy, C., *Teachers College Record,* Volume 114, Number 7. http://www.tcrecord.org ID Number: 16473, Date Accessed: 7/13/2011 12:42:27 PM, 2012.

Shaughnessy, H., "lessons from The Top Ten Tends in Business," *Forbes*, Sept 23, 2011, http://www.forbes.com/sites/haydnshaughnessy/   2011/09/22/lessons-from-the-top-10-trends-in-business/, September, 2011.

Swart, W., Hall, C. Duncan, S. and Chia, R., "Professionalism and Work Ethic among U.S. and Asian University Students in a Global Classroom: A Cross-Cultural Comparison" *The Journal of Systemics, Cybernetics and Informatics: JSCI*, Vol.7, No. 1, 2009.

Swart, W., *Leadership for Academic Units: A performance Improvement Model for Department Chairs, Dean, and Academic Vice Presidents (or those who aspire to be),* HRD press, 2010.

Tripp, Michelle,"6 Essential Skills for Exponential Times*",* http://michelletripp.com/index.php/2009/08/12/essential-skills-for-exponential-times/, August 12, 2009

Vitalani, N and Shaugnessy, H.,*The Elastic Enterprise : The new Manifest for Business Revolution.* www.Amazon.com*,* May 16, 2012.

Wellman, J., Desrochers, D., Lenihan, C., Kirshstein, R., Hurlburt, S., and Honegger, S., *Trends in College Spending: Where Does the Money Come From? Where Does it Go? A Report of the Delta Project,* Washington, D.C.: Delta Project on Postsecondary Education Costs, Productivity and Accountability. Accessed 2-13- 09. www.deltacostproject.org, 2009.

In: Handbook of Academic Performance
Editors: Rolf Haumann and George Zimmer

ISBN: 978-1-62417-888-7
© 2013 Nova Science Publishers, Inc.

Chapter 3

ACADEMIC GRADES AND MOTIVATION IN HIGH SCHOOL SCIENCE CLASSROOMS AMONG MALE AND FEMALE STUDENTS: ASSOCIATIONS WITH TEACHERS' CHARACTERISTICS, BELIEFS, AND PRACTICES

Lee Shumow[*] and Jennifer A. Schmidt
Northern Illinois University, IL, US

ABSTRACT

This study compared the academic performance, perceived competence, attitudes, and perceived level of momentary skill of 244 (n =129 male, n = 115 female) high school students in science. While males and females did not differ from one another in their science grades, there were significant gender differences in factors that promote motivation and persistence in science. Female students reported lower perceived competence in science and more negative general science attitudes than male students. Males and females also differed systematically from one another in their perceived level of momentary skill while in science as measured by the Experience Sampling Method. We sought to understand more about the role that teachers' beliefs and practices may play in fostering these experiential and motivational differences. Students' high school science teachers (n=13) were interviewed about their beliefs pertaining to gender and science. Observational data from their classrooms also were coded and examined to describe teachers' interactions with male and female students. In general, teachers spent an average of 39% more time addressing male than female students, which was not explained by student initiation. In particular, teachers addressed males more often than females about content knowledge, elaboration of course content, and classroom management. Most teachers explicitly denied that there were gender differences in science performance, but their talk about males and females in their classrooms revealed

[*] This material is based upon work supported by the National Science Foundation under Grant No: HRD-0827526. Any opinions, findings, conclusions, or recommendations expressed in this material are those of the authors and do not reflect the views of the National Science Foundation. Corresponding author: Lee Shumow, *lshumow@niu.edu.*

implicit beliefs that suggested gender bias. Some consistency was found between the science teachers' implicit beliefs, teachers' practices, and the gendered motivational patterns of their students.

Several recent studies have found that the gender gap in mathematics and science achievement during adolescence has closed (AAUW, 2008; Hyde, Lindberg, Linn, Ellis & Williams, 2008; Xie & Shauman, 2003). In fact, a recent study of three large nationally representative data sets found that high school girls actually had slightly higher GPAs in science and mathematics than boys (Riegle-Crumb, King, Grodsky, & Muller, 2012). Further, that study found that the gender disparity in postsecondary STEM majors was not explained by prior academic performance measured by either grades or achievement test scores. As suggested by the disparity in STEM majors, gender gaps related to STEM motivation, which have been documented during adolescence over several decades (see DeBacker & Nelson, 2000; Freeman, 2004; Jones, Howe, & Rua, 2000; NCES, 2000a, 2000b; Preston, 2004), persist despite recent parity in STEM achievement (see Hill, Corbett & St. Rose, 2010 for a review; Zafar, 2009). Those motivational gaps include differences in interest, course-taking, and career aspirations favoring male over female students. In the current study, we compared high school students' science grades and motivation as revealed by their perceived competence and by their attitudes toward science.

While there are multiple possible explanations for gender differences in students' motivation in science, a likely influence is science teachers themselves. If teachers overtly or implicitly communicate beliefs about gender differences in science, students' attitudes will likely be affected. It is important to understand, then, how science teachers think and talk about gender and how they interact with both male and female students. This study addresses those issues.

MOTIVATIONAL PROCESSES AND GENDER IN HIGH SCHOOL SCIENCE CLASSES

Our recent research focused on adolescents' subjective experience during science class has demonstrated that male and female students experience high school science classes very differently, with females reporting lower science self-efficacy and lower engagement in response to challenge in science than males (Schmidt, Kackar & Strati, 2010; Schmidt & Shumow, 2012). In the present study, we expand the motivational outcomes we examined previously by comparing students' perceptions of competence, their attitudes toward science, as well as grades in science by gender. Perceiving oneself as competent is considered a basic human need in Self Determination Theory (Deci & Ryan, 1991), an influential theory of human motivation. Researchers have found that students who feel competent are more likely to choose to engage in that activity, persist when they experience setbacks and work harder, all ingredients needed to succeed in complex subjects like the sciences. Students' attitudes toward science, which are defined as psychological tendencies expressed through positive or negative evaluations (Eagly & Chaiken, 1993), influence behavior to a considerable degree (Reid, 2011). Students' attitudes are likely to impact the choices they make about course-taking, post-secondary majors, and careers because people tend to prefer to engage in activities for which they have positive as opposed to negative attitudes.

TEACHER BELIEFS ABOUT GENDER AND SCIENCE

Despite numerous scholarly arguments about a gender gap in science (Riegle-Crumb, King, Grodsky, & Muller, 2012) and the evidence that females are less motivated than males to pursue science, many educators currently believe that gender differences in science have been successfully addressed and no longer exist (Sadker, Sadker, & Zittleman, 2009; Sanders, 2010). On the one hand, educators might base their assessment that gender differences in science have been redressed on positive changes that have taken place in practice (see for example Corra, 2007) and by the equivalence in grades noted previously. On the other hand, they might not notice gender differences because they are concentrating on other more immediate issues during their hectic teaching day (Sanders, 2010). It is also possible that teachers think that expressing beliefs about gender differences is socially undesirable and tantamount to endorsing inequality. We investigate high school science teachers' beliefs about and interactions with male and female students, and how those beliefs and behaviors are related to each other and to the performance and motivation of students in their classrooms.

Few U.S. adults openly express stereotypes about gender and STEM fields (Schmader, Johns & Barquissau, 2004; Hyde et al, 1990). There is considerable evidence, however, that people who do not explicitly endorse stereotyped views nevertheless do reveal implicit beliefs and act in concert with these stereotypes. This pattern is observed with stereotypes in general, and in relation to gender and science in particular. Such implicit beliefs are related to student performance in STEM during the eighth grade (Nosek et al, 2009). Thus, a study of teacher beliefs about gender should be designed to tap into teachers' implicit (likely subconscious) beliefs in addition to their explicitly stated beliefs, a strategy which we adopt here.

TEACHERS' INTERACTION PATTERNS WITH MALE AND FEMALE STUDENTS

One way that teachers have historically enacted stereotypes about gender and science in the classroom is through the way that they talk to, interact with, and respond to students. Trends in general gender-bias in classrooms emerge from discussions with and observations of teachers. Research across a variety of subjects has documented some gender biases in classrooms. For instance, physically active males are often viewed as troublemakers, and, because females are often viewed as compliant, they receive less teacher attention than male students (Ruble, Martin & Berenbaum, 2006; DeZolt & Hull, 2001). Many studies which have examined interaction patterns in science classes were conducted a generation ago (Altermatt, Jovanovic, & Perry, 1998; Jones & Wheatley, 1990; Kahle, 1990; Wilkinson & Marrett, 1985). Those studies showed that teachers called on males more than females, interacted with males more than females about procedures and behavior in class, and communicated higher expectations to males than females. Gender gaps in high school course-taking and achievement have closed in the period since these studies were conducted, though large gaps in post-secondary science interest and persistence remain. Given that the landscape of gender and science has changed somewhat in recent decades, exploring possible teacher gender bias in contemporary science classrooms is important.

Of course, observed gender differences in teachers' beliefs and behavior may not manifest bias but rather reflect real differences in male and female students' engagement and interest in science. Altermatt, Jovanovic, and Perry (1998) found, for example, that teachers called on boys more than girls but that was in direct proportion to the fact that more boys raised their hands to participate in science class. For decades, feminist scholars have suggested that individuals differ in stable and reliable ways with regard to how they approach knowledge and learning (Baxter-Magolda, 1992; Belenky, et al., 1986; Galotti et al., 1999; Knight et al., 2000). However, some evidence suggests that the degree to which gender stereotypes are made salient in classrooms impacts whether or not there are gender differences in approaches to learning. Ryan and David (2003) discovered gender differences in students' approaches to knowing only when gender stereotypes were made salient: In situations where they were not made salient, no gender differences in approaches to knowing were evident. Given that many norms and stereotypes of "scientists" are strongly gendered, it is important to explore the degree to which gender appears salient among the teachers of tomorrow's scientists.

McLaughlin and Talbert (2001) argue that the patterns of practice high school teachers pursue in their classrooms "fundamentally shape students' classroom experiences" (p. 32). In order to better understand the experiences of male and female students in high school science classes a descriptive account of what is happening in science classrooms is needed. Two decades ago, Tobin and colleagues observed high school science classrooms in the United States and Australia, and found that females participated less than males during whole class instruction and that whole class instruction accounted for about 70% of instructional time in high school science classrooms (Gallagher, 1985; Tobin & Gallagher, 1987; Tobin & Garnett, 1987; Tobin et al., 1987). The researchers further found that a "typical" high school science lesson included the teacher providing some factual information during whole class instruction and the students completing seatwork consisting of fact oriented worksheets using the textbook as a reference; girls were observed to be more diligent than boys during seatwork. Typically, rote learning was emphasized, questions posed by the teacher were low-level questions, requiring only a yes or no answer. More recent research suggests that whole class instruction, particularly lecture remains the predominant instructional practice in high school science classrooms and that seatwork is common (McLaughlin & Talbert, 2001; Shernoff, Knauth & Makris, 2000) yet there has been considerable emphasis on reforming science education to emphasize activity and thinking. It is not clear however, whether contemporary teachers interact differently with female and male students in terms of content knowledge, thinking, directives, and behavior management as has been observed in the past. Thus, we consider those teacher interactions patterns with students by gender in this study.

Teacher Beliefs and Practices

We expect teachers' implicit beliefs to influence their classroom practice, and that these beliefs and practices will shed light on the results of our study of students' subjective learning experiences in high school science classrooms. Teachers' beliefs about learning and motivation impact their practices (Turner, Christensen, & Meyer, 2009) and teachers' beliefs and practices have been demonstrated to impact student performance in high school science classrooms (McNeill, Pimental, & Strauss, 2010) but studies have rarely focused on teacher beliefs and behavior as potential contributors to student beliefs about themselves as learners in science classrooms. As research on gender and science moves forward, we must understand the many ways that students' beliefs might be shaped by people and experiences.

The lack of women role models has been offered as an explanation for female students' disinterest and lack of aspirations in science (Bickenstaff, 2005;Weinburgh, 1995). Because women have been underrepresented in science, role models including female science teachers have been scarce for female students interested in science. However, this "women-science-teachers-as-role-models" line of inquiry may not be fruitful theoretically or practically as it suffers from a "chicken-and-egg" problem: are there few female role models because girls aren't interested in science, or are girls not interested because they have few female role models? This study goes beyond the simple consideration of teacher gender, and focuses instead on teachers' beliefs about gender and science as they are reflected both in their discussion of teaching science and in their everyday actions and interactions with high school students in their classrooms.

Study Goals

We examine the degree to which contemporary high school science teachers appear to hold gender-related stereotypes regarding science. In order to investigate teachers' instructional practices and their interactions with male and female students, we have analyzed approximately 100 hours of classroom instruction and interviews with high school science teachers in order to address the following research questions:

1. Is there gender disparity in science grades, attitude toward science, global perceived competence, and momentary perceived competence in science among high school students?

2. What explicit general beliefs do teachers express about gender and science learning, and are these explicit beliefs consistent with implicit beliefs revealed through discussions of specific students in their classrooms?

3. Do high school science teachers interact with male and female students in similar ways in terms of the frequency with which students are addressed, the function or purpose of the verbal interaction, and the degree to which higher level thinking is fostered?

4. Are teachers' interactions aligned with male and female students' initiation of verbal exchanges with their science teacher, observed participation in class activities, and observed display of confidence in science tasks?

5. Do teachers' explicit or implicit beliefs align with behavior observed in the classroom and what does observed behavior tell us about teachers' implicit beliefs?

METHOD

Context

The study was conducted in regular track science classrooms in a large public high school (9th - 12th grades; enrollment = 3,323) serving students from a diverse community. Overall, 33% of the student body came from low-income families. The school graduation rate was reported to be 86%. The school's science department had 28 faculty members (16 female, 12 male) offering a total of 23 different courses in AP, honors, regular, applied, and vocational tracks. All science faculty members were white. Three science teachers from each of the regular track general science, biology, chemistry and physics classes participated in the research project. In the regular track science classes, there was no gender gap in science course taking and science test achievement. The science department chairperson reported that an inquiry approach was used throughout the department.

Participants

Students

In total, 244 students participated in the study. The overall student participation rate across all classrooms was 91%, with half of the classrooms studied having 100% participation. The sample was 53% male and 47% female. The student sample was 42% White, 37% Latino, 12% African American, 2% Asian, 1% Native American, and 6% multi-racial. According to school records, 43% of students in the sample were eligible to receive free or reduced lunch. Approximately one-third of the students reported that at least one parent had a college degree.

Teachers

Thirteen teachers in twelve classrooms participated in the study (in one of the general science classrooms, a new teacher was assigned to the class in the spring semester as a result of staffing changes elsewhere in the department). Six of the teachers were male and 7 were female. It is noteworthy that all of the biology teachers were female and all of the physics teachers were male, while the general science and chemistry classrooms studied had both male and female teachers. As is the case in the science department as a whole, all participant teachers were white. The teachers in the study had an average of 8.6 years of teaching experience, and the average age was 35.6. Three teacher participants (n=1 biology, n = 1 chemistry, and n = 1 physics) had earned National Board Certification in Science.

Data Collection and Measures

Student Outcomes

Science achievement was measured using students' end of year grades in the science course in which we observed them. A measure of *global perceived competence in science* was gathered through the survey administered at the outset of the study using the Perceived

Competence for Learning Scale developed by Williams & Deci (1996). This is the mean of 4 items (on a scale of 1-7) measuring students' perceptions of their capability to learn course material and perform well (M=5.01, SD=1.40, Cronbach's α=.93). Students' *momentary perceived competence* in science was computed using data from the Experience Sampling Method (ESM; see Hektner et al, 2007). Students were signaled with vibrating pagers twice per class for 10 days to report on their experience. When signaled, they were asked to report how skilled they felt on a scale from 0-3. For each student, mean momentary skill ratings were computed, so that each student had an average rating that represented as many as 20 individual responses (M=1.4, SD=.57). General *attitude toward science* was measured using Gogolin & Swartz's (1992) 20-item Attitudes toward Science Inventory, which is computed by taking the sum of all items on a 4 point scale (scale range 20-80, mean=51.74, Cronbach's α=.87). In this scale, higher numbers indicate a more positive attitude toward science.

Teacher Student Interactions

Observational data were collected along with the ESM in each classroom on five consecutive days in both the fall and spring semesters. During each day, three researchers were present in the classrooms. One researcher was a videographer who was positioned in the back of the classroom to record the teachers' activities as unobtrusively as possible.

All class sessions were video-recorded, with a focus on the teachers' activities. After each recorded class session the teacher rated on a 5-point scale how typical the class period was. For each teacher, we selected 2 days (1 from fall, 1 from spring) they rated as "most typical" (ratings of 4 or 5) for detailed coding of *teachers' verbal interactions* with students. The video data were coded using the NVivo8 software, which enables direct coding of video data. In total, 20 hours of video representing 24 different 50-minute class sessions from 13 different science teachers were coded in this manner. Classroom video data were coded at the level of teacher "utterances." A teacher's statement was considered a single utterance so long as it had a consistency in the person being addressed and the function of the statement. The end of one utterance and the beginning of the next utterance was defined in terms of a shift in the person(s) being addressed or in the function or purpose of the statement. Teacher utterances could be very short (e.g. "everyone take out your homework") or, in rare cases, much longer (e.g. a two-minute mini-lecture on the differences between exothermic and endothermic reactions). The fifty-minute class sessions observed in this study typically contained 250 – 400 teacher utterances. As one can infer from the large number of utterances, most utterances lasted just a few seconds.

For the purpose of this study, each utterance was coded on the following dimensions: (1) who was addressed by the utterance (whole class, mixed male/female group; males individually or in a group; and females individually or in a group); (2) who initiated the utterance (teacher or student); (3) whether or not the utterance fostered student thinking (an utterance was coded as fostering thinking if the student was included intellectually, e.g., "What does that tell you?" or "Suppose it looks like this" or "So, how does that work?" etc.); and (4) the function or purpose of the utterance. Following procedures previously used by King, Shumow, and Leitz (2001) the function of each utterance was categorized as either a) content (presenting declaratory knowledge about science); b) sequential flow (moving the lesson forward by focusing on what has to happen next, but no content presented); c) elaboration (focus on explanation, conceptual understanding, meaning making); d) classroom management; and e) irrelevant. Ten percent of the videos were coded by two independent coders who had not read the teacher interviews. Reliability was within acceptable limits, with inter-rater agreement ranging from 85% to 100%. Duration and frequency of utterances were accessed from the NVivo8 software.

The "who was addressed" utterances were used to create variables that enabled comparison by gender. First the utterances addressed to all male small groups and those addressed to individual males were combined into an "addresses males" variable; the same procedure was used for females. The distribution of males and females in each class was not half and half. Therefore, in order to make fair estimates of the teachers interactions with students by gender, the "addresses males" variable was divided by the number of males in the class to yield an estimate of how often the teacher addressed each male in the class; the same procedure was used to estimate how often the teacher addressed each female in the class.

For each of the 120 class periods that was observed, observers completed *in-class global-observational ratings*. Observers rated whether certain behaviors were equally distributed between male and female students (M=F) or occurred more frequently with one gender (M>F or F>M) including: (a) teacher engagement of students, (b) student participation in class, (c) teacher behavior management, (d) student cooperation, (e) teacher messages of competence, and (f) student display of competence/confidence. The percent of days that fell into each observed category was calculated. Inter-rater reliabilities were conducted for more than 25% of the in-class observations; percent agreement on specific items ranged from 76% to 87%. Disagreements were resolved by using the rating of the senior coders who developed the coding scheme and who achieved very high reliability (> 90%) both with each other and with actual counts from video data.

Teacher Beliefs

All science teachers participated in a semi-structured interview during the week following data collection. They were asked directly about their observations and beliefs pertaining to gender differences in science. For example, they were asked whether they noticed student gender differences in science interest, ability, aptitude, or behavior. Socially desirable responses indicating few gender differences were expected. So, more implicit beliefs about gender were tapped by first asking teachers to identify a particular student in their class who had the greatest potential for a science career and their reasons for choosing that student. Student gender and the reasons given for selection were noted. Second, teachers identified the highest and lowest achieving male and female student in their class and were asked to compare and contrast them.

RESULTS

Gender Comparisons on Science-related Outcomes

While males and females did not differ from one another in their science course grades, there were significant gender differences in perceived competence in science and general science attitudes. Males and females also differed systematically from one another in their perceived level of momentary competence (skill) while in science as measured by the ESM. Means comparisons for each of these variables are presented in the table below.

Table 1. Mean Comparisons of Possible Gender Differences in Student Outcomes in Science

	Males (n=129)	Females (n=115)	t-value
End-of-year science grades	1.93	2.09	-.96
Global perceived science competence	5.2	4.7	2.7**
Momentary perceived science competence	1.65	1.37	3.91***
General science attitude	53.33	49.96	2.86**

Teacher Beliefs

Explicit Beliefs about Gender

Six of 13 teachers professed the belief that no gender differences existed in students' science experiences; three said they did not know, and four (2 males, 2 females) indicated that they had noticed gender differences in the way their students responded to science. Teachers who were uncertain and those who expressed the belief that there were no gender differences made comments such as: "It's not a gender thing" or "I don't think it exists much, not as compared to when I was in high school." One female teacher who acknowledged gender differences commented: "Well I think, you know, anybody that wants to be honest will definitely tell you that there are differences in gender and in the science field, if they tell you there is not then they're just either unaware or they're lying, uhm, cause there clearly are. I tell people I'm a teacher, one of the first questions out of their mouth is 'oh do you teach English?'". All four teachers who expressed a belief in gender differences indicated that, in their experience, males are more interested and "catch on" faster to science. Two teachers said males participated more while the other two said females participated more in science class.

Implicit Beliefs about Gender

Asking teachers to identify and compare specific students can uncover deeply held implicit beliefs about how teachers think about gender and achievement. For example, although few teachers expressed a belief of general gender differences in students' interest or aptitude for science, when asked to identify a student who might have a future science career, only three out of 13 identified a female. When pressed about whether there were any female students in the class we studied who might pursue science, most could name one and provide a reason why. It is notable, however, that several teachers had difficulty even remembering the name of any of their female students during our interview.

Teachers' comparisons of the characteristics of their highest and lowest achieving male and female students provided additional insight into their implicit beliefs. According to many teachers, high achieving male and female students were both "good workers." However, the high achieving males were more often described as having intellectual capacity (e.g. "smart" "a natural" "curious" "a deep thinker") whereas the females were simply harder workers ("not smarter," as one said) and more motivated by grades than males. Multiple teachers described how females were conscientious in their completion of homework assignments, commenting on their ability to follow directions and the neatness of their work. Interestingly, none of the four teachers who expressed an explicit belief in gender differences made this intellectual/worker distinction. Rather it was the teachers who denied there were gender differences or "didn't know" whose responses suggested this gendered pattern.

Comparing the higher and lower achieving males with one another, one teacher specifically said the high and low achieving male had the same "potential" but two others described the higher achieving male as smarter. Comparing the higher and lower achieving females, not one teacher said the higher achieving female was more intellectually capable, but two teachers said both were "able". Overall, female achievement was attributed to females' extrinsic motivation, attendance, and assignment completion. Teachers identified problems with work habits, attendance, and motivation as commonalities of low-achieving males and females.

Observations of Classroom Practices

Observation Rating Indicators

In the majority of the class sessions we observed, observers indicated no gender differences on the global ratings of teachers' engagement of students, classroom management or direct messages about competence (see Table 2). Nevertheless, while they were not the norm, some gender differences in teachers' more global interaction patterns were present. Fairly consistent patterns emerged when gender inequities were observed such that teachers engaged males more often than females and focused more on managing male behavior. Teachers tended to send messages of competence equally but more messages of lower competence were sent to female students. Males participated and displayed confidence/competence more than girls. Females cooperated more with the teacher.

Who Teachers Talked to and with What Purpose

Because it is always possible that classroom ratings might be influenced by the researcher's expectations, we also coded all the teacher's verbal interactions with students. These are counts made by viewing the video record of the teacher student interactions that occurred during each class; the duration of each instance is also marked. In a typical 50 minute class period, teachers spent an average of 27 minutes speaking with students: For the remaining 23 minutes, students were talking or the classroom was silent (as in the case of independent seatwork, for example). About 56% of teachers' total classroom talk time was spent addressing the whole class (about 15 min/day), with the remaining 12 min/day spent addressing individual students or small groups of students. In general, science teachers spent 39% more class time talking to their male students than their female students. While this figure represents a difference of only a few minutes per day, over the course of a month this means that teachers will have spent close to 40 more minutes (nearly an entire class period) talking with their male students compared with their female students.

When we examined gender differences in the function of teacher utterances, we found that teachers spent more time addressing males than females in every one of the function categories we coded. In other words, teachers spent more time talking with males than females with the purpose of conveying basic content, moving the lesson along (sequential flow), elaborating on content, managing behavior, and discussing irrelevant material like sporting events and weekend plans.

Table 2. Global Observation Rating Frequencies for 120 Class Periods

	Equally	M>F	F>M
Teacher Attempts to Engage	96	19	5
Student Participation	70	39	11
Teacher Behavior Management Focus	82	34	4
Student Cooperation	101	4	15
Teacher Messages of Low Competence	110	3	7
Student Display of low Competence/confidence	76	8	36

Note: Frequency of class periods receiving this rating is entered in the table.

As shown in Table 3, gender gaps were smallest in utterances characterized as sequential flow (only 15% more time addressing males than females), but were much larger in all other categories, with males receiving 31% - 66% more talk time than females.

Even though teachers spent more time speaking to males than females, they spent twice as much time addressing comments and questions that fostered higher order thinking to female students compared to males. The reader should note, however, that such fostering thinking utterances were extremely rare, amounting to less than 1 minute of class time per week for either gender, on average.

Table 3. Time Teachers Spend Talking with Different Functions

	Min/Wk addressing Male Students	Min/Wk addressing Female Students	Min/Wk addressing all students (whole class, groups or individuals)
Functions			
Content knowledge	3.3	2.3	27.5
Sequential Flow	16.9	14.4	79.0
Elaboration	0.7	0.2	6.5
Beh. Management	7.1	3.5	16
Irrelevant	2.5	1.3	6.5
Fostering thinking[a]	0.3	0.6	3
Total of all Functions	30.5	21.7	135.5

[a] The fostering thinking code was applied separately from the function codes, thus the fostering thinking counts are not included in the total for all functions figure.

Initiators of Verbal Interaction

Not surprisingly, the vast majority of teachers' verbal interaction (80%) was initiated by the teacher. A greater proportion of student-initiated verbal interaction was initiated by male students, however. Teachers spent about 27% more time in male-initiated verbal interaction than female-initiated verbal interaction.

Table 4. Explicit Beliefs about Participation and Observational Ratings of Teacher Engaging and Student Participation in Individual Classes by Gender

T ID	Subject	Explicit T Belief about Participation by Gender	Rating of Student Participation by Gender: # of Days		Mean N of Daily T Verbal Interactions per Enrolled Female & Male Student			Alignment	
			M>F	F>M	M	F	Summary	Explicit Belief & Student Participation	Student Participation & T Interaction
1[a]	General	Equal	1/5	0/5	7.8	5.8	M>F	Mismatch	Match
2[b]	General	Equal	0/5	0/5	9.1	8.8	M~=F	Match	Match
3	General	Equal	2/10	0/10	13.1	10.3	M>F	Mismatch	Match
4	General	Equal	4/10	1/10	17.4	9.8	M>F	Mismatch	Match
5	Biology	Equal	0/10	1/10	2.3	4.1	F>M	Mismatch	Match
6	Biology	M>F	5/10	0/10	10.1	9.9	M~=F	Match	Mismatch
7	Biology	M>F	5/10	0/10	9.3	6.4	M>F	Match	Match
8	Chemistry	Equal	3/10	0/10	6.8	6.1	M>F	Mismatch	Match
9	Chemistry	Equal	6/10	0/10	6.8	5.0	M>F	Mismatch	Match
10	Chemistry	F>M	5/10	0/10	16.3	13.9	M>F	Mismatch	Match
11	Physics	Equal	5/10	0/10	7.1	7.2	M~=F	Mismatch	Mismatch
12	Physics	F>M	1/10	5/10	9.9	8.7	M>F	Match	Mismatch
13	Physics	Equal	2/10	4/10	4.1	9.1	F>M	Mismatch	Match

[a] Observed spring only (5 days); b observed fall only (5 days).

Table 5. Global Beliefs about "Catching on" and Observational Ratings of Teacher Messages of Competence and Student Display of Confidence in Individual Classes by Gender

T ID	Subject	Explicit T Belief about Students "catching on" by Gender	Observational Rating: Teacher Messages of Lower Competence		Observational Rating: Student Displays of Confidence		Alignment Between Explicit Belief & Messages of Competence
			M>F	F>M	M>F	F>M	
1[a]	General	M>F	0/5	1/5	1/5	1/5	Match
2[b]	General	Equal	0/5	1/5	2/5	0/5	Mismatch
3	General	Equal	1/10	0/10	3/10	0/10	Mismatch
4	General	Equal	1/10	1/10	1/10	0/10	Match
5	Biology	Equal	0/10	0/10	1/10	2/10	Match
6	Biology	Equal	1/10	0/10	2/10	0/10	Mismatch
7	Biology	Equal	0/10	0/10	4/10	0/10	Match
8	Chemistry	Equal	0/10	0/10	4/10	0/10	Match
9	Chemistry	Equal	0/10	0/10	5/10	0/10	Match
10	Chemistry	Equal	0/10	1/10	5/10	1/10	Mismatch
11	Physics	Don't Know	0/10	1/10	5/10	1/10	Mismatch
12	Physics	Equal	0/10	0/10	0/10	1/10	Match
13	Physics	M>F	0/10	2/10	3/10	2/10	Match

[a] Observed spring only (5 days); [b] observed fall only (5 days).

Alignment of Beliefs and Practices

As discussed previously, most teachers explicitly stated the belief that males and females participated equally in science class. This stated belief generally does not align with our observations of actual student participation in each classroom. Table 3 compares each teacher's explicit beliefs and our observations of their classroom and coding of lessons for the number of utterances addressed directly to males or females in a typical day (frequencies were adjusted for the number of male or females enrolled in the class).

Generally speaking, we observed greater participation of male students across all science classrooms. The exception is two physics classes in which we observed greater participation among females (in the interviews one of these teachers described a pattern of participation consistent with our observations, while the other believed participation was equal).

Results presented in Table 4 suggest that teacher interaction with students and ratings of student's actual participation tend to be aligned with one another in all subjects except physics, whereas teachers' beliefs about student participation in class tend to be somewhat inconsistent with the observations. We investigated the discrepancy between student participation and the counts of interactions in physics classes and found in two cases the frequency counts and duration of the interactions did not match (as they did in other cases). Teacher 2 actually spent much more time talking to boys than girls and teacher 3 actually spent considerably more time talking to girls than boys, which aligned with the student participation ratings.

We also investigated alignment between teacher beliefs about "catching on", their messages of competence, and student display of competence/confidence by gender. As shown in Table 5, ten teachers say females and males are equal in "catching on". Although teachers were not observed to send lower messages of competence often, five did send messages of lower competence to females more often than males. In sum, females got messages of lower competence during 9 class periods compared to 3 class periods when males did. Gender differences were evident in students' actual display of confidence/confidence. Males displayed greater confidence/competence in ten classrooms (total, 37 class periods). Again, we detect some mismatch between teachers professed beliefs about student competence, and what we observe in their classrooms.

DISCUSSION

Like other recent studies, we found no gender gap in high school students' performance as measured by grades in science suggesting that female students were as prepared to continue studying science as male students. Yet, these female students who actually demonstrated equivalent competence felt less competent than male students both in their global evaluation of their own science competence and in their momentary reports during science class. Their attitudes toward science were also more negative than the attitudes of the male students. It would not be surprising, then, to find that the female students would be less likely to choose STEM majors or careers than the male students. Why is this so?

Evidence from a host of studies demonstrates that teachers' beliefs about ability are connected to students' achievement and motivation in science and mathematics. The finding that few teachers held explicit beliefs about gender differences in science was not surprising given recent similar findings (Sadker, Sadker, & Zittleman, 2009; Sanders, 2010). This finding is a matter for serious concern because the explicitly stated beliefs tended to be inconsistent with teachers' implicit beliefs that emerged in more nuanced discussion of specific male and female students. The implicit view of males as scientific intellectuals and females as hard workers motivated by grades was generally more aligned with teacher practices, which also revealed some gender inequity. The discrepancy between teachers' explicit and implicit beliefs points to the need to help teachers assess and reflect on their beliefs about gender. The method used in this study, which entailed asking teachers to compare and contrast exemplars they chose was more successful at revealing their operational ideas about gender and science ability than was asking them directly.

The fact that teachers do not consciously recognize or acknowledge bias is both good and bad news. Presumably, they do not endorse the idea of gender differences in science because they recognize that this view is not positive or desirable, which suggests that they might be open to redressing the inequities. On the other hand, they are unlikely to seek to address the problem on their own if they think there are no differences or inequities. Certainly, then, it is important, at the very least, for science teacher educators to communicate to preservice teachers that gender inequities persist in science classrooms. Anecdotally, in professional development conferences with teachers, we have found that asking teachers to mentally answer the questions we posed in the interview and then asking them to examine their answers elicited surprise and consternation among many teachers who seemed stunned that their implicit beliefs favored male students. We are currently developing teacher self study materials that include this exercise, and will be formally evaluating these materials in the near future.

Teachers' implicit beliefs about gender and science appear to be reflected in differences in the ways that high school science teachers interact with their male and female students in the classroom. Across all examined subject areas, teachers spent more time talking to males than females about science content and matters related to science instruction; the teachers tried to engage males more than females in class activities and interacted with males considerably more than females. When males receive more attention than females in science class, females may very well be getting the message, whether intentionally or not, that males are more capable and suitable for science work than females (Amelink, 2009). Furthermore, a meta-analysis which investigated the impact of instructional strategies in science classrooms found that students were advantaged when teachers varied their interaction patterns with them during lessons by asking different types and levels of questions (Schroeder, Scott, Huang, Tolson, & Lee, 2007). The current study demonstrated that males received more attention than females in almost every type of verbal interaction during class.

Our findings of gender inequities in student interactions with teachers in science classrooms may have important implications for students' perceptions of their abilities in science and in their longer-term interest and persistence in science fields. In fact, data gathered from students in the larger study revealed clear and abiding perceptions among the female students that they were not competent in science whereas the male students felt competent (Schmidt, Kackar & Strati, 2010). These differences are extremely important in light of recent analyses of NELS by Legewie and Di Prete (2012) that demonstrated that a positive orientation toward female students in science at the local school level considerably narrowed the gender gap in STEM undergraduate degrees among students who had attended such high schools.

The knowledge gained by this descriptive study can inform science teacher education programs by suggesting science curricula and instructional practices that could effectively meet the needs of both males and females. Not surprisingly, in most cases any imbalance in verbal interactions with students by gender matched the greater participation of either males or females in the class. Since, in most classes, males participated more than females, males tended to get more attention from the teachers. This suggests that teachers need to find a way to make class participation an expectation and a norm by establishing routines in which students are called on to participate with some system (like drawing names or round robin) that promotes gender blind participation in class. Teachers will need to be convinced of the need for this approach as the vast majority believed there was equal participation.

The greater participation of female students in physics was an interesting finding. Perhaps the teachers called on females more often (in two of the physics classes) because they were anticipating that the girls would answer more readily and enthusiastically, a common practice (Tobin & Garnett, 1987). Another explanation might rest on the fact that in this school physics is an elective course and is not a graduation requirement. Students seeking science credits for college entrance were able to select from several alternatives. So, the female students in physics might be different from female students who enrolled only in required courses, or from those who chose to take other science electives.

Observed trends in teachers' classroom practices aligned well with teachers' implicit beliefs about gender differences in science ability. In the interviews the teachers described males as more "able" students and females as more conscientious students in science. Further, the greater differences in teachers' interactions with males and females in the classroom suggest that teachers communicated their implicit beliefs to their students during instruction, thus reinforcing gender stereotypes. An alarming message that the students likely receive is that science ability is a fixed quality that males inheritably possess and females do not. Years of research in cognitive psychology have shown convincing evidence that all cognitive abilities will improve with learning and practice (Halpern, et al, 2007). It is this message that the teachers need to explicitly and implicitly convey to students to help close the achievement gap in science education.

Of course this study was conducted with a relatively small number of teachers so caution must be used in generalizing the results. Yet, the results do match the observations of other researchers currently (AAUW, 2008; Hyde, Lindberg, Linn, Ellis & Williams, 2008; Riegle-Crumb, King, Grodsky, & Muller, 2012) and from the past (Altermatt, Jovanovic, & Perry, 1998; Jones & Wheatley, 1990; Kahle, 1990; Wilkinson & Marrett, 1985). It is also important to note that teachers are not the only but are likely one of many influences on students' motivation and engagement. Teachers may be more accessible and amenable to change than mass media or families so it is worth pursuing approaches to impact their implicit beliefs and interaction patterns with students.

In conclusion, this study suggests some inconsistency between science teachers' stated beliefs about gender equity in their classrooms and actual observations of their classrooms. Observations suggest that students may receive some (albeit probably unintended) messages about gender and science. Given that many norms and stereotypes of "scientists" are strongly gendered, it was important to explore the degree to which gender appears salient among the teachers of tomorrow's scientists. Our findings suggest that efforts need to be made to address the implicit beliefs and behaviors of science teachers regarding gender.

REFERENCES

AAUW. (2008). *Where the girls are: The facts about gender equity in education.* Washington, DC: Author.

Altermatt, E., Jovanovic, J, & Perry, M. (1998). Bias or responsivity? Sex and achievement-level effects on teachers' classroom questioning practices. *Journal of Educational Psychology, 90(3),* 516-527.

Amelink, C. (2009). *Gender Differences in Science Performanc. SWE-AWE CASEE Overviews.* Retrieved June 20, 2011 www.engr.psu.edu/awe/.../ARP_GenderDifferencesScience_ Overview.pdf.

Baxter-Magolda, M.B. (1992). *Knowing and reasoning in college: Gender related patterns in students' intellectual development.* San Francisco: Jossey-Bass.

Belenky, M.F., Clinchy, B.M., Goldberger, N.R., & Tarule, J.M. (1986). *Women's ways of knowing: The development of self, voice, and mind.* New York: Basic Books.

Bickenstaff, J. (2005). Women and science careers: leaky pipeline or gender filter? *Gender and Education, 17(4),* 369–386.

Corra, M. (2007). Stereotype threat: Male and female students in advanced high school courses. *Journal of Women and Minorities in Science and Engineering, 13,* 95-118.

DeBacker, T. K., & Nelson, R. M. (2000). Motivation to learn science: Differences related to gender, class type, and ability. *Journal of Educational Research, 74,* 1-18.

Deci, E., & Ryan, R. (1991). A motivational approach to self: Integration in personality. In R. Dienstbier (Ed.), *Nebraska symposium on motivation, 1990: Perspectives on motivation,* Vol. 38 (pp. 237-288). Lincoln: University of Nebraska Press.

DeZolt, D.M., & Hull, S.H. (2001). Classroom and school climate. In J. Worell (Ed.), *Encyclopedia of women and gender* (pp. 257-264). San Diego: Academic Press.

Eagly, A.H. & Chaiken, S. (1993). The psychology of attitudes. London: Harcourt Brace Jovanovich.

Freeman, C.E. (2004). *Trends in educational equity of girls and women.* Washington, DC: National Center for Educational Statistics (NCES2005-016).

Gallagher, J.J. (1985). *Secondary school science. Interim report.* East Lansing, MI: Michigan State University, Institute for Research on Teaching.

Galotti, K.M, Clinchy, B.M., Ainsworth, K.H., Lavin, B. & Mansfield, A.F. (1999). A new way of assessing ways of knowing: The Attitudes toward Thinking and Learning Survey (ATTLS). *Sex Roles, 40,* 745-766.

Gogolin, L., & Swartz, F. (1992). 'A quantitative and qualitative inquiry into the attitudes toward science of nonscience college students. *Journal of Research in Science Teaching, 29* (5) 487-504.

Halpern, D., Benbow, C., Geary,D., Gur,R., Hyde, J., Gernsbacher, M. (2007). The Science of Sex Differences in Science and Mathematics. *Psychological Science in the Public Interest , 8*(1), 1-50.

Hektner, J.M., Schmidt, J.A. & Csikzentmihalyi, M. (2007). *Experience Sampling Method: Measuring the quality of everyday life*. Thousand Oaks, CA: Sage.

Hill, C., Corbett, C., & St. Rose, E. (2010). Why so few? Women in science, technology, engineering and mathematics. Washington DC: American Association of University Women.

Hyde, J., Lindberg, S., Linn, M., Ellis, A., & Williams, C. (2008). Gender similarities characterize math performance. *Science Magazine, 321*, 494–495.

Hyde, J.S., Fennema E., Ryan, M., Frost, L., & Hopp, C. *(*1990*)* Gender comparisons of mathematics attitudes and affect: A meta-analysis. Psychology of Women Quarterly, *14*, 299–324.

Jones, M. & Wheatley, J. (1990). Gender differences in teacher-student interactions in science classrooms *Journal of Research in Science Teaching, 27(9)*, 861–874.

Jones, M.G., Howe, A., & Rua, M.J. (2000). Gender differences in students' experiences, interests, and attitudes toward science. *Science Education, 84* (2) 180-192.

Kahle, J. (1990). Real students take chemistry and physics: Gender issues. In K. Tobin, J. Kahle, & B. Fraser (Eds.), *Windows into science classrooms: Problems associated with higher-level cognitive learning* (pp. 92-134). NY: Falmer Press.

King, K., Shumow, L., and Lietz, S. (2001). Science education in an urban elementary school: Case studies of teacher's beliefs and classroom practices. *Science Education, 85*, 89-110.

Knight, K.H., Elfenein, M.H., Capozzi, L., Eason, H.A., Bernardo, M.F., & Ferus, K.S. (2000). Relationship of connected and separate knowing to parental style and birth order. *Sex Roles, 43*, 229-240.

Legewie, J. & DiPrete, T. (2012). High School Environments, STEM Orientations, and the Gender Gap in Science and Engineering Degrees. Available at SSRN: http://ssrn.com/abstract=2008733 or http://dx.doi. org/10.2139/ssrn.2008733.

McLaughlin, M.W. & Talbert, J.E. (2001). *Professional communities and the work of high school teaching*. Chicago: University of Chicago Press.

McNeill, K., Pimental, D., & Strauss, E., (2010). The effect of teachers' beliefs and curricular enactments on student learning in high school science. *Proceedings of the 9th International Conference of the Learning Sciences, 2,* 403-404.

National Center for Education Statistics (2000a). *Educational equity for girls and women*. Washington, D.C.: U.S. Government Printing Office.

National Center for Education Statistics (2000b). *Entry and persistence of women and minorities in college science and engineering education*. Washington, D.C.: U.S. Government Printing Office.

Nosek, B., Smyth, F., Sriram, N., Lindner, N., Devos, T., Ayala, A., Bar-Anan, Y., Bergh, R., Cai, H., Gonsalkorale, K., Kesebir, S., Maliszerwski, N., Neto, F., Olli, E., Park, J., Schnabel, K., Shiomura, K., Tulbure, B., Wiers, R., Somogyi, M., Akrami, N. Ekehammar, B., Vianello, M., Banaji, M. Greenwald, A. (2009). National differences in gender–science stereotypes predict national sex differences in science and math achievement. *Proceedings of the National Academy of Sciences in the USA, 106(26). 10593-10597* Accessed May 2, 2011 http://www. pnas.org/content/106/26/10593.full.

Preston, A.E. (2004). *Leaving science: Occupational exit from scientific careers*. New York: Sage.

Reid, N. (2011). Attitude research in science education. In I. Saleh & M. Khine (Eds.) *Attitude Research in Science Education* (pp. 3-44). Charlotte NC: Information Age Publishing.

Riegle-Crumb, C., King, B., Grodsky, E., & Muller, C. (2012). The more things change, the more they stay the same? Prior achievement fails to explain gender inequality in entry into STEM college majors over time. *American Educational Research Journal.*

Ruble, D.N., Martin, C.L., & Berenbaum, S.A. (2006). Gender development. In W. Damon & R. Lerner (Eds.) *Handbook of child psychology* (6th ed). New York: Wiley.

Ryan, M.K. & David, B. (2003). Gender differences in ways of knowing: the context dependence of the attitudes toward thinking and learning survey. *Sex Roles*, 49, 693-699.

Sadker, D., Sadker, M., & Zittleman, K. (2009). *Still failing at fairness: How gender bias cheats boys and girls in school and what we can do about it.* New York, NY: Scribner.

Sanders, J. (2010). Lessons I have learned in three decades of working with teachers about girls in STEM. *Journal of Women in Science and Engineering,16(2)*, 99-113.

Schmader, T., Johns, M., & Barquissau, M. (2004) The costs of accepting gender differences: The role of stereotype endorsement in women's experience in the math domain. Sex Roles, *50,* 835–850.

Schmidt, J.A., Kackar, H.Z., & Strati, A. (2010). Do motivational processes "work" differently for male and female students in science? Examining the role of situational factors and gender in motivational processes among high school science students. *Paper presented at the annual meetings of the American Educational Research Association.* Denver, May.

Schmidt, J.A. & Shumow, L. (2012). Change in self-efficacy in high school science classrooms: An analysis by gender. In S.L. Britner (Ed.) *Psychology of self-efficacy.* Hauppauge, NY: Nova Science Publishers.

Schroeder, C.M., Scott, T.P., Tolson, H., Huang, T. & Lee, Y. (2007). A meta-analysis of national research: Effects of teaching strategies on student achievement in science in the United States. *Journal of Research in Science Teaching, 44*(10), 1436-1460.

Shernoff, D.S., Knauth, S., & Makris, E. (2000). The quality of classroom experiences. In M. Csikszentmihalyi & B. Schneider (Eds.), *Becoming adult: How teenagers prepare for the world of work* (pp. 142-164). New York: Basic Books.

Tobin, K., & Gallagher, J.J. (1987). What happens in high school science classrooms? *Journal of Curriculum Studies, 19*(6), 549-560.

Tobin, K. & Garnett, P. (1987). Gender related differences in science activities. *Science Education, 71*(1), 91-103.

Tobin, K., Kahle, J. & Fraser, B. (1987). *Teaching for higher cognitive level learning in science.* London: Falmer Press.

Turner, J., Christensen, A, & Meyer, D. (2009). Teachers' beliefs about student learning and motivation. *International Handbook of Research on Teachers and Teaching, 21(5),* 361-371.

Weinburgh, M. (1995). Gender differences in student attitudes toward science: A meta-analysis of the literature from 1970 to 1991. *Journal of Research in Science Teaching, 32*(4), 387-398.

Wilkinson, L. & Marrett, D. (1985). *Gender influences in classroom interaction.* San Francisco: Academic Press.

Williams, G. C., & Deci, E. L. (1996). Internalization of biopsychosocial values by medical students: A test of self-determination theory. *Journal of Personality and Social Psychology, 70,* 767-779.

Xie, Y., & Shauman, K. A. (2003). *Women in science: Career processes and outcomes.* Cambridge, MA: Harvard University Press.

Zafar, (2009, February). *College major choice and the gender gap.* Federal Reserve Bank of New York Staff Report No. 364. Accessed April 27, 2011 http://ssrn.com/abstract=1348219.

In: Handbook of Academic Performance ISBN: 978-1-62417-888-7
Editors: Rolf Haumann and George Zimmer © 2013 Nova Science Publishers, Inc.

Chapter 4

UNDERSTANDING UNSATISFACTORY ACADEMIC PERFORMANCE: A CASE STUDY IN RADIOGRAPHY

Ntokozo Gqweta[*]

Durban University of Technology, Department
of Radiography, Durban, South Africa

ABSTRACT

Unsatisfactory academic performance is a recurring theme to many education and related studies. Numerous methods and techniques have been suggested on improving academic performance. However there seem to be limited data on the opinions of the students with regard to academic performance and improvement strategies. There is also limited data on the influence of these opinions on the lecturer's (facilitator's) practices. The current study is aimed at eliciting students' opinions on academic performance as well as the influence of these on the lecturer's (facilitator's) developmental process.

Method: A qualitative study using the phenomenological and the autoethnographic approaches was employed. The phenomenological section of the study was conducted using a questionnaire with open ended question items as a data collection tool in order to acquire rich qualitative data [10] from a cohort of 35 final year diagnostic radiography students. The autoethnographic approach was utilised to demonstrate the developmental process through a transformative reflective report from the educator (facilitator).

Results: Five themes emerged from the qualitative data that could possible shed light into possible causes of students' unsatisfactory academic performance. These were (i) the application of poor or non existent assessment preparation strategies, (ii) the absence of independent study time, (iii) lack of understanding, (iv) the utilisation of inadequate studying techniques as well as (v) strategies to improve academic performance. The autoethnographic approach demonstrated a developmental transformative reflection (reflective practice) of a junior lecturer (facilitator) in acquiring the necessary skills to act and respond to students educational and psychosocial needs.

---

[*] Corresponding author: Ntokozo Gqweta. Email address: ntokozog@dut.ac.za.

Conclusion: The impact of the students' input within the education environment cannot be underestimated. Furthermore reflective practice should be utilised by both educators and students to allow for maximum developmental transformation within the educational.

Keywords: Radiography students, reflective practice, studying technique

INTRODUCTION

Improving student performance may have a high economic and social payoff. However policy analysts in all countries have surprisingly limited hard data on which to base educational strategies for raising achievement (Carnoy and Chisholm, 2008). Consequently this may have some implications for the educational environment. Success within the educational environment is dependent on many factors,and the student is the pivotal point at which all these factors revolve. Therefore the student's attitude towards learning as well as the relationship between the student and the educator is imperative for success in the academic environment. Consequently a supportive environment, coupled with positive student attitude, is necessary for student success. However in the absence of clear strategies for improving achievements, poor academic performance may result with less student success. Amongst other factors poor academic performance may result from the usage of outdated and unvaried teaching and learning methods. Correspondingly certain teaching methods may encourage a consumer-producer relationship between learners and educators (Taylor, 2006a). Hence learners may become conditioned to receive and educators to give (Gqweta, 2012). Furthermore the students may be utilizing studying methods that are not necessarily effective despite their familiarity with such methods. Conversely students may lack the skills necessary for effective academic engagement. These skills may include but not limited to effective communication, being a team player, being a responsible individual, being able to work independently, searching and consolidating data to make a strong academic stance (Taylor, 2006a). Therefore the lack of data on strategies to improve academic achievement has far reaching implications and goes beyond the learning environment into the industrial sector. The industrial sector is where all the necessary skills are to be applied within a multi disciplinary environment (Taylor, 2006b). However without the necessary skills as stated above students may not be ready to embark on an industrial sector as independent, well communicating, responsible individuals.

The learner-centred approach to teaching and learning was introduced to replace the teacher-centred paradigm in order to address the needs of the leaner and consequently those of society. Furthermore the learner-centred paradigm encouraged learners to become independent, actively involved in and responsible for their learning (Gqweta, 2012). It is on this background that this article is based, on student centeredness. The aim of this study is to identify and understand possible causes of unsatisfactory academic performance from the students' perspective.

A plethora of research has been conducted to understand the reasons for poor academic performance (Gua'rdia *et al.,* 2006; Casiano, 2010; Uwaifo, 2008). The findings contend that there are numerous factors that may contribute to' poor academic performance. However, according to the author's knowledge there is limited research data in South Africa that explores the predictors of unsatisfactory academic performance in radiography. Moreover there are no studies that are focussing on the lived experiences of students in particular. The current study is therefore designed to shed light on the student's understanding of possible causes of unsatisfactory academic performance.

In order to understand the students' lived experiences in context it is important to provide a brief outline of radiography education in South Africa. Undergraduate radiography education in South Africa is a three year (minimum) professional qualification (Gqweta, 2012).

Furthermore it requires the co-operation of the educational and health sectors in order to be successful and sustainable. Thus providing basic health care needs to the country while, at the same time, meeting the demands of higher education (Engel-Hills, 2005). Consequently radiography education is structured such that it has a theoretical aspect that includes laboratory work and a work integrated learning (WIL) aspect. WIL aligns academic and workplace practices for the mutual benefit of students and workplaces (Engel- Hills *et al.,* 2010). Radiography students spend a minimum of two weeks at university and a minimum of two weeks at the workplace (WIL). The duration of such a rotation depends on the agreement between the health and the respective educational institutions (Gqweta, 2012).

Knowledge imparted during theoretical learning is applied and made relevant during WIL.

On noticing that the majority of the students failed to obtain the minimum required mark to pass a science subject the lecturer investigated the matter further. The investigation was aimed at finding possible causes of this unsatisfactory performance as well as possible remedial actions from the students. The said lecturer was new in lecturing in general and in lecturing the subject specifically. It was then important for him that he find strategies that will improve the teaching and learning in order to improve the academic performance of the students. For the purposes of this article, the operational definition of unsatisfactory academic performance is a pass mark that is less than 50%, which is the minimum pass mark.

METHODOLOGY

Aim

The aim of the study was to understand possible attributes of unsatisfactory academic performance from the students' perspective in order to improve teaching and learning and academic performance.

Objectives

1   To determine possible factors that contributes to unsatisfactory academic performance.
2   To identify strategies to improve academic performance.
3   To establish the role of the students' perceptions on the developmental process of the educator.

Study Design

A qualitative study utilising two methodological designs the phenomenological and the autoethnographic approaches was used. The phenomenological section of the study was conducted using a questionnaire with open ended question items as a data collection tool in order to acquire rich qualitative data (Terre Blanche *et al.*, 2006). The population was a cohort of 35 final year diagnostic radiography students. The autoethnographic approach was utilised to elicit the developmental process, through transformative reflections, of a junior lecturer. Autoethnography is a methodology that uses personal experiences as a primary data and interprets self as a cultural being in relation to others through a systematic investigative process of data collection, analysis and interpretation (Forster, McAllister and O'Brien 2006).

This methodology was chosen because it is a reflexive enquiry for narrative research and practice that specifically addresses the stories of the scientist and the practitioner (McIlveen, 2008). It is therefore impossible to dissociate the lecturer or facilitator from the learners when you are researching a topic in academic performance. The author believes that the aim of the teaching and learning environment is the development of both the student and the educator.

Methodology

The study extended through two phases, phase one was the perceptions and the input of students on their academic performances. Phase two focused on the lecturer and his developmental process through self and student feedback. Thus the study is qualitative, utilising the interpretive design and the autoethnographic design.

Section One

A questionnaire was administered to third year diagnostic radiography students following feedback on an assessment written two weeks prior. The questionnaire was completed by the students and submitted to the researcher at the end of the feedback session. The aim of this qualitative study was to try and understand the individual students in their life world (Van Rooy *et al.*, 2006). An interpretative design was utilised in order to explain the student performances in the context of their personal experiences. The research study was voluntary, and only twenty one (n=21) students returned the questionnaire at the end of the feedback session.

Table 1. The questionnaire items

1. What are your results for this test, pass or fail? (If you passed go to question 3)
2. Why do you think you failed?
3. What can you do to improve?
4. How did you study?
5. How can the lecturer assist you?

Ethics

Permission was obtained from the Head of Department: Radiography. Students were subsequently approached and their participation to the study meant consent as the study was voluntary. Confidentiality and privacy were maintained at all times.

SECTION ONE

Data Analysis and Coding

In order to protect the privacy and to uphold confidentiality of each participant, each questionnaire was allocated a category specific pseudonym. Two broad categories were identified, that is, those respondents that did not meet the minimum pass mark and those that passed the assessment.

The following codes were then devised RF= Respondent Failed and RP =Respondent passed respectively. Each respondent was then given a number which was subsequently attached to the category code for example Respondent F1, represented respondent one from the category fail. Manual analysis of the questionnaire was then conducted, the data were coded and themes were subsequently identified.

RESULTS

Results are divided into two sections, section one reports the phenomenological aspect, demonstrating lived experiences of the students with regards to academic performance. Section two uses an autoethnographic method to demonstrate a reflective transformative developmental process of the lecturer involved in the subject discussed.

In this section the lecturer is the subject of research and a reporter. This section demonstrates developmental transformation through reflections from the lecturer.

Twenty one (n=21) students participated in the study out of the cohort of 35 students. A response rate of 60 % was achieved .Of the twenty one (n=21) students that participated in the study eighteen (n=18) 86 % were females and three (n=3) 14% were males. These gender based demographics are consistent with those of all the students enrolled within the radiography course. Twelve (12) 57 % of these participants obtained less than the minimum requirement to pass that particular assessment.

It is however, relevant to note that the subject in question is assessed on a continuous assessment basis and the above results reflect only the particular written assessment not the overall performance at the end of the academic year. Content analysis of the questionnaire responses revealed 5 themes (see Table 2).

Table 2. Emergent themes

Themes:
1. Assessment preparedness.
2. Independent Study.
3. Understanding and retention.
4. Studying techniques.
5. Improving academic performance.

Summary of Themes

Assessment Preparedness

The majority 57% of the respondents failed to obtain the minimum required mark to pass the particular assessment. These individuals attributed their failure to poor preparation and poor time management.

In alignment with Sansgiry *et al.* (2006) findings these students noted that effective time management skills are imperative for academic success. They learned that the consequence of poor time management is poor academic performance and subsequent lower probability of succeeding in an academic program.

These students acknowledged that the lack of time management skills may have contributed to their current unsatisfactory academic performance.

Respondent F3 felt that she needs to change aspects of her current assessment preparation methods and study well in advance in order to see a change in her academic performance.

'...... I need to learn everything in advance, give myself more time to study.'

This sentiment was also shared by those respondents who managed to pass the current assessment. Respondent P7 noted that if he could start studying well in advance his academic performance would improve '*I can improve my studying by starting earlier than I did.*'

There are many factors that may contribute to poor or absence of assessment preparedness. These may include but not limited to numerous deadlines from different lecturers whereby students are expected to complete different modules, papers, assignments and projects within a specific time frame. These stringent deadlines coupled with psychosocial problems may exert an enormous amount of pressure on the students. However optimum functioning and success within the academic arena is possible through planning, dedication and consistency. The consequence of inadequate planning may lead to unfavourable outcomes. These outcomes may include, but not limited to, missing of stipulated deadlines, penalisation for late submissions and a general feeling of being overwhelmed, hopeless and helpless. A combination of these circumstances (and others) may result in a student failing to meet the required outcomes of a particular subject/module. Subsequently prolonging the time spent studying towards the degree or diploma. These factors may further be exacerbated by procrastination whereby a task is needlessly delayed until the point of some discomfort (Akinsola *et al.,* 2007). The pressures of the university academic life coupled with procrastinating may have serious psychosocial implications and may in turn lead to poor academic performance, failure and eventual dropping out of the course. Therefore it is important to note that optimum academic performance may be achieved through effective time management, planning, consistency and effective study techniques (Sansgiry, *et al. 2006).*

Independent Study

Students at the third level of learning are expected to engage with their learning material independently or with minimum assistance. This was however not demonstrated in the current study. The students in the current study did not engage with their learning material outside the classroom. Even though independent study is the function of academic success and life long learning. However students did acknowledge their fallacy with regard to independent studying. Respondent F6 felt that independent studying is one of the strategies he will have to utilise in order to improve his academic performance.

'In order to improve I will have to do a lot of studying at home and not only rely on the lecturer'. It is however important to note that a variety of factors may have an influence on whether a student does review work at home/outside the classroom or not. These factors may include but not limited to, motivation to learn, fear of failure, home backgrounds and student's maturity including the lifestyle of the student.

Casiano *et al.* (2010) noted that a students' healthy lifestyle is related to attendance of classes, working diligently, socializing, and maintaining healthy interpersonal relationships.

Furthermore home study or independent study is achievable through willingness to minimise or sacrifice certain aspects of one's social life. This is achievable through reducing exposure to aspects of social life that might interfere with academic performance (Williams and Decker, 2009). Accordingly independent study requires the ability to resist the temptation to engage in instant pleasurable experiences that usually occur parallel to studying. Thus effective execution of independent studying requires discipline, maturity and goal orientation in order to be executed successfully.

Understanding and Retention

The majority of the respondents explained that they studied, however they did not understand what they were studying. They also alluded to the fact that they struggled to understand the assessment questions. This may have resulted in assessment question misinterpretation.

Respondent F2 was surprised to learn that she has failed the assessment despite her confidence to the contrary immediately post writing the paper. She explains that

'.... after the paper I didn't feel that I might fail it, I thought i wrote what was expected.'

The lack of understanding was also demonstrated by other respondents. For example respondent F11 exclaimed,

'I guess I learnt but did not understand what..... I'm studying'

This lack of understanding is well demonstrated particularly in students that failed to obtain the minimum mark required to pass the assessment. Evidently this was one of the major contributors to students' not meeting the minimum requirement to pass the assessment. Many variables may play a role in whether a student understands a particular learning material or not. These variables may include, but not limited to, students' listening skills, cognitive ability, psychosocial issues, the level of complexity of the learned material and the lecturer's approach to the teaching and learning environment as well as studying techniques (Gqweta, 2012). There is no single cause for poor or lack of understanding. A systematic process should be employed to investigate the causal factors that may have led to poor or lack of understanding. Academic success is achievable through a combination of varying the support systems and applying various parameters and techniques within the learning and teaching environment. It is also achievable through an effective and conducive working relationship between student and educator.

Studying Techniques

Students at the third level of study are said to be more or less stabilised, well oriented, well adjusted and more knowledgeable about the course (Ugwu *et al.* 2010). Therefore it is also an assumption that they are more knowledgeable about different types of studying techniques. They are able to utilise these different studying techniques in order to be successful in an academic programme. However studying techniques utilised by the current respondents proved to be inefficient and may have contributed to poor performance. Respondent P9 stated that her source of learning material to study was solely the lecture notes.

> 'I just learnt from the notes', and respondent P4 also committed the same fallacy 'I just read the power point slides and the notes' . This resulted in respondent F5 feeling cheated on when .....'some of the things in the test were not in our notes'. Respondent F 21 said 'I didn't study with an understanding so I crammed most of the stuff, when I saw the paper I panicked then I went blank'

These students demonstrated a surface approach to learning. Their main aim was to study merely for the intention of reproducing information without any further analysis (Montgomery and Groat, 1998). These students' studying techniques demonstrated that they disregarded the knowledge that lectures are designed to sensitise them to the required and relevant information for a particular learning area.

Lectures are also designed to introduce basic as well as difficult and novel concepts that are not readily acquired, assimilated and understood when studying independently (Gqweta, 2012).

Consequently lectures do not contain in-depth information that is enough to master a particular learning area, further independent study and analysis of the learning material needs to take place before one can successfully comprehend all the concepts. However an interesting point to note was that some students were well aware of their inadequate studying techniques. For example respondent F12 explained that,

> 'I studied from the notes given but clearly it was not enough'.

Improving Academic Performance

Further analysis of the participants' responses revealed the following improvement strategies.

These included studying in advance of assessment, data triangulation, independent study,and effective lecturer support.

- Studying well in advance of an assessment- the majority of the respondents explained that they can only improve their academic performance by starting to study well in advance of an assessment.
- Searching and utilising other sources of information other than lecture notes to prepare for an assessment (data triangulation) - the respondents noted that the lecture notes are not adequate on their own for academic success. They noted the importance of triangulating their learning material and using different sources of information to enhance understanding and analysis.

- Engaging with the learning material outside the classroom (independent study)- Respondents explained that independent study allows one to identify early areas of difficulty and seek appropriate assistance. They also noted that independent study will allow them to engage with areas relevant learning areas not necessarily covered in the classroom.
- The need for the lecturer to provide printed handouts, past papers as well as worksheets (lecturer support)- These respondents also felt that there is a need to get some guidelines in the form of previous question papers in order to inform them on the expected assessment questioning style. Students also felt that there is a need for tutorials to supplement the learning conducted in the classroom.

These strategies to improve academic performance fall within the domains of the student and the educator. Thus an effective combination of student independence, responsibility, accountability with support from educator is imperative for student success in an academic environment.

SECTION TWO

An autoethnographic reflective report was obtained from the lecturer concerned and some quotes from the participants in section A were used to demonstrate possible blind spots and thus areas of improvements. In an effort to make this section accountable to the scientific rigor, some data excerpts from the student's responses were utilised. This section is based on the autoethnographic method and is aimed at demonstrating a transformative developmental process of a junior lecturer. This section demonstrates developmental transformation through reflections from the lecturer.

Data was collected using unstructured student questionnaires, observations, and interactions of the lecturer with others within the teaching and learning environment. Furthermore this section is reflective in nature and thus all these other methods of data collection were utilised to support and demonstrate the role of others, especially students, in the development of a junior lecturer. Published literature was also used to demonstrate the current status of higher education with regard to human resource.

The Beginning

I am the lecturer of the subject that was evaluated. My professional background is in clinical radiography. Within the radiography profession a large amount of time is spent interacting with patients and many other healthcare practitioners. This interaction at best requires an individual who is self assured, competent, caring, professional and who acts within demarcated ethical codes of conduct. This individual must constantly seek to improve their performances and professional standing. This improvement is amongst other things achieved through keeping abreast with current trends (nationally and internationally) in order to provide the best of care to the patient.

The clinical environment allowed me to develop myself academically and ethically through the interaction with different types of people sometimes under challenging circumstances. Occasionally I was exposed to students that came to do their work integrated learning (WIL) at the clinical venue I worked at. My interaction with these students was through mentoring, monitoring and evaluation (providing them with feedback) on their performance at the end of the week. The students' clinical practice was improving noticeable. The development of these students fascinated me, especially the fact that I also played part in nurturing and fostering it. When an opportunity presented itself and a junior lecturing post was advertised, in 2008, I applied. I went for interviews and was successful. I started working as a junior lecturer in the beginning of year 2009. I was 27 years of age. In the same year an audit conducted by the department of higher education and training revealed that almost 50% of staff working at universities at the time were within the age group between 45 years and older (Department of Higher Education and Training, 2012).

Entering the Educational Sector

From the beginning I began to notice that there were differences between the educational sector and the clinical environment that I was familiar with . The image provided by the interaction with the few students within the clinical environment was different from what confronted me at the educational institution. Firstly, here there were large numbers of students. Apart from this, new duties that were previously non-essential within my scope of practice were the pillars of the new job. These included but not limited to, administration, lecture preparation, lecturing, self-directed and supported research, mandated meeting attendance and certain committee membership. Thirdly a new language was necessary and a new way of being became apparent. More time was spent on thinking and conceptualising and applying the conceptual plans strategically and then evaluating the effectiveness of these plans as well as the impact of their implementation.

Over and above these demands there were the subtle stereotypical expectations. As a young male lecturer in a profession dominated by female students I constantly felt that my conduct was under a microscope from senior staff members and perhaps students as well. During my first year of lecturing I had a student that felt obligated to 'look out' for me. He warned me to be 'careful around the female students' as they may be manipulative and use any interaction with me to their advantage. He explained that they may use the gender difference and the age equivalence as a point of departure in manipulating me through seduction. There was this expectation, from his side, that there is a possibility that, I will step on the wrong side of practice. This, I believe, was also a reflection of the minimum age difference between the two of us. The student felt that I probably do not have enough experience to deal with the demands of the job under these circumstances. Another example is that of a particular senior academic member who noted that he has confidence in me as long as I was over the age of 23 years. It seemed as if when I am over a certain age category I will be able to deal with the demands of the academic arena. It became evident that maybe there is an unwritten rule about age within the higher education sector. The university environment is dominated by seniors in terms of age, experience and qualifications (Department of Higher Education and Training, 2012). Consequently apart from the expressed potential for greatness that youthfulness provides there is also an underlying assumption from others about its potential for self-destruction. These expectations and assumptions about junior individuals may lead to an enormous amount of pressure and increased stress levels on those affected. The subtle expectations and assumptions explained above led me as a junior lecturer to be strict and not yield to any of the student demands. Furthermore I became oppositional in my thinking and in decision making, there was either a right or wrong, a yes or no,and a black or white. Howard *et al.,* (1996) explain that people with this type of thinking have a 'tendency to seem aloof and detached; need to look for flaws in everything; negative, cynical attitude' I felt that I had to make my position clear so that I am not taken 'advantage of' by the students. I needed to demonstrate who was in charge within the teaching and learning interaction. Thus in the beginning of my education and training career the only form of teaching that I utilised was lectures/presentations. It seemed easy to have a group of students listening to me while I presented and hopefully absorbing the information. This meant that I had the upper hand, I was in control and was not going to be taken lightly; I was making a 'statement' demonstrating who was in charge in that situation. Consequently I was not varying my teaching methods which could have been to the disadvantage of the students. I received the respect, or so I thought, that I needed but to the detriment of the students. I also expected the student to be able to independently interrogate the learning material and only seek assistance where necessary. However looking in retrospect I can now see that it was impossible for students to engage with me in this manner even though they may have had issues to discuss. For example one student, respondent P20 felt that I was being too strict with the marking and I needed to have more examples as I teach.

> '...... try to use more example as you teach and loosen up on the way you set the paper. Dont make it too hard and challenging. Set in the way that you want us to pass not fail.

The students felt that I was 'out there' to 'get them'. It therefore would have been impossible for them to summon enough courage and confront me. These students were only able to use this research platform to engage with me constructively. The students' perceptions about me could have resulted in them being resistant to any constructive criticism and suggestions that I might have provided to support their learning. The oppositional approach that I utilised portrayed me as an unapproachable lecturer that was impenetrable, impractical and un-reasonable in the eyes of the students. I became aware of the inadequacy of the experience provided by my previous interactions with the students in the clinical environment.

Furthermore I became aware of the fallacy of demanding too much respect even in lieu of good academic practice. The research results made me question my conduct and seek ways to change it in order to benefit me, students and the institution.

The institution had its own demands on me which may have compounded the situation. I was mandated to complete a qualification higher than the one I was employed with . The combination of stresses of the new territory and the demands placed on me by the institution made the transition process a bit more challenging. However, the institution provided me and other new employees with a chance to go through an induction programme which was useful and assisted me during this period.

Noticing a Disjuncture

The induction programme made me aware of the full extent of requirements of the teaching and learning environment. As well as strategies to deal with a large number of students in a classroom as opposed to the five students that I was accustomed to in the clinical environment. However an induction programme was not enough to elaborate on the extent of the teaching and learning environment. It became apparent that perhaps a teaching diploma or degree would be that much more helpful.

There was a need for knowledge and understanding of the basis for the pedagogical strategies employed. Furthermore the advantages of certain strategies over others within different teaching and learning situations needed further exploration and theoretical knowledge base. Even though currently a teaching qualification is not a requirement for university lecturing I felt that I needed more. I then enrolled for a Post Graduate Diploma in Tertiary Education.

At the same time I conducted a research study to gather data on how students perceive the learning and teaching environment as well as their performance. I believed that student' perceptions of the teaching and learning environment may have an impact on their academic performance. So, when the results of the study came highlighting the shortcomings of the students, and indirectly mine, I began to search for possible remedial actions and solutions. I asked myself 'what can I do to ensure that the students are supported academically, how can I change the learning and teaching environment to ensure maximised student engagement and performance. The answer to these questions had to start with the alteration of my perceptions about the teaching and learning environment. It became apparent that it is no longer necessary for me to demand respect through systematic and stringent processes.

I later understood that respect was and can be obtained through self surety, understanding and unwavering principles. Therefore the enrolment into post graduate diploma was aligned with the time of my personal re-evaluation and redefinition in terms of the teaching and learning environment.

Understanding the Students

The Post Graduate Diploma in Tertiary Education enhanced my knowledge of how to deal with tertiary students in general and those at risk of failing specifically. Previous experience through trial and error and support from colleagues, coupled with knowledge gained from the diploma saw me utilising different teaching strategies within the classroom. This change was aligned with the current needs expressed by stakeholders within the educational environment thatit is no longer satisfactory for educators within the health profession to simply develop the knowledge base of their students.

Educators are increasingly obliged to ensure their students develop the kind of personal and intellectual capacities that will lead to defensible and ethical decision-making that is grounded in the best available "evidence" (Baird, 2008). Therefore different teaching and learning strategies develop different skills, which are necessary in order to encompass all developmental aspects of students.

Lessons Learned

The health related teaching and learning environment may be discipline specific but it encompasses many facets of moulding a developing human being. The academic development alone is no longer enough for a successful, all round and contributing member of the community. This then mean that the educators need to be able to harness within their students, optimum academic functioning and effective psychosocial skills. For an individual to be able to inculcate these dimension, he or she need to have a particular level of maturity that allows them to provide sufficient support for learning in these areas. I am now well aware that it is no longer enough for an educator to be extremely discipline specific in the teaching and learning environment. There is a need for educators to have knowledge and skills to identify factors that may lead an individual student to be at risk of failing a particular subject. Thus accordinglyproviding the necessary support and referral where appropriate . There is also a need for sensitivity to different socioeconomic divides and be able to respond appropriately to issues of this nature that require sensitivity, support and referral. Now as a lecturer being in the industry for just over 3 years I have learned the importance of variation in teaching methods. I have also learned that there is a need for sensitivity and understanding when responding to students issues including psychosocial issues. Student academic performance and subsequent development is equally dependent on them as well as the educator/ facilitator.

DISCUSSION

The emergent themes from the study illustrate the latent effects of the former teacher-centred paradigm, which is still utilised in some secondary schools and higher education institutions (Lowe and Cook, 2003). Students' perceived poor performing more as a consequence of poor learning and application techniques than teaching methods. It is important to note that students' poor academic performance may result from numerous factors including incongruence of the teaching strategy to the students' learning styles, lack of motivation, self efficacy doubts as well as inefficient studying techniques. Furthermore the type of assessment utilised may also have an impact on the students' performance. Written assessments have demonstrated a decreased performance pattern from students as opposed to other forms of assessments. Assignments, group projects, presentations and practical assessments enhanced student performance in the particular program.

It is relevant to note that the students' suggested improvement strategies were aligned with the principles of the learner centred paradigm. These strategies were also aligned with the critical cross fields' outcomes (CCFO's), developed by the South African Department of Education (DoE) (South Africans Qualifications Authority, SAQA, 1997).

The CCFO's were developed in an effort to encourage independent and well developed individuals that can make a positive contribution in their societies and globally. However, the students in this study demonstrated a lack of practical application of these strategies. Therefore the educator needs to harness and nurture these concepts by employing protocols and methods that encourage their application.

Is the Teaching Congruent to the Learning?

Students have different learning styles and educators need to utilise a variety of teaching methods to accommodate most, if not all, leaning styles. One of the emerging points here is that the lecturer utilised one method of teaching in the beginning. This may have had a negative impact on the academic performance of students. Educators must be aware that they have the capacity to widen their teaching styles in ways that can meet the versatility of their students' learning preferences (Arthurs, 2007). Consequently this will enhance students' achievements (Naimiea et al., 2010). Varying one's teaching methods ensures that a wide audience is reached and can access the information. Furthermore it promotes retention and application of new knowledge (Arthurs, 2007). Accordingly educators should be sensitive to different learning styles and be equipped to apply different teaching methods. Misalignment of teaching methods and students' learning styles may lead to students' inattentiveness, poor performance, loss of interest, and ultimately dropping out of the course (Naimiea et al., 2010). The congruency of the teaching methods and learning styles may also enhance students' studying techniques and subsequent responsibility for one's learning.

Responsibility within the Teaching and Learning Environment

Even though the current student's improvement plans were mainly a matter of self development and reported so. These students also strongly felt that their success depended mainly, if not solely, on the educator. This view is in stark contrast to the learner-centred approach, where students are within the centre of the learning phenomenon and as such also responsible for their learning. The comments from students demonstrated the lack of responsibility for their learning. Respondent F1 felt that the lecturer should 'Set *an easier paper...*' conversely Respondent F5 wanted pointers that could possible make them aware of what to expect in future assessments... '*The lecturer must give us past papers to work with*''

Respondent P8 wanted hard copies of notes that can be easily referred to during a lecture... '*The lecturer should print us notes before lecture so that we can learn or study something that we can see.*'

Some of these requests are important and valid in order for students to succeed in an academic programme. However, these requests can also be fulfilled by students: some universities have previous question papers repositories available for students to download. The university where the study was conducted was in the process of setting up this previous question paper repository. Alternatively the current students can obtain these papers from previous students. Conversely students can compile and keep their own notes before a lecture. This is possible because students are given schemes of work with all the learning areas and learning objectives with dates of delivery per particular subject at the beginning of each year (Gqweta, 2012). There is a need to encourage a sense of responsibility from the students with regard to the teaching and learning environment.

Support from educators and other supporting departments within the institution designed to deal with student development is invaluable in this regard. Furthermore programmes designed to develop students' independency such as library orientation, library skills, use of internet and search engines for scientific information, self study and strategies in communication are vital to nurture student development. It is also necessary to allocate extra resources in the first year of study if successful retention strategies by higher education institutions are to be realised (Williams and Decker, 2009). These strategies and resources are designed to break the students' study habits formed in secondary school (Lowe and Cook, 2003). Arguably universities imbed student development strategies within subjects or modules where students are encouraged to engage with their work independently. Accordingly educators create learning opportunities that re-enforce independent learning and research skills through student presentations, assignment projects and group projects. However, some students respond negatively to these strategies (Gqweta, 2012). This negative response could be as a result of the generation of learners coming to higher education. The current generation of students' values, ideas and ideals may prelude this resistance. These learners are referred to as generation NEXT learners whose characteristics include but not limited to consumer orientation, instant gratification, entertainment orientation and scepticism (Taylor, 2006a). These students only respond to information that they perceive to be relevant to their needs. Value systems driven by consumerism do limit these students from exploring other options that might need more effort and appear less attractive with seeming fewer returns. However success in academic programme requires the utilisation of strategic studying techniques which in turn require attention, effort and consistency (Phan, 2006). The strategic studying techniques require one to be attentive, consistent and motivated in order to execute the learning successfully.

Apart from independent studying, learner responsibility and effective time management skills, motivation is a central phenomenon to student success in academic programmes. Furthermore motivation, achievement and academic self-confidence have the strongest relationship to college grade point average (Naimiea *et al,* 2010). Therefore highly motivated students may demonstrate higher performance patterns. These students may either possess intrinsic motivation or extrinsic motivation.

Extrinsically motivated individual may perform activities because they are perceived to be instrumental in achieving valued outcomes that are distinct from the activity itself (Ramayah *et al* n.d). Meanwhile intrinsically motivated individuals engage in activities for inherent satisfaction rather than for some separable consequence. Furthermore intrinsically motivated learners learn to satisfy an inner need for knowledge that is accompanied by experiences of pride, achievement and development (Ryan and Deci, 2000). The lack of motivation to learn may demonstrate poor or absence of intrinsic motivation as well as a perceived lack of positive reinforcing agents. Therefore the role of the educator extends beyond provision of a conducive environment to learn and it includes applying motivating factors within this environment in order to optimise student learning. The ability to ignite and sustain motivation of learners is a skill on its own that is independent of the teaching ability of an individual. Furthermore it may be argued that learners may succeed in academe with minimum assistance as long as they are motivated to learn.

CONCLUSION

The students in the current study reported poor preparation, absence of independent study, lack of understanding and retention, lack of responsibility and poor time management skills as contributing factors to poor academic performance. Furthermore assessment preparedness, effective studying skills, information triangulation, effective lecturer support and independent study are strategies that can be used to improve academic performance. Poor academic performance can be attributed to many factors and can be equally addressed using a variety of strategies (Sansigiry *et al.*, 2006).

It is imperative that educators conduct research studies on their teaching practices to find out what the student's needs and views are about the teaching environment. Student opinions are invaluable in the learner-centred approach. Strategies to combat poor academic performance should be made in consultation with various stake holders including the students. It is evident in this study that the students' perceived improvement strategies are aligned with the principles of the learner-centred paradigm. However there is a lack of practical application which is evidenced by the students' current studying techniques and demonstrated lack of responsibility within the learning environment.

Conversely there are challenges facing junior lecturers in higher education institutions; however these can be minimised by effective support and ongoing application of improvement strategies.

Limitations of This Study and Recommendations for Further Studies

The sample selection was limited to the views of the core group in a particular university and is not representative of third year diagnostic radiography students in all South African universities.

A more representative research study that will include all the universities could yield results that are more inferential. Further probing of the student responses would have yielded the meaning to their responses and perhaps further areas of study and improvement.

The views demonstrated under autoethnography are emotive and aimed at evoking reactions from those with similar experiences, or those who were not aware of such occurrences, to see this as an area of further research. Therefore these views are those of the author and do not necessary reflect those of the institution of employment.

REFERENCES

Akinsola, K. M., Tella, A. and Tella, A. 2007. Correlates of Academic Procrastination and Mathematics Achievement of University Undergraduate Students. *Eurasia Journal of Mathematics, Science and Technology Education.* 3(4): 363-370.

Arthurs, B. J. 2007. A juggling Act in the classroom: Managing different learning styles. *Teaching and Learning in Nursing.* 2: 2-7.

Carnoy, M. and Chisholm, L. Towards understanding student's performance in South Africa: A pilot study of grade 6 mathematics lessons in Gauteng Province. 2008; 1-76 Available at: http://www.hsrc.ac.za/research/output/outputDocuments/5199_Carnoy_Towards understandingstudentacademic.pdf Accessed on March 2011.

Casiano, I. L. The relationship among living situation, health and college academic performance. 2010; Available at: http://clearinghouse.missouriwestern.edu/manuscripts/512.php Access on: 3 August 2010.

Engel-Hills, P. 2005. An Intergrated Approach to Curriculum. *The South African Radiographer*. 43(2): 24-27.

Engel-Hills, P., Garraway, J., Jacobs, C., Volbrecht, T., and Winberg, C. 2010. Work-Integrated Learning (WIL) and the HEQF. Unpublished paper presented at the NQF research conference.

Foster, K., MacAllister, M. and O'Brien, L. 2006. Extending the boundaries: Autoethnography as an emergent method in mental health nursing research. *International Journal of Mental Health Nursing*. 15, 44–53.

Gqweta, N. 2012. Poor Academic Performance a perspective of third year diagnostic students. *Radiography*. 18: 212-217.

Gua'rdia, J., Freixa, M., Pero, M., and Turbany, J. 2006. Factors Related to the Academic Performance of Students in the Statistics Course in Psychology. *Quality and Quantity* . 40(4): 661–674.

Howard, H. W., Brinkman, G. L. and Lambert, R. 1996. Thinking Styles and Financial Characteristics of Selected Canadian Farm Managers. Available at: http://dx.doi.org/ 10.1111/j.1744-7976.1997.tb00157.x. Accessed on 14 November 2012.

Lotkowski, A. V., Robbins, S. B. and Noeth, J. R. 2004. The role of academic and non academic factors in improving college retention: available at http://www.act.org/research/ policymakers/pdf/college_retention.pdf Accessed on 10 October 2011

Lowe, H. and Cook, A. 2003. Mind the gap: are students prepared for higher education. *Journal of Further and Higher Education*. 27(1): 54-76.

McIlveen, P. 2008. Autoethnography as a method for reflexive research and practice in practice in vocational psychology. *Australian Journal of Career Development,* 17 (2); 13-20. Retrieved from http://eprints.usq.edu. au accessed October 2011.

Montgomery, M. S. and Groat, N. L. Student learning styles and their implications for teaching. Centre for Research for Teaching and Learning at the University of Michigan. Occasional paper No. 10. 1998; 1-8. Available at: http://www.crlt.umich.edu/publinks/ CRLT_no10.pdf accessed on March 2011.

Naimiea, Z., Sirajb, S., Piawc, C. Y., Shagholid, R., and Abuzaide, R. A. 2010. Do you think your match is made in heaven? Teaching styles/learning styles match and mismatch revisited. *Procedia Social Sciences Behavioural Sciences*. 2: 349-353.

Phan, H. P. 2006. Examination of learning approaches, reflective thinking, and epistemological beliefs: A latent variables' approach. *Electronical Journal of Research of Educational Psychology*.; 4(3):577-610.

Ramayah, T., Jantam, M. and Ismail, N.n.d. Impact of intrinsic and extrinsic motivation on internet usage in Malaysia. 1-10: available at http://www.ramayah.com/journalarticles pdf/impact of intrinsic.pdf accessed on 10 October 2011.

Republic of South Africa. Department of Higher Education and Training. 2012. Green Paper for Post School Education and Training. Available at: www.dhet.gov.za . Accessed on November 2012.

Ryan, M. R. and Deci, L. E. 2000. Intrinsic and extrinsic motivation: Classic definitions and new directions. *Contemporary Education Psychology*. 25: 54 -67.

Sansgiry, S. S., Bhosle, M. and Sail, K. 2006. Factors That Affect Academic Performance Among Pharmacy Students. *American Journal of Pharmaceutical Education*. 70(5): 1-9.

South African Qualifications Authority (SAQA). Critical Cross-Field Education and Training Outcomes Decision: 0204/96 . Bulletin - Volume One Number One May/June 1997;

Available at: http://www.saqa.org.za/ show.asp?include=docs/pubs/bulletins/bulletin97-1.html Accessed on 6 June 2011.

Stahl, J. D. Parental involvement in education. n.d; 1-16. Available at: http://www.jeffdstahl.com/worksfiles/parentalinvolvement.pdf Accessed on 1 June 2011

Taylor, M. Generation NeXt Goes to Work: Issues in Workplace Readiness and Performance. Chapter 2: Leadership Development Programs and Strategies. Programs, Strategies, and Structures to Support Student Success. 2006a; 2: 35-41 Available at: http://www.cacubo.org/pdf/2007Chicago/Gen%20NeXt%20article%20HLC%2007.pdf Accessed on April 2011.

Taylor, M. Generation NeXt Comes to College: 2006 Updates and Emerging Issues. Chapter 2: Understanding and Supporting All Types of Learners. Focusing on the Needs and Expectations of Constituents.2006b; 2:48-55. Available at: http://www.taylorprograms.com/images/Gen_NeXt_article_ HLC_06.pdf Accessed on June 2011.

Terre Blanche, M., Gurrheim, K. and Painter, D. 2006. *Research in Practice: Applied methods for the Social Sciences.* 4th ed. Cape Town. UCT Press.

Ugwu, A. C., Ukwueze, A. C., Erondu, O. F., and Nwokorie, E. 2010. Affective and cognitive learning outcomes of radiography students in a Nigerian university. *The South African Radiographer.* 48 (2):13-16.

Uwaifo V. O. 2008. The Effects of Family Structure and Parenthood on the Academic Performance of Nigerian University Students. *Stud. Home Comm. Sci.* 2(2): 121-124.

Van Rooy, T., Claassen, C. and Schulze, S. 2006.*Teaching, Learning and Development in Adult Education.* Pretoria. Unisa.

Williams, M. and Decker, S. 2009. Mature students' perspectives of studying radiography. *Radiography.* 15: 77e85.

In: Handbook of Academic Performance
Editors: Rolf Haumann and George Zimmer

ISBN: 978-1-62417-888-7
© 2013 Nova Science Publishers, Inc.

Chapter 5

GENDER AND COMPENSATION: AN EDUCATIONAL ANALYSIS

João Paulo Vieito[*]

Dean, School of Business Studies,
Polytechnic Institute of Viana do Castelo, Portugal

ABSTRACT

Using data from 30 different countries, this investigation is among the first to analyze the impact the education level of the person who one chooses to marry or cohabit with has on personal earnings and if a certain combination in levels of education (qualifications) between the couple leads to higher total family remuneration when compared to other combinations. The results describe something quite new in the area: the education level of the person who one chooses to live or cohabit influences the total remuneration of the other member of the couple; the impact of the husband's education level on the wife's total remuneration is higher than when the inverse is compared; and when it is the man who has the higher educational level, on average, total family earnings are higher than when it is the woman. Finally the total earnings of the other member of the couple and a person's own remuneration are influencing factors which drive male or female to spend more time on housework. The findings of this paper are very important, essentially to executive compensation area, because until the moment literature only focuses on the impact of executive personal characteristics in terms of total executive compensation, but the education level of the person who married or cohabites with this executive seems to have also a positive effect in his personal compensation.

Keywords: Gender Gap; education; marriage

JEL Classification: J16; J12; J3; D13

---

[*] School of Business Sciences - Polytechnic Institute of Viana do Castelo, Avenida Miguel Dantas, 4930 Valença (Portugal). Tel: 0351-251-8000840.Fax: 00351-251-800841. E-mail: joaovieito@esce.ipvc.pt

INTRODUCTION

This investigation is among the first to analyze if the education level of the person that one chooses to marry or cohabit with influences the compensation of the other member of the couple and if a certain combination in education levels between male and female leads to higher total family compensation when compared to others. Additionally the factors which make married or cohabiting male or female spend more time on housework were also analyzed. A wide range of literature, essentially from the area of finance and labor economics, describes female as receiving, on average, lower compensations than male (Weisskoff, 1972; Weinberg, 2000; O'Neil, 2003; Escriche, 2007; Rizzo and Zeckhauser, 2007, Constant et al. 2005; Lauerova and Terrell, 2007 among several others). However, these studies do not take the person's education level into account or the education level of the person who they choose to live or cohabit with, in terms of their personal compensation. Husband and wife, or partners, were classified in relation to their education level: University degree, post-secondary education (undergraduate), secondary education, above compulsory education and below compulsory education. Data was retrieved from the "*International Social Survey Programme* (ISSP) 2002: Family and Changing Gender Roles (III)" which analyzed the attitudes towards family and gender roles, marriage, as well as children and financial support.

The study was conducted on 40 countries but for the purpose of this investigation, only 30 countries were considered and analyzed, those which provided more detailed information (Australia, Germany (West), Germany (East), Great Britain, Northern Ireland, United States, Austria, Hungary, Netherlands, Norway, Sweden, Czech Republic, Poland, Bulgaria, Russia, New Zealand, Philippines, Japan, Spain, Latvia, Slovak Republic, France, Portugal, Republic of Chile, Denmark, Switzerland, Flanders, Finland, Mexico and Taiwan). Working with data from such a vast group of countries would suggest that this study is one of the most relevant and extensive in the area. The results describe something quite new: The education level of one member of the couple has a positive and statistically significant effect on the remuneration of the other member and this impact reduces when the education level also reduces. Most interesting is the fact that an educated husband/partner, with a university degree, has a stronger and more positive effect on his wife/partner's total compensation level than when the inverse is compared. Results are similar, however, with a smaller impact, when the analysis is performed on other lower levels of education (above secondary education). Based on the results, it is possible to conclude that men's education level have a higher impact on their wife/partner's total remuneration than in the opposite situation. The results also describe that when it is the male who has the higher educational level, on average, total family earnings are higher than when it is the female. Finally the total earnings of the other member of the couple and a person's own remuneration are influencing factors which drive male or female to spend more time on housework.

The findings of this investigation are very important to corporate governance area - essentially to executive compensation - because until the moment researches in this area focused essentially on the impact of the executive personal characteristics in terms of his compensation but didn't include in the analysis how much the education level of the person who married or lives with this executive influences his personal compensation. In terms of practitioner and policy implications this study suggests that normally corporate governance, and essentially executive compensation area, until the moment focused on executives individual characteristics and firm characteristics when defining compensation mechanisms to incentive and retain executives but omitted the influence of personal characteristics of the people that he/she chose to marry of cohabit. Our findings seem to prove that the education level of the people that the employee choose to live with makes, in some way, pressure to this person to achieve an higher compensation level than when he/she lives with a low level education person and in terms of total family compensation also matters if it is the men or the women that has the highest education level. This way, Boards and Compensation Committees must include in their analysis not only the personal characteristics of the executives but also the education level of the people that are married or cohabit with these executives when defining the compensation packages to incentive and retain the executives. The study makes an overview of existing literature and provides the specific research hypotheses in Section 2. Section 3 describes the data and methodology used in the research and Section 4 describes the statistics and discusses the results. Section 5 draws the conclusion, and Section 6 provides the references.

LITERATURE REVIEW AND HYPOTHESES DEVELOPMENT

A wide range of literature describes female as receiving, on average, lower compensation than male (Weisskoff, 1972; Weinberg, 2000; O'Neil, 2003; Escriche, 2007; Rizzo and Zeckhauser, 2007; Schmidt and Sevak, 2006; Constant et al., 2007; Lauerova and Terrell, 2007; Davis et al., 2007, and Blau and Kahn, 2006). According Platt (2006) "Female have been paid less than men for doing the same job as a man or a job requiring the same level of skill, effort and responsibility as a job done by a man". However, Vieito and Khan (forthcoming) report that in the U.S. this gap has decreased following the year 2000 even though there is still a difference.

Literature describe married people as generating higher monetary wealth than single households, even after controlling the presence of two income earners in a married household. Díaz-Giménez et al. (1997) and Schmidt and Sevak (2006) report that marital status is an important factor which explains the variation in terms of wealth, however, literature in the area of finance has not taken into account the possible impact the education level of each member of the household may have on personal compensation.

A limited number of existing studies have been carried out essentially in the area of labor economics and these have only investigated the impact of the number of years of education of the wife on the husband's compensation but have not analyzed the inverse situation. Amin and Jepsen (2005) found a positive and statistically significant relationship between the number of years of a wife's education on her husband's compensation in Malaysia. Similar results were obtained in Israel (Neuman and Ziderman, 1992), Iran (Scully 1979), Philippines (Boulier and Rosenzweig 1984), and Brazil (Tiefenthaler, 1997). However, no studies have been carried out to investigate if a husband's qualification influences his wife's total compensation. Due to the unique characteristics of the database that was used for the purpose of this investigation, it was possible to identify the gender of the respondent and the compensation of each member of the couple. Based on this information this first hypothesis was developed:

Hypotheses 1: The education level of one member of the couple has a positive effect on the total compensation of the other member.

When the respondent is a male, it is expected that the education level of the wife/partner's will influence his personal compensation and when the respondent is a female, the husband/partner's education level will also influence the wife/partner's compensation.

Cole and Mehran (2008) complement the information describing that more qualified people normally have access to better remunerate jobs and based on this information the second null hypotheses was formulated:

Hypotheses 2a: On average, a more qualified couple has a higher total family earnings than a couple with a lower level of qualifications.

Hypotheses 2b: Couples with different levels of education, when it is the male who have the higher education level this will lead to higher total family earnings than when it is the female who have the higher education level.

For hypotheses 2a it is expected that couples with higher education level, on average, will have a higher total family compensation than couples with lower qualifications. When the couple has different levels of education, a higher impact on total family compensation is expected when it is the man who has the highest level of education. The reason being that literature states there is a gap in terms of compensation between executive male and female. According to Platt (2006) female receive less than male doing the same jobs that require the same level of skill, effort and responsibility. Booth et al. (2003) report that married female, or female who live in a relationship, female with young children, or female who have spouses who have top positions may be less mobile when compared with the male. This may influence the possibilities of female being promoted as the number of employment opportunities is more reduced. Yurtoglu and Zulehner (2009b) defend that having young children, or more children, or having a husband with a good position can negatively influence the female compensation. In the case of male, on average, compensation normally increases after having children, however, with female, there is on average, a slight decrease in their income after the birth of their first child. The gender compensation gap and marital status was also analyzed by Bertrand et al. (2009), using a sample of graduating MBAs students from the University of Chicago during the period 1990-2006. They found that, before having children, male and female seemed to follow the same career paths, however, when female had children, there was a tendency for them to earn less and male earn more. As can be expected, the career of some female is negatively influenced by having children. The study also reported that female who were married to spouses who receive high remuneration worked less hours than female who were married to spouses with lower compensations.

If literature suggests that having young children or more children has a negative influence on a female's compensation and positive influence on a male's compensation, the following research question was developed:

Hypotheses 3: Having children, on average, has no impact on total family average compensation.

It is expected that, on average, if female have a decrease in their compensation when they have children and if there is an increase in their husbands/partner's total compensation, the total family compensation will not change much. In other words, male attempt to find a way to increase their total remuneration to compensate the decrease of their wife/partner's compensation. In this manner, no significant relationship between the number of children and total family compensation is expected. Some literature also reports that the number of hours spent on housework influences the compensation of each member of the couple. Based on information from the UK, Brya and Sevilla-Sanz (2010) state that housework has a negative impact on the compensation of male and female who work full time, both for married and single households. They also described that the negative influence of housework on compensation is practically identical across full time occupations. As far as part-time jobs, it seems that some jobs are more compatible with housework than others. Hersch (2000) states that married female, on average, spend more time on housework than their husbands and this can have a negative impact on their compensation. The author also found a negative relationship between housework and compensation regardless of marital status and this relationship is higher in the case of routine tasks that are done on a daily basis, such as cleaning and cooking. However, the author did not investigate if the woman's level of education influenced the amount of housework that male do. Consequently the flowing research question was developed:

Hypotheses 4a: A husband married or cohabiting with woman who is highly qualified and who has a well remunerated position spend more time on housework than a man married to a woman who has a lower level of education.

Hypotheses 4b: A woman married to a man who has good qualifications does not influence the number of hours she spent on housework.

History states that normally female spend more time on housework than their husbands. Due to several changes in cultures around the world in last decades, female have had more access to education in a way similar to male in a vast group of countries, especially developed countries. As such, when a wife/partner has a high education level and a well remunerated position, it is expected that the husband/partner will be more collaborative in terms of housework, as he will understand that a significant part of the total family compensation will depend on his wife's work level. Consequently a positive relationship between the number of hours that the husband spends on housework and his wife's education level is expected. When a woman is married to a husband with a high education level, it is expected that the woman will continue to spend, on average, the same hours on housework.

DATA AND METHODOLOGY

Data was obtained from the *International Social Survey Programme* (ISSP) 2002: Family and Changing Gender Roles (III), which analyzes the attitudes towards family and gender roles, marriage, as well as children and financial support. This programme also surveyed household management and partnership, decision-making within partnership/family, work versus family conflict, happiness and satisfaction, information about the occupation of the respondent's mother, and additional demographic and background variables. The survey was made either during a face-to-face interview or by self-completion of a questionnaire. The survey was done in 40 countries (Australia (AUS), Germany (West) (D-W), Germany (East) (D-E), Great Britain (GB), Northern Ireland (NIRL), United States (USA), Austria (A), Hungary (H), Italy (I), Ireland (IRL), Netherlands (NL), Norway (N), Sweden (S),Czech Republic (CZ), Slovenia (SLO), Poland (PL), Bulgaria (BG), Russia (RUS), New Zealand (NZ), Canada (CDN), Philippines (RP), Israel Jews, Arabs (IL), Israel Arabs (IL-A), Japan (J), Spain (E), Latvia (LV), Slovak Republic (SK), France (F), Cyprus (CY), Portugal (P), Republic of Chile (RCH), Denmark (DK), Switzerland (CH), Flanders (FLA), Brazil (BR), Venezuela (YV), Finland (SF), Mexico (MEX),Taiwan (TWN), South Africa (ZA)). Due to lake of information to conduct this study the following countries have been excluded: Italy (I), Ireland (IRL), Canada (CDN) Israel Jews, Arabs (IL), Israel Arabs (IL-A),), Brazil (BR), Venezuela (YV), and South Africa (ZA).

From the total database, which include 46638 observations, only the respondents that were married or leaving with a partner were considered. This totaled 26847 observations. From this sample, only the observations where the variable v252 (household composition: children + adults) corresponding to a family composed of 2 adults with or without children were considered.

. The reason behind this choice is that this database collected information about respondent and total family earnings and based on the difference of these two values it was possible to achieve the earnings of the other member of the couple and consequently develop a more in-depth analysis based not only on the respondent but also on the other member of the couple. Monetary values have been converted to USD based on 31-12-2002 exchange rates.

To select married and cohabiting male and female the variable V202 (marital status) was used to identify couples that were married or living in common law. Finally observations which included "refused" answers (code 999997), "don´t respond" (code 99998) or "no answer" (code 999999) were excluded. The resulting total number of observations was 15956.

DEPENDENT VARIABLES

The dependent variables that were used were Ln (Total Respondent Compensation) that is the natural logarithm of the respondent earnings (v249). To identify the impact of the education level of each one of the partners on total family compensation the LN (Total Family Compensation) was used.

It is the natural logarithm of variable (v250). The compensation of the other member of the couple was obtained based on the difference between variables v250 and v249. To select the gender of the respondent and of the other member of the couple the variable V200 (respondent sex) was used to identify the respondent as male or female. Observations classified with the code 9 (Na, refused) were excluded. Finally, dependent variable LN (Number hours HH), that is the number of hours that respondent spend on housework per week (v36) were also used.

INDEPENDENT VARIABLES

To analyze if the education level of the person to whom one is married or lives with influences the respondent's total compensation and the number of hours spent on housework, and if a certain combination in the level of education lead to a higher total family compensation when compared to others, several independent variables were employed. The education level of each member of the couple was found based on variable v70 which describes the spouse's degree (highest qualification) and variable v205 that identifies the highest education level of the respondent. Both variables classify education level on the following categories: 0-No formal qualification; 1- Lowest formal qualification; 2- Above lowest qualification; 3- Secondary Education; 4-Post-secondary education (undergraduate); 5 - University degree, 8- No answer, Refused 9 –NAP no partner, that means that the information was not provided. Observations with 0, 8 and 9 were excluded. Based on these variables and variable v200, which corresponds to the respondent sex, several dummies were set up which identified the education level of both the man and woman. Education level 5 (Ed level 5) is a dummy that assume the value equal to one when the person has a completed university degree and zero when not. Education level 4 (Ed Level 4), education level 3 (Ed level 3) and education level 2,1 (Ed level 2 or 1) are also a dummy that assume the value equal to one when the person has post-secondary education (4), secondary education (3), above lowest qualification and lowest formal qualification (2 or 1). These two last variables were joined together as the impact of having no qualification or having above lowest qualification is not significant for our study. The same methodology was used for the other member of the couple. Based on these two variables (male and female's education level) a dummy variables was set up to control the education level of the couple (couple education mix) which will make it possible to analyze if certain combinations in education level, on average, receive more total remuneration than others. The following dummies were created for this purpose: "M5 –W5" correspond to a dummy that assume the value equal to 1 when the husband/partner has a completed university degree and is married or cohabiting with a female with the same education level and zero when not; "M5 - W4" is a dummy that assumes the value equal to 1 when the husband/partner has a completed university degree and the wife/partner has post-secondary qualifications and zero when not. The same methodology was applied to other possible education combination (M5 – W3; M5 – W2 or 1; M4 – W5; M4- W4; M4-W3; M4-W2 or 1; M3-W5; M3-W4; M3 – W2 or 1; M2 or 1- W5; M 2 or 1- W4; M2 or 1- W3; M2 or 1 – W 2 or 1). It is reasonable to think that if both members of the couple have a degree, on average, they will receive more than other couples. However, what happens when the couple has different education levels? Does it matter who has the highest education level in terms of total family earnings? One may expect that the higher the education level of the couple, the higher the total family remuneration will be. As existing literature on executive compensation states that there is a remuneration gap between male and female (Vieito and Khan, forthcoming), male receiving, on average, a little more than female for the same jobs and requiring the same level of skills, effort and responsibility (Platt, 2006), one may expect that when the couple has different education levels, if it is the male who has the highest qualification this will lead to higher total family earnings than when it is the female who has the higher qualification. Yurtoglu and Zulehner (2009b) state that having young children or more children has a negative impact on female's remuneration; however, this is not true for male, as their remuneration usually increases. Accordingly, the variable NKIDS was used to control the effect of the number of children on the man and woman's total remuneration. The variable corresponds to variable v66 (how many people in house: children 6,7-17 years). Similar to Bertrand et al. (2009) a negative relationship between the interaction of gender and the number of children is expected. The dummy NKIDS was also used to analyze the impact on total family compensation and it is expected that NKIDS has no effect on total average family remuneration. In other words, if female normally have a reduction in their remuneration and male an increase, I expect that total family earnings will not change in global terms. Husband/partner will make efforts to increase his total earnings to compensate for the reduction in his wife's remuneration. To analyze the impact of the respondent's total compensation and also his/her partner's total compensation on the number of hours that the respondent spends on housework, the variable LN (Total Respondent Compensation) and LN (Total Partner Compensation) were used. These are the natural logarithm respondent earning (v249) and the natural logarithm of the difference between total family compensation (v250) and respondent earnings (v249), respectively. One would expect that when the respondent is a man, he will spend a greater number of hours on housework when his wife has a high education level and a well remunerated job. As the wife/partner represents a significant part of the total family earnings, it is expected that the husband/partner will collaborate more in housework duties. As such, one may expect a positive relationship between wife/partner's education level and the number of hours that the husband/partner spends on housework. When the respondent is a woman, I do not expect that the education level of the husband will influence the number of hours that the woman spends on housework. Gender is a dummy variable that assumes the value equal to one when respondent is a female and zero when it is a man. I use the variable to explain the number of hours spent on housework. A positive relationship between these two variables is expected, meaning that female normally spend a lot more time on housework than male. I also use the variable Supervisor that is built in based on variable v244, and assumes the value equal to one when the respondent supervises a team and zero when not. I expect a negative relationship between this variable and the number of hours that the respondent spends on housework. If the person supervises a team it is expected that they will have less time to spend on housework than a person who does not supervise a team. I also control if the life of respondent at home is stressful or not based on variable (v v45: My life at home is rarely stressful). The variably is a dummy that assumes the value equal to one when it is true and zero when not. It is expected that people who spend more hours doing housework have less stressful lives. Finally the country effect is also controlled by inserting a dummy for each analyzed country.

STATISTICS

Univariate Statistics

Table 1 describes summary statistics on average earnings by respondent and gender, total average family earnings, average number of year of education and average number of children by family.

Table 1. Summary Statistics

	Earnings by Gender/month (US Dollars)						Family Earnings	Age	Year Education	Average children by Family
	Women		Men		T Test		Mean	Mean	Mean	Mean
	N	Mean	N	Mean	Dif					
A	244	922.41	208	1605.23	682.82***		1236.63	--	--	2.11
AUS	172	17708.79	192	31611.06	13902.27***		25041.85	50.06	12.01	2.07
BG	196	64.41	155	104.65	40.24***		82.18	50.99	12.71	--
CH	104	4815.13	172	10483.55	5668.42***		8347.63	50.90	11.95	2.19
CZ	243	250.14	155	384.77	134.63***		302.57	44.71	12.40	1.97
D-E	87	933.15	94	1447.8	514.65***		1200.43	54.09	11.77	--
D-K	306	31314.28	281	43852.18	12537.90***		37316.24	51.38	17.09	--
DW	145	954.91	180	2551.5	1596.59***		1839.18	50.70	12.44	--
E	163	906.74	301	1259.701	352.96***		1135.71	48.97	18.91	2.10
F	384	1425.63	259	2560.33	1134.70***		1882.69	46.26	13.70	2.06
FLA	1	770.00	51	1334.72	564.72		1323.86	51.72	12.00	2.24
GB	279	24347.85	266	46027.8	21679.95***		34929.25	48.37	12.39	--
H	172	198.39	141	294.69	96.30***		241.77	50.27	11.05	2.00
J	129	741.20	132	5419.03	4677.83***		3106.99	49.62	12.98	2.07
LV	60	37.55	72	60.9	23.35***		50.29	53.82	14.55	1.78
MEX	123	370.64	135	628.23	257.59**		505.43	40.40	16.63	--
N	313	27793.55	309	48634.82	20841.27***		38147.17	50.19	13.25	--
NIRL	126	16904.08	125	30601.22	13697.14***		23725.37	47.94	--	--
NZ	155	15235.35	170	29400.04	14164.69***		22644.57	51.88	13.34	--
P	150	602.93	143	855.08	252.15***		725.99	49.07	14.48	2.19
PL	81	303.88	102	416.89	113.01**		366.87	47.26	14.88	2.13
RCH	172	168.59	181	350.78	182.19***		262.01	45.15	12.66	2.61
RP	83	79.66	198	113.73	34.07**		103.67	38.70	11.69	2.63
RUS	249	66.41	231	83.82	17.41***		74.79	47.04	13.47	1.87
S	210	2047.57	172	2490.58	443.01***		2247.04	53.76	12.01	--
SF	357	1990.41	310	2657.02	666.61*		2300.23	45.88	12.25	--
SK	211	178.90	211	273.08	94.18***		225.99	43.33	13.37	--
TWN	128	1098.81	182	1526.45	427.64***		1349.88	46.48	18.30	2.56
USA	164	23713.41	122	39680.34	15966.93***		30524.48	46.12	13.71	2.50

Note1: Some countries do not provide info on number of children per family. IRL and NL have also been excluded due to the fact that the database has no value to perform statistics.

Note 2: (Australia (AUS), Germany (West) (D-W), Germany (East) (D-E), Great Britain (GB), Northern Ireland (NIRL), United States (USA), Austria (A), Hungary (H), Netherlands (NL), Norway (N), Sweden (S),Czech Republic (CZ), Poland (PL), Bulgaria (BG), Russia (RUS), New Zealand (NZ), Philippines (RP), Japan (J), Spain (E), Latvia (LV), Slovak Republic (SK), France (F), Portugal (P), Republic of Chile (RCH), Denmark (DK), Switzerland (CH), Flanders (FLA), Finland (SF), Mexico (MEX),Taiwan (TWN). Statistical significance: † $p < 0.10$; *$p < 0.05$; ** $p < 0.01$; *** $p < 0.001$.

All the monetary values, as previously stated have been converted to USD based on exchange rates on 31.12.2002. From table 1 is possible to see that total average compensation across countries is very different and there is also some disparity in terms of years of education and the number of children by couple.

Multivariate Statistics

A. The impact of the education level of the other member of the couple on respondent's total earnings

In this part hypotheses 1 was tested: "The education level of one member of the couple has a positive effect on the total compensation of the other member."

Table 2. The impact of the wife/husband's (or partner) education level on respondent's remuneration

	LN (Total Respondent Compensation)			
	Women		Men	
	Coef.	t-Stat	Coef.	t-Stat
(Constant)	6.881	125.418***	10.240	227.727***
Respondent Education Level				
Ed Level 5	0.669	14.326***	0.591	15.571***
Ed Level 4	0.441	9.669***	0.359	8.325***
Ed Level 3	0.282	7.663***	0.269	6.144***
Husband /Wife (Partner) Education Level				
Ed Level 5	0.186	4.152***	0.038	6.144***
Ed Level 4	0.183	3.645***	0.044	7.215***
Ed Level 3	0.088	2.395***	0.025	4.174***
Country Dummies	YES	YES	YES	YES
N^a		7686	3865	
R Square	87.4%		88.6%	
			Chow Test	
	F=2.198 p value 0.000			

Note: Data was obtained from the *International Social Survey Programme* (ISSP). Education levels are: 5-University degree; 4- Post-secondary education (undergraduate); 3- Secondary education. The dependent variable is LN (Total Respondent Compensation) which is the natural logarithm of the total respondent earnings. Country differences were also controlled by inserting a dummy for each country.

Statistical significance: † $p < 0.10$; * $p < 0.05$; ** $p < 0.01$; *** $p < 0.001$.

In other words, I test to what degree the education level of the male respondent compensation is influenced by the wife's education level and vice versa. There are only a reduced number of studies which analyze how the education level of one member of the couple may influence the total earnings of the other member and these have only focused on the wife's influence on the husband's total earnings but have not analyzed the inverse situation. Table 2 describes the results for both situations. The results describe something quite new in the area: the education level of the person that one chooses to marry or cohabit with has a positive and statistically significant impact on the respondent total earnings and, as can be expected, the higher the qualification of this person the greater the impact. By comparing male and female respondents it was possible to verify that the impact of the husband's education level on his wife's earnings is slightly higher than the impact of the female's education level on her husband's compensation. Also interesting is the fact that the impact of the husband's education level on his wife's total earnings decreases when the education level of the man is lower but the same is not true for male respondent. The highest impact of a woman's education level on her husband's earnings is found when the woman has a post-secondary school education (Ed Level 4) and not when she has a university degree (Ed level 5). From the table it is also possible to verify that having a university degree (Ed Level 5) significantly impact total earnings when compared to other situations (Ed Lev el 4 or Ed Lev 3). This impact is greater with female, however for both genders, the difference is higher between education levels 5 and 4 and the difference increases substantially when the education level of both female and male is secondary education (Ed level 3). From the results it is possible to conclude that the impact of education on earnings is a little higher for male than for female.

B.   The impact of the couple's education level and number of children on the family's total compensation

Hypotheses 2a and 2b are tested in this section "On average, a more qualified couple has a higher total family earnings than a couple with a lower level of qualifications." Couples with different levels of education, when it is the male who have the higher education level this will lead to higher total family earnings than when it is the female who have the higher education level". Additionally is also investigate Hypotheses 3 "Having children, on average, has no impact on total family earnings" Table 3 first analyzed the impact of the couple's education level in terms of family total remuneration. From the table it is possible to verify that, as expected, if male and female have a university degree (Male 5-Female 5) this will lead to a positive and statistically significant impact on the family's total earnings compared to other combinations in education and the intensity of this impact is higher than in other combinations of education levels. In cases where the couple have the same education level, but it is a post-secondary education (Male 4 - Female 4) the impact on total family earnings is positive but not as strong as in the last example; and in the case of couples where male and female have secondary education (Male 3-Female 3) the impact on total remuneration is positive but practically half of the "Male 4-Female 4" impact. Couples that have Male 2,1 and Female 2,1 (above lowest qualification "2" and Lowest formal qualification "1") the relationship with total family compensation is not statistically significant.

It is possible to conclude that the education level of the couple has a positive impact on total family earnings and that the higher the education level of the couple the higher the total family earnings will be. The second part of the regression analyzed something quite new in the area: there is a variation in results if it is the man or the woman who has the highest level of education. In other words, let us consider two situations: Male 5 - Female 4 or Male 4 - Female 5. The first couple is composed of a man with a university degree and a woman with a post-secondary education (undergraduate) while the second couple has the inverse situation. The methodology of analysis was applied to all other possible combinations in education level between the couple. Then the first regression only analyzed how the couple's education level impacted on their total family earnings while the second added the impact of having children.

Table 3. The impact of the couple's education level and number of children on the family's total compensation

Independent Variables	LN(Total Family Compensation)			
	Coef.	T Stat	Coef.	T Stat
Constant	10.399	39.434***	4.396	95.745***
Equal education level between men and women				
M5 - W5	0.732	2.777***	0.894	21.393***
M4 - W4	0.621	2.349*	0.916	17.704***
M3 - W3	0.305	1.157	0.456	13.009***
M2 or 1 - W2 or 1	-0.175	-0.666	---	--
Mixed education levels between couple members				
M5 - W4	0.614	2.320***	0.871	15.413***
M4 - W5	0.570	2.139*	0.706	8.645***
M5 - W3	0.549	2.074**	0.721	12.681***
M3 - W5	0.554	2.085**	0.692	10.705***
M5 - W 2 or 1	0.367	1.383	0.597	8.048***
M2 or 1 - W 5	0.414	1.551	0.614	7.747***
M4 - W3	0.414	1.556	0.571	10.933***
M3 - W4	0.440	1.667 †	0.574	11.355***
M4 - W 2 or 1	0.680	0.180	0.478	7.501***
M2 or 1 - W 4	0.229	0.864	0.404	6.618***
M3 - W 2 or 1	0.118	0.448	0.263	6.392***
M2 or 1 - W 3	0.076	0.288	0.277	5.831***
Number of children	--	--	-0.009	0.440
Country Dummies	Yes		Yes	
Nº Observations	9958		3468	
R square Adjusted	93.9%		94.4%	

Note: When the regression is performed with the variable "number of children" in "Men 2 and 1 - Women 2 and 1" there are not a sufficient number of observations to consider in order to obtain a result.

Statistical significance: † $p < 0.10$; *$p < 0.05$; ** $p < 0.01$; *** $p < 0.001$.

As literature suggests that children influence the remuneration of a couple. In the first case it was possible to verify that when it is the male who holds a university degree and the woman, a post-secondary education (Male 5 - Female 4) the impact on total family earnings is higher than when it is the female who has the university degree and male the post-secondary education (Male 4 – Female 5). The same happened when the analysis was controlled for the number of children. It would seem that the person (man or woman) holding the university degree in a couple will effect total family earnings. The results are congruent with literature which describes a gap in terms of earnings between male and female (Vieito and Khan, forthcoming). Platt (2006) also states that "female have been paid less than male for doing the same job as a man or a job requiring the same level of skill, effort and responsibility as a job done by a man."

When the analysis was performed to couples where one member has an university degree and other a secondary education (Male 5 - Female 3; Male 3 - Female 5) the impact in terms of total family earnings is practically the same. With the rest of the situations, when the analysis was performed without controlling for the number of children, the results were not statistically significant with the exception of Male 3 - Female 4. When the analysis included the number of children, it was possible to verify that in a couple where the man had a university degree and woman had a level 2 or 1 education, there was a different impact on total family earnings if it was the man or the woman who had the higher level of education. The positive impact of the couple's education level is higher when it is the woman who has a level 4 education (post-secondary education). The same happened in cases where the education level was 4 vs. 2,1 and 3 vs. 3 and 2,1, however, the difference were smaller in both these two cases.

C.   Housework level, compensation and children

In this part I analyze hypotheses 4a: "A husband married or cohabiting with woman who is highly qualified and who has a well remunerated position spend more time on housework than a man married to a woman who has a lower level of education." and hypotheses 4b: "A woman married to a man who has good qualifications does not influence the number of hours she spent on housework.". The analysis of male and female respondents was performed separately to achieve eventual differences in terms of the number of hours spent on housework. A Chow test was used to analyze if the difference between the coefficients was statically significant or not. Table 4 describes the results.

Table 4 analyzes the impact total earnings from the other member of the couple may have on the number of hours the respondent (man or woman) spends on housework. The impact of the respondent's earning on the number of hours spent on housework was also analyzed. As expected, for both male and female respondents, the number of hours that they spent on housework had a negative and statistically significant impact on their personal earnings and the impact was higher for female. When the analysis was done to investigate the partner's total earnings, it was possible to verify that the relationship was only positive and statistically significant for male respondents (female total compensation). The results imply that when the wife/partner receives higher remunerations, the husband/partner will help with housework as they probably understand that part of the family's wealth depends on the wife's earnings. In the case of male, when their total earnings increase, as expected the wife/partner continues to spend the same number of hours on housework. A gender dummy was used to control the gender effect in the case of the samples which included male and female at same time. The relationship between the number of hour spent on housework and gender is positive and statistically significant implying that female spend more hours on housework than male. The results are congruent with literature in the area.

To supervise a team has a negative and statistically significant impact on the number of hour spent on housework but this relationship is only statistically significant for female respondents. In the case of male, it seems that to be a supervisor does not have an impact on the number of hours spent on housework.

Table 4. Housework level, earnings and children

| | Dependent variable: LN(number hours HH) | | | | Ln(Number Hours HH) Men and Women | |
| | Men | | Women | | | |
	Coef.	t- Stat	Coef.	t-Stat	Coef.	t Stat
(Constant)	2.428	4.252***	3.273	8.95***	2.392	7.385***
NKids	0.051	1.485	0.03	1.137	0.044	2.02*
LN (Total Respondent Compensation)	-0.178	-3.585***	-0.122	-4.13***	-0.156	-5.738***
LN (Total Partner Compensation)	0.036	3.079***	-0.005	-0.315	0.029	3.304***
Gender	..	..	..	..	0.716	18.094***
Supervisor (v244)	-0.043	-0.663	-0.098	-1.914*	-0.072	-1.726 †
Final say: choosing weekend activities	0.059	1.959 †	0.027	1.479	0.041	2.445*
My life at home is rarely stressful	0.028	0.994	0.053	3.057***	0.044	2.746***
Husband /Wife (Partner) Education level						
Ed Level 5	0.246	2.734***	0.042	0.699	0.138	2.584**
Ed Level 4	0.172	1.852 †	0.006	0.079	0.104	1.733 †
Ed Level 3	0.030	0.386	0.098	1.827 †	0.067	1.437
Country dummies		Yes			Yes	
Nº Observations	934		984		1918	
R Square	16.3%		24.5%		35.7%	
	CHOW TEST					
F test	F(9. 13091) =2.25				.	
P Value	0.000					

Statistical significance: † p < 0.10; *p < 0.05; ** p < 0.01; *** p < 0.001.

A very interesting result is also the fact that when male spend more time on housework this will give them the power to negotiate with the family what they will do during the weekend. In the case of female, the relationship is not statistically significant. The relationship between a stressful life and the number of hours doing housework is positive only for female and also for the full sample. The results seam to suggest that female who spend more hours on housework have less stressful lives. Finally the relationship between the education level of the other member of the couple and the number of hours that the respondent spends on housework was analyzed. When the respondent was a man, the relationship between the number of hours spent on housework was positive and statistically significant when the wife had a university degree or a post secondary school education. As such it seems that a man married or cohabiting with a woman with qualifications accepts to spend more time doing housework. When the analysis was done to investigate the impact of a husband's education level on the number of hours his wife spends on housework, the relationship is only positive and statistically significant when the husband has a secondary level education.

CONCLUSION

This investigation is among the first to analyze to what degree the education level of the person who one chooses to live or cohabit with affects our total personal earnings. Additionally it also analyzed if certain combinations in education levels led to higher total family earnings when compared to other combinations, and also which factors drive female and male to spend more time on housework. This study is also the first to use information from a vast group of countries (Austria, Australia, Brazil, Bulgaria, Chile, Cyprus, Czech Republic, Denmark, Finland, Belgium, France, Germany, Great Britain, Hungary, Ireland, Israel, Japan, Latvia, Mexico, Netherlands, New Zealand, Northern Ireland, Norway, Philippines, Poland, Portugal, Russia, Slovenia, Slovakian Republic, Spain, Sweden, Switzerland, Taiwan, and the United States) which make the results very robust and important in the area. I found that the education level of the person that one chooses to live or cohabit with influences the total earnings of the other member of the couple. It is not only the wife's education level that has a positive impact on the husband's total remuneration but the inverse situation is also true. More important, the impact of the husband's education level on the wife's total remuneration is higher than the impact of the wife's education level on the husband's total earnings.

The education level of both members of the couple, as can be expected, influences the family's total earnings and the higher the education level of the couple, the higher the total family earnings are. By comparing couples with different education levels, it was possible to obtain very interesting and innovative results: when one member of the couple has a university degree and the other a post secondary education, on average, the impact on total family earnings is higher when it is the man who has the highest qualification. It seems that the fact of whether it is the man or the woman who has the university degree impacts differently on the family's total earnings. The results are congruent with the literature that reports a gap in terms of compensation between male and female (Vieito and Khan, forthcoming; Platt, 2006).

Finally the factors which drive a man or woman to spend more hours on housework were analyzed. It would seem that the education level of the other member of the couple and their earnings are important elements which affect how much time a woman or man spends on housework. More interesting is the fact that empirical evidence seem to suggest that male spend more time on housework when they are married or live with a woman who has a high level of education and has a well remunerated position. However, the inverse is not true. This study presents, however, certain limitations which must be considered: the first one is related with the fact that data emanated from one year survey and this compromised the generalization of the results across the years. Further evidence from other years is needed to strengthen these arguments. The second limitation is that this database only has information if the respondent to the survey supervises a team, or not, but says nothing about the positions of each one according to company hierarchical levels, what limits this investigation in terms of a deeper focus in top executives.

Theoretical and Practical Implications

Despite these limitations, I believe that this study makes a valuable contribution to corporate governance literature. Until the moment most part of the literature about executive compensation didn't analyze the impact of the education level of the person that one chooses to marry or cohabit in terms of executive compensation. The results of this investigation seem to prove that husband/wife or partner education level has a positive impact on the other member of the couple remuneration and future research must explore also this important variable on the analysis. In terms of practical implications, this study suggests that education level of the people that are married, or cohabit, influences the compensation of the other member of the couple, and Boards and Executive Compensation committees must include this information when defining the compensation packages to incentive and retain the executives. To have a husband/wife or partner with high education level seems to be a collateral mechanism that exerts pressure to employees, if he/she is not remunerated according to your expectations, to search in the future for better compensations, and boards and Compensation Committees should consider these elements when they define compensation policies to incentive and retain executives.

REFERENCES

Amin, S., Jepsen, L., 2005. The Impact of a Wife's Education on Her Husband Earnings in Malaysia. *Journal of Economics* 31, 1-18.

Becker, G., 1981. A Treatise on the Family. Cambridge, MA: Harvard University Press.

Bertrand, M., Goldin, C., Katz, L., 2009. *Dynamics of the Gender Gap for Young Professionals in the Corporate and Financial Sectors*, NBER Working Paper Series 14681, Cambridge MA.

Blau, F., Kahn, L., 2006. The U.S. Gender Pay Gap in the 1990s: Slowing Convergence'. *Industrial and Labor Relations Review* 60(1), 45-66.

Booth, A., Johnson, D., Amato, P., Rogers, S., 2003. Marital Instability over the Life Course (United States): *A six-wave panel study*, 1980, 1983, 1988, 1992-1994, 1997, 2000 (1st ICPSR version'. University Park, PA: Alan Booth et al., Pennsylvania State University (Producers), 1998.

Bryan, M., Sevilla-Sanz, A., 2011. Does Housework Lower Wages? Evidence for Britain. *Oxford Economics Papers* 63(1), 187-210.

Boulier, B., Rosenzweig, M., 1984. Schooling, Search, and Spouse Selection: Testing Economic Theories of Marriage and Household Behavior. *Journal of Political Economy*, 92(4), 712-32.

Cole, R., Mehran, H. 2008. What do we Know about Executive Compensation at Privately Held Firms? *Federal Reserve Bank of New York Staff Reports*, 314.

Constant, A., Zimmermann, K. and Shachmurove, Y., 2005. What Makes an Entrepreneur and does it Pay? Native Men, Turks, and Other Migrants in Germany. *International Migration* 45: 60-100.

Davis, S., Greenstein, T., Marks, J., 2007. Effects of Union Type on Division of Household Labor: Do Cohabitating Men Really Perform More Housework? *Journal of Family Issues* 28(9), 1247-72.

Díaz-Giménez, J., Quadrini, V., Ríos-Rull, J., 1997. Dimensions of Inequality: Facts on the U.S. Distributions of Earnings, Income, and Wealth. *Federal Reserve Bank of Minneapolis Quarterly Review* 21(2): 3–21.

Escriche, L., 2007. Persistence of Occupational Segregation: The Role of the Intergenerational Transmission of Preferences. *Economic Journal* 117(520), 837-57.

Hersch, J. 2000. Marriage, Home Production, and Earnings, Harvard Law School, Law-Econ. Discussion Paper No. 275.

Hersch, J., Stratton, L., 2000. Housework and Wages. *Journal of Human Resources* 37(1), 217-229.

Lauerova, J., Terrell, K. 2007. What Drives Gender Differences in Employment? *Comparative Economic Studies* 49(1), 128-55.

Neuman, S., Ziderman, A., 1992. Benefits of Female's Education within Marriage: Results for Israel in a Dual Labor Market Context'. *Economic Development and Cultural Change* 40(2): 413-24.

O'Neil, J. 2003. The Gender Gap in Wages, Circa 2000. *American Economic Review 93*(2): 309-14.

Platt, L. 2006. Pay Gaps: The Position of Ethnic Minority Female and Men. Manchester: Equal Opportunities Commission. ISBN 1-84206-197-6.

Rizzo, J., Zeckhauser, R., 2007. Pushing Incomes to Reference Points: Why Do Male Doctors Earn More? *Journal of Economic Behavior and Organization* 63(3), 514-36.

Schmidt, L., Sevak, P., 2006. Gender, Marriage, and Asset Accumulation in the United States. *Feminist Economics* 12(1-2), 139–166.

Scully, G. 1979. Mullahs, Muslims, and Marital Sorting. *Journal of Political Economy* 87(5), 1139-43.

Tiefenthaler, J. (1997). The Productivity Gains of Marriage: Effects of Spousal Education on Own Productivity across Market Sectors in Brazil. *Economic Development and Cultural Change* 45(3): 633-50.

Vieito, J., Khan, W. *Executive Compensation and Gender*: SandP 1500 Listed Firms. *Journal of Economics and Finance* (forthcoming).

Watson, T., McLanahan, S. 2011. Marriage Meets the Joneses: Relative Income, Identity, and Marital Status. *Journal of Human Resources* 46(3): 482-517.

Weinberg, B. 2000. Computer Use and the Demand for Female Workers. *Industrial and Labor Relations Review* 53(2), 290-308.

Weisskoff, F. 1972. Female's Place in the Labor Market. *The American Economic Review*, 62(1/2): 161-66.

Yurtoglu, B., Zulehner, C., 2009a. Equity-Based Compensation and the Gender Pay Gap in Top Corporate Jobs. Mimeo. *Austrian Institute of Economic Research*, Vienna.

Yurtoglu, B., Zulehner, C., 2009b. Sticky Floors and Glass Ceilings in Top Corporate Jobs. Mimeo. *Austrian Institute of Economic Research*, Vienna.

In: Handbook of Academic Performance
Editors: Rolf Haumann and George Zimmer

ISBN: 978-1-62417-888-7
© 2013 Nova Science Publishers, Inc.

Chapter 6

A PREDICTIVE MODEL OF ACADEMIC PERFORMANCE

B. Chares Tatum[*]

Department of Psychology, College of Letters and Science,
National University, La Jolla, CA

ABSTRACT

Variables that predict work performance are often the same variables that predict academic performance. For example, both job performance and class performance are affected by achievement motivation, cognitive ability, personal characteristics, and self-efficacy, just to name a few commonly investigated factors. Research in organizational psychology and education seems to converge on a common model that applies to both academic and work performance.

The purpose of this chapter is to report on a test of a predictive model of academic performance based largely on findings from organizational psychology and education. The model was tested using a path model framework. The critical components of the model were (a) motivation, (b) ability, (c) personal attributers (e.g., locus of control, self-esteem, self-efficacy), (d) class performance, (e) satisfaction, and (f) outcome. The results showed that the model was a plausible representation of the relationship among these different components.

The findings revealed that motivation and ability predicted student expectations, expectations predicted exam performance, exam performance predicted grade satisfaction, and grade satisfaction predicted the final course grade and estimated college grade point average. Limitations, implications, applications, and future research directions are noted. In general, this chapter shows how research in organizational psychology and education can be integrated into a common predictive model.

Keywords: work performance, academic performance, expectancy theory, self-efficacy, motivation, ability, personal attributes, performance satisfaction

---

[*] Correspondence concerning this article should be addressed to B. Charles Tatum, Email:ctatum@nu.edu

INTRODUCTION

Research has shown that both ability traits (e.g., intelligence, aptitude, talent) and non-ability traits (e.g., personality, interest, motivation, self concept, attitude) influence job performance and skill training (Barrick, Mount, and Judge, 2001; Colquitt, LePine, and Noe, 2000; Schmidt and Hunter, 1998). These same variables have often proven effective in educational settings for predicting classroom performance, grades, and academic success (Arneson, Sackett and Beatty, 2011; Chamorro-Premuzic and Furnham, 2003; Kuncel, Hezlett, and Ones, 2001; Sackett, Kuncel, Arneson, Cooper, and Waters, 2009). The intersection between organizational studies and educational research suggests that a common model should apply to both academic and work performance. As a case in point, in a study that compared performance in school and on the job, Kanfer, Wolf, Kantrowitz, and Ackerman (2010) showed that a variety of ability (e.g., verbal ability, numerical ability) and non-ability (e.g., self concept, self management, achievement) measures predicted both academic and job performance.

A MODEL OF WORK AND ACADEMIC PERFORMANCE

Many models could be considered that would integrate the two bodies of knowledge (organizational and educational). Here, I will propose a variation on a motivational model that has been used successfully by organizational researchers based on expectancy theory. Expectance theory (Ajzen, 1991; Rotter, 1954; Vroom, 1964) is a broad collection of motivational theories, but at the core it describes the relationship between ability, effort, performance expectations, actual performance, and, to lesser degree, dispositional traits such as self esteem, locus of control, attitude, and general self-efficacy (see Donovan, 2001, and Kanfer, 1990, for reviews). Although traditional expectancy theory has been criticized for being overly rational and not temporally dynamic (Steel and Konig, 2006), it has an excellent tack record for predicting work related behaviors (Van Eerde and Thierry, 1996).

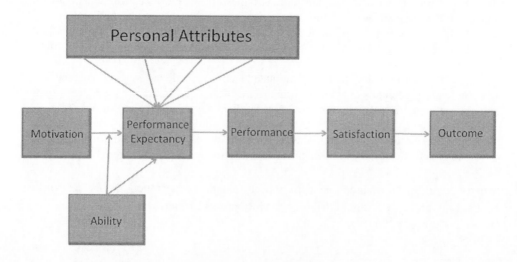

Figure 1. A model of motivation and performance in an academic setting.

A generic model of job performance (which should apply equally as well to school performance) based on expectancy theory is shown in Figure 1. The model has its origins with Vroom (1964), with further developments and refinements by Porter and Lawler (1968), Riedle, Nebeker, and Copper (1988), and Steel and Konig (2006). As seen in Figure 1, the critical components of the model are (a) motivation (which includes many sub-elements such as goals, instrumentality, achievement orientation, effort, etc.), (b) ability (e.g., intelligence, aptitude, talent), (c) performance (e.g., expected performance, goal achievement, task success), (d) satisfaction, and (e) outcomes. Despite the fact that the model in Figure 1 derives from industrial and organizational research, it should be clear that it is highly relevant to educational and academic environments. Causal models have been proposed and tested in educational settings (Akey, 2006; Brown, Park, and Jung; 2010; Drew and Watkins, 1998; Murray-Harvey, 1993; Ofori and Charlton, 2002), but none is based on research outside the education sphere. The purpose of this study was to apply a work performance model based on expectancy theory to a classroom setting, and test the predicted relationships using a causal/path model methodology.

SOME KEY CONSTRUCTS

The generic model in Figure 1 suggests a number of constructs that have been investigated in both work and school environments. The discussion below reviews some of the literature on the effects of these constructs on work and scholastic performance. Following this review, the article will report on the results of a study that attempted to support the interrelationships among these constructs as depicted in Figure 1.

Ability

It is well established that there is a positive relationship between traditional measures of ability (e.g., cognitive ability, aptitude, crystallized knowledge) and performance on the job and in school (Ackerman, 2000; Arneson, Sackett, and Beatty, 2011; Horn and Noll, 1997; Kuncel, Hezlett, and Ones, 2001; Schmidt and Hunter, 1998). Moreover, even measures of self-estimated ability can predict performance (Kanfer et al., 2010) and in some cases these self-estimates are as good as more objective measures (Riedel et al., 1988). Researchers have proposed various multiplicative patterns between ability and motivation (e.g., Feather, 1982; Porter and Lawler, 1968; Riedel et al., 1988; Vroom, 1964), but the general agreement is that motivation and ability interact to produce subsequent expectations, performance, or outcomes. One version of this moderator effect is shown in Figure 1: ability and motivation interact to produce expected performance.

Motivation

Motivation is a broad term and refers to a wide variety of constructs. Sometimes it refers to effort (Porter and Lawler, 1968), and sometimes it refers to a drive for mastery

(McClelland, Atkinson, Clark, and Lowell, 1953) or high levels of performance (Hermans, 1970). These latter meanings of motivation are often referred to as achievement motivation and are reflected in individuals who set high standards of excellence and aspire to achieve difficult goals. One method for assessing achievement motivation is to measure the performance of people against what would be expected given their level of ability (Farquhar and Payne, 1964; McCall, 1994). For example, if a student achieves low grades despite objective evidence of high ability (high intelligence, high scores on standardized tests, excellent performance on pre-tests), we would classify that student as low in achievement motivation (an underachiever). Similarly, a highly productive worker with limited abilities and skills would demonstrate high achievement motivation (an overachiever). Using this approach, studies have shown that achievement motivation is related to persistence and later career success (Mandel and Marcus, 1988; McCall, Evaln, and Kratzer, 1992).

Expectancy/Self-Efficacy

Expectancy has also come to mean different things to different researchers. Sometimes it means a person's belief in the likelihood of improve performance with sufficient effort (Porter and Lawler, 1968). Sometimes expectancy means the expected outcome given certain levels of performance (Vroom, 1964). Sometimes it just means a person's expectation of success (Nagengast et al., 2011). Self-efficacy (a kind of expectancy) has received much attention in both the job and school domains (e.g., Bandura, 1977, 1989, 1991, 1997; Prat-Sala and Redford, 2010). Self-efficacy reflects the belief people have in their capability to perform a specific task (e.g., a work or class assignment). Compared with people who have low levels of self-efficacy, high self-efficacy individuals are more likely to persevere when faced with difficulties, more likely to show intrinsic motivation, and less likely to show disappointment when their efforts are thwarted (Bandura, 1997). In educational settings in particular, self-efficacy is positively related to academic performance (Bong, 2001; Bouffanrd, Boileau, and Vezeau, 2001; Lane and Lane, 2001; Lane, Lane, and Kyprianou, 2004; Ofori and Charlton, 2002; Richardson, 2007), motivation to succeed (Bong and Clark, 1999), and self regulation (Pintrich and De Groot, 1990; Schunk and Zimmerman, 1997). Self efficacy has be viewed as both task-specific and as a more general personal trait (Liem, Lau, and Nie, 2008; Prat-Sala and Redford, 2010; Schwarzer and Jerusalem, 1995), and both orientations have been shown to predict behavior (Bandura, 1997; Schwarzer and Jerusalem, 1995).

Personal Attributes

Many personal and dispositional characteristics have been investigated in work and school performance studies. Constructs that often appear in the organizational and academic literature are self-esteem, locus of control, and attitudes. Many studies (reviewed below) demonstrate that these personal attributes predict job and academic performance. Some of this research suggests that the relationship between personal characteristics and performance is wholly or partially mediated by performance expectations as shown in Figure 1 (e.g., Akey,

2006; Brown et al., 2010; Drew and Watkins, 1998; Murray-Harvey, 1993; Porter and Lawler, 1968; Riedel, et al. 1988).

Locus of control. One variable that tends to cross the boundary between organizational and educational research is locus of control (Rotter, 1966). Locus of control reflects the degree to which individuals believe that they are in command of their performance outcomes. People who score high on internal locus of control tend to believe that their performance is a result of their own efforts and internal motivation. Those who score high on external locus of control tend to consider outcomes as a result of forces beyond their control (e.g., good or bad luck, poor supervision, inadequate teachers). Research in the organizational and educational fields has consistently shown that workers and students who rate high on internal locus of control (versus external locus of control) show greater persistence at tasks, are better at self-regulation, and demonstrate higher levels of performance (e.g., Brockett and Hiemstra, 1991; Chen and Toffelson, 1989; Drew and Watkins, 1998; Perry and Penner, 1990; Ramanaiah, Ribich, and Schmeck, 1975; Salili, 1994; Sandler, Reese, Spenser, and Harpin, 1983; Watkins, 1984, 1987; 1989; Watkins and Astilla, 1984).

Self-esteem. Although self-esteem sounds like just another variation on self-efficacy, there is an important difference. Self-esteem (Fleming and Courtney, 1984; Rosenberg, 1965) refers to a person's overall evaluation of worth and ability to cope. In a sense, it is the sum total of a person's self confidence and self-respect. Self-efficacy, by contrast, relates to confidence in performing tasks, or dealing with situations, rather than a person's overall sense of self-worth or self concept. There is a notion of "general self-efficacy" proposed by some (e.g., Schwarzer and Jerusalem, 1995) which is similar to self-esteem and will be examine later. But, the research literature with regard to self-esteem per se supports the idea that self-esteem is related to academic achievement (Hansford and Hattie, 1982; Miujs, 1997). The causal sequence, however, is not entirely clear. In other words, does high self-esteem lead to good performance or does good performance engender high self esteem (Baumeister, Campbell, Krueger, and Vohs, 2003, 2005)? The evidence seems to suggest that the relationship is actually reciprocal; it can go both ways (Byrne, 1996; Hattie, 1992; Marsh, 1984; Skaalvik and Hagtvet, 1990).

Job and academic attitudes. Several reviews and meta-analyses have shown that job attitudes (defined in various ways such as commitment, involvement, identification, continuance, engagement) are positively related to job performance (Bakker, 2011; Harrison, Newman, and Roth, 2006; Judge, Thoresen, Bono, and Patton, 2001; Meyer, Stanley, Herscovitch, and Topolnytsky, 2002; Riketta, 2002). Riketta (2008) also provides evidence that the casual relationship is from attitude to performance (i.e., positive attitudes produce positive job outcomes) and not the reverse. With respect to the relationship between academic attitudes and scholastic performance, the evidence also suggests a positive relationship. For example, Oliver and Simpson's (1988) longitudinal study reported a strong relationship between attitudes toward science and school performance and learning. Three meta-analyses (Hembree, 1990, and Ma and Kishor, 1997a, 1997b) report positive relationships between math attitudes and math achievement. Partin et al. (2011) demonstrated a significant positive relationship between math attitudes and performance in college biology, and Akey (2006) showed that the attitude of engagement was positively related to math and reading achievement. House and Prion (1998) demonstrated that student attitudes predicted subsequent achievement in college English. None of the education studies addressed the issue of the direction of the relationship, but it is reasonable to suggest that the attitudes mostly drive the performance as it does in the work setting.

Clearly, the literature on worker performance and student performance demonstrates many parallels. The model shown in Figure 1 is an attempt to integrate these two domains. The following study tests this model in an academic environment using a path-model methodology. The details of the methods used were published in an earlier study that tested a simplified version of the model in Figure 1, and so the following method section will be abbreviated (see Tatum, 2012 for details)

METHOD

Participants

The participants were 130 students (80% female, 51% white, mean age 21) who completed a survey in a sophomore-level, Psychology of Learning class taught at a large university in the Southwestern region of the United States.

General Procedure

The students were given a paper and pencil survey three times during the one-semester class. After completing the first exam (a 50-point objective exam covering approximately one-third of the class material), the students were given several self-report measures: (a) exam self-efficacy (described below), (b) estimated exam performance if the student worked at "maximum effort," (c) locus of control, (d) general self-efficacy, (e) self esteem, and (f) academic attitudes. After the second exam (50-point objective test), the exam self-efficacy and estimated exam score measures were repeated relative to Exam 2. Students were also asked to rate their satisfaction with the results of Exam 2. At the completion of the third exam (50-point objective test) at the end of the class, the exam self-efficacy and estimated exam score measures were once again repeated, this time relative to Exam 3. In addition, the students were asked to estimate the grade they thought they might get for the class and to estimate their grade point average (GPA) when they completed their college degree.

Measures

Ability. Ability and effort are compensatory; people can compensate for lack of ability by working hard and vice versa. In this study, effort was assessed by the students' estimates of their scores on the first exam if they worked at their "maximum effort" (see Reidel et al., 1988). This effort measure was then regressed on the score they received on the first exam. Ability was defined as the residual score from this regression because the residual is performance with effort removed. By removing effort from performance, what remains is "ability" (see Grimm and Yarnold, 1995. p. 37 for further discussion of this procedure).

Motivation. Farquhar and Payne (1964) and McCall (1994) describe a technique for assessing student motivation by comparing actual exam performance against expected performance based on ability. In this study, exam performance was the score on the second exam. Ability was the measure described above. Following a regression procedure similar to that used above, scores from Exam 2 were regressed on ability. The residual score (i.e., the difference between actual performance and predicted performance) was the measure of motivation. Students with low motivation were those who performed below the expected (predicted) performance ("underachievers"). Students with high motivation were those who performed above expectation ("overachievers"). Despite the use of common variables and procedures, the measures of ability and motivation used in this study were not correlated (see the correlation matrix in Table 1).

Performance expectancy. Expectancy was defined by combining two separate, but related, measures. The first measure was based on asking the students to report their expected grade in the class.

The second measure was an assessment of the students' self-efficacy (Bandura, 1977). Students were presented with a range of possible test scores (from 24 to 50) and asked to indicate "yes" or "no" with regard to whether they believed they were "capable" of performing at the different levels. A student's self-efficacy score was the highest score marked before responding "no" (not capable of performance at that level). Performance expectancy was calculated as the self-efficacy value from Exam 3 multiplied by the expected grade. The combined score reflected not only the grade the students expected, but also the highest test score that was within their perceived capability.

Performance. There were two performance measures. First, performance was gauged by the score earned on Exam 2. Second, performance was measured as the end-of-semester grade. Final grades were assigned by totaling the three exams and assigning letter grades according to this total. The letter grades were converted ·into numerical scores by the following scheme: A = 4.0, A- = 3.7, B+ = 3.3, B = 3.0, B- = 2.7, C+ = 2.3, C = 2.0, C- = 1.7, D+ = 1.3, D = 1.0, D- = .7, F = 0.

Satisfaction. This was defined as the student's satisfaction (rated on a 5-point scale ranging from "very dissatisfied" to "very satisfied") with their scores on the second exam. Ideally, there should have been a satisfaction rating for the third exam and the final grade, but this was not possible given that these grades were determined after the class had ended and students were not available to take another survey.

Outcome. The best outcome measure would be GPA at graduation. However, it was not feasible to follow each student through his or her four years of school, nor was it likely that these data would be released by the university.

Therefore, the students were asked to estimate their GPA upon graduation, and this was used as a proxy measure for outcome. This is not entirely an unreasonable measure because a meta-analysis by Kuncel, Crede, and Thomas (2005) found that the correlation between self-reported and actual GPA was .90.

Locus of control. This personal attribute measure was based on research by Rotter (1966), but altered to reflect perceived control in an academic setting (e.g., "How well I perform in class is determined by my own efforts…Grades are a very subjective thing that students can't always control…"). Six items were used and the responses were made on a 1 (Strongly Disagree) to 7 (Strongly Agree) Likert-type scale. High ratings reflected high levels of internal control (after reverse scoring).

Table 1. Descriptive statistics and correlations among the major study variables

	Mean	SD	Correlations										
			Motivation	Ability	Expect/ Efficacy	Locus of Control	General Efficacy	Self-Esteem	Academic Attitudes	Earned Exam Grade	Grade Sat	Earned Class Grade	Estimated GPA
Motivation	0	4.43	1	-.01	.35(**)	.02	.06	.00	.180(*)	.88(**)	.45(**)	.44(**)	.27(**)
Ability	.4	5.34		1	.41(**)	.00	-.01	.04	.04	.46(**)	.17(*)	.80(**)	.23(**)
Expectancy/ Self-Efficacy	121.10	31.88			1	.23(**)	.21(**)	.17(*)	.25(**)	.58(**)	.27(**)	.57(**)	.34(**)
Locus of Control	4.82	.94				1	.33(**)	.43(**)	.42(**)	.05	.02	.04	.25(**)
General Self-Efficacy	5.24	.77					1	.63(**)	.55(**)	.08	.05	.04	.26(**)
Self-Esteem	4.91	.82						1	.40(**)	.03	.06	.07	.21(**)
Academic Attitudes	4.49	.65							1	.22(*)	.09	.14	.26(**)
Earned Exam Grade	38.49	5.12								1	.48(**)	.80(**)	.36(**)
Grade Satisfaction	3.06	1.27									1	.34(**)	.12
Earned Class Grade	2.44	.82										1	.32(**)
Estimated GPA	3.28	.37											1

** Correlation is significant at the 0.01 level (2-tailed).

* Correlation is significant at the 0.05 level (2-tailed).

General self-efficacy. This measure of general self-efficacy was based on a series of general statements (not exam specific) about how confident the student felt about dealing with unexpected or difficult situations (e.g., "I can always manage to solve difficult problems if I try hard enough…I am confident that I could deal efficiently with unexpected events…"). The measure was developed by Schwarzer and Jerusalem (1995) and contained ten items with response options on a Likert-type scale (1-Strongly Disagree to 7-Strongly Agree).

Self-esteem. The self-esteem measure consisted of 20 items modified from those developed by Fleming and Courtney (1984). The items were slightly altered to reflect a school or academic environment (e.g., "I often worry about criticisms that might be made of my work by my teacher…I am intellectually better than most of my fellow students…"). The 20 items were rated on a 7-point Likert-type scale (1-Strongly Disagree to 7- Strongly Agree) with some items reverse scored to produce a consistent range from low to high esteem.

Academic Attitudes. This measure was composed of 17 statements reflecting positive and negative attitudes about school work, grades, criticism, teachers, and other features of school and academic work (e.g., "Students should be graded on effort rather than the quality of their work…Students should not be criticized for poor work…Teachers should not correct students when they make mistakes…"). Each statement was rated by the students on a 7-point Likert-type scale (1-Strongly Disagree to 7-Strongly Agree).

After conducting a factor analysis, the 17 items were reduced to nine. Cronbach Alpha reliabilities for the four personal attributes (Locus of Control, General Self-Efficacy, Self-Esteem, and Academic Attitudes) were .73, .88, .86, and .64 respectively.

RESULTS

Demographics and Descriptive Statistics

The means, standard deviations, and correlation coefficients for the major variables are shown in Table 1. There were no significant or meaningful demographic effects to report.

Path Analysis

The path model shown in Figure 2 was derived from the generic model in Figure 1. The path analysis followed the procedure outlined by Grimm and Yarnold (1995). Several regression analyses were performed, beginning with estimated GPA as the criterion variable and earned class grade as the predictor variable. Additional analysis with different criterion and predictor variables were then performed as determined by the arrows in the path model. The path coefficients for all the predictor variables (i.e., the beta coefficients) are shown in Figure 2. Significant path coefficients are designated by an asterisks.

The results of the path analysis show remarkable agreement with the model described in Figure 1. Two findings should be highlighted. First, the path coefficients for two of the personal attributes (self-esteem and academic attitudes) failed to reach statistical significance. This finding will be discussed below. Second, the interaction between ability and motivation (shown by the arrow that bisects the path between motivation and expected grade) was significant. This finding supports several theories that postulate that ability and motivation have a multiplicative (moderator) effect on expectancy (e.g., Feather, 1982; Porter and Lawler, 1968; Riedel et al. 1988; Vroom, 1964).

DISCUSSION

Work and school are connected in many ways. The line between employment and academics is becoming blurred. Workers go to school; students work jobs. It shouldn't be a surprise that what motivates an employee to do a good job also motivates students to do well in school. What is surprising is that there have been few studies that link the work and scholastic domains. This study attempted to show the commonality of work and school by testing a motivation and performance model (developed in organizational research) in an educational setting.

The model shown in Figure 1 was developed from theory and research in the industrial and organizational fields by several researchers over many years (Ajzen, 1991; Porter and Lawler, 1968; Riedle, Nebeker, and Copper, 1988; Rotter, 1954; Steel and Konig, 2006; Vroom, 1964). The issue addressed in this study was whether this model applies as well to college students in a typical undergraduate class. The results of a path analysis (Figure 2) showed a very good fit with the predicted path relationships (Figure 1).

Ability and motivation predicted student grade expectations. Expectancy was significantly related to the actual performance (grade on Exam 2), and this grade was positively related to satisfaction. Satisfaction, in turn, positively predicted the class grade, which was significantly related to the estimated GPA upon college completion.

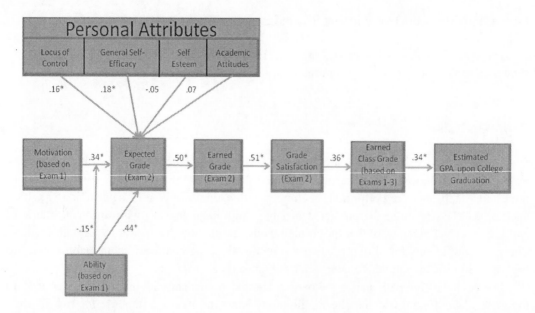

Figure 2. Path model of academic motivation and performance.

The most surprising result was that two of the personal attributes (self esteem and academic attitudes) failed to predict the students' expectancy, as predicted by the model. There are at least three reasons this might be the case: (a) measurement error (although the reliabilities of these constructs were at acceptable levels), (b) these two attributes were not independent of the other two (see Table 1), and (c) these personal attributes are not important in determining expectations, but are better predictors of other parts of the model. There was considerable prior research (reviewed above) to suggest that these two attributes should have been significant, so the lack of significance is an anomaly.

LIMITATIONS

One limitation with this study, which applies to almost all psychological research, deals with the question of generality. The study was done in a classroom setting at one university. Would these finding generalize to other classrooms, other disciplines, other universities, or other educational situations? Clearly, the study should be replicated and more data should be collected. A larger study with more participants and observations would also allow for a full structural equation model analysis (Kline, 1998; Tabachnick and Fidell, 2001). As with any structural model, the model in Figure 1 is only one of several possible conceptions. The data do, however, show that the model as tested is a plausible representation of the interrelationships among the variables. Another limitation is that the path model suggests that the sequence of events from left to right in Figures 1 and 2 form a causal chain, when in fact these relationships are correlational and not causal. Although the timing of events was correct (e.g., ability was assessed before expected class grade, expected grade was estimated before the actual grade was given), not all of the conditions for inferring causality were present (e.g., other unmeasured variables could have been the causal agents). Most survey research, such as this, suffers from this limitation; a limitation that can only be completely overcome with controlled, experimental research. Nonetheless, the causal sequence is plausible given the empirical results. Another limitation to the study might be common method/common source bias (Podsakoff, MacKenzie, Lee, and Podsakoff, 2003). This is often an issue with survey research. This problem is mitigated, however, because the self-report survey measures are combined with performance measures. This mixture of measures means that the measurement source and measurement methods are often not shared. For example the self-report measure of expected class grade does not predict another self-report measures; it predicts the earned class grade (a performance measure). Motivation and ability are predictors of performance expectancy, but these are mixtures of performance and survey measures and not purely derived from self-report responses. The only relationships that might be subject to common method/source variance are the correlations between two personal attributes (locus of control and general self-efficacy) and performance expectancy.

IMPLICATIONS

The study has at least two broad implications. One, it demonstrates that the model derived from organizational research (shown in Figure 1) has broad application. Not only does the model predict work performance (as demonstrated repeatedly in organizational studies), it now has been shown to predict school performance. Many of the variables in the model have been investigated in isolation in past organizational and educational studies, but this current research shows how these variables can be integrated into a more complete understanding of their influence from a broader perspective. Integrating two important domains in psychology (i.e., organizational studies and educational research), and finding common ground, is an important step in our understanding of human behavior.

A second implication of the study is that educational institutions are organizations, just like other organizations such as manufacturing, retail, health care, defense contracting, etc. Industrial/Organizational psychologists and educators should attempt to search for variables and constructs that reveal the underlying structures and processes of organizations in general. Admittedly, this study only examines a small component of an educational organization (i.e., students in class working for grades and a degree), but it now seems that this is not so different from employees on a job working for a salary and a career. The positive results from this study indicate that it might be beneficial to apply more organizational models to other areas of education (e.g., leadership, group processes, adaptation to new technology).

PRACTICAL APPLICATIONS

These findings might be used to predict students' success and then create strategies to that produce greater success, especially for those at risk. Based on the path model in Figure 2, teachers and educators might be able to evaluate ability and motivation, and then predict the expected and actual performance of their students.

This study showed that educators do not necessarily need sophisticated or expensive tests of motivation or ability; these constructs can be measured with information normally collected in class (e.g., test scores, self-reported capabilities). Tailored programs and selected encouragement could be provided to students with low ability or little motivation. For example, tutors could be provided, or study aids supplied, to help increase any shortcomings in ability. Likewise, counseling or workshops could be made available to bolster feelings of efficacy or expectations of success. At the other end of the spectrum, students identified with high levels of expected success could be provided with "enrichment" programs to build on their strengths and create an even higher degree of expected success and achievement. Such enrichment could produce Pygmalion and Galatea effects (Chapman and McCauley, 1993) that could lead to improved scholastic performance, increased graduation rates, and higher post-graduation success. Whatever comes of either remedial assistance or enrichment, the hope is that these activities would also carry over into the workplace and foster better work expectations and performance.

FUTURE RESEARCH

At the micro level, future research should continue to expand on the findings from this study. The model should be tested in more classes, more students should be surveyed, more colleges should be sampled, different measures should be used, and other educational activities should be investigated. At the macro level, research should spread into other domains of education. The model could be applied to leadership (e.g., What motives school principles or college deans?), could be tested on groups of educators (e.g., Does the theory work as well for predicting the performance and outcomes of school departments or committee members?), and could be examined in the context of introducing new instructional technology (e.g., What combination of ability and motivation best predicts who adopts and who resists innovations like social networking, online instruction, and web-based multi-media?).

GENERAL CONCLUSION

We live in a global, interconnected (flat) world (Friedman 2005). The stove pipes, turfs, and borders that once separated corporate departments, academic disciples, and countries are now starting to fall away. We are seeing how communication, cooperation, and coordination achieve better results than secrecy and competition. A greater effort should be made to integrate knowledge across wide domains. This study has shown how the research in industrial and organizational psychology is relevant to education. The findings from this study should be expanded and other cross-disciplinary models should be tested in a diverse set of domains.

REFERENCES

Ackerman, P. L. (2000). Domain-specific knowledge as the "dark matter" of adult intelligence: Gf/Gc, personality and interest correlates. *Journal of Gerontology: Psychological Sciences, 55,* 69–84.

Ajzen, I. (1991). A theory of planned behavior. *Organizational Behavior and Human Decision Processes, 50,* 179-211.

Akey, T. M. (2006). *School context, student attitudes and behavior, and academic achievement: An exploratory analysis.* MCRD, New York, NY.

Arneson, J. J., Sackett, P. R., and Beatty, A. S. (2011). Ability-performance relationships in education and employment settings: Critical tests of the more-is-better and the good-enough hypotheses. *Psychological Science, 20*(10), 1-7.

Bakker, A. B. (2011). The evidence-based model of work engagement. *Current Directions in Psychological Science, 20(4),* 265-269.

Bandura, A. (1977). Self-efficacy: Toward a unifying theory of behavior change. *Psychological Review, 84(2),* 191-215.

Bandura, A. (1989). Human agency in social cognitive theory. *American Psychologist, 44,* 1175-1184.

Bandura, A. (1991). Social cognitive theory of self-regulation. *Organizational Behavior and Human Decision Processes, 50,* 248-287.

Bandura, A. (1997). *Self-efficacy: The exercise of control* New York: W.H. Freeman.

Barrick, M. R., Mount, M. K., and Judge, T. A. (2001). Personality and performance at the beginning of the new millennium: What do we know and where do we go next? *International Journal of Selection and Assessment, 9*, 9–30.

Baumeister, R. F. Campbell, J. D., Krueger, J. I., and Vohs, K.D. (2003). Does high self-esteem cause better performance, interpersonal success, happiness, or healthier lifestyles? *Psychological Science in the Public Interest, 4(1)*, 1-44.

Baumeister, R. F. Campbell, J. D., Krueger, J. I., and Vohs, K.D. (2005). Exploding the self-esteem myth. *Scientific American,* http://www.scientificamerican.com/article.cfm?id=exploding-the-self-esteem-2005-12.

Bong, M. (2001). Role of self-efficacy and task-value in predicting college students' course performance and future enrolment intentions. *Contemporary Educational Psychology, 26,* 553-570.

Bong, M., and Clark, R. E. (1999). Comparison between self-concept and self-efficacy in academic motivation research. *Educational Psychology, 34.* 139-153.

Bouffard, T., Boiteau, L., and Vezeau, (2001). Students' transition from elementary to high school and changes of the relationship between motivation and academic performance. *European Journal of Psychology of Education, 17,* 589-604.

Brockett, R. G., and Hiemstra, R. (1991). *Self-direction in adult learning: Perspectives on theory, research, and practice.* London: Routedge.

Brown, U. J., Park, Y., and Jung; S. (2010). The effects of students' knowledge and attitude on the classroom performance. *Journal of Higher Education in Learning, 8,* 1-8.

Byrne, B. (1996). *Measuring self concept across the life span.* Washington: American Psychological Association.

Chamorro-Premuzic, T. and Furnham, A. (2003). Personality predicts academic performance: Evidence from two longitudinal university samples. *Journal of Research in Personality, 37,* 319–338.

Chapman, G. B. and McCauley, C. (1993). Early career achievements of National Science Foundation (NSF) graduate applicants: Looking for Pygmalion and Galatea Effects on NSF winners. *Journal of Applied Psychology, 78(5),* 815-820.

Chen J. S. and Toffelson, N. (1989). College students, causal attributions for their achievement. *College Student Journal.* 23 (2), 169-177.

Colquitt, J. A., LePine, J. A., and Noe, R. A. (2000). Toward an integrative theory of training motivation: A meta-analytic path analysis of 20 years of research. *Journal of Applied Psychology, 85,* 678–707.

Donovan, J. J. (2001). Work motivation. In N. Anderson, D. S. Ones, H. K. Sinangil, and C. Viswesvaran (Eds.). *Handbook of industrial and organizational psychology, vol. 2 (pp. 53-76).* Thousands Oaks, CA: Sage.

Drew P.Y. and Watkins D. (1998) Affective variables, learning approaches and academic achievement: A causal modeling investigation with Hong Kong tertiary students. *British Journal of Educational Psychology, 68,* 173–188.

Farquhar, W. W. and Payne, D. A. (1964). A classification and comparison of techniques used in selecting under- and overachievers. *Personnel and Guidance Journal, 42,* 874-884.

Feather, N. T. (1982). Expectancy-value approaches: Present status and future directions. In N. T. Feather (Ed.), *Expectations and actions: Expectancy-value models in psychology (pp. 395-420).* Hillsdale, NJ: Erlbaum.

Fleming, J. S. and Courtney, B. E. (1984). The dimensionality of self-esteem: II. Hierarchical facet model for revised measurement scales. *Journal of Personality and Social Psychology, 46*, 404-421.

Friedman, T. L. (2005). *The world is flat: A brief history of the twenty-first century*. New York: Farrar, Straus and Giroux.

Grimm, L G. and Yarnold, P. R. (1995). *Reading and understanding multivariate statistics*. American Psychological Association: Washington, DC.

Hansford, B. C. and Hattie, J. A, (1982). The relationship between self and achievement performance measures. *Review of Educational Research, 52*,123-142.

Harrison, D. A., Newman, D. A., and Roth, P. L. (2006). How important are job attitudes? Meta-analytic comparisons of integrative behavioral outcomes and time sequences. *Academy of Management Journal, 49*, 305–325.

Hattie, J. (1992). *Self-Concept*, Hillsdale, NJ: Lawrence Erlbaum Associates.

Hembree, R. 1990. The nature, effects, and relief of mathematics anxiety. *Journal for Research in Mathematics Education, 21(1)*, 33–46.

Hermans, H. J. M. (1970). A questionnaire measure of achievement motivation. *Journal of Applied Psychology, 54*, 353–363.

Horn, J. L., and Noll, J. (1997). Human cognitive capabilities: Gf-Gc theory. In D.P. Flanagan, J.L. Genshaft, and P.L. Harrison (Eds.), *Contemporary intellectual assessment: Theories, tests, and issues (pp. 53–91)*. New York: Guilford Press.

House, J. D., and Prion, S. K. (1998). Student attitudes and academic background as predictors of achievement in college English. *International Journal of Instructional Media, 25(1)*, 29-43.

Judge, T. A., Thoresen, C. J., Bono, J. E., and Patton, G. K. (2001). The job satisfaction–job performance relationship: A qualitative and quantitative review. *Psychological Bulletin, 127*, 376–407.

Kanfer, R. (1990). Motivation theory. In M. Dunnette and L. Houghs (Eds.). *Handbook of industrial and organizational psychology, vol. 1 (2nd ed.). (pp. 124- 151)*. Palo Alto, CA: Consulting Psychologist Press.

Kanfer, R., Wolf, M. B., Kantrowitz, T. M., and Ackerman, P. L (2010). Ability and trait complex predictors of academic and job performance: A person-situation approach. *Applied Psychology: An International Review, 59(1)*, 40-69.

Kline, R. B. (1998). *Principles and practice of structural equation modeling*. New York: Guilford.

Kuncel, N. R., Crede, M., and Thomas, L. L. (2005). The validity of self-report grade point average, class rank, and test scores: A meta-analysis and review of the literature. *Review of Educational Research, 75*, 63-82.

Kuncel, N. R., Hezlett, S. A., and Ones, D. S. (2001). A comprehensive meta-analysis of the predictive validity of the Graduate Record Examinations: Implications for graduate student selection and performance. *Psychological Bulletin, 127*, 162–181.

Lane, J. and Lane, A. (2001). Self-efficacy and academic performance. *Social Behavior and Personality, 29*, 687-693.

Lane, J., Lane, A., and Kyprianou, A. (2004). Self-efficacy, self-esteem and their impact on academic performance. *Social Behavior and Personality, 32*, 247-256.

Liem, A. D., Lau. S., and Nie, Y. (2008). The role of self-efficacy, task value, and achievement goal in predicting learning strategies, task disengagement, peer relationship, and achievement outcome. *Contemporary Educational Psychology, 33,* 486-512.

Ma, X., and Kishor, N. (1997a). Assessing the relationship between attitude toward mathematics and achievement in mathematics: A meta-analysis. *Journal for Research in Mathematics Education, 28(1), 26–47.*

Ma, X., and Kishor, N. (1997b). Attitude toward self, social factors, and achievement in mathematics: A meta-analytic review. *Educational Psychology Review, 9(2)*, 89–120.

Mandel, H. P. and Marcus, S. I. (1988). *The psychology of underachievement: Differential diagnosis and differential treatment.* New York: Wiley.

Marsh, H.W. (1984). Relations among dimensions of self-attribution, dimensions of self-concept, and academic achievements. *Journal of Educational Psychology, 76,* 1291-1308.

McCall, R. B. (1994). Academic underachievers. *Current Directions in Psychological Science, 3(1),* 15-19.

McCall, R. B., Evahn, C., and Kratzer, L. (1992). *High school underachievers: What do they achieve as adults?* Newbury Park, CA: Sage.

McClelland, D. C., Atkinson, J. W., Clark, R. A., and Lowell, E. L. (1953). *The achievement motive.* New York: Appleton-Century-Crofts.

Meyer, J. P., Stanley, D. J., Herscovitch, L., and Topolnytsky, L. (2002). Affective, continuance, and normative commitment to the organization: A meta-analysis of antecedents, correlates, and consequences. *Journal of Vocational Behavior, 61,* 20–52.

Miujs, D. (1997). Symposium: Self perception and performance. Predictors of academic self-concept: A longitudinal perspective. *British Journal of Educational Psychology, 67*, 263-277.

Murray-Harvey, R. (1993). Identifying characteristics of successful tertiary students using path analysis. *Australian Educational Research, 20(3)*, 63-81.

Nagengast, B., Marsh, H.W., Scalas, L. F., Xu, M. K., Hau, K., and Trautwein, U. (2011). Who took the "X" out of Expectancy-Value Theory: A psychological mystery, a substantive-methodological synergy, and a cross-national generalization. *Psychological Science, 20(10)*, 1-9.

Ofori, R. and Charlton, J. P. ((2002). A path model of factors influencing the academic performance of nursing students. *Journal of Advanced Nursing, 28(5)*, 507-515.

Oliver, J. S., and Simpson, R. D. (1988). Influences of attitude toward science, achievement motivation, and science self concept on achievement in science: A longitudinal study. *Science Education, 72(2)*, 143–155.

Partin, M. L., Haney, J. J., Worch, E. A., Underwood, E. M., Nurnberger-Haag, J. A., Scheuermann, A., and Midden, W. R. (2011). Yes I can: The contributions of motivation and attitudes on course performance among biology nonmajors. *Journal of College Science Teachers, 40(6,)* 86-95.

Perry, R.P. and Penner, K.S. (1990). Enhancing academic achievement in college students through attributional retraining and instruction. *Journal of Educational Psychology, 82,* 262-271.

Pintrich, P. R., and De Groot, E. V. (1990). Motivational and self-regulated learning components of classroom academic performance. *Journal of Educational Psychology. 82,* 33-40.

Porter, L. W. and Lawler, E. E. (1968), *Managerial attitudes and performance*. Homewood, IL; Dorsey.

Podsakoff, P. M, MacKenzie, S. B., Lee, J., and Podsakoff, N. P. (2003). Common method bias in behavioral research: A critical review of the literature and recommended remedies. *Journal of Applied Psychology, 88(5)*, 879-903.

Prat-Sala, M. and Redford, P. (2010). The interplay between motivation, self-efficacy, and approaches to studying. *British Journal of Educational Psychology, 80*, 283-305.

Ramanaiah, N. V., Ribich, F. D. and Schmeck, R. R (1975). Internal/external control of reinforcement as a determinant of study habits and academic attitudes. *Journal of Research in Personality, 9*, 375-384.

Richardson, J. T. E. (2007). Motives, attitudes and approaches to studying in distance education. *Higher Education, 54,* 385-416.

Riedel, J. A., Nebeker, D. M., and Cooper, B. L. (1988). The influence of monetary incentives on goal choice, goal commitment, and task performance. *Organizational Behavior and Human Decision Processes, 42*, 155-180.

Riketta, M. (2002). Attitudinal organizational commitment and job performance: A meta-analysis. *Journal of Organizational Behavior, 23,* 257–266.

Riketta, M. (2008). The causal relation between job attitudes and performance: A meta-analysis of panel studies. *Journal of Applied Psychology, 93(2)*, 472-481.

Rosenberg, M. (1965). *Society and the adolescent self-image*. Princeton, NJ: Princeton University Press.

Rotter, J. B. (1954). *Social learning and clinical psychology*. New York: Prentice-Hall.

Rotter J.B. (1966) Generalised .expectancies for internal versus external control of reinforcement. *Psychological Monographs, 80*, 1–28.

Sackett, P. R., Kuncel, N. R., Arneson, J. J., Cooper, S. R., and Waters, S. D. (2009). Does socioeconomic status explain the relationship between admissions tests and post-secondary academic performance? *Psychological Bulletin, 135*, 1–22.

Salili, F. (1994). Age, sex, and cultural differences in the meaning and dimensions of achievement. *Personality and Social Psychology Bulletin, 20*, 635-648.

Sandler, I., Reese, F., Spencer, L. and Harpin, P. (1983). Person environment interaction and locus of control: Laboratory therapy, and classroom studies. In H. M. Lefcourt (Ed.) *Research with the locus of control construct: Developments and social problems, Vol. 2. (pp. 187–251),* Hillsdale, NJ: Erlbaum,

Schmidt, F. L., and Hunter, J. E. (1998). The validity and utility of selection methods in personnel psychology: Practical and theoretical implications of 85 years of research findings. *Psychological Bulletin, 124*, 262–274.

Schunk. D. H.. and Zimmerman, B. J. (1997). Social origins of self-regulatory competence. *Educational Psychologist. 32,* 195-208.

Schwarzer, R. and Jerusalem, M. (1995). Generalized self-efficacy scale. In J. Weinman, S. Wright and M. Johnson (Eds.), *Measures in health psychology: A user portfolio. Causal and control beliefs (pp. 35-37)*. Windsor, UK: NFER-NELSON.

Skaalvik, E. M. and Hagtvet, K. A (1990). Academic achievement and self-concept: an analysis of causal predominance in a developmental perspective. *Journal of Personality and Social Psychology*, 58, 292-307.

Steel, P. and Konig, C. J. (2006). Integrating theories of motivation. *Academy of Management Review, 31(4)*, 889-913.

Tabachnick, B. G. and Fidell, L. S. (2001). *Using multivariate statistics*. Boston: Allyn and Bacon.

Tatum, B. C. (2012). Testing a model of work performance in an academic environment. SAGE Open, 2(2), 1-8. doi:10.1177/2158244012443543.

Van Eerde, W. and Thierry, H. (1996). Vroom's expectancy models and work-related criteria: A meta-analysis. *Journal of Applied Psychology, 81*, 575-586.

Vroom, V. H. (1964). *Work and motivation*. New York: Wiley.

Watkins, D. (1984). Student learning processes: An exploratory study in the Philippines. *Human Learning, 3*, 33-42.

Watkins, D. (1987). Academic locus of control: A relevant variable at tertiary level? *Higher Education, 16*. 221-229.

Watkins, D. (1989). Causal relationships among self-concept, attributions, and achievement in Filipino students. *Journal of Social Psychology, 130* (5), 625-631.

Watkins, D. and Astilla, E. (1984). The dimensionality, antecedents and study method correlates of the causal attribution of Filipino children. *Journal of Social Psychology, 124*, 191-199,

In: Handbook of Academic Performance   ISBN: 978-1-62417-888-7
Editors: Rolf Haumann and George Zimmer   © 2013 Nova Science Publishers, Inc.

Chapter 7

DEVELOPMENTS IN THE MEASURE OF INTELLIGENCE

Natalia Herranz Torres
África Borges del Rosal, University of La Laguna, Spain

ABSTRACT

This chapter shows the different conceptions of intelligence and the procedures that have been developed to measure it. First, we are going toexplain the main models that have been used to define the concept of intelligence. Subsequently, are going to be developed the first techniques to quantify the intelligence and how they have evolved into the theories that today allow the development of intelligence tests.

1. THE CONCEPT OF INTELLIGENCE

The intelligence is a concept that has interested to different professionals since ancient times. First of all, many philosophers talked about the "intelligent person" in their statements. Next are mentioned, according to Sternberg (1990) the main conceptions about the intelligence from the great philosophers:

Plato thought that intelligence meant the ability to learn. Later *Aristotle* added the importance of a quick learning.

Hobbes talked about "wit" and thought that was divided into the "Natural wit" which were the intellectual skills that are acquired by use and experience; and the "Acquired wit", which is learned by culture and instruction. He believed that the differences in intelligence were due to differences in motivation or "passions".

Locke also believed in the existence of two kinds of intelligence. On the one hand, the "wit" is the ability to link with quickness a set of ideas in which can be found any resemblance or congruity. On the other hand, the "judgment" is the ability to separate one idea from another wherein can be found the least difference. He also talked about the importance of the mental speed in the intelligence.

Finally, *Kant* referred to intelligence as "the higher faculties of cognitions", which he divided in three parts: understanding, judgment and reason.

Intelligence form the Psychological Point of View

Following the tradition of many philosophers, numerous professionals of psychology attempted to define the concept of intelligence.

The main problem that arose was that each author defended his own definition of intelligence, therefore, emerged as many definitions as authors interested in the study of this concept.

To reach a consensus on this term, in 1921 was held a symposium which aimed to know, on the one hand, the concept of intelligence of the participants and, on the other hand, what were the next steps to advance the investigation on this concept.

Below are the main answers obtained from the participants in the symposium (Sternberg, 1990; Andrés-Pueyo, 1997).

After this symposium psychology professionals were unable to reach any consensus about the nature of the intelligence. For this reason, in 1986, Detterman and Sterrnberg conducted a new symposium, this time by mail, with the objective of replicate the definitions obtained in the 1921 symposium (Andrés-Pueyo, 1997).

Following is a table with the main definitions obtained in this symposium, compiled by De Juan-Espinosa (1997) and Andrés-Pueyo (1997).

Table 1. Definitions and conceptions about intelligence given at the 1921 symposium

1921 Symposium	
Objective:Discuss problems related to the nature and measure of intelligence	
Author	**Definition of intelligence**
Thorndike	The capacity to give good responses from the point of view of the truth and facts.
Terman	The ability to think abstractly.
Freeman	Sensory capacity, perceptual recognition capacity, quickness, range or flexibility of association, facility and imagination, attention span, quickness in response.
Colvin	Have learned or ability to learn to adapt to the environment.
Pintner	Ability to adapt oneself adequately to relatively new situations in life.
Thurstone	The capacity to inhibit an instinctive adjustment, the capacity to redefine the inhibited instinctive adjustment in the light of imaginarily experienced trial and error, and the capacity to realize the modified instinctive adjustment in overt behavior to the advantage of the individual as a social animal.
Woodrow	The capacity to acquire capacity.
Henmon	The capacity for knowledge and knowledge possessed.
Peterson	A biological mechanism by which the effects of a complexity of stimuli are brought together and given a somewhat unified effect in behavior.
Dearborn	The capacity to learn o to profit by experience.
Haggerty	Sensation, perception association, memory, imagination, discrimination, judgment, and reasoning.

The Structure of Intelligence

The study of intelligence has numerous difficulties associated. As seen above, the first of them was the lack of agreement between the different professionals on a definition that encompasses the concept of intelligence. Furthermore, this disagreement does not end there, because there have also been wide differences of opinion with respect to the structure of intelligence.

There are two main positions, on the one hand are the psychologist who defend that the intelligence has a hierarchical structure, that is, the intelligence consists in the existence of some general factors which explain it and other factors more specific. On the other hand, are those who think that the structure of intelligence is not hierarchical, that is, people who defend the existence of independent factors.

Table 2. Definitions and conceptions about intelligence given at the 1986 symposium

1986 Symposium	
Objective: To replicate the definitions about the nature of intelligence obtained in the 1986 simposium.	
Author	**Definition of intelligence**
Anastasi	Quality of adaptive behavior in so far as it represents effective ways of satisfying the demands of a constantly changing environment.
Baron	The set of aptitudes involved in achieving rationally chosen goals, whether they are. Two types of intelligence: 1) capabilities such as speed and mental energy, and 2) the provisions, such as being self-critical.
Berry	The final product of the individual development in the field of cognitive psychology. Is different from driving, emotional, motivational and social performance. It is adaptive for a particular cultural group in so far that allows members to operate effectively in a given ecological context.
Carroll	It is a concept that resides in the minds of a society in a broad sense, depending on the nature of this society. Distinguishes between three basic areas to which are applied the concept of intelligence: the academic and technical, practical, and social.
Hunt	Defines intelligence in terms of individual differences in mental competence in cognitive tasks statistically associated to personal variables.
Detterman	Understands intelligence as a system composed of many cognitive processes, independents of each other, but they can work together. This contributes to the appearance of a general factor of intelligence.
Eysenck	The human biological intelligence has its base on the efficiency of neural processing.
Gardner	Es un conjunto independiente de las capacidades que actúan por la demanda de ambiental.
Jensen	The intelligence is based on the speed of information processing and the ability to retain information in the immediate memory.
Sternberg	It is a "*kind of self-government or mental self-management*" of higher order.

a) Hierarchical Structure Theories

First will be presented the conceptions of those professionals who defend a hierarchical structure of intelligence and, next will be explained the non hierarchical theories of this concept.

Spearman, during the first decade of the twentieth century, developed a statistical procedure (the factor analysis), through are identified the components of a particular construct.So, he studied the correlations between different intelligence tests. Through this study he found that the variance of the scores could be decomposed into two parts, obtaining a common factor in all the tests, that he called general factor of intelligence or <<g>> and a specific factor or <<s>>, formed by the specific information of each test.These results led to his bi-factor theory of intelligence. Spearman stated that the g factor is the source of knowledge, since is a comprehensive activity that is necessary to perform complex tasks (Matud, Marrero & Carballeira, 2004). According to the author, the general factor of intelligence is a fundamental ability because it is involved in mental operations. Spearman´s important contributions to psychology were strengthened by his insistence on the great utility that had the measure of the general factor of intelligence to the personnel selection and vocational guidance, favoring the creation of measuring instruments whose objective is to provide an estimation of this general factor of intelligence.

Burt (1909, 1917) proposes some changes to Spearman´s theory. Like him, Spearman extracted which were the factors involved in the intelligence and found that this capacity was structured as follows: firstly it would be the general factor of intelligence, which emerges from the correlation of what he called group or primary factors; at a lower level than these factors would be found the specifics factors of each trait and, finally, its error sources (Matud et al, 2004).

Vernon (1950) distinguishes three kinds of intelligence:

- "A" Intelligence: It can not be measured from the behavioral point of view, since it is inborn or inherited.
- "B" Intelligence: It is related to the acts that people develop daily and the effectiveness they have and, therefore, it has a cultural component.
- Finally, "C" Intelligence: It is which develops in controlled situations, measured through tests and structured tasks.

Regarding how to structure the intelligence, he considers that it is hierarchically divided into three levels. At the top of the hierarchy is the general factor of intelligence. In the second level there are the two secondary factors which he identified: the *verbal-educational (v:ed)*, which comprises the verbal, numerical and attention abilities, among others; and the *spatial mechanical factor (k:m)*, which refers, for example, to perceptive, physical or spatial tasks. In the last level, there is a small group of factors related to the tests that are used to check the performance.

R. B. Cattell (1971) proposed a theory similar to Vernon. His conception of intelligence establishes the existence of two types of skills that are at the basis of the g factor. These skills are the *Crystallized Ability* and the *Fluid Ability*. The first one is similar to the Vernon´s verbal-educational factor, since it consists in the accumulation of knowledge and tools for action throughout life and is measured by tests such as vocabulary, general information or reading comprehension.

Fluid Ability, meanwhile, is similar to the spatial mechanical factor of the same author and its refers to the ability to reason abstractly and the flexibility of thought (Sternberg, 1990).

b) Non-hierarchical Structure Theories

The structure of intellect model of *Guilford* (1967) defines 120 different abilities, which are formed by three dimensions. These three dimensions are: operations, products, and contents.

Mental operations, that is, the processes which are activated to develop a task, are five:

1. Cognition: the capacity to discover or understand information quickly.
2. Memory: the capacity to retain information. It differs in short and long term memory.
3. Divergent production: the capacity to develop different alternatives for a task or situation.
4. Convergent production: the capacity to solve a problem that has only one solution.
5. Evaluation: the capacity to compare something new with something which is already known according to a logical criteria and develop a response basedon that criterion.

The products defined by Guilford are six and with this concept he refers to how the information is connected to produce a reply:

1. Units: individual items of information.
2. Classes: items grouped into sets based on some common characteristic.
3. Relations: established connections between information, according to some predefined criteria.
4. Systems: organized or structured information series.
5. Transformations: modifications of the information.
6. Implications: refer to expectations, anticipations and predictions about the information.

Finally, the contents are referred on the way the information is presented and we can distinguish four types:

1. Figural: the information is presented in a specific way, generally, pictorial.
2. Symbolic: signs that have no meaning in themselves, such as letters or numbers.
3. Semantic: words or concepts with meaning.
4. Behavioral: information reflected in the interaction between people.

As mentioned, the dimensions of Guilford result in 120 independent intellectual abilities but then to reformulate his theory and divide the figurative content and memory into two components, the model explained 180 capabilities.

Gardner (1984) has developed his theory about the multiple intelligences. According to the author, there are seven kinds of intelligences that are independents. Moreover,he argues that intelligence is not fixed, but changes according to the contexts and their influence (Resnick, 1976). The seven intelligences that form his theory are:

1. Linguistic intelligence.
2. Musical Intelligence.
3. Logical-mathematical intelligence.
4. Spatial intelligence.
5. Corporal-kinesthetic intelligence.

6. Intrapersonal intelligence.
7. Interpersonal intelligence.

In this section we have described different conceptions of the term intelligence and its structure. With respect to the definition of this aptitude, although there is controversy, we can find some commonalities between the different authors. For example, there is some agreement to talk about the nature of intelligence, emphasizing concepts such as the ability to adapt to the environment, basic mental processes or higher order thinking.

In terms of structure, even today there is no agreement between the two main positions: those authors who advocate a hierarchical structure, with a general factor of intelligence and a number of specific factors, and of those who speak of independent capabilities.

2. First Approaches to the Measure of Intelligence

As emerged the interest in the study of human capacities, psychology professionals not only were dedicated to try to define the concept of intelligence, but joined to this theoretical interest appeared the motivation to achieve quantify this quality. So, Anderson (1999) states that since the early development of quantification in the social sciences, in the field of psychology, the concept of intelligence has been the most closely associated with the measurement.

It is considered that systematic experimentation on individual differences in behavior was caused by the accidental discovery of differences in reaction time between astronomers. In 1796, an assistant of the Greenwich Observatory recorded, with great accuracy, the instant when certain stars crossed the field of the telescope. It was found that his results showed a difference of 8 tenths of a second with respect to the comments from his boss, this suggested that the assistant did not perform his work properly and was fired. Years later, it was discovered that these differences between observers were due to the different speeds at which they could respond to stimuli. From that moment, it was found that these differences were part of human nature (Cronbach, 1972). This type of data caused that the interest of researchers in analyzing the differences between the abilities of people grow.

Since the beginning of interest in human skills, many professionals have tried to quantify it. This has been done for various procedures. Initially, it was assumed that every aptitude was reflected and could be measured by its physiological correlates. Once abandoned this hypothesis and with the emergence of the first objective tests, were developed different theories of the tests. Below are the most widely used measurement procedures in the field of intelligence.

i. Psychophysiological Measures

As we mentioned before, the firsts attempts to measure the intelligence assumed that the intellectual functioning was manifested, mainly, in coarse physical aspects (Anderson, 1999).

Already in the mid-nineteenth century Paul Broca used measurements of head circumference and brain volume as intellectual performance indicators.His investigations were refined as his studies progressed, until he got to demonstrate that the damage in certain areas of the brain affected the performance of individuals in different areas. Specifically, he found that the left frontal lobe damage affected the speech, showing the relationship between the brain physiognomy and certain human abilities (Anderson,1999).

The interpretation of intelligence through its correlates continued with the work of Francis Galton, who continued the line of research on individual differences initiated by Darwin.In his investigation about this topic, he called to his tests *anthropometric tests* and introduced the concept *mental test*, to refer to the tests or procedures used to measure different human attributes. His procedures were focused on measuring physical characteristics, such as the acuity of the senses.He developed several sensory discrimination tests such as the discrimination of the length of different elements visually, the use of a whistle to determine the highest audible tone, etc., because he believed that such tests could be used to estimate the intellect and thus claimed that *"the only information concerning the external events which reaches us seems to go down the avenue of senses, and the more perceptive the senses are the differences, the greater the field that can act on our judgment and our intelligence will be"* (Galton, 1883, cited in Anastasi and Urbina, 1998). One of the greatest contributions of this author to the development of the scientific science is that he recognized the need for standardization in the examination of subjects, that is the need to introduce to all the same problem under uniform conditions (Nunnally, 1970), which in the future would be reflected in statistical standardization of psychological tests.

Galton had a great influence on James McKeen Cattell who, knowing his work, strengthened his interest in the study of intelligence through objective measures (De Juan-Espinosa, 1997). Like its predecessor, McKeen Cattell focused on tests consisting of sensory discrimination measures and widespread use of anthropometric tests to a wider range of mental abilities, among which are included since skin sensitivity to the associative memory (Andrés-Pueyo, 1997). For this author the study of reaction time was critical, considering that was the indicator of time it took to execute the mental operations needed to solve a task.Through the measure of the reaction time he studied how fatigue, attention or practice effects affecting implementation.In 1890 he wrote the article *Mental Tests and Measurements,* in which proposed a series of 50 psychophysiological tests. In the same year he published a set of studies suggesting that the psychological tasks should correlate with school success.

Following these predictions, Clark Wissler, a student, conducted an investigation using Cattell tests with students from Columbia University and finding the correlation between them and academic success. In this study (Wissler, 1901, cited in De Juan-Espinosa, 1997) was the first time it was used massively the correlation coefficient to measure the relationship between sets of measures of simple psychological processes. However, the attempt to find relationships between measures of simple cognitive processes and a criteria as the academic success was not paid off.First, the correlations between the tests did not exceed the value that could be expected by random. Moreover it was found that although academic qualifications correlated with each other at a high level, its correlation with the psychological tasks was trivial.Light of these results, Wissler concluded that mental tests did not provide any information on the general ability of the students and even questioned the existence of such general ability.

Despite the problems arising by the investigations of Wissler, Cattell (De Juan-Espinosa, 1997) continued his research in the field of intelligence and psychological tests, modifying the way in which presentedthe tests.

In the seventies, Posner (1978, cited by Andrés-Pueyo, 1997) introduced the term *Mental Chronometry*, which is based on the measurement of the speed and mental efficiency. This author understood the mental chronometry as the *"study of the temporal course of information processing in the human central nervous system"* (Andrés-Pueyo, 1997).

The procedures of the mental chronometry presupposed that mental operations that occur in a series of stages that take place in the time interval that occurs between the receipt of the stimulus and the response issuing occupy a time which is reflected in the reaction time. For this reason, the studies framed under this label used reaction time as a measure of performance and cognitive performance.

Early work on this subject were intended to relate general intelligence with simple tasks of information processing. Thus, was used a stimulus to which the subjects had to pay attention and respond. The time between the presentation of the stimulus and the response of the subject is called reaction time (RT).

As the studies were developed, the reaction time was not the only element analyzed, but introduced other terms, such as movement time (MT) or inspection time (IT), measures which finally was shown that did not have a direct relationship with the intelligence. As stated Wissler (1901, cited in Muñiz, 2010), after some early studies was found that these early tests based on sensorimotormeasurements were not adequate predictors of cognitive abilities of individuals.

The difficulties arising from the lack of relationship between measures of intelligence and mental chronometry were quickly overcome by research in the field of mental testing and the contributions of the theories of the tests.

ii. Assessment Derived of the Academic Demands

In France, in theearly twentieth century, Alfred Binet developed a measurement method of human faculties completely different from its predecessors since argued that, because the intelligence is manifested in the performance on different tasks, the study of the participants´ responses to these tasks would be an appropriate way to measure it (Aiken, 2003).

While Binet began to worry about the measure of human faculties, in French schools had been concern about the performance of children, so, this author was asked to develop tests to measure intelligence of students in order to distinguish those children who had difficulty to learn from those without.

In 1905, with his colleague Simon, completed his first test, which assessed the child´s ability to reason about the objects of the cultural environment. This test was revised in 1908, categorizing the items depending on the age level they belonged according to their difficulty.In this way arose the term *mental age*, which referred to the highest level at which a child could respond appropriately.Later, Stern suggested that mental age were divided by the chronological order to obtain IQ (Nunnally, 1970).

The use of this kind of tests, developed by Binet, soon spread to the rest of Europe and America, leading to several revisions.Among them, the most important was done by Terman in 1916, leading the Stanford-Binet test, in which was used for the first time the intelligence quotient. Furthermore, it recognizes the importance of intelligence tests for preschoolers.

The interest for the measure of the human abilities keep on growing, rising its importance at the beginning of the First World War. It was thought that this kind of tests would allow to select adequately the participants in the war, separating those who were useful to deal with the conflict. Was developed the *Army Alpha* test, it was an easy test to administer and interpret.

This test valued the simple reasoning and the level of information that the subject had and, depending on the results, people were classified in various occupational categories (Cronbach, 1972). Thus it was found that the response of a test to a practical need consolidated the interest for the measure of intelligence. The development of tests found the impulse that needed from long time when it was shown that these tests were very useful for the classification of personnel in matters as important as war.From this moment, there was a growth in the development and application of psychological tests in order to measure human skills.

iii. Tests Theories

Tests are sophisticated measuring instruments, by which psychologists make inferences and make decisions on important aspects about people.For this reason, it is necessary to ensure that these inferences are appropriate (Muñiz, 2010). This is the reason of the emerge of the tests theories. They are statistical theories which allow estimation of the psychometric properties of the tests to ensure that inferences are appropriate. The birth of formal test theory can be located in the first works of Spearman, who established the foundations of Classical Test Theory (CTT).

Its main goal was to find a statistical model that support adequately the test scores and allow the estimation of measurement errors associated with the measurement process (Muñiz, 1998). There are two main theories of tests: the Classical Test Theory (CTT) and Item Response Theory (IRT). The following sections will explain in detail each of these theories and their major contributions to the development of measure instruments.

3. CLASSICAL TEST THEORY

The beginning of the Classical Test Theory (CTT) can be found in the first works of Charles Spearman. His main objective was to find a statistical model to support the tests scores and, through it, to obtain an estimation of the measurement errors associated. This author proposed the classic linear model, which assumes that the empirical score of a person in a test (X) consists of two components: the true score of the person in the test (T) and the error (e) associated with the process measurement, the model being formulated as follows (Muñiz, 1998):

$$X_i = T_i + e_i$$

This theory was developed mainly during the first half of the twentieth century, and boasts a number of assumptions, taken from Martinez et al. (2006) as detailed below:

1. For a population of measures with the same tests, or for an infinite repetition of measurements on the same person, the expected value for the measurement error is zero.
2. There is no relationship between the true score and error, this implies that subjects with different values in the attribute measured are affected by error quantities that have nothing to do with their status in the attribute.
3. If you apply two different tests to a population, the measurement errors of both tests are not correlated.
4. Since the measurement errors are random, derivatives of a test are not correlated with the true scores of other different test. That is, the TCT considers the measurement error as a random and non-systematic deviation of the true score.

Quickly the assumptions of the use of the Classical Test Theory were spread and, along with them, the use of a number of indices related to two concepts that have become very important in the field of the construction of tests: reliability and validity.

Reliability

With this concept it is intended that psychological measurements are free of errors of measurement, that is, that will be reliable measurements.For this, it is considered that an instrument (test) doesn't have measurement errors when the measures that carry out are consistent. Reliability refers to the stability of the measurements when there are no reason to suppose that the measured variable has been modified differentially for the subject, so that it is assumed its stability (Muñiz, 1998).

The way to find the reliability is through the reliability coefficient, which can be obtained through the following procedures:

- Correlation between the scores obtained by the participants in two parallel forms of a test.
- Correlation of scores from the same test, applied on two different occasions to the same participants.
- Correlation of the two halves into which the test is divided.

Validity

According to Muñiz (1998), validity refers to the set of evidences that must be collected to ensure that it is possible to make inferences about the behavior of people through their answers to a test. There are numerous types of validity, including, we can refer to the content, predictive or construct validity. The first one refers to the importance of ensuring that a test constitutes a representative sample of the contents we attempt to evaluate. Predictive validity is related to the capacity of the test to predict the behavior that is being assessed.

Regarding the construct validity, it refers to the empirical evidence testing to ensure the existence of a psychological construct that defines the trait or behavior the test is intended to measure. Although Classical Test Theory has been and still is a method widely used in the construction of measurement instruments, soon many authors found some drawbacks in its use. Below are some of the problems found in successive revisions of the CTT (Martinez et al., 2006):

1. Dependence of item statisticians of the population and/or sample in which have been calculated. This affects the need for comprehensive measures that can be applied, with the same results, to different populations. That is, the result of each item of the test is dependent largely on the conditions and participants to which they apply.

2. Dependence of the test statisticians of the population and / or sample in which have been calculated. That is, the statisticians which expressing both characteristics of each of the items as the overall test depend on the variability of the groups are calculated.

3. Practical difficulties arising from the concept of parallelism of the measures. In the CTT, the reliability coefficient is defined as the correlation between scores on parallel forms of a test. But in practice it is very difficult to satisfy the definition of parallelism, which affects this coefficient.

4. In this theory there is a unique and undifferentiated concept of error, under that there are hiding different error sources that give a different meaning to the interpretation of reliability. As shown subsequently, each of these error sources must be taken in consideration separately.

5. Dependence of the scores of the particular set of items used in the test. Although the emphasis is on the overall score of the test, it depends on each particular item that forms it, therefore is not possible to speak of the ability of the subject in general terms.

6. The usual estimator of the true score depends on the population and / or reference.

7. The CTT does not provide a theoretical model for item responses. That is, it not allows to determine the behavior of a person based on the trait quantity that has faces when an item.

8. Measurements without optimal adequacy to the characteristics of the subjects. The test developed under this theory does not produce measures equally appropriate for all subjects.

These difficulties led many professionals in psychology who were interested in the measurement of intelligence or alternative theories seek ways through which to develop measurement instrument to quantify this ability properly.Next will be explained the two main procedures that emerged in response to these problems: Generalizability Theory and Item Response Theory.

4. ALTERNATIVE PROCEDURES
(GENERALIZABILITY THEORY AND ITEM RESPONSE THEORY)

In order to solve the limitations presented by the Classical Test Theory have been proposed several theories. First, the Generalizability Theory (GT) has, as major contribution, the possibility of distinguishing various sources of error, but not introduces major changes from the CTT. The Item Response Theory (IRT) is going to be which get answer many of the problems presented by the CTT.

4.1. Generalizability Theory (GT)

Generalizability Theory (GT) has, as main objective, to determine what are the different sources of error that affect the measurements and estimate its value.Fundamentally, what the GT tries to resolveis whether the value or score that is obtained from the sample is generalizable to the population.

The procedure to check the generalizability begins designing the measurement situation and then through the analysis of variance, will be estimated the amount of the error sources.Therefore, the GT is summarized in two big steps: First, the analysis of designs that can be raised and, secondly, to make the analysis of variance for these designs.

The main concepts that underpin the GT are (Muñiz, 1998):

- *Facet:* Are all factors listed in the design of the measurement. It will take into account all those areas that could affect scores of subjects and constitute potential sources of error. The design complexity depends on the number of facets considered.
- *Universe of admissible observations:* This is all the scores of the subjects that are considered acceptable in the proposed design.
- *Universe of generalization:* The factor or facet in which the researcher intends to investigate whether the data are generalizable.
- *Generalizability coefficient:* It is equivalent to the coefficient of reliability of Classical Test Theory, and indicates the extent to which a measurement is generalizable to the population of measurements referred to, that is, the extent to which a sample of measurements represents the universe of generalization.

Despite these contributions, the Generalizability Theory introduces no major changes from the Classical Theory, so the development of test is still subject to the problems presented above. The alternative that has brought major changes regarding the CTT is the Item Response Theory, which is detailed below.

4.2. Item Response Theory (IRT)

In an attempt to respond to the problems presented by the Classical Test Theory arises *Item Response Theory (IRT)*. Thus, following Lord (1980, cited in Muñiz, 1997), the IRT does not contradict the fundamental assumptions or conclusions of the Classical Theory, but makes additional assumptions, allowing to answer questions that CTT couldn´t answer.As stated Rebollo et al. (2010), the Item Response Theory allows to overcome some of the limitations presented in the context of the Classical Test Theory as, for example, IRT allows to obtain high accuracy measurements using fewer items that the procedures required by the CTT.

The main characteristic of this theory is that the IRT is a procedure which is based on the properties of the items, not the overall test. Thus, Eysenck (1987, cited in De Juan-Espinosa, 1997) suggests that to address the intelligence from a causal point of view, in terms of the underlying cognitive processes, the fundamental unit of analysis should be the item and not the score total in a test with high loadings on factor g.

This theory has its origins with Richardson's proposals in 1936, but its greatest growth comes after the publication of Rasch´s book in 1960 and the work of Birnbaum, Lord and Novick, in 1968.

In the beginning, this theory was called *Latent Trait Theory*, since each item and therefore the test measures a variable or trait, called Θ.

As discussed above, to measure a variable through the CTT, the result obtained will always depend on the test used. Therefore, this represents a major limitation because it creates problems when we try to compare the same measured variable with different tests.Also in this case, the properties of the test are a function of the subjects who have to pass the test. Given these drawbacks, the IRT has, as main objectives to obtaining measurements that are independent of the instruments used and of the subjects tested.

This theory consists of a number of concepts that are explained below. First, the Item Response Theory assumes that there is a functional relationship between the values of the variable measured by the items and the probability of endorse them called Item Characteristic Curve (ICC) (Muñiz, 1997). As the name suggests, each item has its curve, which is defined by three parameters:

- *a parameter or discrimination index* shows the magnitude of the change in the probability of endorse the item according to the skill level of the person changes, and its value is proportional to the point of maximum slope of the tangent of the ICC (Muñiz, 1997).
- *b parameter or difficultyindex*, as the name suggests, indicates the item difficulty depending on the ability level of the individual, and is located at the point of maximum slope of the curve.
- Finally, *c parameter* represents the probability of endorse an item at random when you don´t know theanswer.

Therefore, when we find these three parameters is formed the Characteristic Curve for each item.

Assumptions of Item Response Theory

To achieve the main goal of the IRT (to obtain invariant measures from the subjects measured and instruments used) is required to observe two fundamental assumptions: latent space unidimensionality and local independence (Embretson and Reise, 2000).

Regarding the first, states that the probability of endorsing an item depend only on a factor, corresponding with Θ or the trait that is being measured. In other words, the items that make up a test to measure a particular variable are unidimensional.

Local independence refers to an individual's response to an item is not influenced by the response to others.

Therefore, the development of items under these IRT assumptions enables that the combination of different elements lead to the creation of tests which measure reliably a particular trait.

Applications of IRT

The developing of models of Item Response Theory has allowed the application of this procedure in many areas (Muñiz, 1997), among which highlight the following:

1. Development items' banks: A bank of items refers to a set of items of known psychometric properties. As seen, the IRT allows the creation of items that are independent of the person tested and its parameters are known, being an ideal method for the construction of such items' banks.
2. Equalization scores: The IRT is also helpful for equating scores on two or more tests. This refers to establish correspondence between scores of various tests (which measure the same variable and with the same reliability), so that is indifferent which of them is applied.
3. Study of the differential item functioning: this is the collection of techniques by which various groups of people are compared andis studied if an item works the same for all groups or, however, differs.
4. Adaptive Tests: The defining characteristic of such tests is that are built based on the person to whom they apply. That is, they are tests whose difficulty level adapts at the subject's skill level. IRT's role in this type of test is to allow the comparison of the scores on the different items in a particular variable. As a result of the combined application of Item Response Theory and technological advances arise Computerized Adaptive Test, which allow quick and accurate assessment using a computer as a way of presentation of the items (Rebollo et al., 2010).

5. COMPUTERIZED ADAPTIVE TESTS (CAT)

Advances in the measurement of intelligence have also been reflected in the way the items or tests are presented. Thus, it has been increasing the number of tests in which the items are presented and respond through a computer, which has greatly facilitated the application of psychological tests (Olea, Abad and Barrada, 2010).

By combining the use of Item Response Theory with computer science is possible to create Computerized Adaptive Tests (CATs), whose main characteristic is that the items that are tailored to the level of skill or trait that manifests the person assessed, based on their responses to previous items.Following Olea and Ponsoda (2003), we can define a computerized adaptive test as "*a test, built for psychological or educational evaluation, and whose items are answered using a computer, and its fundamental characteristic is that adapts to the progressive level of competence that is manifesting the person*".

As can be seen, the fundamental idea of CAT is to present only the most informative items for each subject, so that, with a limited number of elements can be derived the trait level of each participant. This requires first having a large item bank calibrated properly.

Following Olea, Abad and Barrada (2010), the process of implementing a Computerized Adaptive Test can be summarized in the following steps:

1. First, it is necessary to establish a starting strategy, ie you have to establish what level of initial trait is assigned to the participant. One way is to select an item that represents the average level that the population has.
2. After answering each item, through statistical procedures, is made an estimate of the level of trait evaluated.
3. It is necessary to apply an algorithm, usually based on the extent of the information provided by each item, for the selection of each of the items to be submitted subsequently to the participant.
4. Finally, it should be a criterion to finish the presentation of the items. Normally this criterion is based on achieving a certain level of accuracy, or after having applied a given number of items.

Below are the main advantages of using Computerized Adaptive Tests:

- The fact that the items presented are different for each assessed improves the validity of the test, as it prevents participants can know beforehand what are the elements that are going to present and their answers.
- Is achieved an estimate of the trait level of the evaluated with a reduced number of items, so that the application time is substantially reduced.
- Allow more precise estimates than a conventional test using the same number of items, since under similar conditions to a traditional test, a CAT allows higher guarantees for the trait levels estimated.

As has been observed, the Computerized Adaptive Tests are great improvements to facilitate the application of psychometric tests. Therefore, their use has increased in recent years.

CONCLUSION

This chapter has presented the development and changes over the years in the study of intelligence. First, has been explained the difficulty of reaching a consensus on the definition and structure of this construct, and the different proposals of major authors involved in this issue. Subsequently have been developed various procedures that have been used to measure this attribute, ending with current procedures, such as the use of Item Response Theory and Computerized Adaptive Tests developing.

REFERENCES

Aiken, L. R., (2003). *Tests psicológicos y evaluación.* México: Pearson Educación.
Anderson, M. (1999). *Desarrollo de la inteligencia.* México: Oxford.

Anastasi, A., y Urbina, S. (1998). *Tests Psicológicos.* México: Prentice Hall.

Andrés-Pueyo, A. (1997). *Manual de Psicología Diferencial.* Madrid: McGraw Hill.

Cronbach, L. J., (1972). *Fundamentos de la exploración psicológica.* Madrid: Biblioteca Nueva.

De Juan-Espinosa, M. (1997). *Geografía de la inteligencia humana. Las aptitudes cognitivas.* Madrid: Pirámide.

De Juan-Espinosa, M. (1997). La inteligencia según Hans Jürgen Eysenck. *Revista de Psicología General y Aplicada*, 50(4), 513-537.

Embretson, S.E, & Reise, S.P. (2000). *Item Response Theory for Psychologist.* New Jersey: Lawrence Erlbaum Associates.

Martínez, M. R., Hernández, M. J.,& Hernández, M. V. (2006). *Psicometría.* Madrid: Alianza Editorial.

Matud, M. P., Marrero, J. & Carballeira, M. (2004). *Psicología diferencial.* Madrid: Biblioteca Nueva.

Muñiz, J (1991) *Inteligencia y procesos básicos.* En J. Mayor y J.L. Pinillos Tratado de Psicología General. Tomo 5 Pensamiento y Lenguaje. Madrid: Alhambra Universidad.

Muñiz, J. (1997). *Introducción a la Teoría de Respuesta a los ítems.* Madrid: Pirámide.

Muñiz, J. (1998). *Teoría Clásica de los Tests.* Madrid: Pirámide.

Nunnally, J. C., (1970). *Introducción a la medición psicológica.* Argentina: Paidós.

Olea, J., Abad, F. J., & Barrada, J. (2010). Test informatizados y otros nuevos tipos de tests. *Papeles del Psicólogo,* 3(1), 94-107.

Olea, J., & Ponsoda, V. (2003). *Tests Adaptativos Informatizados.* Madrid: Universidad Nacional de Educación a Distancia.

Nunnally, J. C., (1970). *Introducción a la medición psicológica.* Argentina: Paidós.

Rebollo, P., Castejón, I., Cuervo, J., Villa, G., García-Cueto, E., Díaz-Cuervo, H., Zardaín, P., Muñiz, J., & Alonso, J. (2010). Validation of a computer-adaptive test to evaluate generic health-related quality of life. *Health and quality of life outcomes,* 8, 147-156.

Resnick, L. B. (1976). *The nature of intelligence.* New Jersey: Lawrence Erlbaum Associates.

Sternberg, R. J. (1990). *Metaphors of mind. Conceptions of the Nature of Intelligence.* Cambridge University Press: Cambridge.

In: Handbook of Academic Performance
Editors: Rolf Haumann and George Zimmer
ISBN: 978-1-62417-888-7
© 2013 Nova Science Publishers, Inc.

Chapter 8

DISCIPLINARY CONSEQUENCE EFFECTS ON THE ACHIEVEMENT OF STUDENTS WITH DISABILITIES: A STATEWIDE EXAMINATION

Kirsten L. Allman[1] and John R. Slate[2]
[1]Klein Independent School District, Klein, TX, US
[2]Sam Houston State University, Huntsville, TX, US

ABSTRACT

In this investigation, we analyzed the effect of disciplinary action (i.e., in-school suspension, out-of-school suspension, and disciplinary alternative education program placement) on the academic achievement (i.e., reading and math) of Texas Grade 9 students ($n = 33,389$) with disabilities (i.e., Learning Disability, Emotional Disturbance, and Other Health Impairment) for the 2008-2009 school year. Students with a disability who received a disciplinary consequence had statistically significantly lower scores in reading and in math on the Texas state-mandated assessments than did students with a disability who did not receive a disciplinary consequence. Effect sizes were small. Implications of our findings are discussed.

For students with disabilities, provisions for assigning school discipline are outlined in the Individuals with Disabilities Act (IDEA) of 1997. Specified in the law was the provision for school administrators to remove a student with disabilities from his or her regular educational environment for up to a total of 10 school days (IDEA, 1997). Once the 10 days are used, a change in placement procedure must be followed as outlined by the IDEA. The exception to this 10-day rule, however, was established in 2004 when Congress reauthorized the IDEA allowing schools to remove students from their regular educational placement for up to 45 school days regardless of disability, if student offenses included weapons or drugs, or if their behavior inflicted serious bodily injury toward other students or persons (Individuals with Disabilities Education Improvement Act, 2004). The continued use of school consequences in which students are removed from their regular educational placement has been a recent area of interest with the accountability measures of the No Child Left Behind Act (NCLB, 2001). Called for in the NCLB Act are high standards of learning by all students; the act specifically addresses students with disabilities because students served in special education have consistently performed lower than their non-disabled peers on standardized assessments (Amuso, 2007; O'Reilly, Fafard, Wagner, Schiller, and Brown, 2006). Because student achievement has been consistently documented to be directly related to students' opportunities to learn (Baker et al., 2001; Sailor, Stowe, Turnbull, and Kleinhammer-Tramill, 2007; Wang, Haertel, and Walberg, 1997), the impact of school discipline that removes students with disabilities from their general education placement must be examined. Each time students are removed from their regular educational placement, they receive one less opportunity for learning to occur in the classroom environment. Negative relationships have been established between removal from class and academic achievement. This removal from students' educational placement might be a contributing factor to the current educational gap that exists between students with disabilities and their non-disabled peers (Christle et al., 2004; Costenbader and Markson, 1998; Krezmien, Leone, and Achilles, 2006; Williams, 2007). For educators to meet the standards set by the NCLB Act and to continue to make Adequate Yearly Progress (AYP) as outlined in federal legislation, the academic achievement of special education students must increase. In fact, the most recent federal regulations (34 C.F.R. Part 200) mandated that states include scores of no less than 97% of all students with disabilities in state assessment reporting (U. S. Department of Education, 2007). This regulation raises the standard for the academic achievement of students with disabilities and calls for a high level of performance, because the passing standard is the same for both students with and without disabilities. Now that components of AYP encompass the monitoring and analysis of the performance of subgroups such as students with disabilities, it is critical that school discipline be evaluated to identify the possible effects that school consequences might have on the academic achievement of students with disabilities. If a school fails to meet AYP for two consecutive years, the school or district will be required to provide students with supplemental educational services, a choice of schools for students to attend, and other corrective actions (Texas Education Agency, 2009a). In addition to AYP accountability, if the removal of students with disabilities from their educational environment is not addressed, students might continue to suffer academically, become at risk for dropping out of school and for more serious behaviors as they become older (Achilles, McLaughlin, and Croninger, 2007; Dunn, Chambers, and Rabren, 2004). Numerous researchers have demonstrated the presence of negative relationships between academic achievement and discipline consequences that remove students from the general education environment without regard to disability status. For example, Christle, Nelson, and Jolivette (2004) analyzed the effect of school suspension on student achievement as measured by the Kentucky state assessment for students in Grade 6, Grade 7, and Grade 8. They documented the presence of statistically significant differences in academic achievement between students who received school suspension and students who did not receive suspensions. Similar findings have been reported by other researchers (e.g., Amuso, 2007; Kralevich, 2007; Lassen, Steele, and Sailor, 2006; Sheffield-Coley, 2009; Warren, 2007; Waters-Maze, 2002; Zentner, 2001) who have examined the relationship between academic achievement and student discipline for students in middle school. Warren (2007), for example, analyzed students' disciplinary infractions and academic achievement for students in Grade 8 across four different states. He established that a statistically significant relationship was present between student discipline and reading achievement. In fact, as the number of discipline infractions increased, achievement in reading decreased (Warren, 2007). Waters-Maze (2002) determined that a statistically negative correlation between school suspension and academic achievement was present for students in Grades 6 through 11. Most recently, Sheffield-Coley (2009) analyzed in-school suspension and out-of-school suspension and established the presence of statistical significance between in-school suspension and academic achievement, and out-of-school suspension and academic achievement for English language arts, math, science, and social studies.

SIGNIFICANCE OF THE STUDY

Student achievement has been linked to students' opportunities to learn (Baker et al., 2001; Sailor et al., 2007). Each time students are removed from their general educational environment for school consequences, they have fewer opportunities to learn than students who are not removed from the general education environment. Although researchers (e.g., Amuso, 2007; Rysewyk, 2008; Sheffield-Coley, 2009; Warren, 2007) have documented the negative relationship between the removal of students from their general education environment and academic achievement, limited research is available regarding the impact disciplinary sanctions might have on the academic achievement of students with disabilities. An analysis of the discipline consequences and test scores for students with disabilities might result in consideration for a change of disciplinary practices that currently remove students from their general educational environment. Students receiving special education services appear to have a greater risk for disciplinary actions that remove them from the general education setting more often than their non-disabled peers (Drakeford, 2006; Texas Appleseed, 2010; Texas Education Agency, 2009b). Moreover, students receiving special education services consistently perform at an academic level lower than their non-disabled peers. This overrepresentation of school discipline resulting in the removal of students with disabilities from educational programs, and the current achievement gap of students with disabilities, creates the need for the discipline rates to be examined further (Cooley, 1995; Leone et al., 2000; Zhang, Katsiyannis, and Herbst, 2004).

Research Question

The following research question was addressed in this study: What is the effect of disciplinary action on the academic achievement of students with disabilities in Grade 9?

METHOD

Participants

All students who received special education services and who were enrolled in Texas public schools for the 2008-2009 school year represented the population for this study. The sample size selected for the study included only students with disabilities in Grade 9 . Participants must have received a score for the Texas Assessment of Knowledge and Skills/ Texas Assessment of Knowledge and Skills-Accommodated English Language Arts/Reading and Mathematics assessment for the 2008-2009 school year. In addition, students must have had a primary disability classified as either a learning disability, emotional disability, or other health impairment. Frequency counts for each of the variables included in the study for students in Grade 9 for the 2008-2009 school year in Texas are presented in 1.

The total sample of students with disabilities in Grade 9 was 33,389 students. Out of this sample size, 15,648 students received a disciplinary consequence during the 2008-2009 school year, and 17,741 students did not receive any disciplinary consequences during the 2008-2009 school year.

Four disciplinary actions were included in this study. The first disciplinary action is out-of-school suspension. The term *out-of-school suspension* refers to any disciplinary action that excludes a student from the school property for a specified period of time (Christle et al., 2004).

Students may return to their regular education setting after the assigned number of days of out-of-school suspension has been served. Another common disciplinary action that will be utilized in this study is in-school suspension. *In-school suspension* is a discipline program in which school administrators assign a student to a designated amount of time in a removed setting because of disruptive behavior (Sheets, 1996). In-suspension programs are usually implemented in separate classrooms on the regular school campuses and are overseen by certified classroom teachers (Short, 1988).

During in-school suspension, students must also eat lunch in isolation. The third disciplinary action that will be included in this study is disciplinary alternative education programs. A *disciplinary alternative education program* (DAEP) is a campus within a school district that serves as a different placement for students for committing a disciplinary offense (Carpenter-Aeby and Kurtz, 2000). A DAEP is a temporary placement wherein students receive their academic instruction (Texas Education Agency, 2007a).

Table 1. Frequency Counts of Variables for Students with Disabilities in Grade 9

Variable	n
Grade 9 Students	33,389
Students receiving any disciplinary consequences	15,648
Students receiving no disciplinary consequences	17,741
Black students	7,045
Hispanic students	15,411
White students	10,673
Students with emotional disturbance	3,541
Students with a learning disability	24,723
Students with other health impairment	5,125
Students receiving in-school suspension	13,919
Students receiving out-of-school suspension	7,346
Students receiving disciplinary alternative education placements	3,156
Students expelled from school	14

Disciplinary alternative education programs also provide special education services to students who receive these services in their general school setting. Finally, this study will also include expulsion. When a student receives an *expulsion* from school, the student must withdraw from the school completely and is removed from school (Kemerer and Walsh, 2000). The student is also not permitted to attend the school district's disciplinary alternative education program (Kemerer and Walsh, 2000).

In this study, three disability categories within special education were explored. These disabilities are Learning Disability, Emotional Disturbance, and Other Health Impairment. Federal legislation under the IDEA defines a *learning disability (LD)* as:

> A disorder in one or more of the basic psychological processes involved in understanding or in using language, spoken or written, that might manifest itself in the imperfect ability to listen, think, speak, read, write, spell, or to do mathematical calculations, including conditions such as perceptual disabilities, brain injury, minimal brain dysfunction, dyslexia, and developmental aphasia. (U.S. Department of Education, 2006, para. 10)

Additionally the student must be identified by a multidisciplinary team as having a "severe discrepancy" between his or her academic achievement and intellectual ability (Texas Education Agency, 2006, p. A-8). *Emotional Disturbance (ED)* is defined by Federal legislation under IDEA as:

> A student who exhibits one or more of the following characteristics over a long period of time and to a marked degree that adversely affects a child's educational performance: (a) an inability to learn that cannot be explained by intellectual, sensory, or health factors; (b) an inability to build or maintain satisfactory interpersonal relationships with peers and teachers; (c) inappropriate types of behavior or feelings under normal circumstances; (d) a general pervasive mood of unhappiness or depression; or (e) a tendency to develop physical symptoms or fears associated with personal or school problems. (U.S. Department of Education, 2006, para. 4ii)

The final disability to be included in this research study is *Other Health Impairment (OHI)*. According to federal legislation for students with disabilities, a student with OHI is defined as a student who has:

> Limited strength, vitality, or alertness, including a heightened alertness to environmental stimuli, that results in limited alertness with respect to the educational environment that— 1)Is due to chronic or acute health problems such as asthma, attention deficit disorder or attention deficit hyperactive disorder, diabetes, epilepsy, a heart condition, hemophilia, lead poisoning, leukemia, nephritis, rheumatic fever, sickle cell anemia, and Tourette syndrome; and 2)Adversely affects a child's educational performance. (U.S. Department of Education, 2006, para. 9)

Instrumentation and Procedures

In this study, archival data were utilized from the Texas Education Agency (TEA) for the 2008-2009 school year. Data for all students attending Texas public school in Grade 9 who qualified as a student with a disability were received. Data consisted of students' scaled scores for the Texas Assessment of Knowledge and Skills English Language Arts (ELA)/Reading and Math measures. Additionally, data were obtained that included the students' disciplinary placements, ethnic membership, and disability type. These data were obtained from the TEA as reported in the Public Education Information Management Systems database.

The Texas Assessment of Knowledge and Skills (TAKS) is an assessment program measuring student mastery of the state-mandated curriculum for varying grade levels and content areas to help teachers determine the degree to which students are mastering the content. It is also designed to help educators evaluate their effectiveness in schools and districts throughout Texas. The TAKS measures were developed as a result of Senate Bill 103, enacted during the 76th Session of the Texas Legislature in 1999. Called for in Senate Bill 103 was a new testing program to be implemented statewide (Texas Education Agency, 2008c).

To assist the TEA in meeting this new state mandate, a committee of educators and individuals from the general public examined the Texas Essential Knowledge and Skills (TEKS) and identified objectives for each subject area in every grade level that should be assessed. After a series of reviews and drafts, the objectives were finalized and published and the new assessment was named the TAKS.

The Texas Assessment of Knowledge and Skills Accommodated (TAKS-A) is an accommodated version of the TAKS assessment for students with disabilities. Students must meet eligibility for special education services and meet eligibility requirements for specific accommodations. Specific accommodations are allowed on the TAKS-A assessment, however, they must be determined on an individual basis by each student's Annual Review Dismissal committee.

The committee must meet at least once a year and among other things, they must determine student eligibility for the TAKS-A assessment and make accommodation recommendations. Embedded field-test questions are not included in the TAKS-A assessment; however, it includes format accommodations that are not included on the TAKS assessment. Examples of format accommodations for the TAKS-A assessment include larger font size and fewer test items per page (Texas Education Agency, 2008c).

Permission was obtained from the Texas Education Agency (TEA) to utilize data included in the Public Education Information Management System (PEIMS) database as the instrument for this study. The TEA requires all school districts to provide data that are collected into the PEIMS. These data are placed into the reporting system by school district personnel and are compiled by the TEA for reporting (Texas Education Agency, 2008a). School districts are required by TEA to report data four times throughout each school year. The collection includes the following groups of information: (a) organization, (b) finance, (c) staff, and (d) students. For the purpose of this study, variables included in the student information section of the PEIMS were analyzed. This database provided archival data collected by the TEA from local education agencies. The database included all of the necessary information needed to address the research questions previously delineated, as it included the following student information: (a) disability type, (b) discipline reports, (c) ethnic membership, (d) TAKS ELA, Reading, and Math scores, and (e) TAKS-A ELA, Reading, and Math scores.

The TEA provides school districts with detailed information on the requirements for submission and timelines for when the data must be submitted (Texas Education Agency, 2008a). Data submitted to the TEA by school districts are entered electronically through a software program that allows data to be extracted from school district data systems and are sent to TEA for reporting in the PEIMS. This method has:

> (a) a standard set of definitions, codes, formats, procedures and dates for the collection of data published as the PEIMS Data Standards, (b) standard edit procedures, (c) an established database design, (d) a production system to format and load data into the TEA enterprise database, and (e) written documentation describing the numeric and alphanumeric values stored in the database published as the Data Documentation. (Texas Education Agency, 2007b, para. 1)

As discussed previously, the PEIMS database encompasses student information such as ethnicity and disability type. Moreover, also provided in this database was the number of times each student received a disciplinary consequence that removed the student from the general education setting and included the number of days the student was removed from the classroom. The TAKS and TAKS-A scores, in the form of scaled scores in the areas of reading, ELA, and math were provided from the PEIMS database (Texas Education Agency, 2009d). A scale score is used for the TAKS assessments rather than a raw score because a scale score allows for "direct comparisons of student performance between specific sets of test questions from different test administrations" (Texas Education Agency, 2009d, para. 1). To determine a student's scale score, the raw score (the number of questions a student answered correctly on a particular set of questions) is converted into a:

> Scale that is common to all test forms for that assessment. The scale score takes into account the difficulty level of the specific set of questions on which it is based. It quantifies a student's performance relative to the passing standards or proficiency levels. (Texas Education Agency, 2009d, para. 1)

Scoring and reporting for the TAK-A assessment is the same as described for the TAKS assessments. The TAKS-A is a form of the TAKS assessment that provides formatting accommodations for students with disabilities and does not include embedded field-test items (Texas Education Agency, 2009c). However, it is still a measure of students' mastery of the TEKS. As such, the TEA includes results of students' performances on the TAKS-A assessments in campus and district reports for the Academic Excellence Indicator System (Texas Education Agency, 2008b). Students' scores on the TAKS-A assessments are included for state accountability ratings. Therefore, TAKS and TAKS-A scores were analyzed together to measure academic achievement in this study.

The data file, obtained from the TEA on a compact disc in a SAS file, contained information for the Reading/ELA TAKS. Math data were sent electronically and were merged with the SAS file.

The file was opened and analyzed in SPSS. The first step in data analysis was to obtain the frequency counts of students by ethnic membership and by disability type. Next, string variables were recoded to numeric values to permit SPSS to perform statistical operations. Once this relabeling and recoding had occurred, further analysis was conducted for each variable.

RESULTS

To determine the extent to which disciplinary consequences influenced the academic achievement of students with disabilities in Grade 9, several statistical analyses were conducted. Independent variables for the multivariate analysis of variance procedure (MANOVA) were disciplinary consequences (i.e., in-school suspension, out-of-school suspension, disciplinary alternative education programs, or expulsion), followed by each disciplinary sanction. Dependent variables were students' scaled scores on the TAKS Reading assessment and TAKS Math assessment.

A MANOVA was conducted to determine if a difference was present in academic achievement between students who received discipline consequences that removed them from the general education environment and students who did not receive such discipline consequences. The results of the MANOVA were statistically significant, Wilks Λ = .97, F(2, 33386) = 444.42, p < .001, n^2 = .026. Using Cohen's (1988) criteria for effect size associated with this difference, as defined by Partial Eta squared, the effect size was small. A follow-up ANOVA yielded statistical significance for the TAKS Reading scores, F(1, 33387) = 382.93, p < .001, n^2 = .011, a small effect size (Cohen, 1988). Similar results were yielded for the TAKS Math measure, F(1, 33387) = 789.70, p < .001, n^2 = .023, a small effect size (Cohen, 1988). Table 2 presents the descriptive statistics for the TAKS Reading and TAKS Math assessments for students with disabilities in Grade 9. As observed in Table 2, students who did not have disciplinary consequences that removed them from their general education setting had higher mean scores on both the TAKS Reading and TAKS Math assessments than students who received a disciplinary consequence. Next, each individual disciplinary sanction was examined to determine if a difference was present in academic achievement between students who received that particular disciplinary sanction and students who did not receive that specific disciplinary sanction. However, a sufficient number of cases were not present in the analysis for expulsion because of the very few ninth-grade students with disabilities who were expelled during the 2008-2009 school year. Therefore, results were not reported for expulsion.

Table 2. Descriptive Data for Discipline Consequences, TAKS Reading, and TAKS Math for Students with Disabilities in Grade 9

Variable	n	M	SD
Students not receiving discipline consequences			
Reading	17,741	2,120.65	193.57
Math	17,741	2,025.40	221.05
Students receiving discipline consequences			
Reading	15,648	2,076.00	223.39
Math	15,648	1,951.89	256.91

In-School Suspension and Academic Achievement

A MANOVA was conducted to determine if a difference was present in TAKS reading scores between students who received in-school suspension and students who did not receive in-school suspension in Grade 9. The results were statistically significant, Wilks Λ = .98, $F(2, 33386)$ = 287.56, p < .001, n^2 = .017. This effect size was small (Cohen, 1988). Table 3 presents the descriptive statistics for the TAKS Reading and TAKS Math assessments and in-school suspension for students with disabilities in Grade 9.

Table 3. Descriptive Data for In-School Suspension, TAKS Reading, and TAKS Math for Students with Disabilities in Grade 9

Variable	n	M	SD
Students not receiving in-school suspension			
Reading	19,470	2,115.22	199.63
Math	19,470	2,015.87	229.56
Students receiving in-school suspension			
Reading	13,919	2,078.05	220.23
Math	13,919	1,956.09	252.81

The results of a follow-up ANOVA were also statistically significant for the TAKS Reading scores, $F(1, 33387)$ = 258.10, p < .001, n^2 = .008, a trivial effect size (Cohen, 1988). Similarly, results were statistically significant for the TAKS Math measure, $F(1, 33387)$ = 505.65, p < .001, n^2 = .015, a small effect size (Cohen, 1988). As observed in Table 3, students who did not receive in-school suspension had higher mean scores on both the TAKS Reading and TAKS Math assessment than students who received in-school suspension.

Out-of-School Suspension and Academic Achievement

A MANOVA, performed to determine whether a difference was present in academic achievement between students who received out-of-school school suspension and students who did not receive out-of-school suspension, was statistically significant, Wilks Λ = .97, $F(2, 33386)$ = 571.36, p < .001, n^2 = .033. Using Cohen's (1988) criteria for effect size, this difference reflected a small effect size. Table 4 presents the descriptive statistics for the TAKS Reading assessment, TAKS Math assessment, and out-of-school suspension for students with disabilities in Grade 9. The follow-up ANOVA was statistically significant for the TAKS Reading scores, $F(1, 33387)$ = 496.58, p < .001, n^2 = .015. Using Cohen's (1988) criteria for effect size, this difference reflected a small effect size.

Table 4. Descriptive Data for Out-of-School Suspension, TAKS Reading, and TAKS Math for Students with Disabilities in Grade 9

Variable	n	M	SD
Students not receiving out-of-school suspension			
Reading	26,043	2,113.18	197.17
Math	26,043	2,012.91	223.50
Students receiving out-of-school suspension			
Reading	7,346	2,052.03	241.46
Math	7,346	1,913.07	282.59

Similarly, results were statistically significant for the TAKS Math measure $F(1, 33387) = 1010.30$, $p < .001$, $n^2 = .029$. Using Cohen's (1988) criteria for effect size, this difference reflected a small effect size. As observed in Table 4, students who did not have out-of-school suspension had higher mean scores on both the TAKS Reading and TAKS Math assessment than students who received out-of-school suspension.

Disciplinary Alternative Education Programs and Academic Achievement

A MANOVA, calculated to determine whether a difference was present in academic achievement between students who received placements in a disciplinary alternative education program and students who did not receive such placements, yielded a statistically significant result, Wilks $\Lambda = .98$, $F(2, 33386) = 390.49$, $p < .001$, $n^2 = .023$. This effect size was small (Cohen, 1988). Table 5 presents the descriptive statistics for the TAKS Reading and TAKS Math assessment for students with disabilities in Grade 9 and disciplinary alternative education programs.

A follow-up ANOVA, calculated to determine whether a difference was present in TAKS reading scores between students who received placements in a disciplinary alternative education program and students who did not receive such placements, yielded a statistically significant result, $F(1, 33387) = 332.94$, $p < .001$, $n^2 = .01$. This effect size was small (Cohen, 1988). Similar results were yielded for the Math TAKS measure, $F(1, 33387) = 696.75$, $p < .001$, $n^2 = .02$. This effect size was also small (Cohen, 1988). As observed in Table 5, students who did not attend a disciplinary alternative education program had higher mean scores on the TAKS Reading assessment than students who had received a placement in a disciplinary alternative education program.

A statistically significant difference was observed in academic achievement between students who received disciplinary consequences and students who did not receive such consequences for students with disabilities in Grade 9.

In addition, a statistically significant result was present between each of the three disciplinary sanctions and TAKS scores for both reading and math. Table 6 provides a summary of the statistical outcomes regarding the academic achievement of students with disabilities in Grade 9.

Table 5. Descriptive Data for Disciplinary Alternative Education Programs, TAKS Reading, and TAKS Math for Students with Disabilities in Grade 9

Variable	n	M	SD
Students not attending discipline alternative education program			
Reading	30,233	2,106.44	201.94
Math	30,233	2,002.10	230.79
Students attending discipline alternative education program			
Reading	3,156	2,035.37	260.93
Math	3,156	1,884.16	305.50

**Table 6. Summary of Discipline and Academic Achievement Results
for Students in Grade 9**

Disciplinary Type	Outcome	Effect Size	Higher Mean Score
Any disciplinary consequence			
Reading	Significant	.011 (small)	No consequence
Math	Significant	.023 (small)	No consequences
In-school suspension			
Reading	Significant	.008 (trivial)	No suspensions
Math	Significant	.015 (small)	No suspensions
Out-of-school suspension			
Reading	Significant	.015 (small)	No suspensions
Math	Significant	.029 (small)	No suspensions
Disciplinary alternative education program			
Reading	Significant	.01 (small)	No disciplinary alternative education program
Math	Significant	.02 (small)	No disciplinary alternative education program

DISCUSSION

In the research question, the effect of school discipline on the academic achievement of students with disabilities was examined. Statistically significant differences were present between students who did not receive discipline consequences and students who received such consequences for both the TAKS Reading and the TAKS Math measure. These differences might be interpreted to mean that students with disabilities in Grade 9 who did not receive school consequences had higher academic achievement than students who received such consequence. Moreover, a close examination of the TAKS reading scores revealed a passing mean score on the TAKS Reading test for students with disabilities who did not receive any discipline consequences. However, the mean score for students who received school consequences had a mean score below the passing standard as established by the TEA (2009d).

The effect of each type of disciplinary consequence was also examined to address the research question. Students with disabilities who received in-school suspension had lower mean scores for both reading and math than students with disabilities who did not receive in-school suspension. Mean differences in TAKS scores were also present between students with disabilities who received out-of-school suspension and students with disabilities who did not receive such consequences, and students who attended disciplinary alternative education programs had lower mean scores for reading and math than students who did not attend disciplinary alternative education programs. An examination of the mean scores for each type of disciplinary consequence (i.e., in-school suspension, out-of-school suspension, disciplinary alternative education programs) revealed a passing mean score on the TAKS Reading test for students who did not receive any of the school disciplinary sanctions. However, students who received an in-school suspension, out-of-school suspension, or disciplinary alternative education program had a failing mean reading score on the TAKS Reading test.

Much attention has been given to the overrepresentation of students with disabilities in in-school suspension and out-of-school suspension. However, little research is available on the impact these removals have on the academic achievement of students with disabilities (Krezmien et al., 2006). The current achievement gap between students with disabilities and their non-disabled peers, and the overrepresentation of students with disabilities in school disciplinary sanctions has highlighted the need for more research in this area (Krezmein et al., 2006; Severns, 2008; Texas Appleseed, 2010). Therefore, the results of this study provide empirical data on the impact of school disciplinary consequences that remove students with disabilities from their general education environment and academic achievement.

The findings of the present study on the impact of school disciplinary consequences on academic achievement support these findings from earlier research studies (Amuso, 2007; Kralevich, 2007; Lassen et al., 2006; Sheffield-Coley, 2009; Warren, 2007; Waters-Maze, 2002; Zentner, 2001). The present research study also extends the current literature base on the impact of school disciplinary consequences and academic achievement because most researchers have focused their research efforts on the effects of student discipline on the academic achievement of students in Grades 6 through 8. However, data on students with disabilities in Grade 9 were analyzed in this study. Because the early high school years lay the foundation for the rest of high school and result in the highest rates of dropout, more data for students in these grades are needed.

Two researchers who examined school discipline and the academic achievement of high school students reported similar results with the present study (Arcia, 2006; Rysewyk, 2008). In fact, both authors demonstrated statistically significant differences between the academic achievement of students who were removed from their general education environment for discipline consequences and students who did not receive such consequences (Arcia, 2006; Rysewyk, 2008). Additional studies that replicate this study could extend the findings both across regions and time.

Although some researchers have used state assessments similar to the assessments utilized in this study, no research studies were reviewed that specifically examined the population of the present study. Researchers have identified discipline consequences as a possible contributing factor to the low academic achievement of students with disabilities, yet the populations of students with disabilities have not been studied specifically. Subsequently, this study provides empirical data to support the claims that a relationship exists between the academic achievement of students with disabilities and school disciplinary consequences.

One contradiction established as a result of the present study, however, is related to disciplinary alternative education programs. Some researchers reported optimism for the outcome of students who attended disciplinary alternative education programs because disciplinary alternative education programs provided an educational environment for learning in which problematic behavior could be simultaneously addressed (Kemerer and Walsh, 2000). However, the findings from the present study indicated a negative relationship between students who attended a disciplinary alternative education program and student who did not attend such programs and their academic achievement. This negative relationship was present for students with disabilities in Grade 9 on both measures of academic achievement.

IMPLICATIONS

Several alternatives are available to the traditional discipline practices that remove students from the general education environment (IDEA, 1997). Positive Behavior Support, for example, is one alternative that has been documented to decrease student misbehavior that otherwise results in their removal from class or school (Edmonson and Turnbill, 2002; Turnbull et al., 2002; Warren et al., 2003). However, traditional models are still being used in schools today. The results of the present study indicate the need to utilize positive behavior supports. School district leaders and policy makers should consider the impact that school suspensions, disciplinary alternative education programs, and expulsion may have on students with disabilities before developing policies and practices that result in these disciplinary consequences. Current policies should be modified to include more alternative models to address school discipline issues for students with disabilities. An emphasis on appropriate interventions for students with disabilities who exhibit behavior difficulties may also help increase these students' opportunities to learn and improve their overall academic achievement.

Although the effect sizes in this study were all determined to be trivial or small for the present study, these statistical differences accounted for a failing mean score on the TAKS Reading and TAKS ELA assessment for students who received discipline consequences for several of the examined variables. These findings have implications for educational practice, as best practices for teaching students with disabilities should be examined, and ways to increase these students' opportunities to learn should be explored.

RECOMMENDATIONS FOR FUTURE RESEARCH

The present study adds empirical data to the limited base of literature that exists on the impacts of school discipline on the academic achievement of students with disabilities. Further studies are needed in which the impact of school discipline on the academic achievement of high school students with disabilities is examined. In addition, an examination of the effects of alternative disciplinary practices such as positive behavior support that include more opportunities for students to learn could be conducted. This type of study could help school administrators develop more effective disciplinary practices in schools that do not inhibit the academic success of students with disabilities.

Another recommendation for further research is to explore the reasons for the low math achievement of students with disabilities. In the present study, students with disabilities in Grades 9 had failing mean scores on the TAKS Math exam. These failing scores highlight the achievement gap between students with disabilities and their non-disabled peers. Possible factors contributing to these low passing means on the TAKS exam should be explored.

Because the present study only included students in Texas, further studies should be replicated that include students with disabilities in other states. Alternative measures for academic achievement could also be examined. Course grades and national exams are examples of other measures for academic achievement. Research findings from these studies could be helpful in identifying the effects of school discipline on academic achievement for students with disabilities.

REFERENCES

Achilles, G. M., McLaughlin, M. J., and Croninger, R. G. (2007). Sociocultural correlates of disciplinary exclusion among students with emotional, behavioral, and learning disabilities in the SEELS national database. *Journal of Emotional and Behavioral Disorders, 15*(1), 33-45. doi:10.1177/10634266070150010401

Amuso, J. G. (2007). *The occurrence of student absenteeism from the regular school setting and student achievement on the seventh grade mathematics Mississippi curriculum test* (Doctoral dissertation). Available from ProQuest Dissertations and Theses database. (UMI No. 3300838)

Arcia, E. (2006). Achievement and enrollment status of suspended students: Outcomes in a large, multicultural school district. *Education and Urban Society, 38*, 359-369. doi:10.1177/0013124506286947

Baker, J. A., Derrer, R. D., Davis, S. M., Dinklage-Travis, H. E., Linder, D. S., and Nicholson, M. D. (2001). The flip side of the coin: Understanding the school's contribution to dropout and completion. *School Psychology Quarterly, 16*, 406-426. doi:10.1521/scpq.16.4.406.19901

Carpenter-Aeby, T., and Kurtz, P. D. (2000). The portfolio as a strengths-based intervention to empower chronically disruptive students in an alternative school. *Children and Schools, 22*, 217-231.

Christle, C., Nelson, C. M., and Jolivette, K. (2004). School characteristics related to the use of suspension. *Education and Treatment of Children, 27*, 509-526.

Cohen, J. (1988). *Statistical power analysis for the behavioral sciences* (2nd ed.). Hillsdale, NJ: Lawrence Erlbaum.

Costenbader, V. K., and Markson, S. (1998). School suspension: A survey of current policy and practices. *NASSP Bulletin, 78*, 103-107. doi:10.1177/019263659407856420

Drakeford, W. (2006). Racial disproportionality in school disciplinary practices. *Practitioner Brief.* Tempe, AZ: The National Center for Culturally Responsive Educational Systems: Education For All.

Dunn, C., Chambers, D., and Rabren, K. (2004). Variables affecting students' decisions to dropout of school. *Remedial and Special Education, 25*, 314-323. doi:10.1177/07419325040250050501

Edmonson, H., and Turnbill, A. (2002). *Positive behavioral supports: Creating supportive environments at home, in schools, and in the community.* In W. Cohen, L. Nadel, and M. Madnick (Eds.), *Vision for the 21st century* (pp. 357-375). New York, NY: Wiley.

Individuals with Disabilities Education Act Amendments of 1997, 20 U.S.C. § 1400 et seq.

Individuals with Disabilities Education Improvement Act of 2004. Pub.L. No. 108-446. 118 STAT.2647.

Kemerer, F., and Walsh, J. (2000). *The educator's guide to Texas school law* (5th ed.). Austin, TX: University of Texas Press.

Kralevich, M. R. (2007). *Disciplinary placement and student achievement among Texas middle school students.* (Doctoral dissertation). Available from ProQuest Dissertations and Theses database. (UMI No. 3274061).

Krezmien, M. P., Leone, P. E., and Achilles, G. M. (2006). Suspension, race, and disability: Analysis of statewide practices and reporting. *Journal of Emotional and Behavioral Disorders, 14*, 217-226. doi:10.1177/10634266060140040501

Lassen, S. R., Steele, M. M., and Sailor, W. (2006). The relationship of schoolwide positive behavior support to academic achievement in an urban middle school. *Psychology in the Schools, 43*, 701-712. doi:10.1002/pits.20177

No Child Left Behind Act (NCLB) of 2001 (PL 107-110), 20 U.S.C. § 1000 *et seq.*

O'Reilly, F., Fafard, M., Wagner, M., Schiller, E., and Brown, S. C. (2006). *Improving results for students with disabilities: Key findings from the 1997 National Assessment Studies*. Retrieved from http://www.centerforpubliceducation.org/site/apps/nlnet/content3.aspx?c=lvIXIiN0JwEandb=5112895andcontent_id=%7BE2AC61D9-BFFB-4F12-9CA1-710B79CAE5C5%7Dandnotoc=1

Rysewyk, J. W. (2008). *Factors predicting academic success for impoverished urban high school freshman.* (Doctoral dissertation). Available from ProQuest Dissertations and Theses database. (UMI No. 3308030)

Sailor, W., Stowe, M. J., Turnbull, H. R., and Kleinhammer-Tramill, P. (2007). A case for adding a social-behavioral standard to standards-based education with schoolwide positive behavior support as its basis. *Remedial and Special Education, 28*, 366-376. doi:10.1177/ 07419325070280060601

Severns, J. (2008). *Disruptive student behavior: An evaluation study to identify, evaluate and address the problem.* (Doctoral dissertation). Available from ProQuest Dissertations and Theses database. (UMI No. 3350564)

Sheets, J. (1996). Designing an effective in-school suspension program to change student behavior. *NASSP Bulletin, 80*(579), 86-90. doi:10.1177/019263659608057915

Sheffield-Coley, N. V. (2009). *The relationship among the use of corporal punishment, office discipline referrals, in-school suspensions, and out-of-school suspensions on middle school students' achievement in a Georgia school system.* Doctoral Dissertation. (Doctoral Dissertation). Available from ProQuest Dissertations and Theses. (UMI No. 3342224).

Short, P. M. (1988). *Planning and developing in-school suspension programs.* Monographs in Education, C. T. Holmes ed., No. 9. Athens, GA: College of Education.

Texas Appleseed. (2010). *Texas' school-to-prison pipeline: School expulsion-on the path from lockout to lockup.* Austin, TX: Texas Appleseed. Retrieved from http://www.texasappleseed.net/

Texas Education Agency. (2006). *Special Education Rules and Regulations: Individuals with Disabilities Education Act State Board Education Rules Commissioner's Rules Texas State Laws.* Retrieved from http://www.tea.state.tx.us/special.edu/rules

Texas Education Agency. (2007a). *Disciplinary Alternative Education Program Practices.* Retrieved from http://ritter.tea.state.tx.us/ research/pdfs/prr17.pdf

Texas Education Agency. (2007b). *PEIMS - Public Education Information Management System.* Retrieved from http://www.tea.state.tx.us/peims/

Texas Education Agency. (2008a). *PEIMS Data Standards 2008-2009.* Retrieved from http://ritter.tea.state.tx.us/peims/standards/0809/i ndex.html

Texas Education Agency. (2008b). *Scoring and reporting information.* Retrieved from http://ritter.tea.state.tx.us/student.assessment/resources/conferences/tac/2007/2007TACandESCReportingSystemsUpdate.pdf

Texas Education Agency. (2008c). *Student Assessment Division: Texas Assessment of Knowledge and Skills (TAKS) resources.* Retrieved from http://www.tea.state.tx.us/ student.assessment/taks/

Texas Education Agency. (2009a). *Adequate Yearly Progress.* Retrieved from http://ritter.tea.state.tx.us/ayp/

Texas Education Agency. (2009b). *Counts of students and discipline actions by discipline action groupings.* Retrieved from http://ritter.tea.state.tx.us/ cgi/sas /broker?_service=marykayand_program=adhoc.download_ static_DAG_summary.sasanddistrict=andagg_level=STATEandreferrer=Download_State _DAG_Summaries.htmlandtest_flag=and_debug=0andschool_yr=08andreport=01andrep ort_type=htmlandDownload_State_Summary=Submit

Texas Education Agency. (2009c). *TAKS assessment comparison chart for students receiving special education services.* Retrieved from http://ritter.tea.state.tx.us/ student.assessment/resources/ard/TAKS ComparisonChart.pdf

Texas Education Agency. (2009d). *Testing and Accountability: Student Assessment Raw Score Conversion Tables.* Retrieved from http://www.tea.state.tx.us/ index3.aspx?id=3270andmenu_id=793

Turnbull, A., Edmonson, H., Griggs, P., Wickham, D., Sailor, W., Beech, S.,…Warren, J. (2002). A blueprint for schoolwide positive behavior support: full implementation of three components. *Exceptional Children, 68*, 337-402.

U.S. Department of Education. (2006). *Building the legacy of IDEA 2004. Regulations: Part 300/A/300.8 Child with a Disability.* Retrieved from http://idea.ed.gov/ explore/view/p/ %2Croot%2Cregs%2C300%2CA%2C 300%252E8%2C

U.S. Department of Education. (2007). *34 CFR Parts 200 and 300 Title I—Improving the academic achievement of the disadvantaged; Individuals with Disabilities Education Act (IDEA); Final Rule.* Retrieved from http://www.ed.gov/legislation/ FedRegister/finrule/ 2007-2/040907a.pdf

U.S. Department of Education. (2009). *Building the legacy of IDEA 2004. Q and a:* Wang, M. C., Haertel, G. D., and Walberg, H. J. (1997). Learning influences. In H. J. Walberg and G. D. Haertel (Eds.), *Psychology and educational practice* (pp. 199-211). Berkeley, CA: McCatchan.

Warren, A. F. (2007). *The relationship between reported incidents of student discipline and student achievement across four eastern states.* (Doctoral dissertation). Available from ProQuest Dissertations and Theses database. (UMI No. 3300074)

Warren, J., Edmonson, H., Griggs, P., Lassen, S., McCart, A., and Sailor, W. (2003). Urban applications of school-wide positive behavior support: Critical issues and lessons learned. *Journal of Positive Behavior Interventions, 5,* 80-92. doi:10.1177/10983007 030050020301

Waters-Maze, J. (2002). *The effect of school suspension on academic achievement.* (Doctoral dissertation). Available from ProQuest Dissertations and Theses database. (UMI No. 3061765)

Williams, S. D. (2007). *Factors affecting academic achievement of elementary students in the metropolitan Nashville public schools.* (Doctoral dissertation). Available from ProQuest Dissertations and Theses database. (UMI No. 3259040).

Zentner, S. M. (2001). *The relationship between student discipline and student achievement: A multi-linear approach* (Unpublished doctoral dissertation). University of Wisconsin-Madison, Madison, WI.

Zhang, D., Katsiyannis, A., and Herbst, M. (2004). Disciplinary exclusions in special education: A 4-year analysis. *Behavioral Disorders, 29*, 337-347. doi:10.1177/10634266060140040501.

In: Handbook of Academic Performance
Editors: Rolf Haumann and George Zimmer

ISBN: 978-1-62417-888-7
© 2013 Nova Science Publishers, Inc.

Chapter 9

NEW HIGH SCHOOL TEACHERS AND ACCOUNTABILITY RATINGS: A FIVE-YEAR STATEWIDE STUDY

Cynthia Martinez-Garcia and John R. Slate
Sam Houston State University, Huntsville, TX US

ABSTRACT

In this study, we examined 5 most recent years of data (2003-2004 through 2007-2008) from the Academic Excellence Indicator System of the State of Texas regarding new teachers on high school campuses (n of schools > 1000). In particular, we focused on the accountability rating of each high school as it was related with new teachers, new teacher salaries, and minority students. Across all 5 years, statistically significant differences were present, primarily between the Exemplary and Academically Unacceptable high school campuses, in the percent of minority students and in teacher salaries. In 3 of the 5 years, Academically Unacceptable schools had higher percentages of new teachers than did Exemplary high schools. Results were quite consistent across the 5 years of data analyzed. Implications of these findings and suggestions for further research are discussed.

Keywords: beginning high school teachers, statewide educational database analysis, teacher salaries, minority students

INTRODUCTION

Our nation faces great challenges as America seeks to reform its educational system with the goal of leaving no child behind (Joftus and Maddox-Dolan, 2002). With the current policy demands on states and districts to improve school outcomes, many states have implemented programs to address policy mandates. The challenge to reform the American educational system is being addressed through a variety of strategies and approaches; however, perhaps the most essential strategy in achieving success in this endeavor is the need to attract and to retain highly qualified and effective teachers (Joftus and Maddox-Dolan, 2002). Since the early 1980s, teacher quality has been and continues to be a major concern for policymakers, researchers, and educators (Stedman, 2004).

Teacher quality is a critical topic in education reform because of the valuable role that teachers play in improving students' academic success (Darling-Hammond, 2000; Darling-Hammond and Sykes, 2003). This assertion is supported by the findings delineated in an increasing number of research studies. For example, present in the Alliance for Excellent Education (2004) report *Tapping the Potential: Retaining and Developing High-Quality New Teachers* was the comment that the quality of the teacher was the most important factor influencing student achievement. As Whitehurst (2002) stated, "Teacher quality is affected by general knowledge and ability, certification and licensure, experience, intensive and focused in-service training, and alignment between teacher training and standards based reform" (p. 40). Whitehurst (2002) extracted this information from the Elementary and Secondary Education Act (ESEA) provisions. Recent focus on teacher quality and the quality of teaching has been emphasized in numerous research studies (Darling-Hammond, 2000; Darling-Hammond and Sykes, 2003; Obama, 2005; Rice, 2003; Rowland and Coble, 2005; Whitehurst, 2003). Ingersoll (2003) documented that the most important factors influencing the knowledge and the development of students are the quality of teachers and teaching.

Boyd, Lankford, Loeb, and Wyckoff (2005) noted that a highly qualified teacher is defined by teacher certification exam scores and experience. For the past 10 years, many researchers have acknowledged that students at the lowest achieving schools are frequently taught by teachers who lack teaching experience (Allen, Palaich, and Anthes, 1999; Darling-Hammond, 1998; Ingersoll, 1999, 2002; Nieto, 2003; Orfield and Lee, 2005; Peske and Haycock, 2006; Rowland and Coble, 2005). Researchers generally agree that new teachers require from 3 to 7 years of teaching experience to sharpen their teaching abilities and to make gains in promoting their student's academic success (Claycomb and Hawley, 2000). Provasnik and Dorfman (2005) stated that new teachers are typically the least effective teachers, and more experienced teachers are more effective than teachers with 3 or less years of experience. Similarly, the National Center for Educational Statistics (2000) asserted that teachers with more than a few years of experience tend to be the most effective teachers. The Education Trust (2008) stressed that beginning teachers without any teaching experience, who are still developing their skills, are less likely to be as effective in preparing students to meet state standards and in facilitating students' academic achievement as their colleagues with some experience. Regardless of these consistent findings, beginning teachers are assigned to teach the lowest-performing students at risk of failing or dropping out of school (Alliance for Excellent Education, 2004, 2008).

In our opinion, it is unfortunate that many of the teachers considered to be highly qualified are not teaching in the schools where their expertise and skills are needed the most. That is, many researchers have documented that the lowest performing schools have teachers with the least amount of teaching experience although students at the poorest achieving schools desperately need highly qualified teachers (Allen et al., 1999; Darling-Hammond, 1998; Ingersoll, 1999, 2002; Peske and Haycock, 2006; Nieto, 2003; Orfield and Lee, 2005; Rowland and Coble, 2005).

The difference in the types of schools and students that beginning teachers are assigned to teach and the lack of feedback, training, and professional support aimed at helping their most difficult students succeed may increase the likelihood of teachers departing prematurely from the teaching profession (Alliance for Excellent Education, 2004, 2005). As such, this situation results in a deplorable cyclical process for low performing schools and for at risk students. Clear evidence exists that teacher attrition is particularly high with teachers during their first years in the profession (e.g., Ingersoll and Smith, 2003). In fact, Ingersoll (2003) emphasized that new teachers leave the profession at startling rates; after the first year about 14% of beginning teachers leave, after the third year around 33% of the teachers leave, and within five years almost 50% of the teachers leave. Martinez-Garcia, Slate, and Tejeda-Delgado (2008), in a comprehensive study of Texas school districts, noted that teacher turnover was almost twice as high in school districts with higher percentages (i.e., 75% or higher) of minority students than in school districts with lower percentages (i.e., less than 25%) of minority students. These researchers also stated that teacher turnover was 1.5 times greater in Texas school districts with higher percentages (i.e., 50% or higher) of economically disadvantaged students than in Texas school districts with lower percentages (i.e., 50% or less) of economically disadvantaged students (Martinez-Garcia et al., 2008).

In a comprehensive 5-year study on beginning teachers and minority student enrollment in Texas high schools, Martinez-Garcia and Slate (2010a) indicated that beginning teachers were more likely to be hired at Texas high schools with higher percentages of minority students than at Texas high schools with lower percentages of minority students. In a separate study, Martinez-Garcia and Slate (2010b) revealed that Academically Unacceptable elementary campuses had the highest percentages, 82% to 91%, of minority students and the highest percentages of new teachers. Again, in a recent study, Martinez-Garcia and Slate (2012) documented that new teachers were more likely to be employed in Texas elementary schools with higher percentages of minority students and with higher percentages of economically disadvantaged students than at Texas elementary with lower percentages of each.

In the State of Texas schools are rated through its state-mandated accountability system. This state-mandated accountability system provides ratings for both the individual campuses and the school districts. For schools to receive the highest rating, *Exemplary*, the following criteria must be met: at least 90% of students passing the Texas Assessment of Knowledge and Skills (TAKS), as well as subgroups; 95% of the completion standard met; and no more than a 0.2% dropout rate (Texas Education Agency, 2004, 2005, 2006, 2007, 2008). For schools to receive the next highest rating, *Academically Recognized*, the following criteria must be met: at least 75% of students passing the TAKS, as well as subgroups; and 85% of the completion standard; and no greater than a 0.7% dropout rate (Texas Education Agency, 2004, 2005, 2006, 2007, 2008).

For schools to receive the next rating, *Academically Acceptable,* the criteria that must be met are: at least 65% of students pass the English/Language Arts, Writing, and Social Studies portions of the TAKS, as well as subgroups; at least 45% of students pass the TAKS Math, including subgroups; at least 40% of students pass the Science portion of the TAKS, including subgroups; 75% of the completion standard met; and no greater than a 1.0% dropout rate (Texas Education Agency, 2004, 2005, 2006, 2007, 2008). Finally, a rating of *Academically Unacceptable* is assigned to schools that do not meet the aforementioned criteria. Given the tremendous attention placed on accountability in the country today, it should not be surprising that receiving a label of Academically Unacceptable results in sanctions and consequences for the school and school staff.

We were particularly interested in the employment of beginning teachers and teacher characteristics that might be related to the accountability ratings assigned to the Texas public high school campuses in this study. Specifically, to what extent are more beginning teachers present at public high schools with less positive or lower accountability ratings than at public high schools with more positive or higher accountability ratings? Moreover, to what extent are results consistent across five years of data?

Purpose of the Study

Our purposes in conducting this study were twofold: (a) to determine the extent to which high school campus accountability rating was related with new teacher characteristics, and (b) to ascertain the extent to which any findings would be consistent across five years of statewide data. These purposes, if achieved, could provide useful information both to teacher education preparation programs and to educational administrators.

Research Questions

The following research questions were addressed in this study: (a) What is the difference among high school campus accountability ratings in their percent of new teachers, average salary of new teachers, and percent of minority students? and (b) To what degree are any findings consistent across five years of statewide data?

METHOD

Participants

Data from all high public school campuses ($ns > 1000$) in the State of Texas for the school years 2003-2004, 2004-2005, 2005-2006, 2006-2007, and 2007-2008 were utilized in this study. Charter schools were eliminated from consideration. The research questions previously delineated were individually addressed for each of the five years obtained from the State of Texas educational database. Each year the Texas Education Agency posts online aggregated data for each of its school campuses and school districts through the Academic Excellence Indicator System (AEIS).

Instrumentation

Archival data were acquired on all public high school campuses ($ns > 1000$) in the State of Texas for the 2003-2004, 2004-2005, 2005-2006, 2006-2007, and 2007-2008 school years. Through accessing and downloading files from the Academic Excellence Indicator System, data that were reported by each high school campus were gathered. Specifically, data on the number and percent of beginning teachers, the average beginning teacher salary, and the accountability rating at each high school campus were obtained. The Texas Education Agency defines a beginning teacher as "a teacher reported with zero years of experience" (Public Education Information Management System [PEIMS], 2007). Because the data for each of these variables are self-reported by the individual school campuses, traditional reliability and validity estimates are not appropriate. Rather, any errors in these self-reported figures are assumed to be minimal.

Regarding accountability rating, Texas labels school campuses and school districts based on campus and district performance on pre-specified variables. As discussed previously, to receive the highest label of Exemplary, the following criteria must be met: no more than a 0.2% dropout rate; at least 90% of students passing the Texas Assessment of Knowledge and Skills (TAKS), as well as subgroups; and 95% of the completion standard met (Texas Education Agency, 2004, 2005, 2006, 2007, 2008). *Academically Recognized*, the next highest rating, is assigned when these criteria are met: no greater than a 0.7% dropout rate; at least 75% of students passing the TAKS, as well as subgroups; and 85% of the completion standard (Texas Education Agency, 2004, 2005, 2006, 2007, 2008). The lowest minimum label, *Academically Acceptable*, is assigned when: no greater than a 1.0% dropout rate; at least 65% of students pass the English/Language Arts, Writing, and Social Studies sections of the TAKS, as well as subgroups; at least 45% of students pass the TAKS Math, including subgroups; at least 40% of students pass the TAKS Science measure, including subgroups; and 75% of the completion standard met (Texas Education Agency, 2004, 2005, 2006, 2007, 2008). For school campuses and school districts that do not meet the criteria delineated in the Academically Acceptable rating, the designation of *Academically Unacceptable* is assigned.

Procedures

After accessing the Texas Education Agency's Academic Excellence Indicator System website, each specific year of interest was accessed. Connection to each AEIS data file of interest (i.e., campus, teacher, and student) was made. Data from each data file were downloaded as .dat files and then merged using the Statistical Package for the Social Sciences-Version 15. Prior to conducting statistical procedures, the underlying assumptions (e.g., normality of data) were checked and verified. Accordingly, the use of parametric statistical procedures was justified.

RESULTS

Overall Analyses

To determine whether (a) the percent of new teachers, (b) the average salary of new teachers, and (c) the percent of minority students enrolled on campus differed as a function of campus accountability rating, a multivariate analysis of variance (MANOVA) was conducted. This analysis yielded a statistically significant result, $\Lambda = .85$, $p < .001$, $n^2 = .05$, small effect size (Cohen, 1988), for the 2007-2008 school year. The same statistical procedure, conducted for the 2006-2007 school year, yielded similar results, $\Lambda = .87$, $p < .001$, $n^2 = .05$, small effect size (Cohen, 1988). For the 2005-2006 school year, the MANOVA, after aggregating the Exemplary high school campuses ($n = 10$) with the Academically Recognized schools, resulted in a statistically significant difference, $\Lambda = .83$, $p < .001$, $n^2 = .09$, moderate effect size (Cohen, 1988).

The MANOVA, performed for the 2004-2005 school year, yielded a statistically significant result, $\Lambda = .91$, $p < .001$, $n^2 = .05$, small effect size (Cohen, 1988). For the 2004-2005 school year, the Exemplary schools ($n = 7$) were merged with the Academically Recognized campuses so that an adequate sample size was present.

Finally, the MANOVA, conducted for the 2003-2004 school year, resulted in a statistically significant difference, $\Lambda = .83$, $p < .001$, $n^2 = .06$, moderate effect size (Cohen, 1988). For all five years of data analyzed, statistically significant results were present, with two effect sizes being moderate and three effect sizes being small.

Percent of New Teachers

For the 2007-2008 school year, the univariate follow-up F revealed a statistically significant difference for the percent of beginning teachers, $F(3, 1044) = 9.22$, $p < .001$, $n^2 = .03$, small effect size (Cohen, 1988). Scheffe` post hocs revealed that the percent of beginning teachers was statistically significantly higher for the Unacceptable high school campuses than for the other three campus accountability ratings. The other high school campuses did not differ in their average percent of beginning teachers. Readers are referred to Table 1 for the descriptive statistics for the percent of beginning teachers by campus accountability rating.

Concerning the 2006-2007 school year, the univariate F did not yield a statistically significant difference for the percent of beginning teachers, $F(3, 1030) = 1.05$, $p = .37$. All four accountability ratings had similar percentages of beginning teachers. Regarding the 2005-2006 school year, the univariate follow-up F did not reveal a statistically significant difference for the percent of beginning teachers, $F(2, 1007) = 1.24$, $p = .29$. This result was similar to the 2006-2007 school year. For the 2004-2005 school year, the univariate follow-up F did not result in a statistically significant difference for the percent of beginning teachers, $F(2, 1017) = 1.99$, $p = .14$.

Concerning the 2003-2004 school year, the univariate follow-up F yielded a statistically significant difference in the percentage of beginning teachers, $F(3, 966) = 5.49$, $p = .001$, $n^2 = .02$, small effect size (Cohen, 1988). Scheffe` post hocs revealed that the Academically Unacceptable high school campuses had higher percentages of beginning teachers than did the Exemplary and Academically Acceptable campuses, but not higher than the Recognized campuses. No other differences in beginning teacher percentages were observed.

Average Salary of Beginning Teachers

Concerning the 2007-2008 school year, the univariate follow-up F revealed a statistically significant difference for the average salary of beginning teachers, $F(3, 1044) = 8.41$, $p < .001$, $n^2 = .02$, small effect size (Cohen, 1988). Scheffe` post hocs indicated that the highest average teacher salaries for beginning teachers were at the Exemplary high school campuses and at the Academically Unacceptable high school campuses.

**Table 1. Descriptive Statistics for the Percent of Beginning Teachers
by Accountability Rating for All School Years**

Variable	n of schools	M	SD
2007-2008			
Percent of Beginning Teachers			
Exemplary	31	6.37	6.99
Recognized	166	8.42	9.43
Acceptable	791	8.59	6.19
Unacceptable	60	13.03	7.24
2006-2007			
Percent of Beginning Teachers			
Exemplary	15	10.25	10.25
Recognized	102	7.90	5.77
Acceptable	839	8.71	6.33
Unacceptable	78	9.25	5.37
2005-2006			
Percent of Beginning Teachers			
Exemplary/Recognized	144	8.49	8.97
Acceptable	778	8.25	6.06
Unacceptable	88	9.40	6.58
2004-2005			
Percent of Beginning Teachers			
Exemplary/Recognized	120	7.64	7.59
Acceptable	869	8.32	7.03
Unacceptable	31	10.47	5.34
2003-2004			
Percent of Beginning Teachers			
Exemplary	11	4.96	3.34
Recognized	237	8.09	8.02
Acceptable	708	9.93	6.10
Unacceptable	14	12.80	8.65

Both of these accountability ratings had statistically higher average beginning teacher salaries than either the Academically Recognized or the Academically Acceptable high school campuses. Academically Recognized and Academically Acceptable high school campuses did not differ in their average salaries for beginning teachers. Readers are referred to Table 2 for the descriptive statistics for beginning teacher average salaries.

Regarding the 2006-2007 school year, the univariate follow-up F yielded a statistically significant difference for the average salary of beginning teachers, $F(3, 1030) = 12.04$, $p < .001$, $n^2 = .03$, small effect size (Cohen, 1988). Scheffe` post hocs indicated that the highest average teacher salaries for beginning teachers were at the Exemplary high school campuses. No other differences were present between accountability rating and beginning teacher average salary.

For the 2005-2006 school year, the univariate follow-up F revealed a statistically significant difference for the average salary of beginning teachers, $F(2, 1007) = 6.80$, $p = .001$, $n^2 = .002$, small effect size (Cohen, 1988). Scheffe` post hocs revealed that the highest average teacher salaries for beginning teachers were at the Academically Unacceptable high school campuses than at either the Exemplary/Recognized or Academically Acceptable campuses.

Concerning the 2004-2005 school year, the univariate follow-up F revealed a statistically significant difference for the average salary of beginning teachers, $F(2, 1017) = 6.12$, $p = .002$, $n^2 = .012$, small effect size (Cohen, 1988). Scheffe` post hocs revealed that the highest average teacher salaries for beginning teachers were at the Academically Unacceptable high school campuses than at either the Exemplary/Recognized or at the Academically Acceptable high school campuses. No difference was present between the Exemplary/Recognized and the Academically Acceptable campuses.

Regarding the 2003-2004 school year, the univariate follow-up F yielded a statistically significant difference in the average salary of beginning teachers, $F(3, 966) = 4.08$, $p = .007$, $n^2 = .01$, small effect size (Cohen, 1988). Scheffe` post hocs revealed that, though an overall difference was present, no pair of accountability ratings differed.

Though not statistically significant, the highest average beginning teacher salary was present at Exemplary high school campuses and the lowest average beginning teacher salary was at the Academically Unacceptable high school campuses.

Minority Student Enrollment

Regarding the 2007-2008 school year, the univariate follow-up F revealed a statistically significant difference for the percent of minority students on campus, $F(3, 1044) = 49.26$, $p < .001$, $n^2 = .12$, large effect size (Cohen, 1988). Scheffe` post hocs revealed that the Academically Unacceptable high school campuses had the highest average percent of minority student enrollment than the other three accountability ratings. Academically Recognized high school campuses had the lowest percentage of minority students. Exemplary and Academically Acceptable did not differ in their percentages of minority student enrollment. For the 2006-2007 school year, the univariate follow-up F resulted in a statistically significant difference for the percent of minority students on campus, $F(3, 1030) = 43.25$, $p < .001$, $n^2 = .11$, near-large effect size (Cohen, 1988). Scheffe` post hocs indicated that the Academically Unacceptable high school campuses had the highest average percentage of minority students than the other accountability ratings, except for the Exemplary campuses. Academically Recognized high school campuses had the lowest percentage of minority students. The Exemplary and the Academically Acceptable also did not differ in their percentages of minority student enrollment. Readers are referred to Table 3 for the descriptive statistics for the percent of minority student enrollment by campus accountability rating.

Concerning the 2005-2006 school year, the univariate follow-up F yielded a statistically significant difference for the percent of minority students on campus, $F(2, 1007) = 98.59$, $p < .001$, $n^2 = .16$, large effect size (Cohen, 1988). Scheffe` post hocs revealed that the Academically Unacceptable high school campuses had the highest average percentage of minority students than did the other accountability ratings. Exemplary/Recognized high school campuses had the lowest percentage of minority students. Regarding the 2004-2005 school year, the univariate follow-up F revealed a statistically significant difference for the percent of minority students on campus, $F(2, 1017) = 46.98$, $p < .001$, $n^2 = .08$, moderate effect size (Cohen, 1988). Scheffe` post hocs revealed that the Academically Unacceptable high school campuses had the highest average percentage of minority students than did the other accountability ratings.

Table 2. Descriptive Statistics for Average Salaries of Beginning Teachers by Accountability Rating for All School Years

Variable	n of schools	M	SD
2007-2008			
Average Salary of Beginning Teachers			
Exemplary	31	$40,448.19	$6,295.68
Recognized	166	$36,146.22	$6,510.59
Acceptable	791	$37,424.60	$5,671.66
Unacceptable	60	$39,654.58	$5,378.15
2006-2007			
Average Salary of Beginning Teachers			
Exemplary	15	$42,227.87	$3,389.27
Recognized	102	$33,267.78	$6,414.40
Acceptable	839	$35,967.60	$5,801.18
Unacceptable	78	$35,538.99	$7,711.52
2005-2006			
Average Salary of Beginning Teachers			
Exemplary/Recognized	144	$31,200.35	$6,643.96
Acceptable	778	$32,851.56	$5,614.85
Unacceptable	88	$33,800.25	$5,220.14
2004-2005			
Average Salary of Beginning Teachers			
Exemplary/Recognized	120	$31,121.41	$7,306.68
Acceptable	869	$31,654.42	$5,337.35
Unacceptable	31	$35,023.97	$5,440.07
2003-2004			
Average Salary of Beginning Teachers			
Exemplary	11	$33,352.00	$7,661.84
Recognized	237	$30,497.40	$5,103.99
Acceptable	708	$31,453.95	$5,266.92
Unacceptable	14	$28,215.29	$5,167.59

Exemplary/Recognized high school campuses had the lowest percentage of minority students, with Academically Acceptable high school campuses being in the middle in terms of their percentages of minority student enrollment. For the 2003-2004 school year, the univariate follow-up F yielded a statistically significant difference in the percent of minority students on campus, $F(3, 966) = 53.36$, $p < .001$, $n^2 = .14$, large effect size (Cohen, 1988). Scheffe` post hocs revealed that the Academically Unacceptable high school campuses had the highest average percentage of minority students than the other accountability ratings except for the Academically Acceptable campuses. The Recognized high school campuses had the lowest percentage of minority students but did not differ from the Exemplary campuses.

**Table 3. Descriptive Statistics for Minority Student Percentage
by Accountability Rating for All School Years**

Variable	n of schools	M	SD
2007-2008			
Percent of Minority Students on Campus			
Exemplary	31	57.44	33.66
Recognized	166	32.32	25.37
Acceptable	791	55.34	28.94
Unacceptable	60	79.78	25.46
2006-2007			
Percent of Minority Students on Campus			
Exemplary	15	64.13	36.19
Recognized	102	26.62	22.59
Acceptable	839	52.15	29.52
Unacceptable	78	74.96	28.76
2005-2006			
Percent of Minority Students on Campus			
Exemplary/Recognized	144	26.45	23.42
Acceptable	778	51.75	29.25
Unacceptable	88	78.79	23.46
2004-2005			
Percent of Minority Students on Campus			
Exemplary/Recognized	120	30.82	25.87
Acceptable	869	50.74	29.72
Unacceptable	31	83.82	23.36
2003-2004			
Percent of Minority Students on Campus			
Exemplary	11	41.14	39.16
Recognized	237	29.23	23.52
Acceptable	708	55.26	29.66
Unacceptable	14	74.01	34.42

DISCUSSION

In this study, we examined characteristics of high schools in the State of Texas concerning the employment of beginning teachers over a 5-year time period. Of the five multivariate analyses performed, all 5 procedures resulted in statistically significant differences. Effect sizes, or practical importance of these analyses, ranged from small to moderate (Cohen, 1988). What these overall analyses revealed was that differences were present in where beginning teachers were employed for each of the last five school years, particularly in terms of the accountability rating of each high school campus.

Out of the 5 years of data analyzed in this study, as the accountability rating of the school improved, the percent of beginning teachers declined in 3 of the 5 years, albeit statistically significantly so in only 2 of the 5 years. For example, in the most recent school year, 2007-2008 (see Table 1), 13.03% of beginning teachers were present at high schools rated as being

Academically Unacceptable, compared with only 6.37% of beginning teachers at Exemplary high schools. The percent of beginning teachers at the Academically Unacceptable high schools was more than twice the percent of beginning teachers at the Exemplary high schools for two years. In 3 of the 5 years, beginning teacher percentages were notably higher in Academically Unacceptable high schools. Though our results were not as strong in this study, our findings were commensurate with a multi-year study conducted by Martinez-Garcia and Slate (2010b) about beginning teachers employed at Texas elementary schools. They documented that beginning teacher percentages statistically significantly increased as the elementary school accountability rating decreased. More specifically, Martinez-Garcia and Slate (2010b) reported that the percent of beginning teachers was almost twice as high at the Academically Unacceptable elementary schools than at the Exemplary elementary schools.

Interestingly, the average salary of beginning teachers was highest at the Exemplary high school campuses for 3 of the 5 school years examined. In fact, the average beginning teacher salary at Exemplary high schools was higher than the average salary of beginning teachers at Academically Unacceptable schools for 3 of the 5 school years. These results are commensurate with the findings of Martinez-Garcia and Slate (2011) in their study on average salaries of beginning teachers at middle school campuses. We believe that further research needs to be conducted to determine the reasons for these findings.

Our third set of results involved higher percentages of minority students being enrolled at the Academically Unacceptable high schools than at Academically Acceptable, Recognized, and Exemplary high schools. In 3 of the 5 years of data analyzed, as the accountability rating improved, the percentage of minority students decreased. Of interest is that the effect sizes for the five years analyzed were moderate to large (Cohen, 1988) in which the Academically Unacceptable high schools had the highest percentages, 74% to 84%, of minority students. A strong and clear difference exists in the accountability rating of high school campuses and the percentage of enrolled minority students. Interesting, our findings in regard to minority student enrollment are congruent to the strong findings of Martinez-Garcia and Slate (2010b) in their study of minority student enrollment and beginning teachers at Texas elementary schools in which the Academically Unacceptable elementary schools had the highest percentages, 82% to 91%, of minority students.

Also, our findings were similar to the findings of Martinez-Garcia and Slate (2012) study in which the new teachers were more likely to be employed in Texas elementary schools with higher percentages of minority students and with higher percentages of economically disadvantaged students. Additionally, our findings were congruent to the findings of Martinez-Garcia and Slate (2010a) study in which new teachers were likely to be employed in Texas high schools with higher percentages of minority students.

Based on results obtained in this study, higher percentages of beginning teachers were employed at Texas high schools determined to be low-performing schools. Unfortunately, minority students at underprivileged schools usually have the highest concentration of beginning teachers who are still learning the profession rather than having more experienced teachers (Education Trust, 2008; Jepsen and Rivkin, 2002; Peske and Haycock, 2006; U.S. Department of Education, National Center for Education Statistics, 2000) who are familiar with the profession and know how to help students with many learning needs succeed academically.

As mentioned previously, beginning teachers are often assigned to the most difficult classrooms with little support (Alliance for Excellent Education, 2004). Though no evidence was present about support, results in this study support the assignment of beginning teachers to schools with high-needs students. In addition, the Education Trust (2008) documented that, in Texas school districts, 43 of the 50 largest school districts had higher percentages of beginning teachers in their underprivileged schools and had a larger impact on the achievement gaps by student subgroups.Several caveats are presented to avoid overgeneralizing.

First, this study represents a causal-comparative research design and, as such, cause-and-effect results are not yielded. Second, a limited set of variables were investigated that relate to the employment of beginning teachers at high school campuses. Third, data from only one state were examined. Accordingly, readers are urged to be cautious to the extent that they generalize from the results delineated in this investigation. Researchers are encouraged to extend this study by examining other schooling situations and student characteristics related to beginning teachers. In particular, beginning teachers and their employment in other states or in school districts at various school levels (i.e., elementary schools, middle schools, and high schools) need to be addressed.

REFERENCES

Allen, M., Palaich, R., and Anthes, C. (1999). *Teacher recruitment, preparation and retention for hard-to-staff schools*. A Report of the August 29-20, 1999 Meeting in Chicago, IL. Denver, CO: Education Commission of the States. Retrieved from http://www.ecs.org/ initiatives/geringer/chicago%20hard-to-staff%20meeting%20report.htm

Alliance for Excellent Education. (2004). *Tapping the potential: Retaining and developing high-quality new teachers*. Washington, DC: Author.

Alliance for Excellent Education. (2005, August). *Teacher attrition: A costly loss to the nation and to the states*. (Issue Brief). Retrieved from http://www.all4ed.org/files/archive /publications/TeacherAttrition.pdf

Alliance for Excellent Education. (2008, February). *What keeps good teachers in the classroom? Understanding and reducing teacher turnover*. (Issue Brief) Retrieved from http://www.all4ed.org/files/TeachTurn.pdf

Bolich, A. M. (2001). *Reduce your losses: Help new teachers become veteran teachers*. A Report Prepared by the Southern Regional Educational Board. Retrieved from http://www.sreb.org/main/highered/reducelosses.asp

Borman, G. D., and Dowling, N. M. (2008). Teacher attrition and retention: A meta-analytic and narrative review of the research. *Review of Educational Research, 78*, 367-409.

Cohen, J. (1988). *Statistical power analysis for the behavioral sciences* (2nd ed.). New York, NY: Wiley.

Darling-Hammond, L. (1998, September). *How can we ensure a caring, competent, qualified teacher for every child?* National Commission on Teaching and America's Future. Paper presented at the American Federation of Teachers/National Education Association Joint Conference, Washington, DC. Retrieved from http://www.middleweb.com/ TchRcrtLDH.html

Darling-Hammond, L. (2000). Teacher quality and student achievement. A review of state policy evidence. *Education Policy Analysis Archives, 8*, 1. Retrieved from http://epaa.asu.edu/epaa/v8n1/

Darling-Hammond, L., and Sykes, G. (2003). Wanted: A national teacher supply policy for education: The right way to meet the "highly qualified teacher" challenge. *Education Policy Analysis Archives, 11*, 33. Retrieved from http://epaa.asu.edu/epaa/v11n33/

DePaul, A. (2000). *Survival guide for new teachers*. U.S. Department of Education. Office of Research and Improvement [on-line]. Retrieved from http://ed.gov/pubs/survivalguide/

Education Trust. (2008). *Their fair share: How teacher salary gaps shortchange poor children in Texas*. Retrieved from http://www.theirfairshare.org/resources/TheirFairShareFeb08.pdf

Hirsch, E. (2005). *Teacher working conditions are student learning conditions: A report of Governor Easley's 2004 working conditions initiative*. Chapel Hill, NC: Southeast Center for Teaching Quality. Retrieved from http://www.teachingquality.org/pdfs/TWC_FullReport.pdf

Hirsch, E., Emerick, S., Church, K., and Fuller, E. (2006). *Working conditions survey report: Kansas*. Chapel Hill, NC: Center for Teaching Quality.

Ingersoll, R. M. (1999). The problem of underqualified teachers in American secondary schools. *Educational Researcher, 28*(2), 26-37.

Ingersoll, R. M. (2001a). *Teacher turnover, teacher shortages, and the organization of schools*. Seattle, WA: University of Washington, Center for the Study of Teaching and Policy.

Ingersoll, R. M. (2001b). Teacher turnover and teacher shortages: An organizational analysis. *American Educational Research Journal, 38*, 499–534.

Ingersoll, R. M. (2002). *Out-of-field teaching, educational inequality, and the organization of schools: An exploration analysis*. Seattle, WA: University of Washington, Center for the Study of Teaching and Policy.

Ingersoll, R. M. (2003a). *Is there really a teacher shortage?* Seattle, WA: University of Washington, Center for the Study of Teaching and Policy.

Ingersoll, R. M. (2003b). *Out-of-field teaching and the limits of teacher policy*. Seattle, WA: University of Washington, Center for the Study of Teaching and Policy.

Ingersoll, R. M., and Smith, T. M. (2003). The wrong solution to the teacher shortage. *Educational Leadership, 60*(8), 30-33.

Jepsen, C., and Rivkin, S. (2002). *Class size reduction, teacher quality, and academic achievement in California public elementary public schools*. San Francisco, CA: Public Policy Institute of California. (ERIC Document Reproduction Service No. ED 497298)

Joftus, S., and Maddox-Dolan, B. (2002). *New teacher excellence: Retaining our best*. (Report). Alliance for Excellent Education. Washington, DC. Retrieved from http://www.all4ed.org/publications/NewTeacherExcellence/NTE.pdf

Martinez-Garcia, C., and Slate, J. R. (2012). Elementary school campuses and new teachers: A multi-year study. *Education and Urban Society, 44*(1), 83-96. Retrieved from http://eus.sagepub.com/content/early/2010/06/16/0013124510380907doi:10.1177/0013124510380907

Martinez-Garcia, C., and Slate, J. R. (2011, April). *New middle school teachers and accountability rating: A five-year statewide study*. Paper presented at the annual conference of the American Educational Research Association, New Orleans, LA.

Martinez-Garcia, C., and Slate, J. R. (2010a). High school campuses and new teachers: A multi-year statewide study. *Current Issues in Education, 13*(3). Retrieved from http://cie.asu.edu/ojs/index.php/cieatasu/article/view/524

Martinez-Garcia, C., and Slate, J. R. (2010b, April). Elementary schools, new teachers, and minority students: A multi-year study. Paper presented at the annual conference of the American Educational Research Association, Denver, CO.

Martinez-Garcia, C., Slate, J. R., and Tejeda-Delgado, C. (2008). Teacher turnover and student demographics: A three-year analysis of Texas statewide data. *National Journal of Urban Education and Practice, 2*(2), 59-70.

National Commission on Teaching and America's Future. (2002). *Unraveling the "teacher shortage" problem: Teacher retention is the key.* Washington, DC: Author.

National Commission on Teaching and America's Future. (2008). *Learning teams: Creating what's next.* Washington, DC: Author.

National Center for Education Statistics. (2000). *Monitoring school quality: An indicators report.* NCES 2001-030. Washington, DC: U.S. Department of Education, Office of Educational Research and Improvement. Retrieved from http://nces.ed.gov/pubs2001/2001030.pdf

Nieto, S. M. (2003). Going? *Educational Leadership, 60*(8), 15-18.

Obama, B. (2005). *Teaching our kids in a 21st century economy.* Remarks as prepared for delivery at the Center for American Progress, Washington, DC. Retrieved from http://obama.senate.gov/speech/051025-teaching_our_ki/

Orfield, G., and Lee, C. (2005). *Why segregation matters: Poverty and educational inequality.* The Civil Rights Project. Cambridge, MA: Harvard University. (ERIC Document Reproduction Service No. ED 489186).

Orfield, G., Losen, D., Wald, J., and Swanson, C. (2004). *Losing Our Future: How Minority Youth are Being Left Behind by the Graduation Rate Crisis*, Cambridge, MA: The Civil Rights Project at Harvard University. Contributors: Advocates for Children of New York, The Civil Society Institute. Retrieved from http://www.urban.org/UploadedPDF/410936_LosingOurFuture.pdf

Peske, H. G., and Haycock, K. (2006). *Teaching inequality: How poor and minority students are shortchanged on teacher quality.* Washington, DC: The Education Trust. Retrieved from http://www2.edtrust.org/NR/rdonlyres/010DBD9F-CED8-4D2B-9E0D-91B446746ED3/0/TQReportJune2006.pdf

Provasnik, S., and Dorfman, S. (2005). *Mobility in the teacher workforce* (NCES 2005-114). U.S. Department of Education, National Center for Educational Statistics. Washington, DC: U.S. Government Printing Office.

Public Education Network. (2003). *The voice of the new teacher.* Retrieved from http://www.publiceducation.org/pdf/Publications/Teacher_Quality/Voice_of_the_New_Teacher.pdf

Rice, J. K. (2003). *Teacher quality: Understanding the effectiveness of teacher attributes.* Washington, DC: Economy Public Institute.

Rowland, C., and Coble, C., (2005, November). *Targeting teacher recruitment and retention policies for at-risk schools.* (Policy Issues No. 20). North Central Regional Educational Laboratory. (ERIC Document Reproduction Service No. ED 489524).

Stansbury, K., and Zimmerman, J. (2000). *Lifelines to the classroom: Designing support for beginning teachers* (Publication No. RJ96006901). San Francisco, CA: WestEd.

Stedman, J. B. (2004). *K-12 Teacher quality: Issues and legislative action*. Congressional Research Service. The Library of Congress. Washington, DC.

U.S. Department of Education, National Center for Education Statistics. (2000). *Monitoring school quality: An indicators report*. NCES 2001-0300 by Daniel P. Mayer, John E.

Mullen, and Mary T. Moore. John Ralph Project Officer. Washington, DC. (ERIC Document Reproduction Service No. ED 450473).

Whitehurst, G. (2003). *Research on teacher preparation and professional development*. Whitehouse Conference on Preparing Tomorrow's Teachers. Washington, DC. Retrieved from   http://www.ed.gov/admins/tchrqual/learn/preparingteachersconference/white hurst.html

Wilson, B., Ireton, E., and Wood, J. (1997). Beginning teacher fears. *Education, 117*(3), 396-380.

In: Handbook of Academic Performance
Editors: Rolf Haumann and George Zimmer

ISBN: 978-1-62417-888-7
© 2013 Nova Science Publishers, Inc.

Chapter 10

ACADEMIC PERFORMANCE: KEYS TO IMPROVING

Maryurena Lorenzo Alegría and África Borges del Rosal

University of La Laguna,
Santa Cruz de Tenerife, Spain

ABSTRACT

Education has been of concern to different groups from time immemorial; there have been many efforts of professionals, politicians, families, etc., so that children have a quality education. And yet, the problem of low performance is unresolved. Although there are many resources for education, changes of models and laws, the school failure is still a pending issue for many countries. Researchers from different disciplines have tried to find the cause of poor academic performance and what variables are associated with good performance in order to intervene and achieve more successes in education.

1. ACADEMIC PERFORMANCE

The definition of achievement is not without criticism and difficulties. In the literature there are many perspectives and models. However, we could simplify by saying that the adequate performance is one that achieves the best results in the shortest time and effort possible.

Academic performance may be influenced by different elements:

- The students and their knowledge about their progress.
- Teachers and the school activity programming.
- Parents and their monitoring about the children's school performance.
- The administration, which seeks to improve the quality of the system.
- The society, which assesses the effectiveness of the functioning of schools.

As shown, define the concept of academic performance is not an easy task because it is influenced by many variables and all agents have some responsibility on the final product (Brueckner and Bond 1969, cited in Adell, 2002).

1.1. Academic Performance Measures

1.1.1. School Grades

The most common indicator of achievement in the scientific literature is the qualifications. There is consensus about its use because it is a useful measure, socially and legally accepted. However, the discrepancies about the exclusive use of them are also common. So, we find those who say that the rating is not always a true indicator of the conceptual, procedural and attitudinal answers. In fact not always cover the participation and involvement of students, attention or willingness to learn from others. Additionally, is possible to put scores when are not considered the procedures used, the ability to express themselves, to reason or to apply learning to new situations (Adell, 2002).

It is important to consider the role of teachers in school marks; there are a number of factors relating to teachers that could affect the objectivity of the ratings. For example, the fatigue of correcting numerous exams, positive or negative judgment having the teacher on the student, or calligraphy and organization issues.

Also have an important role the type of school, the teacher training or society. For all these influential variables, it is considered that school grades are an indicator, with limitations, to evaluate academic performance (Álvaro-Page et al., 1990).

1.1.2. Objective Test

Objective tests are those in which the answers can be properly evaluated without depending on the judgment of the teacher or examiner. This kind of measurement has many advantages: they have high degree of objectivity because the answers are short and precise and the ratings are independent of the evaluator; have a high degree of validity, as they measure what they purport to measure, in other words, that for which they were developed, and finally, they could be used to compare the answers with other centers, courses, levels or students. However, these tests also have some limitations: the inability to measure some variables such as, composition, writing and organization; there are random responses, and their elaboration has a high degree of difficulty to fulfill the requirements (Álvaro-Page et al., 1990).

2. PREDICTORS OF ACADEMIC PERFORMANCE

There are numerous predictors of academic performance, as many variables that can influence the teaching-learning process. In the scientific literature we can find multiple classifications, depending of performance model is chosen. In this chapter we have selected those that appear with more frequently in literature. First, you could find cognitive factors, then personality factors, and finally, a new predictor variable: the emotional intelligence.

Some authors relate Emotional Intelligence with cognition components and others with personality.

2.1. Cognitive Factors

2.1.1. Intelligence and Skills

The field of mental abilities is almost as wide as the situations where the people can demonstrate, through behavior, their performance according to the demands of the situation. These capabilities can include mental creativity, learning and reading ability and intelligence. In everyday language, there are many synonyms of intelligence that allow us to characterize individuals in reference to their mental capacity. However, in science, the precise meaning of the terms is a prerequisite. Today, the debate continues about the definition of intelligence and its different models (Andrés-Pueyo, 1996).

The intelligence term was introduced by Ciceron. The word intelligence comes from the Latin intellegere, term composed of inter 'between' and legere 'read, pick', so that, etymologically, intelligent is who knows to choose. In other words, intelligence allows you to choose the best options to resolve an issue (Yela, 1987). Starting in the early years twentieth century, the concept of intelligence changed, it was put aside the idea that intelligence was an ability of the soul and were made the first psychological theories. The Phrenology has been contributed to give light to the scientific study of intelligence, and definitely concepts as judgment and perception, among others, were made important and were associated with identifiable parts of the brain (Andres-Pueyo, 1996).

The measurement of intelligence and mental capacity began with Binet and Simon (Binet, Simon and Kite, 1916). Spearman (1927) was the first author to propose a monolithic theory of human intelligence, understood as a general capacity that remains stable over time, the general intelligence factor. The proposal of g factor by Spearman was not accepted by all authors. So that, Thurstone (1938) proposed that the general factor proposed by Spearman was only one of the possible groupings of data through factor analysis. This author extracted seven factors considered equally important mental abilities.

At the end of the sixties, emerged a concern for another point of view about intelligence. So much so, that some authors postulate away models from the g factor to explain what general intelligence could not. Along these lines, Guilford (1967), formulated the Model Structure of Intellect and the existence of other skills such as creativity, divergent thinking or social intelligence. In contrast to the monolithic positions, Gardner (1983) defends the flexibility and plasticity of human capabilities and the resulting effects of specialization and multiplicity. He proposed the Theory of Multiple Intelligences and, later, nine types of intelligence: linguistic-verbal, logical-mathematical, visual-spatial, bodily-kinesthetic, musical, interpersonal, intrapersonal, naturalist and spiritual. Afterwards, Eysenck (1985) proposed the existence of a natural intelligence, psychometric intelligence and social intelligence, claiming that IQ tests only covered a portion of intelligence. So that social intelligence is broader, complex and difficult to delimit. (Andrés-Pueyo, 1996). In this line, Yela (1996) stated that intelligence emerges and enriches along life and he said that it is a complex structure of multiple covariates skills integrated into a dynamic hierarchy. (De Juan-Espinoza, 1997). Similarly, Sternberg (2005) introduced the term successful intelligence to try to explain individual differences.

The evidence collected by Vernon (1950) indicate that a large part of the differences in educational outcomes for individuals can be explained by differences intellectual in the *"g" factor* but part of the variation comes from the *"v:ed " factor* and in a non-intellectual factor he calls*" x "*, which is a set of traits of personality, interests and background characteristics (Tyler, 1975 cited in Casanova, 1988).

Intelligence and intellectual skills are variables with a considerable weight on the academic performance of students, even when it was repeatedly proven that they are not the only determinants of academic success. Intelligence has been the success factor long studied Gilly (1978). In the 50s, several authors showed that general intelligence tests were the best predictors of academic success, especially in mathematics and language. The term intelligence covers many cognitive skills, the distinction between intelligence and skills is quite controversial. Cognitive Skills are part of a taxonomy that helps the description and understanding of intellectual functioning. In studies in this field there are correlations ranging from 0.40 to 0.60 between intelligence and school performance (Álvaro-Page et al., 1990).

Contrary to expectations, in a study that addresses the relationship between emotional intelligence and IQ with academic performance in college students, there are no significant relationship between the variables related to academic performance and traditional psychometric intelligence, defined as IQ. According to the authors, this result could be explained by the fact that these are college students and, in many cases at this level of education, the correlations between intelligence and performance have disappeared (Perez and Castejón, 2006).

In a study with 539 students in the 3rd and 899 in the 4th year of basic education (EGB), it was calculated the correlation between intelligence and skills with overall academic performance, using the instrument of Lorge-Thorndike tests and the Goodenough test. It was found that, in general, in the 4th year, performance is affected more by intelligence and intellectual skills than in the 3rd year. According to the authors, could be that the first years are more affected by non-intellective variables. The authors emphasize the weight that has verbal intelligence and verbal comprehension. The most expressive factors are those with lower relationship but one should consider that the relationship with performance is always conditioned by their own performance criteria. In the traditional school system, the expressive are inconsiderate (Hernández, 1883).

In studies of type M-G, Cronbach pointed out multiple correlations of the Multidimensional Battery with global academic performance with university student, these correlations were of the order of 0.60 to 0.70. Correlations were higher in women. Using the Thurstone PMA, V and R factors were those that have shown higher correlation with student performance at secondary school, correlations ranged between 0.60 and 0.70. The remaining obtained factors correlations very low or non-significant. However, when taken in overall, the multiple correlation output reaches values of between 0.40 and 0.73 (Casanova, 1988).

Recent research asserts that general intelligence and cognitive skills are keys variable in predicting students' academic performance. They are, virtually, the most important predictor variables but it is important to consider other modulating variables and its effects (Miñano and Castejón, 2011).

In a study on predictors of academic achievement through structural equation, we conclude that there is an unquestionable relationship between intelligence and academic achievement (Borges, Hernández-Jorge and González, 2012).

In short, intelligence seems to be a good predictor of academic performance, except, perhaps, the best marks obtained in previous courses but it is not the only predictor.

2.1.2. Thinking Styles

The theory mental self-government proposes 13 styles of thought in its first order factorial structure that are grouped into five dimensions of second order function (including styles legislative, executive and judicial), shape (styles hierarchical, oligarchic, monarchic and anarchic), level (global and local styles), field (internal and external styles), and trend (conservative and liberal styles). People with a thinking style of legislative are, often, individuals who like to create their own procedures, are involved in performing tasks using personal forms, prefer not pre-structured problems or tasks, decide how and with what strategy to solve the tasks, and prefer creative and innovative activities. People with a predominant judicial style often involved in the evaluation of procedures developed by others, judging the strategies and structures, they prefer tasks that have to analyze and judge the ideas present in these tasks. Also, they are inclined to develop activities that can develop their judicial style like writing critical comments, review comments, judging the opinions of others, evaluate programs, assess the work of others, and so on, and, consequently, they try to get a job that allows them to fully utilize their style predominant. By contrast, people with an executive style prefer, rather than create, follow the plans developed by others, they prefer to work on problems or tasks pre-engineered. Likewise they tend to choose tasks with clear structures in which they only have the responsibility of filling content and finally, executive type prefer occupations (González-Pienda et al., 2004 cited in Bernardo et al., 2009). In this line, in an investigation that took into account only the dimension "function" it was found that performance in core curriculum areas, is mainly predicted by the legislative style and, to a lesser extent, by the judicial style, but never by the executive style. These results support the idea that increased use of highly complex cognitive styles and personal involvement and creativity generators (e.g. judicial and legislative), will do a higher yield in the core curriculum areas (Bernardo et al., 2009).

2.2. Personality Factors

2.2.1. Personality

After the low percentage of variance explained by IQ tests or intellectual abilities, many researchers have been worried for the relationships between personality and academic performance. The current state of research does not allow, for the time, to establish a predictive relationship between intelligence and personality. However, it is possible to refer to some studies related to this subject. In the study INCIE of Madrid (1976, cited in Hernandez, 1983), is not got no significant correlation between personality traits and performance. In the same vein, it was also found no significant correlations between personality and performance (Pelechano 1977, cited in Hernandez, 1983). Importantly in this field there are moderating variables that may affect the study variables and the relationship between them (Hernández, 1983).

In two longitudinal studies, with sample of British university students, it was studied the character predictor of personality traits on academic performance. To this end, academic performance was evaluated over three years and multiple criteria such as exams and final projects. Correlations and regressions were calculated which provided strong evidence to support the hypothesis that personality is related significantly to academic entity. Thus, it was found that neuroticism proved a negative predictor of performance. It was found that in the first sample, the Big Five personality factors, particularly Neuroticism and responsibility, are predictors of performance. The results suggest that neuroticism may affect performance and accountability can lead to greater achievement. In sample 2, the results showed that the three superfactors were the best predictor of academic performance, accounting for nearly 17% of unique variance in overall exam results. This study demonstrates that psychotics and neuroticism could limit academic success (Chamorro-Premuzic and Furnham, 2003).

2.2.1.1. Extraversion

Extraversion is a typical attitude characterized by the concentration of interest in an external object. Extroverts are interested in the outside world of people and things, they try to be more sociable and be more aware of what is happening in their environment. There is a controversial relationship between extraversion and performance. Some studies suggest that extroverts may have better yields. Others studies, nevertheless, found no relation between the two constructs. Differentiated of these two positions is that of Byner (1972 cited in Alvaro Page et al., 1990), who states that extraversion is a flattering influence in elementary school, is void to the secondary school and a negative influence at the university.

2.1.1.2. Anxiety

Anxiety is an unpleasant response set including subjective feelings of restlessness, tension and discomfort associated with changes in the physiological activity of the autonomic nervous system. The relationship between anxiety and performance can be affected by other variables such as school, sex or other personality variables. The findings of many studies are that one can not consider anxiety as a predictor of performance, if not a variable that modifies the predictive value of other variables more consistent as intelligence and motivation (Lavin, 1965; Rodriguez, 1982; cited in Alvaro-Page et al., 1990).

2.1.1.3. Motivation

The motivation involves inner states that direct the body towards certain goals or purposes are the impulses that drive a person to perform certain actions and persist in them for completion. Motivation can be defined as something that activates and directs behavior. In the literature, a theoretical level, it seems that there is a relationship between motivation and school performance, the fact that a student has an interest and experience with the tasks, will lead to better achievement. Nonetheless, the motivation construct is multidimensional and complex, which complicates the measurement and makes it difficult to establish relationships with other constructs such as performance. (Álvaro-Page et al., 1990). The trigger level, the choice between different courses of action, focus attention and persevere with an activity are the main motivational indicators. Extrinsic motivation is something external to the person who moves the person to act, that is, the effects and consequences that we get after performing a behavior. Intrinsic motivation, on the other hand, occurs when the interest and value are located in the activity in what is being learned. That which moves a person is the personal satisfaction of understanding and learning (Guerrero, 2006). In a study about motivation and academic achievement in students of Secondary School Education LOGSE it was found that motivational dimensions are powerful predictor variables, and the student achievement is predicted, for the most part, based on the marks obtained assessments in previous courses (Broc Cavero, 2006).

The performance problem is explained, in part, by the lack of motivation for studies there. Seemingly motivation research and intervention that is derived from it, is a wrong base approach. It is not the teacher who has to grab the student's attention or is he the protagonist of teaching. Nor should we talk about motivating tasks. Instead, we must investigate and intervene to help students to generate mechanisms of motivation, but not just for the school, but for everything in life. That should be the ultimate goal of education: getting students reach an autonomous and self-regulated learning. However, to think that motivation is all it takes to learn is a mistake, because there are also important variables such as attention, processing, retrieval and transfer of knowledge (Beltrán, 1998). In a research about predictors of achievement, in a secondary students sample, through structural equation. The motivation variable is maintained as part of the model despite the low correlation obtained with academic performance. Authors state that would be interesting to study specific aspects related to motivation, such as task persistence, in order to observe the different relationships in the model (Borges et al., 2012). It is unlikely that learners show motivated with tasks, when they consider themselves unable to do so. Neither if this activity is not interesting, nor if the task generates sadness, frustration or fear. Therefore, the motivation requires some personal balance between competence beliefs, personal interest and emotions it provokes. Only if you get a positive cost/benefit between emotions and personal considerations, will be favorably disposed to the involvement, commitment and investment of time and effort (Guerrero, 2006).

2.1.1.4. Self-Concept

The self-concept is the self-image of each person. That is, how each person perceives herself. This concept includes reviews of all parameters that are relevant to the person as physical appearance, skills for sexual performance or social and intellectual capabilities among others. The self-concept is formed by experience, it is a dynamic construct which is fed back (positive or negative) of the social environment information.

The self-perceptions and beliefs about oneself (self), and the references to one's ability and competence (self-efficacy) are cornerstones of motivation. A student will need to be convinced that it has resources, capacities and competence to perform a task (Guerrero, 2006). Researches that show the relationship between academic performance and self-concept have been numerous. Gimeno Sacristan (1976, cited in Adell, 2002) considered that the self-concept is a determinant of academic performance and he attributed to this factor a correlation of 0.54 specifying which related to academic self-concept. Other authors relativize the importance of self-concept and argue that it is a necessary but not sufficient condition to have good performance. In the same way, in an investigation of Rodriguez-Espinar et al. (1993, cited en Adell, 2002), it was concluded that students who have low self-concept academic obtain worse results than those with a better opinion of their academic potential.

The findings of a study, between researchers from the University of Oviedo and Navarra, shed light on the issue. The results suggest that positive self-concept favors the use of strategic learning procedures, in the sense that the higher self-concept, the greater use of learning strategies, which will facilitate deep processing of information (González-Pumariega, 1998). A recent study found results which suggest that the students' academic performance is correlated with academic self-concept. This self-concept is strongly related to family self-concept, which seems to justify the importance of family in student achievement, and physical self-concept (Costa and Tabernero, 2012).

2.1.1.5. Confidence in the Future as a Predictor of Performance

An optimistic view about the future seems to influence the performance. It can be said that a person who is hoping to reach a goal is motivated and who have not lost interest, which does not imply endeavors (Adell, 2002).

2.3. Emotional Intelligence

The idea that there is an emotional intelligence (EI) emerged with the proposal of Mayer, Salovey and Di Paolo (1990). The original idea was that some individuals have a greater capacity to reason about emotions and to use this reasoning to think more effectively (Mayer, Salovey and Caruso, 2008).

Numerous studies have tried to shed light on the relationship between emotional intelligence and academic achievement. However, the results have been contradictory. Early studies Anglistics showed a direct relationship between emotional intelligent and academic performance (Extremera and Fernández-Berrocal, 2004). The results of Newsome, Day and Catano (2000) did not endorse the positive relationship between emotional intelligence, as measured by the EQ-i, and academic achievement in students of Canadian university. Furthermore, Parker, Summerfeldt, Hogan and Majeski (2004), in a study of adolescents, obtained different results depending on how the variable academic performance was operationalized. When it was examined the relationship between EI and academic performance in the full sample, the predictive ability of emotional intelligence on performance was poor. By contrast, some of the EQ-i subscales (intrapersonal, stress management and adaptability) itself significantly predicted academic success (around 8-10% of the variance in scores). Subsequently, we compared the groups of high and low performance, in this case, appeared linked to academic performance subscales: interpersonal skills, adaptability and stress management. Finally, in this study, discriminant analysis was performed using emotional intelligence as a predictor to assign to the high and low academic achievement. The results showed that emotional intelligence, in general, is a powerful predictor to identify students who were to succeed academically at the end of the semester (82% to 91% higher performance and low performance) were correctly identified and grouped according to their scores on emotional intelligence. Furthermore, Barchard (2003) assessed college students through the MSCEIT, controlling cognitive skills that have traditionally been linked to performance (verbal ability, inductive reasoning, and visualization) and classic personality variables (neuroticism, extraversion, openness, kindness and responsibility). The results obtained support the ideal that emotional intelligence levels in university student could predict the grades at the end of the school year. Finally, Perez and Castejón (2006) found significant correlations between academic performance and emotional intelligence. By contrast, there are studies that oppose this view, like Sanchez, Rodriguez and Padilla (2007) in which it was found that only the factor of emotional attention was related to academic performance significantly. The relationship found was negative which means that the higher the note, lower will be the academic performance (-0.165).

A recent prospective study by Qualter, Gardner, Pope, Hutchinson and Whiteley (2012), examined the impact of emotional intelligence and skill as a feature in future academic performance, it was controlled cognitive abilities and personality. The results showed that cognitive ability is far from being the greatest predictor of academic performance. It was also found that emotional intelligence predicts academic performance, as the results show the relationship between emotional intelligence skill and trait, measured at 11 years of age and academic performance measured five years later. The study also shows that more emotionally intelligent participants, outperformed their peers (with the same capacity cognitive) in academic performance. The findings of this study suggest that the development of emotional intelligence can improve academic success.

3. LEARNING STRATEGIES

Learning strategies have great popularity; however, experts have failed to agree on the definition of strategy or nature. As a result, there are cumbersome boundaries between strategies and other related constructs. It is important to distinguish between the construct at hand, strategies and the learning process that is used to designate the chain of activities and mental operations involved in the act of learning as attention, comprehension or acquisition. Learning techniques, meanwhile, are observable activities, operational and manipulable. They are, for example, the organization of informative data, making abstracts, making sketches, etc. Strategies involve an action plan, unlike the process and learning techniques. Strategies are used to advance the learning process and the techniques are the tools used to implement a strategy. Learning strategies relate to the quality of learning to identify and diagnose because of those are at the base of a low or high performance. The strategies put the differential point in performance, thus, two people with the same intellect, the same degree of motivation and the same educational system but with different learning strategies, could get different academic performance. Identify the strategies used by the students will analyze the causes of performance and help to intervene to optimize learning. The use and quality of the strategies used will influence the quality of learning. Thus, learning that merely repeats the knowledge is repetitive, whereas if you select, organize and develop the knowledge will be a constructive and meaningful learning. Using strategies also promotes autonomous learning, independent, allowing the learning control pass into the hands of students (Beltran, 2003).

There are many classifications of learning strategies, McKeachie and cols. (1986, cited in Roces, González-Pienda and Alvarez, 2002), Pintrich and cols. (1991, cited in Roce et al., 2002), differ into three groups of strategies: cognitive, metacognitive and resource control. Cognitive strategies are involved in learning the art and comprise the comprehension and recall. The resource control strategies are refer to control by the student about variables that influence their involvement in the task, such as time, motivation or the external environment. Finally, metacognitive strategies relate to planning, regulation, monitoring and modification of cognitive processes (Roces, et al., 2002)

In a study about the learning strategies for obtaining good academic performance, conducted with high school students and high school. It was found that the students, who achieved good performance, used more successfully some tactics own process acquisition of information, encoding, and supporting recovery processing information. Beside this, the girls use more metacognitive strategies and are more motivated intrinsically and extrinsically than boys (Lozano, González-Pienda, Nuñez, Lozano, and Álvarez, 2001).

In research on learning strategies, it was extracted that the successful student, facing a material to be learned, first, explores the topic, reads the summary or index, makes a superficial reading, highlights the most important points, and repeats and revises after a while. Second, encodes this information and makes summaries, diagrams and summary tables, memorizes the most important, derives the information to put in his own words and express his doubts using people nearby or at other materials. When reviewing the study, recalls the grouped concepts, sketches and drawings made taking into account the corrections that were made on the subject. In addition, the student is aware of the mental operations that can be done and knows selecting, monitoring its use and effectiveness (metacognitive strategies) (Lozano, et al., 2001).

According to the work of Nuñez et al. (1998), knowing learning strategies, to the extent that enhances the regulation of learning process, promotes self-knowledge of capabilities and limitations and the ability to act on them.

4. SEX AND GENDER DIFFERENCES

The distinction between sex and gender, part of a series of studies which distinguishes the concept of sex as a natural or biological. And the concept of gender which has a cultural significance that refers to a set of roles. This section will discuss the two terms as a whole, noting some research results.

It has always existed the belief that males are more intelligent than females and, therefore, the females´ yield is inferior. Apparently, in view of the results of numerous investigations, these differences in performance are determined by other factors that cause different educational outcomes, as different patterns of socialization and differential reinforcement of different skills.

It can be concluded that sex can be a moderator variable of performance but not because of a possible genetic reason, on the contrary, because of the differentiated socially established structures that determine educational and professional actions differentiated for women and men (Alvaro-Page et al., 1990).

When analyzing the differences by gender, it is possible to find in the scientific literature, that girls tend to get better grades than boys in the area of language and lower marks in math. This results, consequently, in a forced question, are the differences real or these differences are the result of sociocultural factors implicit in the very process educative (De Miguel, 1988)? In this view, the differences in educational achievement between children from basic education (EGB) taking into account the assessment of the teacher and a reading test, are not statistically significant. However, there is a trend for girls to obtain a superior performance in the area of language. (Elices, Riveras, González and Crespo, 1990).

A recent study has addressed identify whether there are gender differences in academic performance. The results show that there are differences in favor of girls in courses of Spanish Language and Literature, and a marginal difference in the Foreign Language course. Furthermore, it appears that there are no differences in academic performance in the subject of mathematics although this should be contrasted with longitudinal studies, according to the authors (Costa and Tabernero, 2012).

CONCLUSION

This chapter has done a review of the factors influencing academic performance and the results of various investigations. Subsequently, there has been talk of learning strategies and their usefulness in the teaching-learning process and ultimately have discussed the differences in academic performance due to the variable sex and gender as a whole. As mentioned earlier, the performance is a complex construct that can be affected by many factors so that further investigations are necessary in this regard to provide quality education and greater achievements in the field of education.

REFERENCES

Adell, M.A. (2002): *Estrategias para mejorar el rendimiento académicos de los adolescentes*. Madrid: Pirámide.

Álvaro Page, M. et al. (1990). *Hacia un modelo causal del rendimiento académico*. Madrid: C.I.D.E.

Andrés-Pueyo, A. (1996). *Manual de Psicología Diferencial*. Madrid: McGraw Hill.

Barchard, K. (2003). Does Emotional Intelligence assist in the Prediction of Academic Success? *Educational and Psychological Measurement*, 63 (5), 840-858.

Beltrán, J. (1998). Claves psicológicas para la motivación y el rendimiento académico. En M. Acosta (Coord.), Creatividad, motivación y rendimiento académico (pp.39-54). Málaga: Aljibe.

Beltrán, J.A. (2003). Estrategias de aprendizaje. *Revista de educación*, 332, 55-73.

Acosta (Coord.), Creatividad, motivación y rendimiento académico. Málaga: Aljibe.

Bernardo, A., Nuñez, J.C., Gonzalez Pienda, J., Rosario, P., Alvarez, L., González-Castro, P., Valle, A., Rodríguez, S., Cerezo, R., Álvarez, D. and Rodríguez, C. (2009). Estilos intelectuales y rendimiento academico: Una perspectiva evolutiva. *Psicothema*, 21(4), 555-561.

Borges del Rosal, Á., Hernández Jorge, C. M., and González Sierra, M. A. (2012). Achievement predictors in a secondary students' sample. *Quality and Quantity*, 46(6), 1687. doi: 10.1007/s11135-011-9547-5.

Broc Cavero, M. (2006). Motivación y rendimiento académico en alumnos de educación secundaria obligatoria y bachillerato LOGSE. *Revista De Educación*, (340), 379-414.

Chamorro-Premuzic, T. and Furnham, A., (2003). Personality predicts academic performance: Evidence from two longitudinal university samples. *Journal of Research in Personality*, 37, 319–338.

Casanova, P. (1988). Predicción del rendimiento escolar a partir de modelos aptitudinales. Tesis doctoral. Universidad Complutense de Madrid.

Costa, S. and Tabernero, C. (2012). Rendimiento académico y autoconcepto en estudiantes de educación secundaria obligatoria según el género. *Revista Iberoamericana de Psicología y Salud*, 3(2), 175-193.

De Juan-Espinosa, M. (1997). Geografía de la inteligencia humana. Las aptitudes cognitivas. Madrid: Pirámide.

De Miguel, M. (1988): Preescolarización y rendimiento académico: Un estudio longitudinal de /as variables psicosociales a lo largo de la EGB. Madrid. C.I.D.E.

Elices, J. A., Riveras, F., González, C. and Crespo, M. A. (1990). El rendimiento escolar en función del sexo al inicio de la EGB. *Revista Interuniversitaria de Formación del Profesorado*, 8, 123-132.

Extremera, N. and Fernández-Berrocal, P. (2004). El papel de la inteligencia emocional en el alumnado: evidencias empíricas. Revista Electrónica de Investigación Educativa, 6 (2). [http://redie.uabc.mx/vol6no2/contenido-extremera.html].

González Pumariega, S. (1998). Estrategias de aprendizaje, autoconcepto y rendimiento académico. *Psicothema*, 10(1), 97-109.

Guerrero, E. (2006). Psicología, educación, métodos de investigación y aprendizajes escolares. Barcelona: Davinci.

Hernández, P. (1983): "Rendimiento, adaptación e intervención psicoeducativa". Secretariado de Publicaciones de la Universidad de La Laguna.

Lozano, L., González-Pienda, J.A., Nuñez, J.C., Lozano, L.M., and Álvarez, L. (2001). Estrategias de aprendizaje, género y rendimiento académico. *Revista Galego-Portuguesa De Psicoloxía e Educación*, (7), 203-216.

Mayer, J. D., Salovey, P., and Caruso, D. R. (2008). Emotional intelligence: New ability or eclectic traits? *American Psychologist*, 63(6), 503-517. doi: 10.1037/0003-066X.63.6.503.

Mayer, J. D. Dipaolo, M. T. and Salovey, P. (1990). Perceiving affective content in ambiguous visual stimuli: A component of emotional intelligence. *Journal of Personality Assessment*, 54, 772-781.

Mayer, J. D., Salovey, P., and Caruso, D. R. (2008). Emotional intelligence: New ability or eclectic traits? *American Psychologist*, 63(6), 503-517. doi:10.1037/0003-066X.63.6.503.

Miñano, P. and Castejón, J.L. (2011). Variables cognitivas y motivacionales en el rendimiento académico en Lengua y Matemáticas: un modelo estructural. *Revista de Psicodidáctica*, 16 (2), 203-230.

Newsome, S., Day, A. L. and Catano, V. M. (2000). Assessing the predictive validity of emotional intelligence. *Personality and Individual Differences*, 29 (6), 1005-1016.

Núñez, J.C., González-Pienda, J.A., García, M., González-Pumariega, S., Roces, C., Álvarez, L. and González, M.C. (1998) Estrategias de aprendizaje, autoconcepto y rendimiento académico. *Psicothema*, 10 (1), 97-109.

Parker, J. D. A., Summerfeldt, L. J., Hogan, M. J. and Majeski, S. A. (2004). Emotional intelligence and academia success: examining the transition from high school to university. *Personality and Individual Differences*, 36 (1), 163-172.

Pérez-Pérez, N and Castejón, J. (2007). La inteligencia emocional como predictor del rendimiento académico en estudiantes universitarios. *Ansiedad y Estrés*, 13 (1), 119-129.

Pérez, N and Castejón, J.L. (2006). Relaciones entre la inteligencia emocional y el cociente intelectual con el rendimiento académico en estudiantes universitarios . *Revista Electrónica de Motivación y Emoción*, 9, 1–15.

Qualter, P., Gardner, K. J., Pope, D. J., Hutchinson, J. M., and Whiteley, H. E. (2012). Ability emotional intelligence, trait emotional intelligence, and academic success in british secondary schools: A 5 year longitudinal study. *Learning and Individual Differences*, 22 (1), 83-91. doi:10.1016/j.lindif.2011.11.007.

Roces, C., González-Pienda, J.A., and Álvarez, L. (2002). Procesos y estrategias cognitivas y metacognitivas. En J.A. González-Pienda, R. González Cabanach, J.C. Núñez and A. Valle (Eds.), *Manual de Psicología de la Educación* (pp. 95-116). Madrid: Pirámide.

Sánchez, M., Rodríguez, M.C. and Padilla, V. (2007). ¿La inteligencia emocional está relacionada con el rendimiento académico? *IPyE: Psicología y Educación*, 1 (1), 54-66.

Yela, M. Estudios sobre Inteligencia y lenguaje. Pirámide, Madrid, 1987.

In: Handbook of Academic Performance
Editors: Rolf Haumann and George Zimmer

ISBN: 978-1-62417-888-7
© 2013 Nova Science Publishers, Inc.

Chapter 11

RELATIONSHIPS BETWEEN TEACHER AND STUDENT ETHNICITY IN TEXAS ELEMENTARY SCHOOLS: AN 11-YEAR ANALYSIS

*Jamie A. Bone[*1], John R. Slate[‡2] and Cynthia Martinez-Garcia[†2]*
[1]Conroe Independent School District, Conroe, Texas, US
[2]Sam Houston State University, Huntsville, Texas, US

ABSTRACT

In this study, relationships between teacher ethnicity and student ethnicity in Texas public elementary schools were investigated. Data from all public elementary schools in the state of Texas were gathered for the school years 1999-2000 through 2009-2010 using the Academic Excellence Indicator System. Data on both student enrollment by ethnic membership and teacher employment by ethnic membership at the elementary school level were downloaded. Statistically significant, positive relationships, with large effect sizes, were yielded between teacher ethnic diversity (i.e., Black, Hispanic, and White) and student ethnic diversity (i.e., Black, Hispanic, and White) respectively in Texas elementary schools. As more Hispanic students were enrolled in an elementary school, the tendency was present for more Hispanic teachers to be employed at that school. The same result was yielded for Black and for White teachers and students. Implications of these findings are provided.

Keywords: student diversity, teacher diversity, Texas elementary schools

In an effort to spread equality for all U.S. citizens, the Civil Rights Act of 1964 was enacted, which served the purpose of protecting U.S. citizens against discrimination on the basis of race and color, among other characteristics, in programs that receive federal funding (Office of Civil Rights, n.d., para 2). Contained within the prominent provisions of the Civil

---

[*] email jbone@conroeisd.net
[‡] email jrs051@shsu.edu
[†] email cmg021@shsu.edu

Rights Act of 1964 was terminology that would allow for the outlawing of discrimination in employment practices, as well as language that would provide for equal educational opportunities for all students. Since the passage of the Civil Rights Act of 1964, U.S. public schools have struggled to increase the ethnic diversity of teaching staff (Orfield & Lee, 2007).

Evidence of the overwhelming changes in the ethnic makeup of students in Texas has been well documented (e.g., Cho & DeCastro-Ambrosetti, 2005; Cloudt & Stevens, 2009; Frankenberg & Siegel-Hawley, 2008; Orfield & Lee, 2007; Petersen & Assanie, 2005; Snyder, Dillow, & Hoffman, 2007). Moreover, multiple researchers (e.g., Alliance for Excellent Education, 2005; Branch & Kritsonis, 2006; Tyler, Yzquierdo, Lopez-Reyna, & Saunders-Flippin, 2004) have reported a positive relationship between teacher ethnicity and student achievement. However, a dearth of studies exist pertaining to teacher ethnicity as it relates to student ethnicity or to the efforts made toward diversifying the teaching force. Therefore, examining the relationship between teacher ethnicity and student ethnicity in public schools is important.

STATEMENT OF THE PROBLEM

The ethnic achievement gap in Texas public schools has been identified as a major contributing factor in the reduction in economic growth and prosperity in the U.S. (Paige & Witty, 2010). Other negative consequences of the ethnic achievement gap include lower earnings, poorer health, and higher rates of incarceration. Each consequence contributes to the national debt and to the financial load that U.S. taxpayers bear (McKinsey & Company, 2009). An obvious way to address the impacts of the achievement gap in Texas elementary schools is to confront the issue of racial inequity in Texas public schools. Tyler et al. (2004) suggested that ethnically diverse teachers could benefit students by providing them with mentors, advocates, and community-to-school liaisons. Thus, ascertaining the relationship between teacher ethnicity and student ethnicity at the elementary school level over time can assist in the determination as to whether progress has been made in providing an ethnically diverse teaching staff that is representative of the diversity among the student population.

PURPOSE OF THE STUDY

The purpose of this study was to determine the extent to which relationships were present among teacher ethnicity and student ethnicity in Texas public elementary schools. Archival data from the Texas Education Agency (TEA) Academic Excellence Indicator System (AEIS) were utilized. Data examined were teacher ethnicity and student ethnicity from Texas public elementary schools for each school year from 1999-2000 through 2009-2010.

SIGNIFICANCE OF THE STUDY

The results of this study are important for multiple reasons. First, an examination of the results provides Texas school district administrators with a basis for the importance of ensuring their teacher ethnicity matches that of their students. Second, results from this study may increase Texas school district administrators' awareness of the impact minority teachers have on the success of students, and ultimately, on the efforts made toward closing the achievement gap for minority students. Third, the information gathered and analyzed in this study may influence the overall understanding of the progress that has been made because of efforts to recruit more minority teachers to public schools in Texas.

Finally, an examination of the results of this study will provide policy makers with the necessary information to make informed decisions regarding the need and importance of increasing minority teachers for minority students.

Theory of Representative Bureaucracy

In his theory of representative bureaucracy, Kingsley (1944) suggested that more positive outcomes for a specific group are produced when that group has a larger representation within an organization. Additionally, Kingsley (1944) noted that when members of a group hold lesser positions within an organization, those members can become active representatives for their group. Consequently, Levitan (1946) suggested that the only way to ensure that individuals in positions of authority utilized their positions appropriately was to ensure that those individuals would be representative of the people they served. Therefore, when minority teachers are better represented among a campus staff, the likelihood of academic success increases among minority students than when minority teachers are not well represented (Kingsley, 1944). Similarly, individuals with common ethnicities often share cultural norms, values, experiences, and world views.

Decisions made by those individuals are likely to reflect those norms and values (Krislov, 1974). Consequently, decisions made by those individuals are likely to reflect the norms and values of the ethnic group to which the individual belongs. That is, employing more minority teachers in Texas public elementary schools would likely result in decisions and actions made in the best interest of minority students, which would contribute to the narrowing of the achievement gap.

Alternatively, Texas public elementary students are taught mostly by White teachers (Frankenberg & Siegel-Hawley, 2008). Accordingly, the decisions and actions made by teachers in Texas public elementary schools are in the best interest of White students. Thus, the theory of representative bureaucracy provides a scaffolding on which the necessity of this study was built.

Theory of Homosocial Reproduction

The phenomenon wherein individuals in positions of authority hire applicants who are most like themselves is referred to as the theory of homosocial reproduction (Kanter, 1977). Most organizations place the strongest emphasis on the product, which places the pressure to perform on managers.

Rather than risk the quality of the product by hiring individuals whose abilities are essentially unknown, managers are more likely to hire applicants who exhibit social characteristics similar to their own (Kanter, 1977). For example, applicants who conform, particularly in the way of appearance, are typically perceived as individuals who will also conform to behavioral norms (Kanter, 1977). In other words, individuals who are similar to the management group, particularly in terms of race, ethnicity, gender, and social class, are the most likely to be trusted by the management group (Kanter, 1977).

Similar to the demands placed on managers in a business setting, school principals are also under tremendous pressure to produce results, particularly in the way of standardized test scores. Hiring teachers who can be trusted to generate impressive standardized test scores becomes critical to the successful career of a school principal. Consequently, principals are likely to hire teachers with whom they are comfortable establishing communication, discretion, and trust (Kanter, 1977).

Currently, principals across the U.S. are overwhelmingly White, which has resulted in a teaching staff that is also overwhelmingly White (Taylor, 1988). What's more, according to the theory of homosocial reproduction, the ethnic makeup of public school teaching staff is unlikely to change in the future because the current White principals are likely to hire and cultivate teachers and leaders who are similar to themselves. Thus, to examine the research questions, both the theory of representative bureaucracy and the theory of homosocial reproduction were used as a theoretical framework.

RESEARCH QUESTIONS

The following research questions were addressed in this study: (a) What is the relationship between teacher ethnic diversity (i.e., Black) and student ethnic diversity (i.e., Black) in Texas elementary schools for each of the 11 school years from 1999-2000 through 2009-2010?; (b) What is the relationship between teacher ethnic diversity (i.e., Hispanic) and student ethnic diversity (i.e., Hispanic) in Texas elementary schools for each of the 11 school years from 1999-2000 through 2009-2010?; and (c) What is the relationship between teacher ethnic diversity (i.e., White) and student ethnic diversity (i.e., White) in Texas elementary schools for each of the 11 school years from 1999-2000 through 2009-2010?

METHOD

Selection of Participants

Data from all public elementary schools in the state of Texas were gathered for the school years 1999-2000 through 2009-2010 using the Academic Excellence Indicator System. Through the AEIS database, information was collected on approximately 1,220 public school districts in Texas. For the purposes of this study, the data gathered focused on AEIS reports regarding elementary schools.

Additionally, Black, Hispanic, and White teacher groups and Black, Hispanic, and White student groups were examined. Because the AEIS results included many more than 380 cases in each academic year from 1999-2000 to 2009-2010, the minimum number of participants needed to make generalizations was met.

INSTRUMENTATION

For the purposes of this study, archival data were gathered using the Texas AEIS for the 11 academic years 1999-2000 through 2009-2010. The AEIS is a comprehensive reporting system, which is used to generate reports about campuses, school districts, and the state, and these data are then used to determine accountability ratings (TEA, 2009a). Data for this study were collected by the TEA and reported through AEIS. Collected data were used to determine the relationship between the percentage of Black teachers and Black students, the relationship between the percentage of Hispanic teachers and Hispanic students, and the relationship between the percentage of White teachers and White students. Each relationship was studied at the elementary school level for the 11 academic school years.

Elementary School Level

School types are assigned to all campuses within the AEIS database according to the lowest and highest grade levels of the students. In an instance where the grade levels served at a campus are not exactly as specified in the AEIS database, the schools are associated with the school type most similar to their grade span. For the purposes of this study, elementary school referred to a campus at which students in grades K-5 are enrolled (TEA, 2009b).

DATA ANALYSIS

Data were analyzed to determine the relationship between the percentage of Black teachers and the percentage of Black students, the percentage of Hispanic teachers and the percentage of Hispanic students, and the percentage of White teachers and the percentage of White students at the elementary school level for each of the school years of data downloaded. To begin this analysis, descriptive statistics were obtained. The accuracy of the dataset was determined first by performing frequencies in SPSS version 17.0 and checking that the output values were within possible limits. For a few variables, several values were present (e.g., -3) that reflected the presence of masking. The TEA (2009b) masks data that have the potential to reveal the performance of a student so that the data will remain in compliance with the federal Family Educational Rights and Privacy Act (FERPA). These values were replaced with system missing values prior to statistical analyses.

Next, the means, standard deviations, skewness, and kurtosis values were obtained from SPSS. From this information, the standardized skewness coefficients (i.e., the skewness value divided by the standard error of skewness) and the standardized kurtosis coefficients (i.e., the kurtosis value divided by the standard error of kurtosis) were calculated. Because all of the standardized skewness coefficients and the standardized kurtosis coefficients were outside the bounds of normality of -3.00 and 3.00 (Onwuegbuzie & Daniel, 2002), a non-parametric correlation procedure (i.e., Spearman's rank order correlation coefficient) was conducted. Scatterplots depicting the association between the variables in each research question for each school year analyzed were examined to determine any departure from linearity. Linearity was present in all of the scatterplots, thereby justifying the computation of a correlational procedure.

RESULTS

First, the relationship between Black teachers and Black students was examined. A statistically significant relationship was yielded between the two variables (r [3819] = .65, p < .001). The effect size was large (Cohen, 1988). By squaring the correlation coefficient, a r^2 of .42 was obtained, indicating an overlap of 42% was present between where Black teachers were employed and where Black students were enrolled in elementary school for the 1999-2000 school year.

Second, the relationship between Hispanic teachers and Hispanic students at the elementary level for the 1999-2000 school year was examined. A statistically significant relationship was yielded between the two variables (r [3819] = .83, p < .001). The effect size was large (Cohen, 1988). By squaring the correlation coefficient, a r^2 of .69 was obtained, indicating an overlap of 69% between where Hispanic teachers were employed and where Hispanic students were enrolled in elementary school for the 1999-2000 school year.

Third, the relationship between White teachers and White students at the elementary level for the 1999-2000 school year was examined. A statistically significant relationship was yielded between the two variables (r [3819] = .87, p < .001). The effect size was large (Cohen, 1988). By squaring the correlation coefficient, a r^2 of .76 was obtained, indicating an overlap of 76% between where White teachers were employed and where White students were enrolled in elementary school for the 1999-2000 school year.

These correlations reported above were calculated for the remaining 10 years of data. With the exception of one school year, 2004-2005, all of the correlations, strength of associations, and effect sizes were similar for each of the ethnic comparisons. These results, again with the exception of one school year, were commensurate with the results for the 1999-2000 school year. Readers should note that data and results for one school year, the 2004-2005 school year, were not congruent with the other 10 school years of data analyzed. This finding parallels that of a recent doctoral dissertation in which Texas secondary school size was analyzed. Greeney (2010) also reported that the data for the 2004-2005 school year were not commensurate with the data for the surrounding school years, although he did not provide any speculations concerning specific reasons for the data anomalies. As such, Greeney (2010) did not analyze data from that school year.

Readers are referred to Tables 1 through 3 for the correlations, strength of associations, and effect sizes. Depicted in Table 1 are the correlation coefficients (r), the coefficients of determination (r^2), and effect sizes for the correlation calculated between Black teachers and Black students in Texas public elementary schools for all academic years of data examined.

With the exception of one school year, the data remained consistent over the 11 school years. Overall, Black elementary teacher employment and Black elementary student enrollment were highly correlated with large degrees of overlap. Represented in Table 2 are the correlation coefficients (r), the coefficients of determination (r^2), and effect sizes for the correlations calculated between Hispanic teachers and Hispanic students in Texas public elementary schools for all school years of data examined.

Table 1. Correlation Coefficients, Coefficients of Determination, and Effect Sizes for Black Teachers and Black Students in Texas Public Elementary Schools

Correlation	r	r^2	Effect Size
Black Teachers and Black Students			
1999-2000	.65	.42	Large
2000-2001	.65	.42	Large
2001-2002	.66	.44	Large
2002-2003	.64	.41	Large
2003-2004	.65	.42	Large
2004-2005	.27	.07	Small
2005-2006	.65	.42	Large
2006-2007	.65	.42	Large
2007-2008	.65	.42	Large
2008-2009	.65	.42	Large
2009-2010	.67	.45	Large

Table 2. Correlation Coefficients, Coefficients of Determination, and Effect Sizes for Hispanic Teachers and Hispanic Students in Texas Public Elementary Schools

Correlation	r	r^2	Effect Size
Hispanic Teachers and Hispanic Students			
1999-2000	.83	.69	Large
2000-2001	.83	.69	Large
2001-2002	.84	.71	Large
2002-2003	.85	.72	Large
2003-2004	.85	.72	Large
2004-2005	.28	.08	Small
2005-2006	.87	.76	Large
2006-2007	.87	.76	Large
2007-2008	.88	.77	Large
2008-2009	.88	.77	Large
2009-2010	.81	.66	Large

Table 3. Correlation Coefficients, Coefficients of Determination, and Effect Sizes for White Teachers and White Students in Texas Public Elementary Schools

Correlation	r	r^2	Effect Size
White Teachers and White Students			
1999-2000	.87	.76	Large
2000-2001	.87	.76	Large
2001-2002	.88	.77	Large
2002-2003	.89	.79	Large
2003-2004	.89	.79	Large
2004-2005	.36	.13	Moderate
2005-2006	.90	.81	Large
2006-2007	.89	.79	Large
2007-2008	.90	.81	Large
2008-2009	.90	.81	Large
2009-2010	.87	.76	Large

As was noted with Black teachers and Black students in elementary schools, with the exception of one school year, the data remained consistent over the 11 school years. Overall, Hispanic elementary teacher employment and Hispanic elementary student enrollment were highly correlated with large degrees of overlap. Illustrated in Table 3 are the correlation coefficients (r), the coefficients of determination (r^2), and effect sizes for the correlation calculated between White teachers and White students in Texas public elementary schools for all school years of data examined. As was noted with the two minority groups, with the exception of one school year, the data remained consistent over the 11 school years. Overall, White elementary teacher employment and White elementary student enrollment were highly correlated with large degrees of overlap.

DISCUSSION

Although a positive relationship between teacher ethnicity and student academic performance has been documented in multiple studies (Alliance for Excellent Education, 2005; Branch & Kritsonis, 2006; Tyler et al., 2004), few researchers have focused on teacher ethnicity as it relates to student ethnicity or the efforts being made toward diversifying the teaching force. Thus, this study was focused on the relationship between teacher ethnicity and student ethnicity in Texas public elementary schools. Nationally, more than $2 million is spent annually on recruiting new teachers to the field of education to replace those who have left the profession (Alliance for Excellent Education, 2005). Similarly, the state of Texas spends more than a half billion dollars each year on teacher recruitment (Alliance for Excellent Education, 2005). Martinez-Garcia, Slate, and Tejeda-Delgado (2009) reported that teacher turnover was almost twice as high in Texas school districts with higher percentages (i.e., 75% or higher) of minority students (Hispanic and Black students) than in Texas school districts with lower percentages (i.e., less than 25%) of minority students (Hispanic and Black students). Moreover, attrition rates increase roughly 50% in high minority populated schools (Alliance for Excellent Education, 2005).

As a result, those campuses that are most in need of spending funds directly on student instruction are instead spending limited funds on replacing teachers who have left the profession. Thus, the results of this study provided implications concerning the effectiveness of minority teacher recruitment and retention throughout public elementary schools in Texas.

With the exception of one school year, the data examined regarding the relationships between teacher ethnic diversity (i.e., Black, Hispanic, and White) and student ethnic diversity (i.e., Black, Hispanic, and White) in Texas public elementary schools remained consistent across the 11 school years included in the study. A strong relationship was present between where Black students were enrolled and where Black teachers were employed. As the numbers of Black students enrolled in elementary schools increased, the numbers of Black teachers employed at the elementary schools increased. Even stronger was the positive relationship between where Hispanic students were enrolled in elementary schools and where Hispanic teachers were employed in elementary schools. The strongest relationship was present between where White students were enrolled in elementary schools and where White teachers were employed in elementary schools.

Unfortunately, the increase in minority teachers at the elementary level was still lacking when compared to the increase in minority students at the elementary level. Overall, the relationships between teacher ethnic diversity (i.e., Black, Hispanic, and White) and student ethnic diversity (i.e., Black, Hispanic, and White) in Texas public elementary schools did not change much across the school years included in the study. Thus, it can be concluded that the minority teacher recruitment strategies employed by school districts in Texas have not been successful at increasing the diversity of the teacher work force and providing ethnic students with more teachers of their same ethnicity in public elementary schools.

Results of this study were congruent with the theory of homosocial reproduction. In this study, elementary schools at which more minority students were enrolled also employed more minority teachers. However, the ethnicity of the elementary school teaching staff consistently remained disproportionate to the ethnicity of the students enrolled in Texas public elementary schools. Moreover, the ethnicity of the elementary school teaching staff remained consistent over the school years examined, in spite of the fact that student ethnic groups in elementary schools were growing, particularly among the Hispanic population. According to the Schools and Staffing Survey (USDE, 2004), 87.5% of public elementary school administrators throughout the nation were White. Thus, the consistency demonstrated in the results of this study was an indication that Texas public elementary school administrators continued largely to hire individuals who were most like themselves. If these trends persist, student ethnic minority groups will continue to diversify, yet school districts will continue to employ a mostly White teaching staff. Accordingly, school districts must implement successful strategies to recruit more minority teachers. Additionally, school districts must begin to hold school administrators accountable for hiring a teaching staff whose ethnicity is reflective of the students' ethnicity.

IMPLICATIONS FOR POLICY

Implications for policy can be ascertained from the results of this study. At a minimum, an examination of the results of this study should convince local, state, and national education agencies to analyze critically the emphasis currently placed on minority teacher recruitment, as evidenced in policy. Additionally, the results of this study generate the need for policy reform from social, academic, and economic standpoints.

Social Standpoint

Some minority students graduate high school without ever having been taught by a teacher of the same ethnicity (NCES, 2003). The disparity between the percentage of minority teachers and the percentage of minority students on campuses throughout Texas is an indication of the lack of understanding of the importance of providing a diverse teaching staff. Furthermore, employing a teaching staff whose ethnicity mirrors that of their students helps to create more equitable and participatory communities (Villegas & Lucas, 2002). According to Villegas and Lucas (2002), efforts to hire more minority teachers assist in the interruption of discriminatory policies and practices in classrooms.

When school districts do not hold administrators accountable for hiring a diverse teaching force, a message is sent to students and to the community regarding the value placed on diversity (Villegas, 1993). In fact, Clewell, Anderson, Bruschi, Goertz, and Villegas (1993) contended that one way an organization, such as a public school district, demonstrates a commitment to diversity is by recruiting, hiring, and retaining minority teachers. However, schools that do not actively recruit and employ minorities in teaching and leadership positions do not reflect a commitment to an inclusive, multicultural climate (Villegas, 1993). If citizens of the U.S. truly want to promote a culture of equality, then the schools must embody that desire. Thus, from a social standpoint, an examination of the outcomes of this study should result in changes to policy. Guidelines must be put into place that would require school administrators to implement strategies to recruit and retain minority teachers. Furthermore, these guidelines must provide for instruments to measure and gauge the effectiveness of the strategies implemented.

Academic Standpoint

The nation has mandated that school districts provide an equal education to all students. However, minority students do not have as many role models in leadership positions throughout the schools to represent their own ethnic and cultural backgrounds (USDE, n.d.). If all students in the state of Texas are to receive a fair chance at learning and succeeding in education, then minority students must be provided with more teachers who represent varying student ethnicity to serve as role models (Branch & Kritsonis, 2006).

According to Tyler et al. (2004), numerous benefits for minority students exist with a diverse teaching force. For example, racially or ethnically diverse teachers have a profound impact on minority students' comfort level in the classroom, provide role models for these students, act as liaisons between the community and the school, and even act as a cultural liaison for the students, introducing them to the school's culture that is largely White, middle class (Tyler et al., 2004). Additionally, diverse teachers might serve as activists for student rights and advocates for student growth and development.

Among minority students in elementary schools, minority teachers are able to impact academic achievement particularly by acting as role models for the students (Ikegulu, 2009). Minority teachers are often some of the only minority professionals with whom elementary minority students come into contact and with whom they can relate (Villegas & Irvine, 2010). Moreover, providing minority teachers as role models for elementary aged minority students decreases the sense of alienation experienced in U.S. schools and classrooms by many minority students (Villegas & Irvine, 2010). As a result, Hess and Leal (1997) reported that providing elementary aged minority students with minority teacher role models increased math and reading scores. Overall, minority teacher role models in elementary schools can have positive effects on minority student academic outcomes (Pitts, 2007).

Regardless of the age, minority students stand to benefit academically from the presence of minority teachers. In fact, researchers identified five practices of minority teachers that result in more successful academic outcomes for minority students at all levels. The five practices include: (a) having high expectations of students; (b) using culturally relevant teaching; (c) developing caring and trusting relationships with students; (d) confronting issues of racism through teaching; and (e) serving as advocates and cultural brokers (Villegas &

Irvine, 2010). Should minority students be provided with more opportunities for academic success, the high dropout rates for minorities (50% of all African-American students and 49% of all Hispanic students) in 2001 (Orfield et al., 2004) would decrease, and the percentage of minority students attending college would increase. In turn, the number of potential minority teacher candidates would also increase.

RECOMMENDATIONS FOR FUTURE RESEARCH

One of the most vital studies to be recommended for future research is to obtain the necessary data to determine which teachers teach which students. With AEIS data, a determination can be made regarding the percentage of minority teachers, as well as the percentage of minority students. However, the AEIS does not provide the number of ethnic minority students by grade or course assignment. Therefore, it is impossible to determine which teachers are teaching which students. In this study, teacher and student ethnicity were examined on a campus level, rather than on a teacher to student level. Thus, a recommendation for future research is for researchers who have access to student level data to pursue a study of teacher ethnicity and student ethnicity at the student level.

A second suggestion for future research is to compare teacher ethnicity and student ethnicity in Texas middle schools, high schools, charter schools, Texas private schools, and Texas alternative placement schools. Such comparisons would shed light on the equal opportunities for employment in middle schools, high schools, charter, private, and alternative schools. Additionally, studies performed in these settings would most definitely provide some insight into the racial achievement gap. Moreover, a study of teacher ethnicity and student ethnicity in Texas alternative schools would add to the existing body of knowledge on the relationship between teacher ethnicity and student ethnicity and referrals to alternative placement schools.

CONCLUSION

Documented in the results of this study were positive relationships between where Black teachers were employed and where Black students were enrolled, where Hispanic teachers were employed and where Hispanic students were enrolled, and where White teachers were employed and where White students were enrolled at the elementary school level. The relationship between the employment of Hispanic teachers and enrollment of Hispanic students was stronger than that of Black teachers and Black students. Moreover, the relationship between the employment of White teachers and enrollment of White students was even stronger than that of Hispanic teachers and Hispanic students. Most importantly, the relationships examined in this study remained consistent over the school years analyzed. This consistency was an indication that the resources devoted to diversifying the teaching force have not been effective.

Therefore, it is critical for school districts to find more accurate methods of measuring the effectiveness of minority teacher recruitment strategies. If school districts do not employ more successful tactics for recruiting minority teachers that better represent the ethnic diversity of the students, then resources expended toward this effort are better spent in other instructional areas. Ultimately, student diversity in Texas public schools will continue to expand, and unless minority teacher recruitment strategies undergo drastic changes, the achievement gap will only continue to widen. Furthermore, the negative consequences of the minority academic achievement gap, such as lower incomes, poorer health, and higher rates of incarceration, will continue to contribute to the national debt and to the financial load that U.S. citizens must shoulder (McKinsey & Company, 2009). Additionally, minorities will continue to have negative consequences and will continue to encumber the states and federal government with large percentages of minorities dependent on welfare or incarcerated.

REFERENCES

Alliance for Excellent Education. (2005). *Teacher attrition: A costly loss to the nation and to the states.* Retrieved from http://www.all4ed.org/files/archive/publications /TeacherAttrition.pdf

Branch, R., & Kritsonis, W. (2006). National agenda: Minority teacher recruitment, development, and retention. *National Journal for Publishing and Mentoring Doctoral Student Research, 3*(1), 1-4.

Cho, G., & DeCastro-Ambrosetti, D. (2005). Is ignorance bliss? Preservice teachers' attitudes toward multicultural education. *The High School Journal, 89*(2), 24-28. doi:10.1353/hsj.2005.0020

Clewell, B. C., Anderson, B. T., Bruschi, B. A., Goertz, M. E., & Villegas, A. M. (1993). *Innovative programs in teacher education: Preparing teachers for diversity in the classroom and increasing the pool of minority teachers.* Princeton, NJ: Educational Testing Service.

Cloudt, C., & Stevens, N. (2009). Texas teacher diversity and recruitment. *Policy Research, 2*(1), 3-25.

Cohen, J. (1988). *Statistical power analysis for the behavioral sciences* (2nd ed.). Hillsdale, NJ: Lawrence Erlbaum.

Frankenburg, E., & Siegel-Hawley, G. (2008). *Are teachers prepared for racially changing schools? Teachers describe their preparation, resources, and practices for racially diverse schools.* Cambridge, MA: The Civil Rights Project at Harvard University.

Greeney, B. (2010). *High school size, student achievement, and school climate: A multi-year study.* (Unpublished doctoral dissertation.) Sam Houston State University.

Hess, F. M., & Leal, D. L. (1997). Minority teachers, minority students, and college matriculation. *Policy Studies Journal, 25*, 235-248.

Ikegulu, T. N. (2009). *Economically disadvantaged student failure: The role of non-minority teachers of elementary school students.* Retrieved from http://www.eric.ed.gov/PDFS/ED507249.pdf

Kanter, R. M. (1977). *Men and women of the corporation.* New York, NY: Basic Books.

Kingsley, J. D. (1944). *Representative bureaucracy.* Yellow Springs, OH: Antioch Press.

Krislov, S. J. (1974). *Representative bureaucracy.* Englewood Cliffs, NJ: Prentice Hall.

Levitan, D. M. (1946). The responsibility of administrative officials in a democratic society. *Political Science Quarterly, 61*, 562-598. doi:10.2307/2144373

Martinez-Garcia, C., Slate, J. R., & Tejeda-Delgado, C. (2009). Teacher turnover and student demographics: A three year analysis of Texas statewide data. *National Journal of Urban Education & Practice, 2*(2), 59-70.

McKinsey & Company. (2009). *The economic impact of the achievement gap in America's schools.* Retrieved from www.mckinsey.com/App_Media/Images /Page_Images/ Offices/SocialSector/PDF/achievement_gap_report.pdf

National Center for Education Statistics. (2003). *The condition of education 2003.* United States Department of Education, Office of Educational Research and Improvement, Washington, DC. Retrieved from http://nces.ed.gov /pubsearch/pubsinfo.asp? pubid=2003067

Office of Civil Rights. (n.d.). In *U.S. Department of Education.* Retrieved from http://www.ed.gov/about/offices/list/ocr/docs/hq43e4.html

Onwuegbuzie, A. J., & Daniel, L. G. (2002). Uses and misuses of the correlation coefficient. *Research in the Schools, 9*(1), 73-90.

Orfield, G., & Lee, C. (2007). *Historic reversals, accelerating resegregation, and the need for new integration strategies.* Cambridge, MA: The Civil Rights Project at Harvard University.

Orfield, G., Losen, D., Wald, J., & Swanson, C. (2004). *Losing our future: How minority youth are being left behind by the graduation rate crisis.* Cambridge, MA: The Civil Rights Project at Harvard University. Retrieved from http://www.urban.org/ UploadedPDF/410936_LosingOurFuture.pdf

Paige, R., & Witty, E. (2010). The Black-White achievement gap: Why closing it is the greatest civil rights issue of our time. *The Education Digest, 75*(8), 69-70.

Petersen, D., & Assanie, L. (2005). *The changing face of Texas: Population projections and implications.* Dallas, TX: Federal Reserve Bank of Dallas.

Pitts, D. W. (2007). Representative bureaucracy, ethnicity, and public schools: Examining the link between representation and performance. *Administration & Society, 39,* 497-526.

Snyder, T. D., Dillow, S. A., & Hoffman, C. M. (2007). *Digest for education statistics 2006.* National Center for Education Statistics, Institute of Education Sciences, U.S. Department of Education, Washington, DC: U.S. Government Printing Office.

Taylor, E. (1998). Toward a coherent theory of race in the education of school leaders: Fly fishing across the racial divide. *Race Ethnicity and Education, 1,* 225-239. doi:10.1080/1361332980010206

Texas Education Agency. (2009a). *Academic Excellence Indicator System.* Retrieved from http://ritter.tea.state.tx.us/perfreport/account/2009/manual/intro.pdf

Texas Education Agency. (2009b). *Academic Excellence Indicator System Glossary.* Retrieved from http://ritter.tea.state.tx.us/perfreport/aeis/2009/glossary.pdf

Tyler, N. C., Yzquierdo, Z., Lopez-Reyna, N., & Saunders-Flippin, S. (2004). Cultural and linguistic diversity and the special education workforce: An overview. *Journal of Special Education, 38*(1), 24-27. doi:10.1177/00224669040380010301

U.S. Department of Education. (2004). *Public school principal, BIA school principal, and private school principal* [Data file]. Retrieved from http://nces.ed.gov /surveys/sass/ tables/sass_2004_27.asp

U.S. Department of Education. (n.d.). *Education Resource Organizations Directory.* Retrieved from http://wdcrobcolp01.ed.gov/Programs/EROD/org_list.cfm?category_ cd=SEA

Villegas, A. M. (1993). *Teaching for diversity: Models for expanding the supply of minority teachers.* Retrieved from http://www.eric.ed.gov/PDFS/ED390920.pdf

Villegas, A. M., & Irvine, J. J. (2010). Diversifying the teaching force: An examination of major arguments. *Urban Review, 42,* 175-192. doi:10.2007/s11256-010-0150-1.

Villegas, A. M., & Lucas, T. (2002). *Educating culturally responsive teachers: A coherent approach.* Albany, NY: State University of New York.

In: Handbook of Academic Performance
Editors: Rolf Haumann and George Zimmer

ISBN: 978-1-62417-888-7
© 2013 Nova Science Publishers, Inc.

Chapter 12

GENDER AS A DETERMINING FACTOR IN THE COPING STRATEGIES AND RESILIENCE OF UNIVERSITY STUDENTS

Jesús de la Fuente[1], María Cardelle-Elawar[2],
José Manuel Martínez-Vicente[1], Lucía Zapata[3]
and Francisco Javier Peralta Sánchez[1]

[1]University of Almería, Spain
[2]Arizona State University, US
[3]Education and Psychology I+D+I, University of Almería, Spain

ABSTRACT

Introduction: *Coping Strategies* and *Resilience* have emerged as two variables that determine behavior when facing stress in academic situations. Current research examines their role among other motivational-affective variables of a cognitive type. The objective of this study was to establish how the gender of university students relates to strategies for coping with stress and to resilience. An interdependence relationship was hypothesized between students' gender and the type of coping strategies used, and between gender and resilience behavior.

Method: The participants were 243 students from the Psychology degree program at the University of Almería (Spain). An ex post-facto design was used. The assessment instruments were: (1) for *Coping Strategies,* the *Escalas de Estrategias de Coping*, a Spanish version of the Coping with Stress Questionnaire by Lazarus and Folman (Chorot & Sandín, 1987, Sandín & Chorot, 2003), assessing coping strategies that either focus on the problem or focus on emotion, when managing academic stress; (2) for *Resilience,* the CD-RISC inventory, Spanish version (Connor & Davidon, 2003). The latter is a likert-type scale made up of 25 items and five factors: (1) personal competence, high standards and tenacity, (2) tolerance of negative affect and strengthening effects of stress, (3) positive acceptance of change, and secure relationships, (4) control and (5) spiritual influences. Cluster analyses, correlation and ANOVAs were performed.

Results: Significant differences appeared in the variables assessed as a function of gender. Female university students scored higher on total coping strategies, and on coping strategies focused on emotion and on the problem. As for resilience, male students had higher scores in withstanding stress, while female students scored higher on the spirituality factor.

Discussion: The results provide evidence of the importance of coping strategies and resilience in the life of the university student, according to students' gender. Furthermore, they concur with other prior evidence. An important line of research is thus marked out for the study of motivational and affective variables involved in how university students learn.

Keywords: Gender, coping strategies, resilience, academic stress, higher education

INTRODUCTION

The study of coping strategies and resilience are highly current topics in the field of Clinical and Health Psychology (American Psychological Association, 2008; Boyden, & Mann, 2005; Bonanno, Galea, Bucciareli, Vlahov, 2007; Carver, & Scheier, 1999; Castro & Murray, 2010). However, there has been insufficient inquiry into the sphere of learning processes, which has been more limited to the study of cognitive processes. Coping strategies and resilience have considerable explanatory value in the area of motivational-affective processes while learning at university. As their name indicates, coping strategies are strategic behaviors that university students employ in response to and in order to manage situations of academic stress. Thus, they can be considered meta-motivational and meta-affective behaviors (Caballero, Abello, & Palacio, 2007; Caballero, Hederich & Palacio, 2010; Jang, 2008; Martin, 2008; Martin, and Liem, 2010; Miñano, Gilar, and Castejón, 2012). In the same way, resilience behaviors may also be classified as such, since they explain how one faces and overcomes adverse situations that are typical to academic settings at university (Zautra, Hall, and Murray, 2010). In addition to the inherent importance of both research topics, due to their role in formal teaching-learning processes, possible gender differences in how students face stressful academic situations is also of interest.

The University Academic Context As a Presage Variable of Stress

The academic context is important because it can operate as a variable that induces or reduces stress. The topic of stress, as seen from different fields of knowledge, has been well studied during the 20th century, generating a series of theoretical perspectives for both pure and applied research in this area (Barraza, 2005). Historically, there have been diverse conceptions of stress. The first studies understood stress from a physiological and biochemical viewpoint, emphasizing the importance of the organic response, and focusing on the internal processes of the subject. The more psychological and social viewpoints are interested above all in the situation that generates stress. More recent approaches, such as the interactive theory of stress by Lazarus and collaborators, place more emphasis on interrelationships and mediational or transactional processes (Lazarus & Folkman, 1984; Folkman & Moskowitz, 2004), in which stress is defined as the appraisal of an event based on the person's perceived ability to cope.

Coping Strategies As a Motivational-affective Variable in the Learning Process

Coping strategies refer to a constellation of strategies which healthy people develop as problem solvers. Several reviews indicate a strong association between the experience of stressors and the presence of emotional and behavioral problems (Dumont and Provost, 1999; Grant *et al.*, 2003; Kim, Conger, Elder, and Lorenz, 2003; Rafnsson, Jonson, and Windle, 2006). However, despite this evidence, it has been suggested that psychological well-being and health are more influenced by the manner of coping with stress than the mere presence of difficult situations (Folkman, Lazarus, Pimley and Novacek, 1987).

According to the classic transactional model of coping proposed by Lazarus and Folkman (1984), stress occurs when a person perceives that environmental demands exceed their capacities and available resources, so it will carry out evaluation of the stressor, which will determine the level of stress that person experiences. According to Lazarus and Folkman (1984), "Psychological stress is a particular relationship between the person and the environment, which is appraised by the person as taxing or exceeding his or her resources and endangering his or her well-being" (Lazarus and Folkman, 1984, p. 19). These authors describe two important types of cognitive appraisal of significance for well-being. Indeed, before actually coping with a situation, it must be cognitively evaluated as potentially stressful. Two cognitive mechanisms, classified as primary and secondary appraisals, are employed. Primary appraisal is an assessment of what is at stake: "Am I in trouble or being benefited, now or in the future, and in what way? Is anything at stake here?" If the answer to this question is yes, then people categorize the situation as being a threat, a challenge or a loss. Loss refers to damages or harms that have already happened; threat and challenge appraisals can refer to past events or to anticipated ones. While threat suggests potential danger to one's well-being or self-esteem, challenge suggests that one focuses on the success, the social rewards, and the personal growth that the situation could bring. It is important to note, however, that threat and challenge appraisals are not necessarily mutually exclusive. As stated by Lazarus and Folkman (1984) threat and challenge appraisals are not two ends of a single continuum. Although they are negatively correlated (Skinner & Brewer, 2002), threat and challenge appraisals can occur simultaneously. For example, Folkman and Lazarus (1985) showed that students waiting for an exam appraised the upcoming event as particularly threatening and challenging.

Secondary appraisal is an assessment of coping resources and answers to the question: "Can I cope with this situation?" It indicates confidence in one's ability to cope with the situation because one has the resources to cope with it. Resources can be physical (e.g., health, energy), social (e.g., social support one can get from family, friends and social network), psychological (e.g., beliefs, self-esteem, perceived control, morale) or material (e.g., financial, tools). Coping refers to "cognitive and behavioral efforts to master, reduce, or tolerate the internal and/or external demands that are created by the stressful transaction" (Folkman, 1984, p. 843; see also Folkman & Lazarus, 1980). Given the diversity of responses to stress that exist, most authors tried to make significant and meaningful categorizations (e.g. active versus passive or avoidant coping, see Suls & Fletcher, 1985; Roth & Cohen, 1986). Lazarus and Folkman proposed that coping serves two major functions (Folkman *et al.*, 1986). One is the regulation of emotions or distresses that come with the stressful situation (emotion-focused coping).

The other is the management of the problem that is causing the stress by directly changing the elements of the stressful situation (problem-focused coping). Although both forms of coping are used in most stressful encounters, they are nevertheless dependent on the way one appraises the situation (i.e., as a threat and/or a challenge) and of the antecedents of the model. For example, Folkman and Lazarus, who analyzed 1300 stressful episodes reported by people, found that both forms of coping were used in most encounters. Nevertheless, people tended to use more problem-focused strategies when the situation was appraised as changeable and more emotion-focused strategies when the situation was appraised as not or less changeable (Folkman & Lazarus, 1980).

In sum, Lazarus and Folkman identified at least two broad categories of antecedents which will directly influence how people appraise and cope with the situation: those that are linked to the characteristics of the individual and those linked to the characteristics of the situation.

Among the former, for example, we can find commitments (which define what is important for the person and so what is at stake in that situation), beliefs, such as beliefs about personal control (Folkman, 1984), and personal traits such as self-esteem (Rector and Roger, 1997). Among situational factors, we can find the novelty or the predictability of the situation, the uncertainty of the event, temporal factors (e.g. time generally enhances threat but can also leave some time to think it through) and the ambiguity of the situation (Lazarus & Folkman, 1984).

Another line of research on coping strategies focuses on two objectives: (a) The development and classification of typologies and (b) the study of relationships between emotional strategies for coping and their manifestation in individual behavior. With regard to typological classification, presently there is neither consensus on the conceptualization of the construct nor on its measurement (Skinner, Edge, Altman, & Sherwood, 2003). However, research conducted by Duhachek and Oakley (2007), suggests that there may be a common thread running through a group of coping strategies for facilitating behavioral change. These strategies represent an effort oriented to modify the stressors attributed to the individual and the environment. The first group of these coping strategies attempt to solve problems, confronting them as an active agent. The second group includes social support, situational change, and psychological adjustment. The third group from the review of the literature relates to avoidance, an individual attitude orientation toward giving up without struggling for control of the conflictive situation, or just accepting it through resignation.

Resilience As a Motivational-affective Variable in the Learning Process

Resilience is the capacity to overcome adversity, recover, and come out stronger and successful, and to develop social, academic and vocational competence despite being exposed to severe psychosocial stress (Bermejo, 2011; Csikszentmihalyi, 1999; Grotberg, 1995; Rutter, 1985). Traditionally, psychology has not given sufficient attention to this phenomenon, but in recent years resilience has become an object of study. From the etymological viewpoint, this term comes from the Latin saliere, meaning to jump backward, rebound, be repelled, come up. The prefix re implies repeating or resuming. Resiliar means "to be revived or go forward, after having suffered a blow or having experienced a traumatic situation" (Cyrulnik et al., 2004, p.12).

In the last several years, the concept of resilience has come to be addressed as that quality of persons to withstand and to recover from traumatic situations or losses. Resilience has been defined as a person or group's capacity to continue moving forward toward the future, despite destabilizing events, difficult life conditions and sometimes serious traumas (Manciaux *et al.*, 2001).

In the educational context, resilience plays an important role. The individual measures his or her own strength in the face of different challenges and demands, not only academic challenges but also psychosocial, dealing with demanding situations that require self-confrontation in order to better understand one's own potential and ability to grow stronger, learn and respond effectively, preserving one's mental health and confidence in one's potential and skills. The few studies that have addressed this topic have focused mainly on identifying resilient characteristics in a childhood population (Bradley *et al.*, 1994), and in populations that are victims of poverty or disasters (Seifer, Sameroff, Baldwin, & Baldwin, 1992), but the student population remains largely unexplored.

The learning process involves a large dose of motivation, not only to adequately withstand the pace and demand for adaptation and all kind of responses, but also to self-regulate and be able to respond adequately without becoming overwhelmed or falling into emotional disturbances such as defencelessness, apathy, depression, anxiety (Álvarez & Cáceres, 2010).

Some prior work on resilience in student populations associates these manifestations with a deficiency in resilience (Bragagnolo *et al.*, 2005). Likewise, research on stress in university students indicates that lack of self-confidence creates a pattern of vulnerability, leaving students with low resistance and lack of optimism about themselves, their environment and their possibilities for getting ahead. This in turn triggers psychological disorders in the educational and social context; these disorders are not always addressed by institutional support services, and end up affecting academic performance, social relationships and the student's own affectivity (Solórzano & Ramos, 2006).

Aims and Hypothesis of the Study

The objective of this study was to establish how the gender of university students relates to coping strategies and to resilience. An interdependence relationship was hypothesized between students' gender and the type of coping strategies used, and between gender and resilience behavior. We hypothesized that there is an interdependent relationship between student's gender and level of the two variables.

METHOD

Participants

The sample was composed of 243 students in the 2nd and 4th years of the Psychology Degree program at the University of Almería (Spain), with a mean age of 21.06 years (SD= 3.10).

Instruments

Coping Strategies

The Coping Strategies Scale, EEC (Sandin & Chorot, 2003; Londoño *et al.*, 2006), with a total of 90 items, was selected for being one of the most validated scales for assessing coping with stress in undergraduate students in Higher Education. It was developed by following the Lazarus and Folkman (1984) model. Prior to this study, the questionnaire was validated in a pilot study with a sample of Spanish undergraduates, in order to assess the *internal validity criteria;* the results from exploratory factor analysis of principal components showed that the questionnaire has a two-factor structure for second level (forced). The Bartlett test, a prerequisite to factor analysis, shows a chi-square value (36) =216.842; *p*<.001, demonstrating that our data structure is valid for the factor analysis. The KMO rate of .768 also demonstrated data suitability for factor analysis. The study of this two-fold dimension of the teaching-learning process was done by principal components with varimax rotation (rotation with no factor limit and ignoring saturations less than .40). The analysis suggested two factors that explained 79.36% of the variance: emotional coping strategies (38.58%) and problem coping strategies (31.78%). *Reliability* results were Cronbach Alpha = .930 (complete scale), .930 (first half) and .904 (second half); Spearman-Brown: .8439 and Guttman: .803.

Resilience

The *CD-RISC* inventory, Spanish version, was used (Connor & Davidson, 2003). This Likert-type scale is made up of 25 items and five factors: (1) personal competence, high standards and tenacity, (2) tolerance of negative affect and strengthening effects of stress, (3) positive acceptance of change, and secure relationships, (4) control and (5) spiritual influences. Reliability and Validity measures reported by the authors are consistent. In our sample, the statistics are Alpha= .868, and Guttman Split Half=.814.

Procedure

The assessment was performed with second- and fourth-year students from the psychology program at the University of Almería (Spain), during academic year 2011-2012. All students participated voluntarily and were informed of the purposes of the research. Assessment was carried out through the same classroom subject, teacher and methodology. The first questionnaire was completed at mid-term, and the second was completed at the end.

Data Analysis

An inferential 2 (year in school) x 2 (gender) design was used, in addition to univariate analyses (ANOVAs) and multi-variate analyses (MANOVAs).

RESULTS

Coping Strategies

No statistically significant effect was found in the ANOVA that took gender x year in school as independent variables, and total mean for coping strategies as dependent variable.

However, a significant main effect did appear for year in school, in favor of students in fourth year, in their average of total coping strategies used, F (1, 239)=10.807, p<001, eta^2= .043. Direct values are shown in Table 1.

Styles of Coping Strategies

The MANOVA which took *gender x year in school* as independent variables and the two types of coping styles (emotion-focused vs. problem-focused) as dependent variables, revealed a main effect of *gender, F* (1,239)=10.807, p<.001, eta^2= .043, in favor of the female gender, and of *year in school, F* (2,238)=2.867, p<.05, eta^2= .024, in favor of the fourth year students. Specifically, there was an effect of *gender* on problem-focused coping, in favor of the female gender, F (2,238)= 3.124, p<.05. There was also an effect of *year in school,* in favor of the fourth year, in both types of coping strategies, emotion-focused coping, F (2,238)=10.241, p<.001 and problem-focused coping, F (2,238)= 10.472, p<.001. Direct values are shown in Table 2.

Table 1. Average values for coping strategies according to gender and year in school

	2nd year (n=42)	*4th year* (n=151)	*Total* (n=243)
Male (n=51)	2.45 (.30)	2.82 (.67)	2.75 (.63)
Female (n=192)	2.57 (.19)	3.04 (.70)	2.94 (.66)
Total (n=243)	2.54 (.22)	2.99 (.70)	2.90 (.66)

Table 2. Average values for styles of coping strategy, according to gender and year in school

Emotion-focused coping			
	2nd year (n=42)	4th year (n=151)	*Total* (n=243)
Male (n=51)	2.20 (.41)	2.58 (.78)	2.51 (.73)
Female (n=192)	2.24 (.27)	2.82 (.81)	2.70 (.77)
Total (n=243)	2.23 (.30)	2.77 (.81)	2.66 (.77)
Problem-focused coping			
	2nd year (n=42)	4th year (n=151)	*Total* (n=243)
Male (n=51)	2.69 (.24)	3.06 (.64)	3.00 (.57)
Female (n=192)	2.90 (.19)	3.26 (.62)	3.18 (.57)
Total (n=243)	2.86 (.21)	3.22 (.62)	3.15 (.66)

Types of Coping Strategies

The MANOVA which took *gender x year in school* as independent variables and the thirteen types of coping strategies as dependent variables showed a significant main effect of gender, F (13,227)= 3.996, p<.001, eta^2= .186 and of year in school, F (3,227)= 1.955, p<.05, eta^2= .101. Specifically, female students showed higher scores on coping strategies of the second type (help seeking and family counsel), F (1, 239)= 5.870, p<.01, the third type (actions directed at the causes), F (1,239)= 9.403, $p<.001$, and the twelfth type (communication of feelings and social support), F (1,239)= 15.173, $p<.001$. See direct values in Table 3.

Table 3. Average values for types of coping strategy, according to gender and year in school

	2nd year (n=42)	4th year (n=151)	Total (n=243)
F2 Help seeking and family support			
Male (n=51)	2.65 (.33)	2.92 (.73)	2.91 (.68)
Female (n=192)	3.03 (.62)	3.31 (.77)	3.25 (.74)
Total (n=243)	2.96 (.59)	3.23 (.77)	3.18 (.74)
F3. Actions directed at the causes			
Male (n=51)	2.31 (.40)	2.79 (.78)	2.71 (.75)
Female (n=192)	2.78 (.36)	3.15 (.70)	3.07 (.66)
Total (n=243)	2.70 (.41)	3.07 (.73)	3.00 (.69)
F12. Communication of feelings and social support			
Male (n=51)	2.62 (.52)	2.90 (.85)	2.85 (.81)
Female (n=192)	3.24 (.65)	3.42 (.71)	3.39 (.70)
Total (n=243)	3.13 (.67)	3.31 (.78)	3.27 (.76)

The factor *year in school* had a significant effect in all types of coping strategies, in favor of fourth year students, with the exception of strategy F12 (communication of feelings and social support).

Table 4. Significant average values of the constituent factors of resilience

	2nd year (n=42)	4th year (n=151)	Total (n=243)
F2. Confidence and tolerance of stress			
Male (n=51)	3.74 (.47)	3.74 (.60)	3.74 (.53)
Female (n=192)	3.33 (.49)	3.51 (.59)	3.39 (.52)
Total (n=243)	3.43 (.51)	3.60 (.60)	3.49 (.55)
F3. Perceived control			
Male (n=51)	3.57 (1.0)	3.64 (.93)	3.60 (1.0)
Female (n=192)	3.92 (.72)	3.98 (.63)	3.94 (.69)
Total (n=243)	3.83 (.83)	3.85 (.77)	3.084(.80)
F5. Spirituality			
Male (n=51)	2.32 (.91)	2.30 (1.1)	2.31 (1.0)
Female (n=192)	2.85 (.83)	2.88 (.87)	2.86 (.84)
Total (n=243)	2.72 (.87)	2.66 (1.0)	2.70 (.93)

Resilience

The ANOVA which took *gender x year in school* as independent variables and total score on resilience as dependent variable did not show stastistically significant effects. However, the MANOVA *gender x year in school* that took the five constituent factors of resilience as dependent variables, did show a significant main effect of *gender, F* $(5,84)$=5.981, p<.001, eta^2=.263. This was not the case for year in school.

Specifically, a significant effect of gender appeared on F2 (tolerance to negative stress situations), in favor of male students, *F* $(1,88)$=6.778, p<.01, on F4 (perceived control), in favor of female students, *F* $(1,88)$= 3.436, p<.05, and on F5 (spiritual influence) in favor of female students, *F* $(1,88)$=6.691, p<.01. Direct values are shown in Table 4.

DISCUSSION AND CONCLUSION

The results allowed us to meet the objectives and to verify the research hypotheses. As proposed, the *gender* factor has a clear effect on both constructs. In the case of *coping strategies*, apart from the lack of general gender differences in the average level of strategies, different ways of coping with stressful situations were found to exist (González-Cabanach *et al,* 2010). Thus, female students were seen with higher averages in problem-centered strategies than male students. These results point in the same direction as others found previously (El-Ghoroury, *et al,* 2012). Also, the year in school, representing a history of learning, reveals an increase in strategies for coping with stress, just as would be expected. However, this result brings into question a different result found earlier, referring to a negative relationship between the number of coping strategies and personal self-regulation (de la Fuente & Cardelle-Elawar, 2011). On the other hand, in the case of *resilience,* no general differences between genders were revealed, but specific differences with regard to how stress is experienced. Male students report higher tolerance for negative stress situations, while female students have more perceived control over the situations and more spirituality in facing them. These results confirm the importance of this topic in the prior evidence (Skinner, Furrer, Marchand & Kinderman, 2008; Skinner, Kinderman & Furrer, 2009; Skinner, Kinderman, Connell & Wellborn, 2009; Skinner & Pitzer, 2012). As for the implications of these results, there is a need for intervention in university students in order to help them manage stressful situations, especially through *mindfulness programs* (de la Fuente, Franco & Mañas, 2010). Based on these results, such programs would appear to be more necessary for male students, due to the lower number of coping strategies used, as well as having less perceived control over stressful situations. Future research should determine other more precise relationships between learning approaches and motivational-affective correlates analyzed here, such as coping strategies, resilience, self-regulation and action-emotion style.

ACKNOWLEDGMENTS

This research was carried out within the framework of the R&D Project ref. EDU2011-24805 (2012-2014). MICINN (Spain) and FEDER Funds.

REFERENCES

Álvarez, L. and Cáceres, L. (2010) Resiliencia, Rendimiento Académico y Variables Sociodemográficas en Estudiantes Universitarios de Bucaramanga (Colombia). [Resilence, Academic Performance and Socio-demographic Variables in University Students of Bucaramanga (Colombia)]. *Psicología Iberoamericana, 18* (2), 37-46.

American Psychological Association, Task Force on Resilience and Strength in Black Children and Adolescents (2008). Resilience in African American children and adolescents: A vision for optimal development. Washington, DC: Author. Retrieved from http://www.apa.org/pi/cyf/ resilience/html.

Barraza, A. (2005). El estrés académico de los alumnos de Educación Media Superior, Hermosillo. [Academic stress in students of Upper Secondary Education, Hermosillo.] Online proceedings of the *VIII Congreso Nacional de Investigación Educativa.*

Bradley, R. H., Whiteside-Mansell, L., Mundfrom, D. J., Casey, P. H., Kelleher, K. J., Pope, S. K. (1994). Early indications of resilience and their relation to experiences in the home environments of lowbirthweight, premature children living in poverty. *Child Development.* 65,346–60.

Bermejo, J. C. (2011). *Resiliencia.* [Resilience.] Madrid: PPC.

Boyden, J. and Mann, G. (2005). Children's risk, resilience, and coping in extreme situations. In M. Ungar (Ed.), *Handbook for working with children and youth: Pathways to resilience across cultures and contexts* (pp. 36). Thousand Oaks, CA: Sage.

Bonanno, G. A., Galea, S., Bucciareli, A., and Vlahov, D. (2007). What predicts psychological resilience after disaster? The role of demographics, resources, and life stress. *Journal of Consulting and Clinical Psychology, 75* (5), 671–682.

Bragagnolo, G., Rinarudo, A., Cravero, N., Fomía, S., Martínez, G., and Vergara, S. (2005). *Optimismo, esperanza, autoestima y depresión en estudiantes de Psicología. Informe de investigación.* [Optimism, hope, self-esteem and depression in Psychology. A research report.] Buenos Aires: Universidad Nacional de Rosario.

Carver, C. S., and Scheier, M. F. (1999). Stress, coping, and self-regulatory processes. In O. P. John & L. A. Pervin (Eds.), *Handbook of personality: Theory and research* (pp. 553–575). New York: Guilford Press.

Castro, F. G. and Murray, K. E. (2010). Cultural adaptation and resilience: Controversies, issues, and emerging models. In J. W. Reich, A. J. Zautra & J. S. Hall (Eds.), *Handbook of adult resilience* (pp. 375–403). New York: Guilford.

Caballero, C., Abello, R., and Palacio, J. (2007). Relación del *burnout* y el Rendimiento académico con la satisfacción frente a los estudios en estudiantes universitarios. [How burnout and academic performance relate to satisfaction with studies, in university students.] *Avances en Psicología Latinoamericana, 25,* 98-111.

Caballero, C., Hederich, Ch., and Palacio, J. (2010). El *burnout* académico: delimitación del síndrome y factores asociados con su aparición. [Academic burnout: delimiting the syndrome and factors associated with its appearance.] *Revista Latinoamericana de Psicología, 42,* 131-146.

Connor, K. M. and Davidson, J. R. T. (2003). Development of a new resilience scale: the Connor-Davidson Resilience Scale (CD-RISC). *Depression and Anxiety 18,* 76–82.

Csikszentmihalyi, M. (1999). If we are so rich, why aren't we happy? *American Psychologist, 54*(10), 821-827.

de la Fuente, J. and Cardelle-Ellawar, M. (2009). Research on action-emotion style and study habits: Effects of individual differences on learning and academic performance of undergraduate students. *Learning and Individual Differences, 19* (5), 567-576.

de la Fuente, J. and Cardelle-Elawar, M. (2011). Personal Self-Regulation and Copyng Style in University Students. En L.B. y R.A. Nichelson, *Psychology of individual Differences* (pp. 171-182). New York: Nova Science Publisher.

de la Fuente, J., Franco, C. and Mañas, I (2010). Efectos de un programa de entrenamiento en conciencia plena (mindfulness), en el estado emocional de los estudiantes universitarios [Results of a training program in mindfulness on the emotional state of university students]. *Estudios sobre Educación, 19*, 31-52.

Duhachek, A. and Oakley, J. L. (2007). Mapping the Hierarchical Structure of Coping: Unifying Empirical and Theoretical Perspectives. *Journal of consumer psychology, 17*(3), 218–233.

Dumont, M. and Provost, M. A. (1999). Resilience in adolescents: protective role of social support, coping strategies, self-esteem, and social activities on experience of stress and depression. *Journal of Youth and Adolescence, 28*, 343–363.

El-Ghoroury, N. H., Galper, D. I., Sawaqdeh, A., and Bufka, L. F (2012). Stress, Coping, and Barriers to Wellness Among Psychology Graduate Students. *Training and Education in Professional Psychology*, 6 (2), 122–134.

Folkman, S., and Lazarus R. S. (1980). An analysis of coping in a middle-aged community sample. *Journal of Health Social Behavior, 21,* 219-239.

Folkman, S. and Lazarus, R. S. (1985). If It Changes It Must Be a Process: Study of Emotion and Coping During Three Stages of a College Examination. *Journal of Personality and Social Psychology, 48*, 150-170.

Folkman, S., Lazarus, R. S., Dunkel-Schetter, C., de Longis, A., and Gruen, R. (1986). The dynamics of a stressful encounter: Cognitive appraisal, coping and encounter outcomes. *Journal of Personality and Social Psychology, 50,* 992-1003.

Folkman, S. and Moskowitz, J. T. (2004). Coping: Pitfalls and promise. *Annual Review of Psychology, 55,* 745–774.

Folkman, S., Lazarus, R., Pimley, S., and Novack, J. (1987). Age differences in stress and coping processes. *Psychology Aging, 2,* 171 -184.

Grant, K. E., Compas, B. E., Stuhlmacher, A., Thurm, A. E., McMahon, S., and Halpert, J. (2003). Stressors and child/adolescent psychopathology: Moving from markers to mechanisms of risk. *Psychological Bulletin, 129*, 447-466.

González-Cabanach, R., Valle, A., Rodríguez, S., Piñeiro, I., García, M., and Mosquera, I. (2009). *Stress University Students. The Subjetive Experience of Stress and Coping.* In A. Valle, J. C. Núñez, R. González- Cabanach, J. A. González-Pienda y S. Rodríguez (eds.), *Handbook of Instructional Resources and Their Applications in the Classroom* (pp. 311-323). New York: Nova Science Publishers.

Grotberg, E. (1995). *A guide to promoting resilience in children: strengthening the human spirit. The International Resilience Project.* Bernard van Leer Foundation. The Hague, Netherlands.

Jang, H. (2008). Supporting students' motivation, engagement, and learning during an uninteresting activity. *Journal of Educational Psychology, 100,* 798-811.

Kim, K. J., Conger, R. D., Elder, G. H., and Lorenz, F. O. (2003). Reciprocal influences between stressful life events and adolescent internalizing and externalizing problems. *Child Development, 74*, 127-143.

Lazarus, R. S. (1983). Costs and benefits of denial. In *The denial of stress* (pp. 1–30) S. Breznitz (Ed.) New York: International Universities Press.

Lazarus, R. S. and Folkman, S. (1984). *Stress, appraisal and coping.* New York: Springer.

Londoño, N. H., Henao, G. C., Puerta, G. C., Posada, S., Arango, D., & Camilo, D. (2006). Propiedades psicométricas y validación de la escala de estrategias de coping modificada (EEC-M) en una muestra colombiana [Psychometric properties and validation of a modified scale on coping strategies in a Colombian sample]. *Universitas Psychologica, 5* (2), 327-349.

Manciaux, M., Vanistendael, S., Lecomte, J., and Cyrulnik, B. (2001). La resiliencia: estado de la cuestión. En M. Manciaux (Ed.), *La resiliencia: resistir y rehacerse.* [Resilience: state of affairs. In M. Manciaux (Ed.), Resilience: resist and rebuild].. Madrid: Gedisa, 2003.

Martin, A. (2008). Enhancing student motivation and engagement: The effects of a multidimensional intervention. *Contemporary Educational Psychology, 33*, 239-269.

Martin, A. and Liem, G. (2010). Academic personal bests (PBs), engagement, and achievement: A cross-lagged panel analysis. *Learning and Individual Differences, 20,* 265-270.

Miñano, P., Gilar, R., and Castejón, J. L. (2012). A structural model of cognitive-motivational variables as explanatory factors of academic achievement in Spanish language and mathematics. *Anales de Psicología, 28,* 45-54.

Rafnsson, F. D., Jonson, F. H. and Windle, M. (2006). Coping strategies, stressful life events, problem behaviors, and depressed affect among Icelandic adolescents: A cross-cultural replication study. *Anxiety, Stress and Coping, 19*, 241-257.

Rector, N. A., and Roger, D. (1997). The stress buffering effects of self-esteem. *Personality and Individual Differences, 23*, 799-808.

Roth, S., and Cohen, L. (1986). Approach, avoidance, and coping with stress. *American Psychologisl, 41*, 813-819.

Rutter, M. (1985). Resilience in the face of adversity: Protective factors and resistance to psychiatric disorder. *British Journal of Psychiatry, 1*(47), 598-611.

Sandín, B. and Chorot, P. (1987). *Escala EEC.* [EEC Scale] Departamento de Psicología de la Personalidad. Madrid. UNED.

Sandín, B. and Chorot, P. (2003). Cuestionario de Afrontamiento del Estrés (CAE): desarrollo y validación preliminar. [Questionnaire on Coping with Stress: preliminary development and validation.] *Revista de Psicopatología y Psicología Clínica, 8* (1), 39-54.

Seifer, R., Sameroff, A. J., Baldwin, C. P., and Baldwin, A. (1992). Child and family factors that ameliorate risk between 4 and 13 years of age. *Journal of the American Academy of Child and Adolescent Psychiatry, 31*, 893-903.

Skinner, N., and Brewer, N. (2002). The dynamics of threat and challenge appraisals prior to a stressful achievement event. *Journal of Personality and Social Psychology, 83, 678-692.*

Suls, J., and Fletcher, B. (1985). The relative efficacy of avoidant and non-avoidant coping strategies: A meta-analysis. *Health Psychology, 4,* 249-288.

Skinner, E., Edge, K., Altman, J., and Sherwood, H. (2003). Searching for the structure of coping: A review and critique of category systems for classifying ways of coping. *Psychological Bulletin, 129* (2), 216-269.

Skinner, E., Furrer, C., Marchand, G., and Kinderman, T. (2008). Engagement and disaffection in the classroom: Part of a larger motivational dynamic? *Journal of Educational Psychology, 100,* 765-781.

Skinner, E., Kinderman, T., and Furrer, C. (2009). A motivational perspective on engagement and disaffection. Conceptualization and assessment of children's behavioral and emotional participation in the academic activities in the classroom. *Educational and Psychological Measurement, 69,* 493-525.

Skinner, E., Kinderman, T., Connell, J., and Wellborn, J. (2009). Engagement and disaffection as organizational constructs in the dynamic of motivational development. In K. Wentzel & A. Wigfield (Eds.), *Handbook of Motivation at School* (pp. 223-245). London: Routledge.

Skinner, E. and Pitzer, J. (2012). Developmental dynamics of student engagement, coping, and everyday resilience. In S. Christenson, A. Reschly & C. Wylie (Eds.), *Handbook of Research on Student Engagement* (pp. 21-44). New York: Springer.

Solórzano, M. and Ramos, N. (2006). Rendimiento académico y estrés académico de los estudiantes de la E.A.P. de enfermería de la Universidad Peruana Unión. [Academic performance and academic stress in EAP nursing students at the Universidad Peruana Unión.] *Revista de Ciencias de la Salud, 1*(1), 34-38.

Zautra, A. J., Hall, J. S., and Murray, K. E. (2010). Resilience: A new definition of health for people and communities. In J. W. Reich, A. J. Zautra & J. S. Hall (Eds.), *Handbook of Adult Resilience* (pp. 3–34). New York: Guilford.

In: Handbook of Academic Performance
Editors: Rolf Haumann and George Zimmer

ISBN: 978-1-62417-888-7
© 2013 Nova Science Publishers; Inc.

Chapter 13

ADVANCED PLACEMENT COURSES: GENDER AND ETHNIC DIFFERENCES IN ENROLLMENT AND SUCCESS

David Clark, George W. Moore and John R. Slate
Sam Houston State University, Hunstville, TX, US

ABSTRACT

Enrollment in Advanced Placement courses in one Texas school district was examined for two years to determine the extent to which student diversity was present. A higher percentage of girls were enrolled in Advanced Placement courses for both years than was boys. In this urban school district, Whites comprised the largest ethnic group of students enrolled in Advanced Placement courses and Black students had the lowest percentage of students for both years. Language Arts, Social Studies, and Math were the three areas with the largest percentage of student enrollment for both years, with Foreign Language having the lowest percentage of student enrollment (4.4%) for the most recent year. Boys had higher percentages than girls in Computer Science and Math Advanced Placement courses for both years. Statistically significant differences were present in Advanced Placement subject area enrollment as a function of gender and ethnicity for both years. Regarding student success, White students had the highest percentage of students with exam scores of at least 3, with Black students having the lowest percentage of exam scores of at least 3. Implications of these findings are discussed.

Advanced Placement (AP) courses have been available to students since the mid-1950s. At that time, the Advanced Placement courses were offered to advanced students as preparation for college. More recently, the College Board has held the position that AP courses are appropriate for all students who desire to work hard and meet the demands of these rigorous courses. According to the *AP Equity Policy Statement*:

> The Board encourages the elimination of barriers that restrict access for AP courses to students from ethnic, racial, and socioeconomic groups that have been traditionally

underrepresented in the AP Program. Schools should make every effort to ensure that their AP classes reflect the diversity of their student population. (*http://apcentral.collegeboard.com/pc/public/program/initiatives/22794.html*).

Since the beginning, the program has grown to the extent that students may earn college credit in 37 courses in 22 subject areas. The rigorous nature of the AP courses have been touted as an important experience leading to readiness for college level work [e.g., Hansen, 2005; Kaye, 2006; Klopfenstein, 2004b; Leonard, Blasik, Dilgen, and Till, 2003]. Furthermore, the Texas AP Report [2006] reported that "45 percent of students who take one AP course and 61percent who take two or more courses are finishing their bachelor's degree in four years or less" (p. 1). Enrollment and completion of AP courses in high school helps students with college admissions [Santoli, 2002]. The acceptance of AP exams for college credit is based on the score attained by the student. That is, Advanced Placement examinations are scored as a 5, 4, 3, 2, or 1. According to the *Advanced Placement Report to the Nation*, these scores are given a definition:

> AP Exam grades of 5 are equivalent to the top A-level work in the corresponding college course. AP Exam grades of 4 are equivalent to a range of work representing mid-level A to mid-level B performance in college. Similarly, AP Exam grades of 3 are equivalent to a range of work representing mid-level B to mid-level C performance in college. (p. 1).

The College Board [2007] stated that scores of 3, 4, or 5 are "predictive of college success and graduation: (p. 2). Most colleges and universities accept scores of 3, 4, or 5 to award credit for courses. Matthews [2002] reported that Harvard was accepting only scores of 5. A review of large flagship universities in the State of Texas revealed credit is given for scores of 3, 4, or 5, with the accepted score being course-specific. Readers should be aware, however, that some universities will accept only a score of a 4 or a 5.

The College Board [2007] indicated an interesting fact about AP students in the United States compared to international students on the Third International Math and Science Study (TIMSSO). Students who completed AP Calculus scored equal to the top leader, France, on the AP Calculus measure. Students who complete AP Physics scored in the top three on the AP Physics measure, only behind Norway and Sweden. Moreover, this finding was also true for students who also scored 1 and 2 on their respective exams. However, when including all students, the United States TIMSS ranking was considerably lower.

"Texas has the second largest population of AP students in the nation" [College Board, 2007, p.11]. The percentage of Black and Hispanic students taking AP courses in Texas has increased since 2000 [College Board]. Nationally growth has occurred in the number of underrepresented students enrolling in AP courses; however, a gap still exists among the types of students who enroll in these AP courses [Ndura, Robinson, and Ochs, 2003].

Beyond the gap between underrepresented and groups and the majority group, a gender gap still remains present. The *Advanced Placement Report to the Nation* [College Board, 2007b] provided the enrollment percentages of males and of females in each subject area. For example, a greater percentage of females enroll in language, literature, and history courses whereas a greater percentage of males enroll in the math and science courses. Moreover, Breland, Danos, Kahn, Kubota, and Bonner [1994] reported that males tend to score higher in the math and sciences, and females tend to score higher in the language, literature, and history courses. Students of color and economically disadvantaged students still are not enrolled in AP courses in the percentages equal to their percentage in their local school's population [Klopfenstein, 2004a; Solórzan and Ornelas, 2002; VanSciver, 2006]. Although Klopfenstein [2004a] suggested the rate of enrollment of students of color and of students who are economically disadvantaged was about one half of the enrollment rate of White students, it is important to keep in mind that White students may also be living in economically disadvantaged situations.

PURPOSE OF THE STUDY

One purpose of the study was to analyze the demographic characteristics of students enrolled in Advanced Placement courses in this school district for the previous two academic years. A second purpose was to determine the demographic characteristics of students who enrolled in specific Advanced Placement course areas. Our third purpose was to ascertain the extent to which students were differentially enrolled in and successful in their Advanced Placement enrollments as a function of gender and/or ethnicity.

RESEARCH QUESTIONS

Research questions addressed in this study were:

a)   What are the characteristics of students, separated by gender, ethnicity, economically disadvantaged, and grade level who are enrolled in at least one Advanced Placement course?

b)   What are the Advanced Placement course areas in which students are enrolled?

c)   What are the characteristics of students, separated by gender and ethnicity, enrolled in Advanced Placement course areas?

d)   What is the difference between boys and girls in their enrollment in an Advanced Placement course?

e)   What is the difference among ethnic groups in their enrollment in an Advanced Placement course?

f)   What is the difference between boys and girls in their success rates on Advanced Placement exams? and

g)   What is the difference among ethnic groups in their success rates on Advanced Placement exams?

METHOD

Participants

Data from one Texas urban independent public school district for the school years 2005-2006 and 2006-2007 were utilized in this study. For the 2005-2006 school year, 1,396 students had enrolled in 2626 sections of Advanced Placement courses. Of this number, 54.3% were female and 45.7% were male. These percentages differed somewhat from the school district's secondary student population wherein 51% of the students were male and 49% were female. Concerning ethnic membership, 64.8% were White, 16.2% were Asian/Pacific Islander, 11.8% were Hispanic, 7.0% were Black, and 0.2% were Native American. These percentages differed substantially from this school district's secondary student population. That is, White students comprised 51% of this district's secondary school population, with Hispanic students constituting 23%. Black students were 18% of the secondary student population and Asian-Pacific Islander students were 8%. The majority of the students were enrolled in the 12th grade (48.6%), followed by the 11th grade (46.3%). The remaining students were in the 9th (0.8%) or 10th (4.4%) grades.

Table 1. Descriptive Statistics for Students Enrolled in Advanced Placement Courses for the 2005-2006 and 2006-2007 School Years

Variable	n	%
Advanced Placement Courses		
2005-2006 School Year		
Boys	638	45.7
Girls	758	54.3
2006-2007 School Year		
Boys	754	44.2
Girls	953	55.8
2005-2006 School Year		
White	904	64.8
Hispanic	165	11.8
Black	98	7.0
Asian-Pacific Islander	226	16.2
2006-2007 School Year		
White	1033	60.5
Hispanic	267	15.6
Black	128	7.5
Asian-Pacific Islander	277	16.2
2005-2006 School Year		
Economically Disadvantaged	123	8.8
Not Economically Disadvantaged	1273	91.2
2006-2007 School Year		
Economically Disadvantaged	216	12.7
Not Economically Disadvantaged	1491	87.4
2005-2006 School Year		
11th Grade Students	646	46.3
12th Grade Students	678	48.6
2006-2007 School Year		
11th Grade Students	775	45.4
12th Grade Students	851	49.9

For the 2006-2007 school year, 1707 students had enrolled in 3550 sections of Advanced Placement courses, with 55.8% being female and 44.2% being male. These percentages also differed from this school district's secondary student population wherein 50% of the students were male and 50% were female. Concerning ethnic membership, 60.5% were White, 15.6% were Hispanic, 16.2% were Asian/Pacific Islander, 7.5% were Black, and 0.2% were Native American. These percentages again were substantially different from the secondary student population of this school district. White students were 50% of the students, followed by Hispanic students at 25%. Seventeen percent of the students in the district were Black, with Asian-Pacific Islanders comprising 8%. The majority of the students were enrolled in the 12th grade (49.9%), followed by the 11th grade (45.4%). The remaining students were in the 9th (0.8%) or 10th (4.0%) grades.

Instrumentation and Procedures

Archival data were acquired from a Texas urban independent public school district for the school years 2005-2006 and 2006-2007. Specifically, data were obtained on: gender; ethnicity; grade level; name of Advanced Placement course; number of Advanced Placement courses enrolled; whether or not the Advanced Placement exam was taken; and whether or not the student was successful on the Advanced Placement exam. The senior researcher selected each of the variables analyzed in this study and downloaded them into an Excel file. From the Excel file, all variables were screened for accuracy and then converted into a *Statistical Package for the Social Sciences-Version 15.0* (SPSS) database.

Results

Table 1 depicts the numbers and percentage of high school students in this urban school district who were enrolled in Advanced Placement courses for the 2005-2006 and for the 2006-2007 academic years, separated by gender, ethnicity, grade level, and economic status. Roughly the same percentage of boys and girls were enrolled in AP courses for both years, with more girls being enrolled than boys.

An examination of ethnicity revealed that the majority of the students enrolled in this school district's Advanced Placement courses were White, followed by Asian-Pacific Islander for the 2005-2006 school year (16.2%). Black students, in both years, had the lowest percentage of students enrolled in Advanced Placement courses, 7.0% and 7.5% respectively. Hispanic students' numbers and percent increased from the 2005-2006 school year ($n = 165$, 11.8%) to the 2006-2007 school year ($n = 267$, 15.6%).

Students with a label of Economically Disadvantaged also enrolled in Advanced Placement courses, with slightly over 8.8% ($n = 123$) of students enrolled in Advanced Placement courses in this school district in the 2005-2006 school year and a higher number and percentage in the 2006-2007 school year ($n = 216$, 12.7%). For both years, the percentage of students enrolled in Advanced Placement courses was approximately equal for the 11th and 12th grades.

Next, specific Advanced Placement subject areas were examined to determine the numbers and percent of student enrollment in these areas for the two school years of data analyzed in this study. Social Studies Advanced Placement courses had the highest percent of student enrollment for both years, followed by Language Arts. Of interest is that Foreign Language Advanced Placement courses had the lowest percentage of student enrollment for both years.

Table 2. Advanced Placement Courses in Which Students were Enrolled for the 2005-2006 and 2006-2007 School Years

Variable	n	%
Advanced Placement Course		
2005-2006 School Year		
Computer Science	122	4.7
Fine Arts	135	5.1
Foreign Language	34	1.3
Language Arts	758	28.9
Mathematics	427	16.3
Science	190	7.2
Social Studies	960	36.6
2006-2007 School Year		
Computer Science	138	3.9
Fine Arts	159	4.5
Foreign Language	155	4.4
Language Arts	988	27.8
Mathematics	586	16.5
Science	226	6.4
Social Studies	1298	36.6

Table 3. Advanced Placement Courses in Which Students were Enrolled Separated by Gender for the 2005-2006 and 2006-2007 School Years

	Boys		Girls	
Variable	n	%	n	%
Advanced Placement Course				
2005-2006 School Year				
Computer Science	98	80.3	24	19.7
Fine Arts	59	43.7	76	56.3
Foreign Language	10	29.4	24	71.0
Language Arts	271	35.8	487	64.3
Mathematics	219	51.3	208	48.7
Science	101	53.2	89	46.8
Social Studies	440	45.8	520	54.2
2006-2007 School Year				
Computer Science	111	80.4	27	20.0
Fine Arts	51	32.1	108	68.0
Foreign Language	43	27.7	112	72.3
Language Arts	392	40.0	596	60.3
Mathematics	299	51.0	287	49.0
Science	108	47.8	118	52.2
Social Studies	570	44.0	728	56.0

Table 4. Percentages of Enrollment in Advanced Placement Courses by Gender for the 2005-2006 and the 2006-2007 School Years

Course	Male %age	Female %age
2005-2006		
Computer Science	8.2	1.7
Fine Arts	4.9	5.3
Foreign Language	0.8	1.7
Language Arts	22.6	34.1
Mathematics	18.3	14.6
Science	8.4	6.2
Social Studies	36.7	36.4
2006-2007		
Computer Science	17.1	1.4
Fine Arts	3.2	5.5
Foreign Language	2.7	5.7
Language Arts	24.9	30.2
Mathematics	19.0	14.5
Science	6.9	6.0
Social Studies	36.2	36.8

Table 5. Advanced Placement Courses in Which Students were Enrolled Separated by Ethnic Membership for the 2005-2006 School Year

	White		Asian-Pacific Islander		Hispanic		Black	
Advanced Placement Course	n	%	n	%	n	%	n	%
2005-2006 School Year								
Computer Science	78	63.9	34	27.9	8	6.6	2	1.6
Fine Arts	101	74.8	17	12.6	12	8.9	5	3.7
Foreign Language	10	29.4	5	14.7	17	50.0	2	5.9
Language Arts	467	61.6	134	17.7	96	12.7	60	7.9
Mathematics	291	68.2	75	17.6	38	8.9	21	4.9
Science	119	62.6	49	25.8	13	6.8	8	4.2
Social Studies	635	66.2	153	15.9	101	10.5	69	7.2

Table 6. Advanced Placement Courses in Which Students were Enrolled Separated by Ethnic Membership for the 2006-2007 School Year

	White		Asian-Pacific Islander		Hispanic		Black	
Advanced Placement Course	n	%	n	%	n	%	n	%
Computer Science	83	60.1	36	26.1	16	11.6	3	2.2
Fine Arts	99	62.3	34	21.4	19	12.0	6	3.8
Foreign Language	64	41.3	20	12.9	64	41.3	7	4.5
Language Arts	577	58.4	174	17.6	149	15.1	88	8.9
Mathematics	370	63.1	124	21.2	63	10.8	29	5.0
Science	125	55.3	78	34.5	18	8.0	5	2.2
Social Studies	810	62.4	232	17.9	169	13.0	86	6.6

Table 7. Advanced Placement Courses in Which Students were Enrolled Separated by Ethnic Membership for the 2005-2006 School Year

Advanced Placement Course	White %	Hispanic %	Black %	Asian/Pacific Islander %
Computer Science	4.6	2.8	1.2	7.3
Fine Arts	5.9	4.2	3.0	3.6
Foreign Language	0.6	6.0	1.2	1.1
Language Arts	27.5	33.7	35.9	28.7
Mathematics	17.1	13.3	12.6	16.1
Science	7.0	4.6	4.8	10.5
Social Studies	37.3	35.4	41.3	32.8

Table 8. Advanced Placement Courses in Which Students were Enrolled Separated by Ethnic Membership for the 2006-2007 School Year

Advanced Placement Course	White %	Hispanic %	Black %	Asian/Pacific Islander %
Computer Science	3.9	3.2	1.3	5.2
Fine Arts	4.7	3.8	2.7	4.9
Foreign Language	3.0	12.9	3.1	2.9
Language Arts	27.1	29.9	39.3	24.9
Mathematics	17.4	12.7	13.0	17.8
Science	5.9	3.6	2.2	11.2
Social Studies	38.0	33.9	38.4	33.2

Table 9. Percentages of Students who Took the Advanced Placement Course Exams and Their Test Scores for the 2005-2006 and the 2006-2007 School Years

Test Score	n	%
2005-2006		
0	0	0.0
1	185	11.9
2	343	22.1
3	470	30.3
4	343	22.1
5	208	13.4
2006-2007		
0	6	0.3
1	274	13.1
2	547	26.1
3	589	28.1
4	429	20.4
5	255	12.1

An analysis was next conducted to determine the course areas in which boys and girls were enrolled. Table 3 depicts these numbers and percentages separately for boys and for girls. For both years, boys comprised a very high percentage of the students enrolled in Computer Science courses, over 80%. Other than Computer Science courses, boys had a higher percentage than girls only in Math courses, about 51%. In all other course areas, girls comprised a higher percentage of the student body in the respective Advanced Placement course areas. To ascertain whether gender differences in Advanced Placement enrollment were present, Pearson chi-squares were conducted. The result was statistically significant for the 2005-2006 school year, $\chi^2(7) = 114.50$, $p < .001$, and for the 2006-2007 school year, $\chi^2(7) = 119.62$, $p < .001$. The effect sizes for these two findings were .29 and .26 respectively, both moderate effects [Cohen, 1988]. Table 4 shows the Advanced Placement areas in which boys and girls were enrolled, out of their total percentages. That is, of the boys who were enrolled in Advanced Placement courses, their percentage is broken down by course area. The same is true for girls.

After analyzing the Advanced Placement course area enrollment by gender, a frequency distribution was conducted by ethnic membership. These numbers and percentages are depicted in Tables 5 and 6. Hispanics had the highest percentage of student enrollment in Advanced Placement Foreign Language courses in 2005-06, and were tied with White students in 2006-07. White students comprised the highest percentage of student enrollment in all other Advanced Placement course areas. Of note to readers should be not only the low enrollment in Science courses but the very low percentages of Black and Hispanic students who are enrolled in Advanced Placement Science courses.

To determine whether statistically significant differences were present in student diversity across the Advanced Placement subject areas, a Pearson chi-square was conducted and yielded a statistically significant finding for the 2005-2006 school year, $\chi^2(21) = 101.22$, $p < .001$, and for the 2006-2007 school year, $\chi^2(21) = 300.43$, $p < .001$. The effect size was .16, small, for the 2005-2006 school year and .24, small, for the 2006-2007 school year [Cohen, 1988]. Tables 7 and 8 show the percentages of student enrollment across the seven Advanced Placement subject areas for each ethnic group. That is, of the White students enrolled in Advanced Placement courses, only 0.6% were enrolled in an Advanced Placement Foreign Language course in the 2005-2006 school year. As can be seen in Tables 7 and 8, Asian/Pacific Islanders were more likely to enroll in Advanced Placement Computer Science and Science courses than were Black and Hispanic students.

Students who enroll in Advanced Placement courses are not required to take an Advanced Placement course exam unless they want to receive college credit for the course. As such, many students who enroll in and complete Advanced Placement courses do not take the exams. As shown in Table 9, 40.3% of students who enrolled in Advanced Placement courses in this urban school district in the 2005-2006 school year did not take an Advanced Placement exam. A similar percentage, 40.9%, of students did not take an Advanced Placement exam in the 2006-2007 school year.

With a score of at least 3 being necessary to receive college credit [College Board, 2007], Table 9 shows the low percentage of students who took the Advanced Placement exams who would be eligible for college credit. For the 2005-2006 school year, 30.3% earned an exam score of 3, 22.1% earned an exam score of 4, and 13.4% earned Advanced Placement exam scores of 5. Thus, almost two-thirds, 65.9%, of the students who took the Advanced Placement course exams received high enough scores to be eligible for college credit. For the 2006-2007 school year, 28.1% earned an exam score of 3, 20.4% earned an exam score of 4, and 12.1% earned Advanced Placement exam scores of 5. Again, more than half, 60.6%, of students who took the Advanced Placement course exams received high enough scores to be eligible for college credit.

To ascertain whether students' demographic characteristics were related to their scores on the Advanced Placement exams, exam scores were recoded into either a could receive college credit (i.e., scores of 3, 4, and 5) or could not receive college credit (i.e., scores less than 3). Then Pearson chi-square procedures were conducted to determine whether students had a different pass rate as a function of their gender and ethnic membership, separately for each of the two school years. For the 2005-2006 and for the 2006-2007 school years, no difference was present in pass rates between boys and girls, $ps > .05$. Boys had a success rate of 58.5% in the 2005-2006 school year, compared with a success rate of 60.7% for girls on the AP exams. In the 2006-2007 school year, boys had a success rate of 60.2% whereas girls had a success rate of 55.8%. In all cases, more than half of the boys and girls had AP exam scores of at least 3.

A statistically significant difference, however, was yielded for the 2005-2006 school year in pass rates as a function of ethnic membership, $\chi^2(3) = 28.02$, $p < .001$. The highest pass rates occurred for White students (65.9%) and for Asian-Pacific Islander (51.9%) students and the lowest pass rates occurred for Black (36.4%) and Hispanic (46.7%) students. A similar statistically significant difference was yielded for the 2006-2007 school year in pass rates as a function of ethnic membership, $\chi^2(3) = 53.23$, $p < .001$. The highest pass rates occurred for White (67.0%), Hispanic (47.4%), and Asian-Pacific Islander (44.2%) and the lowest pass rate occurred for Black (34.0%) students. The effect sizes, Cramer's V, for both results were small, .19 and .23 respectively [Cohen, 1988].

Discussion

In this study we analyzed AP enrollment by the demographic characteristics of students in one urban school district in the State of Texas. Additionally, we analyzed the success rate for AP students. In analyzing data on the characteristics of the students enrolled in AP classes, we found that in both 2005-2006 and in 2006-2007, female enrollment was higher than was male enrollment. In the 2006-2007 school year, females accounted for 55.8% of the students enrolled in the AP courses. These percentages were a little higher than for the 2005-2006 school year percentages, 54.3% females and 45.7% males. In both years the percentage of females enrolled in AP courses was higher than the percentage of females in the entire school district student population. In the 2005-2006 and 2006-2007 school years, the percentage of girls enrolled in AP math courses was smaller than the percentage of males; however, the percentage of girls enrolled in AP science courses was higher than for males in the 2006-07 school year. Girls enrolled in language, arts, and social studies in higher percentages than boys, and a higher percentage of boys were enrolled in computer science than were girls. These results are congruent with information from the College Board indicating that female students tend to enroll in higher percentages in the language, literacy, and history classes. In contrast to the College Board information, however, in our study a larger percentage of female than male students was enrolled in science courses in the 2006-07 school year.

Next, we analyzed differences in AP enrollment as a function of ethnicity. As might be expected, White students were enrolled in most AP courses at a greater percentage than were the Asian-Pacific Islanders, Hispanic, and Black students. Based upon their percentages in this school district's student, Hispanic and Black students are still underrepresented in the AP program. Interestingly, based upon this same comparison, Asian-Pacific Islander students exceeded their percentage in the local school district population.

Further analyses of student characteristics revealed that 8.8% of the students enrolled in AP courses in the 2005-2006 school year were students who were economically disadvantaged. In the 2006-2007 school year, this percentage increased dramatically to 12.7%. For the 2005-2006 school year, 48.6% of the students were in the 12th grade, and 46.3% were in the 11th grade. These figures remained constant for the most part in the 2006-07 school year (49.9% and 45.4% respectively).

Seven AP course areas were identified, and the enrollment was obtained for each course. In 2005-2006 and in 2006-2007, language arts, social studies, and mathematics— respectively--were the top three areas in which students enrolled. Between 2005-2006 and 2006-2007, the percentage of students enrolled in AP foreign language increased and the percentage of students enrolled in AP science decreased. Additionally, when looking at gender and the enrollment in AP areas, males were enrolled in computer science and mathematics in higher percentages than were the female students. Moreover, females were enrolled in higher percentages in four areas (e.g., fine arts, foreign language, language arts, and social studies) than were males.

Examining ethnic membership within specific AP courses revealed that, in both 2005-2006 and 2006-2007, Hispanic students were enrolled in an AP foreign language course at a much higher percentage than were any of the other ethnic groups in the 2005-2006 year, and at the same rate as Whites in 2006-2007. In all other AP course areas, White students were enrolled at the highest percentage. Black students were underrepresented in all subjects, and Hispanics students were underrepresented in all courses except AP foreign language.

Analysis of the enrollment by ethnic membership across each AP course area revealed an interesting finding. In all ethnic groups, language arts, social studies, and mathematics respectively were the top three courses in which students were enrolled in 2005-2006. In the 2006-2007 school year, Hispanic students' top enrollment choices were language arts, foreign language, and social studies. In both years, AP social studies was the one course in which most students from all subgroups were enrolled (with the sole exception of Afircan-Americans and language arts in the 2006-2007 school year).

Finally, an analysis of student success on AP examinations was conducted. In both 2005-2006 and 2006-2007, 59.7% and 59.1% of students who were enrolled in AP courses respectively took an exam. Of those students who took an AP exam, 65.9% in 2005-2006 and 60.6% in 2006-2007 scored a 3, 4, or a 5. In both years, a 3 was scored by the most students. However, in the 2006-2007 school year, the number of students scoring a 2 ($n = 547$) was almost equal to the number of students who scored a 3 ($n = 589$). As a 2 is not accepted by universities for college credit, these scores reflect a negative economic cost of enrollment in AP courses and of taking the AP exams, yet receiving no college credit.

In 2005-2006 and 2006-2007 no statistically significant difference between males and females was determined when examining AP exam scores. However, statistically significant differences were present in AP exam scores as a function of ethnic membership. White students had the highest pass rate on AP exams in 2005-2006 and in 2006-2007. In 2005-2006, Asian-Pacific Islander students had the second highest passing rate on AP exams. In 2006-2007, Hispanic students had the second highest passing rate on AP exams. In both years, Black students scored lower than the other three ethnic groups of students. These findings merit further investigation regarding reasons for differential success in AP courses, in ways related to ethnicity and gender.

Access to AP courses, we believe, is important for all students. According to the College Board [2006]:

- 45% of students who have taken one AP course and 61% of students who have taken two or more AP courses are completing their bachelor's degrees in four years or less.
- Only 29% of students who enroll in colleges without having taken AP are completing their bachelor's degrees on schedule. (p. 5).

In addition, recent reports have indicated a large number of students who are entering college are having to enroll in at least one remedial course [Houston Chronicle, 2007].

Advanced Placement classes may help students with financial considerations because these students are able to receive college credit for which they will not pay tuition [Santoli, 2002]. College admission may also be helped by AP credit [Contreras, 2005; Kyburg, Hertberg-Davis, and Callahan, 2007; Santoli, 2002]. Ndura et al. [2006] stated that minority students want the challenge and the opportunity to earn college credit, and they want to be ready for college. Minority students want to go to college, and they know they need to take courses to prepare them. We must continue to find ways to encourage these students to take more rigorous courses, and we need to work with school cultures that might discourage their participation. More rigorous and supportive curriculum at all levels is needed that will help all learners prepare for AP [Kyburg et al., 2007; Ndura et al., 2003].

Furthermore, highly qualified teachers of high quality must receive the professional development that allow them to work better with all students especially those students who are underprepared for the rigors of AP courses [Klopfenstein, 2003; Kyburg et al., 2007].

Finally, readers are urged to be cautious in the extent to which they make generalizations from our findings. First, these data were obtained from a single urban school district in the State of Texas. The extent to which these findings generalize beyond this school district is not known. Second, these data were obtained for a 2-year time period. More information is needed regarding AP enrollment and exam performance for longer periods of time. Third, these data reflect aggregations of courses within each subject area. That is, several AP foreign language courses were aggregated into AP foreign language. To the extent that student performance differs in specific AP courses within each subject area, then these aggregated data might not accurately reflect performance within individual AP courses. Future research is clearly needed at the individual AP course level. With these cautions in mind, readers should note that our findings are congruent with the national trends as reported by the College Board.

REFERENCES

Breland, H. M., Danos, D. O., Kahn, H. D., Kubota, M. Y., and Bonner, M. W. (1994). Performance versus objective testing and gender: An exploratory study of an Advanced Placement History examination. *Journal of Educational Measurement, 31*(4), 275-293.

Cohen, J. (1988). *Statistical power analysis for the behavioral sciences* (2nd ed.). Hillsdale, N. J.: Lawrence Erlbaum.

College Board. (2006). *Texas public schools: Advanced Placement program participation and performance*. Retrieved from http://www.collegeboard.com/prod_downloads/about/news_info/ap/2006/texas_ap-report_06.pdf

College Board. (2007). *Advanced Placement report to the Nation*. Retrieved from http://apcentral.collegeboard.com

Contreras, F. E. (2005). Access, achievement, and social capital: Standardized exams and the Latino college-bound population. *Journal of Hispanic Higher Education, 4*(3), 197-214.

Hansen, A. L. (2005). *Research brief: Success in Advanced Placement course. The Principals' Partnership*. Retrieved from http://www.prinicipalspartnership.com

Kaye, R. D. (2006). *Progress in Advanced Placement and International Baccalaureate in S. R. E. B. states*. Atlanta, G. A.: Southern Regional Education Board. Retrieved from http://sreb.net/main/Goals/Publications/06E07-Progress AP IB.pdf

Klopfenstein, K. (2003). Recommendations for maintaining the quality of Advanced Placement programs. *American Secondary Education, 32*(1), 39-48.

Klopfenstein, K. (2004a). Advanced Placement: Do minorities have equal opportunity? *Economics of Education Review, 23*(2), 115-131.

Klopfenstein, K. (2004b). The Advanced Placement expansions of the 1990s: How did traditionally underserved students fare? *Education Policy Analysis Archives, 12*(68). Retrieved from http://epaa.asu.edu/epass/v12n68

Kyburg, R. M., Hertzberg-Davis, H., and Callahan, C. M. (2007). Advanced Placement and International Baccalaureate programs: Optimal learning environments for talented minorities? *Journal of Advanced Academics, 18*(2), 172-215.

Leonard, S. T., Blasik, K., Dilgen, A, and Till, F. (2003). Advanced Placement as a means of narrowing the achievement gap. *E. R. S. Spectrum, 21*(2), 4-14.

Mathews, J. (2002). Advanced Placement. *Education Week*. 7 August 2002.

Ndura, E., Robinson, M., and Ochs, G. (2003). Minority students in high school advanced placement courses: Opportunity and equity denied. *American Secondary Education, 32*(1), 21-38.

Santoli, S. P. (2002). Is there an Advanced Placement advantage? *American Secondary Education, 3*(2), 23-35.

Solórzano, D. G., and Ornelas, A. (2002). A critical race analysis of Advanced Placement classes: A case of educational inequality. *Journal of Latinos and Education, 1*(4), 215-229.

Texas Education Agency. (2007). *Overview of the Academic Excellence Indicator System*. Retrieved from http://www.tea.state.tx.us/perfreport/aeis/about.aeis.html

VanSciver, J. H. (2006). Closing the diversity gap in Advanced Placement course enrollment. *Multicultural Perspectives, 8*(3), 56-58.

In: Handbook of Academic Performance
Editors: Rolf Haumann and George Zimmer

ISBN: 978-1-62417-888-7
© 2013 Nova Science Publishers, Inc.

Chapter 14

ETHNIC DIFFERENCES IN SCIENCE: AND THE ACHIEVEMENT GAP CONTINUES

Veronica Vijil[,1], John R. Slate[2,‡] and Julie P. Combs[2,#]*
[1]Spring Independent School District, Houston, TX, US
[2]Sam Houston State University, Huntsville, TX, US

ABSTRACT

In this study, the researchers examined the science achievement of Hispanic students and of White students on the Texas state-mandated assessment for students in Grades 5, 8, and 11 for 3 years (i.e., 2005-2006, 2006-2007, and 2007-2008) for all schools in Texas (*n of schools* > 1,000). Statistically significant differences were present for all comparisons, within each grade level and within each year of data analyzed. All effect sizes were very large, with White students having statistically significantly higher science pass rates than Hispanic students. With the accountability mandates of the No Child Left Behind Act focused in reading and math, the achievement gap in science remains wide.

Keywords: science, achievement gap, Hispanic students

A shortage of qualified workers in the science field challenges the United States to remain economically competitive in a global market (Andres, 2006; U.S. Department of Education, 2005). Comparatively, Europe produces nearly three times as many engineering graduates as the United States whereas Asia produces almost five times as many engineers (Orask, 2008). Well-documented recently in the research literature is an achievement gap between Hispanic and White students (e.g., Haas and Slate, 2010; Rojas-LeBouef and Slate, 2011), particularly in science-related courses and careers (ACT, 2009; College Board, 2007). The percentage of Hispanic children under the age of 18 is reported to be 22% (Fry and

---

[*] E-mail: vgvijil@yahoo.com
[‡] E-mail: profslate@aol.com
[#] E-mail: jcombs@shsu.edu

Passel, 2009). Despite the increase in the Hispanic population in general and in higher education, Hispanic students are underrepresented in science-related courses and careers (Young, 2009). Differing factors are attributed to the gaps that exist. Nonetheless, some researchers ascertain that substantial racial-ethnic differences remain (Muller, Stage, and Kinzie, 2001).

REVIEW OF RELATED LITERATURE

A sense of urgency has been placed on educational institutions to educate students to become proficient in science and mathematics, as well as to encourage students to explore these fields as career options (Graczyk, 2009; U.S. Department of Education, 2005). States such as Texas have increased the number of science courses needed to graduate from high school (Texas Education Agency [TEA], 2006). In 2006, TEA increased the total number of credits needed to graduate to 26 credits and also raised the number of required science credits from three to four in each subject area (TEA, 2008). Overall, students, especially at the middle and high school level, have continued to struggle in science as reflected by scores on state mandated examinations (TEA, 2008). With the inception of the No Child Left Behind (NCLB) Act of 2001, states were mandated to demonstrate adequate yearly progress which is an individual state's measure of progress toward the goal of 100% of students achieving to state academic standards in at least reading/language arts and math (U.S. Department of Education, 2005). Because the results have critical implications in many areas such as state and federal funding, the NCLB Act has resulted in districts placing heavy pressure on teachers and administrators to ensure student gains in test scores (Nichols and Berliner, 2008). Some researchers (e.g., U.S. Department of Education, 2005) have contended that the NCLB Act has benefitted students of color, such as Hispanics. In one report about the effects of the NCLB Act, the U.S. Department of Education (2005) revealed the achievement gap between White and Hispanic 9-year-old students in reading and math was at an all-time low in 2005, thereby indicating that the gaps between the two groups were decreasing.

Currently in Texas fifth-, eighth-, and 11th-grade students are tested in different content areas and fifth graders who qualify have the option of taking a Spanish examination (TEA, 2009). Fifth-grade students must take the mathematics, reading, and science examinations; all examinations in Grade 5 are available in English and Spanish (TEA, 2009). Eighth-grade students are required to take mathematics, reading, science, and social studies examinations but are not available in Spanish (TEA, 2009). The addition of a science examination for eighth graders was enacted by the Texas Legislature in June, 2003 (TEA, 2009). Eleventh-grade students take exit-level examinations in English language arts, mathematics, science, and social studies (TEA, 2009). Students must pass exit level assessments to be eligible to graduate (TEA, 2009). A system intended to assist struggling students in reading and math is the Student Success Initiative [SSI] (TEA, 2009). In 1999, the Texas Legislature adopted a grade advancement component for third, fifth, and eighth-grade students whereby students are allowed to advance to the next grade level only by passing the reading and math TAKS examination (TEA, 2009).

The SSI component began for third-grade students in the 2002-2003 school year in reading; fifth-grade students beginning in the 2004-2005 school year in reading and mathematics; and eighth-grade students beginning in the 2007-2008 school year in reading and mathematics (TEA, 2009). In 2009 the initiative was modified by the 81st Texas Legislature and no longer includes students in third grade (TEA, 2009). Students in fifth and eighth grade must be allowed at least three opportunities to pass the TAKS examination under the SSI guidelines (TEA, 2009). An exception may be made by a grade placement committee to advance the student to the next grade level if the student's parent or guardian submit an appeal and the committee unanimously determine that the student is expected to perform at grade level by the end of the next year with proper intervention (TEA, 2009).

Statement of the Problem

Hispanic students continue to be underrepresented in science-related courses and careers. Given that gaps exist between ethnic groups and begin to emerge as early as in the elementary grades, educators must utilize best practices to attain interest and successful completion in science courses beginning at the elementary level (Oakes, 1990). Stereotypes must be addressed to recognize that barriers exist for subpopulations of students in schools (American Association of University Women [AAUW], 2004). A concerted effort must be made to attract Hispanic students to the sciences.

Significance of the Study

Findings from this study may be used to increase awareness of the impact of science coursework and instructional strategies for subgroups in elementary, middle, and high schools. Although many assertions are made about the impact on student achievement, empirical data demonstrate the need to narrow any gaps that may continue to exist among subgroups. Educators may use the data to recognize the need to plan strategically and to incorporate activities in classrooms and on campuses that will generate an interest among Hispanic students in science activities.

Purpose of the Study

The purpose of this study was to analyze the performance of Hispanic and White students on the TAKS Science examination in Grades 5, 8, and 11 for the years 2006, 2007, and 2008. Specifically, we wanted to determine the extent to which achievement gaps were present between Hispanic students and White students in science for grades at the elementary, middle, and high school levels.

Research Questions

The following research questions were addressed in this study: (a) What is the difference in Grade 5, Grade 8, and Grade 11 TAKS Science passing rates between Hispanic students and White students for 3 school years (i.e., 2006, 2007, and 2008)? and (b) To what extent were findings consistent across the 3 years and three grade levels whose data were analyzed?

METHOD

Participants

Data from the 2006, 2007, and 2008 administration of the Texas Assessment of Knowledge and Skills (TAKS) Science examination were obtained for this study. Data files were downloaded from the Texas Education Agency Academic Excellence Indicator System website (http://ritter.tea.state.tx.us/). Specifically, TAKS Science passing rates for campuses in Texas for all students enrolled in Texas public schools in Grade 5, 8, and 11 were obtained. Information about TAKS science passing rates for select ethnic memberships is available in the file. Thus, passing rates by campuses for the years and grade levels indicated were analyzed.

The number of campuses for which TAKS scores were analyzed in this study varied from a low of 941 campuses (i.e., Hispanic students in Grade 11 for the 2006-2007 school year) to 3,126 campuses (i.e., Hispanic students in Grade 5 for the 2007-2008 school year). The specific numbers of campuses for each group can be obtained by reviewing the tables in this study. Readers should note that the unit of analysis was campus-level aggregated data which represents tens of thousands of Hispanic and White students across the state of Texas.

Moreover, the manner in which the Academic Excellence Indicator System reports data limits the ability to utilize sophisticated statistical procedures. Specifically, demographic characteristics such as ethnicity are merged with examination score information. That is, for purposes of this study, Hispanic student Grade 5 science pass rates and White student Grade 5 science pass rates were downloaded as two separate variables. This merging of demographic characteristic and dependent variable of test scores is different from how researchers code data for analysis purposes.

To conduct multivariate procedures, demographic characteristics and dependent variables are coded as separate, independent variables. Utilizing the data provided by the Texas Education Agency to address the research questions we posed limited our ability to use more sophisticated statistical procedures.

Instrumentation and Procedures

Archival data were downloaded from the Texas Education Agency website (http://ritter.tea.state.tx.us/). The website contains files of TAKS examinations results for the state of Texas for the years 2006, 2007, and 2008. Each of these files contains information on student passing rates by campus separated by gender and ethnic group. Regarding the TAKS Science exam, specific information about its score reliabilities and its score validities are available on the website. Readers are referred to the Technical Digests for each year in which the TAKS Science passing rates were analyzed. The examinations were criterion-referenced tests that measured the mastery of the state mandated science objectives.

RESULTS

Standardized skewness coefficients (i.e., skewness divided by the standard error of skewness) and standardized kurtosis coefficients (i.e., kurtosis divided by the standard error of kurtosis) were calculated. In particular, the coefficients relating to science achievement as measured by TAKS scores for Hispanic students and for White students were calculated. When calculated, 10 of the 12 standardized skewness and kurtosis coefficients for Grade 5 were outside the limits of -3.00 and 3.00, and were, therefore, determined to be non-normal (Onwuegbuzie and Daniel, 2002). Similarly, nine of the 12 standardized skewness and kurtosis coefficients for Grade 8 were outside the limits of -3.00 and 3.00 (Onwuegbuzie and Daniel). Finally, 11 of the 12 standardized skewness and kurtosis coefficients for Grade 11 were outside the limits of -3.00 and 3.00 (Onwuegbuzie and Daniel, 2002). Achievement data, at the state level, are typically not normally distributed on criterion-referenced measures. To the extent that state-mandated assessments, in this case the TAKS, are measuring concepts on which instruction has occurred, then students should be able to demonstrate their mastery, resulting in many students being successful and fewer students being unsuccessful. Because of the lack of normality in our TAKS data, a decision was made to be conservative in the statistical analyses we used. As such, we utilized a nonparametric statistical procedure, specifically a Wilcoxon's dependent samples t-test (Huck, 2007), to examine differences between Hispanic students and White students in their TAKS Science passing rates.

The Wilcoxon's dependent samples t-test analysis between the TAKS Science passing rates for Hispanic students and White students in Grade 5 for the 2006, 2007, and 2008 school years revealed statistically significant differences, $z = -27.73$, $p < .001$; $z = -31.78$, $p < .001$; and $z = -31.88$, $p < .001$, respectively. Cohen's (1988) criteria, using Cohen's d, were used to determine all effect sizes. Effect sizes for the Grade 5 differences between Hispanic students and White students for the 2006, 2007, and 2008 school years were 1.19, 1.17, and 1.00, respectively. These effect sizes were very large. In all cases, the average passing rates on the TAKS Science measure were substantially higher for White students than for Hispanic students. Readers are directed to Table 1 for Grade 5 results.

Table 1. Descriptive Statistics for Grade 5 TAKS Science Passing Rates for Hispanic and White Students by School Year

	Hispanic Students			White Students		
Year	n of schools	M	SD	n of schools	M	SD
2008	3,126	75.78	13.92	2,095	87.67	9.54
2007	2,704	67.65	15.77	1,958	83.90	11.50
2006	2,284	68.71	15.64	1,624	84.97	11.19

Depicted in Figure 1 are the TAKS Science passing rates for Grade 5 Hispanic and White students for the 2005-2006, 2006-2007, and 2007-2008 school years. The achievement gap between Hispanic and White students in science is visibly present. Wilcoxon's dependent t-test analyses between Hispanic and White students in Grade 8 for the 2006, 2007, and 2008 school years yielded statistically significant differences, $z = -25.72$, $p < .001$; $z = -25.84$, $p < .001$; and $z = -27.57$, $p < .001$.

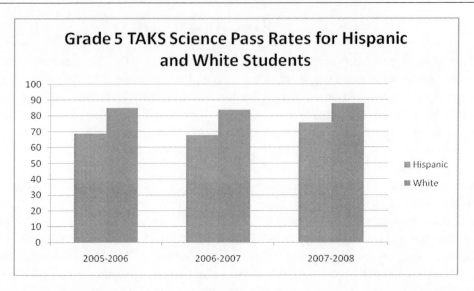

Figure 1. Passing rates on the TAKS Science examination for Grade 5 Hispanic and White students by school year.

Effect sizes for Grade 8 for the 2006, 2007, and 2008 school years were very large, with effect sizes of 1.49, 1.44, and 1.24, respectively (Cohen, 1988). In all cases, the average passing rates on the TAKS Science measure were substantially higher for White students than for Hispanic students. Readers are directed to Table 2 for Grade 8 results. Depicted in Figure 2 are the TAKS Science passing rates for Grade 8 Hispanic and White students for the 2005-2006, 2006-2007, and 2007-2008 school years. The achievement gap between Hispanic and White students in science is visibly present. Of importance is the fact that the gap is greater for these Grade 8 students than was present for our Grade 5 students.

Table 2. Descriptive Statistics for Grade 8 TAKS Science Passing Rates for Hispanic and White Students by School Year

	Hispanic Students			White Students		
Year	*n* of schools	*M*	*SD*	*n* of schools	*M*	*SD*
2008	1,427	60.62	15.79	1,397	78.72	13.20
2007	1,224	58.74	15.33	1,218	79.05	12.55
2006	1,217	63.72	15.37	1,203	83.66	10.98

Table 3. Descriptive Statistics for Grade 11 TAKS Science Passing Rates for Hispanic and White Students by School Year

	Hispanic Students			White Students		
Year	*n* of schools	*M*	*SD*	*n* of schools	*M*	*SD*
2008	1,047	70.29	16.11	1,063	86.97	9.98
2007	941	64.13	16.55	977	82.82	11.72
2006	1,006	62.97	17.03	1,068	83.98	10.21

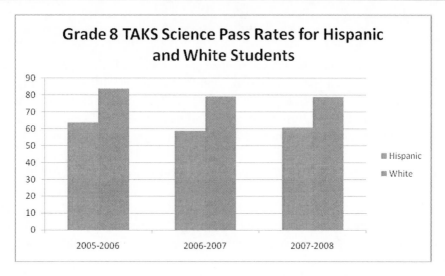

Figure 2. Passing rates on the TAKS Science examination for Grade 8 Hispanic and White students by school year.

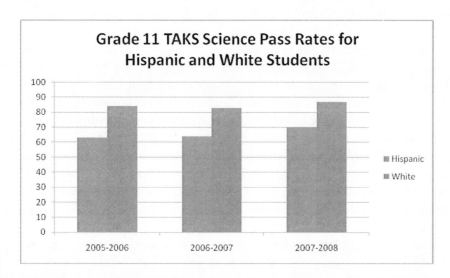

Figure 3. Passing rates on the TAKS Science examination for Grade 11 Hispanic and White students by school year.

For Grade 11, the Wilcoxon's dependent t-test analyses also resulted in statistically significant differences, $z = -23.32$, $p < .001$; $z = -21.93$, $p < .001$; and $z = -22.91$, $p < .001$. Effect sizes for the 3 school years were very large, 1.49, 1.30, and 1.24, respectively (Cohen, 1988). In all cases, the average passing rates on the TAKS Science measure were substantially higher for White students than for Hispanic students. Readers are directed to Table 3 for Grade 11 results.

Figure 3 provides a visual depiction of the achievement gap between Grade 11 Hispanic and White students' performance on the TAKS Science measure. The achievement gap is very visible between the two ethnic groups. Moreover, the achievement gap is greater than for our sample of Grade 5 and of Grade 8 students.

DISCUSSION

In this study, we analyzed the TAKS Science passing rates over a 3-year time period to ascertain the extent to which Hispanic students and White students differed. Passing rates for all Hispanic students and all White students who took the TAKS Science examination in Grade 5, Grade 8, and Grade 11 were analyzed. At all three grade levels and for all 3 years of data analyzed, White students had higher TAKS Science passing rates than did Hispanic students.

The gap between Hispanic students and White students reflected varied results. In Grade 5, the gap remained stable for the 2005-2006 and 2006-2007 school years (i.e., .01 difference), but decreased for the 2007-2008 school year. A large gap existed in Grade 8 in 2005-2006 (M difference = 19.94) and in 2006-2007 (M difference = 20.31). Though still large, a slight decrease in the achievement gap was present in the 2007-2008 school year (M difference = 18.10).

In Grade 11, the gaps were the largest among the three grade levels. The TAKS Science passing rate gap, however, showed a decrease in each of the 3 years: in the 2005-2006 school year, the mean difference was 21.01; in the 2006-2007 school year, the mean difference was 18.69; and in the 2007-2008 school year, the mean difference was 16.68. Delineated in Table 4 are the effect sizes for the achievement gap difference between Hispanic and White students by grade level for each year of data analyzed herein.

According to the U.S. Department of Education (2005), closing the achievement gap is a national priority that has resulted from the passage of the NCLB Act. Furthermore, states continue to make gains to accomplish the task. However, the achievement gap in science does not appear to be narrowing, at least in Texas for the grade levels examined and for the ethnic group of Hispanic students. The student success initiative allows Grade 5 and Grade 8 students to take math and reading examinations three times, however, students would benefit from the same standards being applied to science. Although students in Grade 5 and Grade 8 are required to pass the examination in math and reading, science continues to lag behind other subject areas (TEA, 2009). Accountability for students becoming proficient in science is not present until students take the exit exam in Grade 11.

Differences may exist for a variety of reasons. Some questions that may arise are: (a) What are the teacher expectations for Hispanic students in science classes?; (b) What professional development would assist teachers?; (c) What cultural influences for the Hispanic students might have an impact on their scores?; and (d) What other gaps exist for sub-populations of students such as Black students and economically disadvantaged students? Bias and stereotypical ideas still exist and it is important for teachers to learn about their students and how to motivate them to provide the best learning environment for them.

Table 4. Effect Sizes (i.e., Cohen's d) by Grade Level and School Year

Year	Grade 5	Grade 8	Grade 11
2008	1.00	1.24	1.24
2007	1.17	1.44	1.30
2006	1.19	1.49	1.49

The findings confirm the need that researchers contend is crucial to promote engaging activities in science classes to gain student interest (Holloway, 2002; Lehman, 2009; Wolk, 2008). As with any study, limitations exist. Although 3 years of data were examined, a longitudinal study would provide more information for science achievement. That is, a study in which data from the same students were analyzed over time would be very informative. In addition, data from only a single state were analyzed. The extent to which these findings would generalize to students enrolled in schools in other states is not known. As such, we encourage researchers to investigate student performance in science and in other areas not held to the same degree of accountability as reading and math under the NCLB Act.

REFERENCES

ACT Newsroom. (2009). *ACT profile report – state,* Retrieved from http://act.org/new/aapfacts.html

American Association of University Women. (2004). *Under the microscope: A decade of gender equity projects in the sciences.* Washington, DC: Author.

Andres, G. (2006). The cost of doing business: Should the United States create incentives for stem labor? *Bioscience, 56*(3), 202.

College Board. (2007). *Advanced Placement report to the nation.* Retrieved from http://www.collegeboard.com/prod_downloads/about/news_info/ap/2007/2007/_ap-report-nation.pdf

Cohen, J. (1988). *Statistical power analysis for the behavioral sciences* (2nd ed.). Hillsdale, NJ: Lawrence Erlbaum.

Fry, R., and Passel, J. S. (2009). *Latino children: A majority are U.S.-born offspring of immigrants.* Retrieved from http://www.pewhispanic.org/reports/report.php?ReportID=110

Graczyk, A. C. (2009). *Factors that influence women's dispositions toward science.* (Doctoral dissertation). Available from ProQuest Dissertations and Theses database. (Order No. AAI3334441)

Haas, L., and Slate, J. R. (2010, February). *Ethnic differences in reading and math among K-5th grade.* Paper presented at the Southwest Educational Research Association, New Orleans, LA.

Holloway, J. (2002). Extracurricular activities and student motivation. *Educational Leadership, 60*(1), 80-81.

Huck, S. W. (2007). *Reading statistics and research* (5th ed.). New York, NY: Addison Wesley.

Lehman, C. (2009). Shifting ground. *Principal Leadership, 12,* 18-21.

Muller. P. A., Stage F. K., and Kinzie J. (2001). Science achievement growth trajectories: Understanding factors related to gender and racial-ethnic differences in precollege science achievement. *Educational Research Journal, 38*(4), 981-1012.

Nichols, S. L., and Berliner, D. C. (2008). *Collateral damage.* Cambridge, MA: Harvard Education Press.

Onwuegbuzie, A. J., and Daniel, L. G. (2002). Uses and misuses of the correlation coefficient. *Research in the Schools, 9*(1), 73-90.

Orask, G. (2008). *Closing the gap*: *Thoughts from Dr. Geoffrey Orask*. Retrieved from http://www.infinity-project.org

Rojas-LeBouef, A., and Slate, J. R. (2011). Reading and math differences between Hispanic and White students in Texas: A 16 year analysis. *International Journal of Educational Leadership Preparation, 6*(2). Available online at http://www.ncpeapublications.org/volume-6-number-2/384-reading-and-math-differences-between-hispanic-and-white-students-in-texas-a-16-year-analysis-html

Texas Education Agency. (2006). *State board of education gives preliminary approval to increased high school graduation requirements.* Austin, TX: U.S. Press.

Texas Education Agency. (2008). *Texas student assessment program technical digest for the academic year 2004-2005.* Austin, TX: National Computer Systems.

Texas Education Agency. (2009). *Technical digest 2007-2008.* Austin, TX: National Computer Systems.

U.S. Department of Education. (2005). How No Child Left Behind Benefits Hispanics. Retrieved from http://www2.ed.gov/nclb/accountability/ achieve/nclb-hisp.pdf.

Wolk, S. (2008). Joy in school. *Educational Leadership, 66*(1), 8-15.

Young, H. (2005). Secondary education systematic issues: Addressing possible contributors to a leak in the science education pipeline and potential solutions. *Journal of Science Education and Technology, 14,* 205-216.

In: Handbook of Academic Performance
Editors: Rolf Haumann and George Zimmer

ISBN: 978-1-62417-888-7
© 2013 Nova Science Publishers, Inc.

Chapter 15

GENDER DIFFERENCES IN SCIENCE PASSING RATES: A MULTIYEAR, MULTIGRADE LEVEL STUDY

Veronica Vijil[1,], Julie P. Combs[2,‡] and John R. Slate[2,#]*

[1]Spring Independent School District, Houston, TX, US
[2]Sam Houston State University, Huntsville, TX, US

ABSTRACT

We examined the extent to which boys and girls differed in their performance on the Texas state-mandated science assessment in grades 5, 8, and 11 for three consecutive school years (i.e., 2005-2006, 2006-2007, and 2007-2008) for all public schools in Texas ($ns > 7,000$ schools). For all three grade levels and for all three years, boys demonstrated higher passing rates in science than girls. Given the need for qualified people working in science, the lack of accountability for science proficiency in the No Child Left Behind Act, and the consistent achievement gaps in science documented in this study, we believe that this presence of a gender gap is cause for concern.

Keywords: gender differences, science proficiency

A shortage of qualified workers in the science field challenges the United States to remain economically competitive in a global market (Andres, 2006; U.S. Department of Education, 2009). Comparatively, Europe produces nearly three times as many engineering graduates as the United States whereas Asia produces almost five times as many engineers (Orask, 2008). Well-documented in the research literature is an achievement gap between boys and girls in science-related courses and careers (ACT Inc, 2009; College Board, 2007; Muller, Stage, & Kinzie, 2001). In fact, Haas and Slate (2010) recently documented the presence of gender differences in reading and in math for students enrolled in kindergarten

---

[*] E-mail: vgvijil@yahoo.com
[‡] E-mail: jcombs@shsu.edu
[#] E-mail: profslate@aol.com

through grade 5. They analyzed data from the Early Childhood Longitudinal Study-Kindergarten, thereby permitting generalizations to the nation. At the high school level, Combs, Slate, Moore, Bustamante, Onwuegbuzie, and Edmonson (2010) demonstrated that gender differences were present in college-readiness for a statewide sample.

A sense of urgency has been placed on educational institutions to educate students to become proficient in science and mathematics, as well as encourage students to explore these fields as career options (Graczyk, 2008; U.S. Department of Education, 2009). States such as Texas have increased the number of science courses needed to graduate from high school (Texas Education Agency [TEA], 2006). In 2006, the TEA increased the total number of credits needed to graduate to 26 credits and also raised the number of required science credits from three to four in each subject area (TEA, 2008). Overall, students, especially at the middle and high school level, have continued to struggle in science as reflected by scores on state mandated tests (TEA, 2008). Because students spend so much time at school interacting with their teachers, it is important to emphasize that what happens inside schools has a lasting effect on the development of lifelong learning (Wolk, 2008). Advocates such as Holloway (2002) promoted that student participation in extracurricular activities was one way to obtain student motivation. Holloway (2002) stated that specifically extracurricular science activities may provide structure and challenge, appeal to student interests, and even draw students – especially girls – to science. Lehmann (2009) stated that technology is essential to increase empowerment rather than engagement for students in real-world learning through an inquiry learning process. Still, others contended that to minimize gender differences, it was essential to for teachers to create an environment that encouraged and rewarded the cooperative behavior that was an integral part of scientific investigations (Linn & Hyde, 1989). Popular interventions that have had some success with decreasing gaps included students working with mentors, ensuring a hands-on curriculum, and taking field trips (American Association of University Women Educational Foundation [AAUW], 2004). Recommendations by researchers of AAUW to improve the development and support of projects intended to progress gender equity in the sciences included: (a) incorporate science, technology, engineering and mathematics (STEM) activities into the formal school curriculum; (b) focus on content and skills; (c) increase professional development for educators; (d) allow students to become tutors to students of different ages; (e) increase availability to online programs; and (f) stress the importance of all data collection and evaluation (2004). Educators can benefit from research that enables them to determine activities and lessons that promote engagement in science classrooms.

With the inception of the No Child Left Behind (NCLB) Act of 2001, states were mandated to demonstrate adequate yearly progress which is an individual state's measure of progress toward the goal of 100% of students achieving to state academic standards in at least reading/language arts and math (U.S. Department of Education, 2009). Because the results have critical implications in many areas such as state and federal funding, the NCLB Act has resulted in districts placing heavy pressure on teachers and administrators to ensure student gains in test scores (Nichols & Berliner, 2009). Often the focus for these students is no longer growth and creativity but instead is limited to learning the essential components of the curriculum to obtain meeting standards of the test (Nichols & Berliner, 2009).

Currently in Texas fifth, eighth, and eleventh grade students are tested in different content areas and fifth graders have the option of taking a Spanish test (TEA, 2009). Fifth grade students must take the mathematics, reading, and science test and all tests are available in English and Spanish (TEA, 2009). Eighth grade students are required to take mathematics, reading, science, and social studies tests but are not available in Spanish (TEA, 2009). The addition of a science test for eighth graders was enacted by the Texas Legislature in June, 2003 (TEA, 2009). Eleventh grade students take exit level tests in English language arts, mathematics, science, and social studies (TEA, 2009). Students must pass exit level assessments to be eligible to graduate (TEA, 2009).

Statement of the Problem

Females continue to be underrepresented in science-related courses and careers. Additionally, a regression analysis by researchers of the American Association of University Women (AAUW) revealed that earnings between women and men show that men earned as much as 12% more than women in the same occupations and the gap was most evident the careers with a science focus such as engineering (Corbett, Hill, & St. Rose, 2009). Given that gaps exist between boys and girls in achievement, gaps that begin to emerge as early as in the elementary grades, educators must utilize best practices to attain interest and successful completion in science courses beginning at the elementary level. Stereotypes must be addressed to recognize that barriers exist for subpopulations of students in schools. A concerted effort must be made to attract girls to the sciences.

Purpose of the Study

The purpose of this study was to determine the extent to which boys and girls differed in their science performance at grade 5, 8, and at grade 11. Moreover, we wanted to determine the extent to which an achievement gap in science, if present, was consistent across these grade levels and across three years of statewide data. If gaps existed, we were interested in whether the gaps had changed over the three years of data analyzed.

Research Questions

The following research questions were addressed in this study: (a) What is the difference between boys and girls in grade 5, 8, and 11 in their TAKS Science passing rates for the 2005-2006, 2006-2007, and 2007-2008 school years? and (b) To what extent is any gap consistent across the three years of data analyzed?

METHOD

Data from the 2006, 2007, and 2008 administration of the Texas Assessment of Knowledge and Skills (TAKS) test in science were obtained for this study. Data files were downloaded from the Texas Education Agency website (http://ritter.tea.state.tx.us/). Science passing rates for campuses in Texas for students in grade 5, 8, and 11 were obtained. Information about TAKS Science pass rates was separated by gender in the data file.

The number of campuses for which TAKS Science passing rates were analyzed in this study varied. As depicted in each table, the number of schools differs by school level, with elementary schools or grade 5 having more schools that provided data and high schools or grade 11 having fewer schools that provided data. In addition, the number of schools changed over the 3-year time period. Readers are referred to Tables 1 through 3 for the specific number of campuses by grade level and by school year.

Instrumentation and Procedures

Following written consent from the Institutional Review Board, archival data were downloaded from the Texas Education Agency website (http://ritter.tea.state.tx.us/). The website contains files of TAKS tests results for the state of Texas for the past 20 plus school years. We downloaded data files for the past three years. In particular, we downloaded TAKS Science passing rates for boys and for girls for grade 5, 8, and 11 for each of the three school years previously cited. The TAKS Science measures are criterion-referenced tests in which student mastery of state-mandated science objectives are assessed. The Texas Education Agency provides extensive documentation concerning the score reliabilities and score validities of the TAKS Science measure. Presenting basic information only, the internal consistencies for the TAKS Science exams were .90, .89, and .90 for the 2006, 2007, and 2008 school years. With 1.00 being the maximum possible reliability, these values are reflective of a high degree of score reliability, more than sufficient for research purposes. Concerning score validity, the items for the TAKS Science measure are written in alignment with the state-mandated curriculum standards. For more detailed information, readers are referred to the Texas Education Agency website for the psychometric information concerning the TAKS Science test.

RESULTS

Standardized skewness coefficients (i.e., skewness divided by the standard error of skewness) and standardized kurtosis coefficients (i.e., kurtosis divided by the standard error of kurtosis) were calculated for the TAKS Science passing rates for boys and for girls for the three years of data analyzed. Of the 12 standardized skewness and kurtosis coefficients for grade 5, 10 coefficients were outside the limits of -3.00 and 3.00 (Onwuegbuzie & Daniel, 2002). Similarly, 9 of the 12 standardized skewness and kurtosis coefficients for grade 8 were also outside the limits of -3.00 and 3.00 (Onwuegbuzie & Daniel, 2002). Finally, 11 of the 12 standardized skewness and kurtosis coefficients for grade 11 were outside the limits of -3.00 and 3.00 (Onwuegbuzie & Daniel, 2002). Because almost all of the coefficients indicated that the TAKS Science passing rates were not normally distributed, we decided to use a conservative statistical procedure. Specifically, we used a non-parametric procedure, the Wilcoxon's dependent samples *t*-test (Huck, 2007), to determine the extent to which boys and girls differed in their TAKS Science passing rates for each grade level and for each year of data analyzed.

The Wilcoxon's dependent samples t-test analysis revealed that boys and girls differed on their TAKS Science passing rates for grade 5 for the 2005-2006, 2006-2007, and 2007-2008 school years, $z = -22.05$, $p < .001$; $z = -23.41$, $p < .001$; and $z = -31.05$, $p < .001$, respectively. Cohen's (1988) criteria were used to determine all effect sizes. Effect sizes for grade 5 were 0.30, 0.28, and 0.39, respectively. These values reflected small practical differences in the TAKS Science passing rates of boys and girls. In all cases, boys had higher average TAKS Science passing rates than did girls.

Table 1. Descriptive Statistics for Grade 5 TAKS Science Passing Rates for Girls and Boys by School Year

	Girls			Boys		
Year	n of schools	M	SD	n of schools	M	SD
2008	3550	76.68	14.85	3391	82.17	12.85
2007	3081	70.39	16.68	2995	74.98	15.52
2006	2652	71.64	16.74	2598	76.04	16.07

Similarly, the Wilcoxon's dependent t-test analyses between girls and boys for grade 8 yielded statistically significant differences for the 2005-2006, 2006-2007, and 2007-2008 school years, $z = -23.42$, $p < .001$; $z = -18.30$, $p < .001$; and $z = -19.19$, $p < .001$, respectively. Similarly, the effect sizes for grade 8 were small effect sizes, 0.43, 0.30, and 0.29, respectively (Cohen, 1988). Again, boys had higher TAKS Science passing rates than did girls for all three school years.

Table 2. Descriptive Statistics for Grade 8 TAKS Science Passing Rates for Girls and Boys by School Year

	Girls			Boys		
Year	n of schools	M	SD	n of schools	M	SD
2008	1664	65.11	17.03	1651	69.87	16.20
2007	1447	64.13	17.20	1415	69.09	15.98
2006	1452	68.22	16.82	1390	75.21	14.96

Table 3. Descriptive Statistics for Grade 11 TAKS Science Passing Rates for Girls and Boys by School Year

	Girls			Boys		
Year	n of schools	M	SD	n of schools	M	SD
2008	1302	74.07	16.46	1195	81.19	13.79
2007	1160	70.31	17.17	1138	74.62	16.32
2006	1279	67.96	18.48	1211	76.72	15.24

Finally, the Wilcoxon's dependent t-test analyses between girls and boys for grade 11 for these three school years resulted in statistically significant differences, $z = -23.11$, $p < .001$; $z = -13.62$, $p < .001$; and $z = -21.50$, $p < .001$, respectively. For grade 11, the effect size for

2005-2006 was 0.51, moderate, whereas the effect sizes for the other two years were 0.25 and 0.46, both small effects (Cohen, 1988). Congruent with the results for students in Grades 5 and 8, boys had higher TAKS Science passing rates than did girls for all three school years.

DISCUSSION

In this study, we analyzed the TAKS Science passing rates to determine the extent to which a gender gap might be present in grades 5, 8, and 11 over the most recent three years of statewide data available. For these three grade levels and for the three years of data analyzed, boys demonstrated higher average TAKS Science passing rates than did girls. The gap between girls and boys in grade 5 widened from year to year whereas the science gap between girls and boys decreased slightly in grade 8. Variability was present in the science gap for grade 11. We believe that our results on a statewide sample, across multiple years are supportive of the recent findings of Nichols and Berliner (2008) and are congruent with the recent findings of Haas and Slate (2010). Moreover, we concur with their assertion that the NCLB Act has not accomplished its intended goal of narrowing gaps that exist.

According to the United States Department of Education (2009), closing the achievement gap is a national priority that has resulted from the passage of NCLB and, furthermore, states continue to make gains to accomplish the task. However, the achievement gap does not appear to be narrowing in Texas for the grade levels and ethnicity membership reviewed in this study. The student success initiative allows fifth and eighth grade students to take math and reading tests three times, however, students would benefit from the same standards to be applied to science. Although students in fifth and eighth grade are required to pass the test in math and reading, science continues to lag behind other subject areas (TEA, 2009) and there does not seem to be as much accountability in the area of science until the exit exam in eleventh grade when a passing score is needed to graduate. Math achievement appears to be increasing according to TAKS results; however, the scores may be a reflection of the impact of SSI standards.

Differences may exist for a variety of reasons. Some questions that may arise are: (a) What are the teacher expectations for girls in science classes?; and (b) What professional development would assist teachers in improving the science performance of girls? Bias and stereotypical ideas still exist and it is important for teachers to learn about their students and how to motivate them to provide the best learning environment for them. The findings confirm the need that researchers contend is crucial to promote engaging activities in science classes to gain student interest (Holloway, 2002; Lehman, 2009; Wolk, 2008).

Findings from this study may be used to increase awareness of the impact of science coursework and instructional strategies for diverse student groups in elementary, middle, and high schools. To the extent that our findings are replicable, then modifications in curricula and instructional strategies may need to be addressed. Although many assertions are made about the impact on student achievement, empirical data demonstrate the need to narrow any gaps that may continue to exist among subgroups. Educators may use the data to plan strategically and incorporate activities in classrooms and on campuses that will generate an interest among girls in science activities.

Similar to any study, limitations are present in this investigation. Three years of data were analyzed, not a sufficient number of years to permit generalizations concerning trends in a science achievement gap between boys and girls. Moreover, we analyzed data from only one state and only for three specific grade levels. Thus, we encourage readers to be cautious in the extent to which they make any generalizations from our study, until such time as our study's results are replicated by other researchers. Readers should note, however, that our findings at a statewide level, across multiple years of data, are congruent with the extant literature.

REFERENCES

ACT Newsroom. (2009). *ACT profile report – state,* Retrieved from http://act.org/new/aapfacts.html

AAUW Educational Foundation. (2008). *Behind the pay gap.* Retrieved from http://www.aauw.org

AAUW Educational Foundation. (2004). *Under the microscope a decade of gender equity projects in the sciences.* Retrieved from http://www.aauw.org

Andres, G. (2006). The cost of doing business: Should the United States create incentives for stem labor? *Bioscience, 56*(3), 202.

College Board. (2007). *Advanced Placement report to the nation.* Retrieved from http://www.collegeboard.com/prod_downloads/about/news_info/ap/2007/2007/_ap-report-nation.pdf

Cohen, J. (1988). *Statistical power analysis for the behavioral sciences* (2nd ed.). Hillsdale, NJ: Lawrence Erlbaum.

Combs, J. P., Slate, J. R., Moore, G. W., Bustamante, R., Onwuegbuzie, A. J., & Edmonson, S. (2010). Gender differences in college preparedness: A statewide study. *The Urban Review, 42*(5). doi:10.1007/s11256-009-0138-x

Graczyk, A. C. (2008). *Factors that influence women's dispositions toward science* (Doctoral dissertation). Retrieved from http://unx1.shsu.edu:2048/login?url=?did=1612980181&Fmt=6&clientId=96&RQT=309&VName=PQD

Haas, L., & Slate, J. R. (2010). Gender differences in reading and math for students in K – 5th grade. *Graduate Research Journal, 2.* Retrieved from http://grj.fp.expressacademicorg/article.php?autoID=119&issueID=65

Holloway, J. (2002). Extracurricular activities and student motivation. *Educational Leadership, 60*(1), 80-81.

Huck, S. W. (2007). *Reading statistics and research* (5th ed.). New York, NY: Addison Wesley.

Lehman, C. (2009). Shifting ground. *Principal Leadership, 12,* 18-21.

Lynn, M. C., & Hyde, J. S. (1989). Gender, math, and science. *Educational Researcher, 18*(8), 17-27.

Muller. P. A., Stage F. K., & Kinzie J. (2001). Science achievement growth trajectories: Understanding factors related to gender and racial-ethnic differences in precollege science achievement. *Educational Research Journal, 38*(4), 981-1012.

Nichols, S. L., & Berliner, D. C. (2008). *Collateral damage.* Cambridge, MA: Harvard Education Press.

Onwuegbuzie, A. J., & Daniel, L. G. (2002). Uses and misuses of the correlation coefficient. *Research in the Schools, 9*(1), 73-90.

Orask, G. (2008). *Closing the gap: Thoughts from Dr. Geoffrey Orask.* Retrieved from http://www.infinity-project.org

Texas Education Agency. (2006). *State board of education gives preliminary approval to increased high school graduation requirements.* Austin, TX: U.S. Press.

Texas Education Agency. (2008). *Texas student assessment program technical digest for the academic year 2004-2005.* Austin, TX: National Computer Systems.

Texas Education Agency. (2009). *2009 AYP Guide Sections II-V.* Austin, TX: U.S. Press.

Texas Education Agency. (2009). *Technical digest 2007-2008.* Austin, TX: National Computer Systems.

Wolk, S. (2008). Joy in school. *Educational Leadership, 66*(1), 8-15.

Young, H. (2005). Secondary education systematic issues: Addressing possible contributors to a leak in the science education pipeline and potential solutions. *Journal of Science Education & Technology, 14,* 205-216.

INDEX

D

T